James Caughey, Ralph William Allen

Showers of Blessing from Clouds of Mercy

James Caughey, Ralph William Allen

Showers of Blessing from Clouds of Mercy

ISBN/EAN: 9783337345549

Printed in Europe, USA, Canada, Australia, Japan

Cover: Foto ©Lupo / pixelio.de

More available books at **www.hansebooks.com**

SHOWERS OF BLESSING

FROM

CLOUDS OF MERCY;

SELECTED

From the Journal and other Writings

OF THE

REV. JAMES CAUGHEY;

CONTAINING

MOST STIRRING SCENES AND INCIDENTS, DURING GREAT REVIVALS IN BIRMINGHAM, CHESTERFIELD, MACCLESFIELD, AND OTHER PLACES IN ENGLAND, UNDER HIS MINISTRY; SEVERAL OF MR. CAUGHEY'S AWAKENING ADDRESSES AND SERMONS; THOUGHTS ON HOLINESS; NOTES OF PERSONAL EXPERIENCE, AND OBSERVATIONS UPON PERSONS AND PLACES VISITED.

"*And I will make them, and the places round about my hill, a blessing; and I will cause the shower to come down in his season:* THERE SHALL BE SHOWERS OF BLESSING." Ezek. xxxiv. 26.

SIXTH THOUSAND.

BOSTON:
FOR SALE BY J. P. MAGEE,
AND AT ALL THE
METHODIST BOOK DEPOSITORIES IN THE U. STATES AND CANADA.
1860.

Entered according to Act of Congress, in the year 1857, by
JAMES CAUGHEY & R. W. ALLEN,
In the Clerk's Office of the District Court of the District of Massachusetts.

Stereotyped by
HOBART & ROBBINS,
New England Type and Stereotype Foundery,
BOSTON.

Rand and Avery, Printers, 3 Cornhill.

EDITOR'S PREFACE.

WE present the religious public with another volume, unfolding and illustrating the wonderful success of Mr. Caughey's labors in his revival efforts. It records the events, incidents, and results, of one of the most remarkable revivals of modern times — the revival in Birmingham, England. It also presents the result of his labors in several other places. Descriptions of several places he visited — the scenes of his revival labors — are given in his peculiarly interesting style. Several of his revival sermons and addresses are given. These, by many, will be regarded as the most interesting part of the volume. We think it will be found, in every respect, as interesting and profitable as either of his other works; and, should it find as many readers, will undoubtedly accomplish as much good.

The sale of Mr. Caughey's works has been unprecedented in the history of religious literature in this country. In six years, about seventy thousand volumes have been sold. The good they have done is immense. We trust the present volume will be made a blessing to thousands! That many a sinner may be turned from the error of his way to serve the Lord, and that multitudes of God's people may be led to the highest attainments of Christian experience, by reading its thrilling pages, is the earnest prayer of the editor.

R. W. A.

CONTENTS.

CHAPTER I.
INTRODUCTION.

Invited to Birmingham (England) — Health in activity — Goole visited — A character — Sudden death — Visits Armin — Huddersfield — London — Returns to Sheffield — A successful Sabbath — Home yearnings — The will of God, ... 13

CHAPTER II.
SHEFFIELD.

The metropolis of cutlery — Scenery — Public buildings — Cholera Mount — Montgomery, the poet — A visit to Wharncliff — Trade of Sheffield, ... 20

CHAPTER III.
EXCURSIONS.

Haddon Hall — The old clock — A Roman altar — The "Keep" penalty — The gem of Haddon — Loneliness and decay — A sigh to the past — Chatsworth — The park — The palace — Carvings in wood — The conservatory — Hobbes, the infidel — A surly motto — His death-scene — Derbyshire moors — A touching story, ... 35

CHAPTER IV.
AN EXCURSION.

Hathersage — Grave of "Little John" — A thunder-storm — Peak's Hole Cavern — Entrance — Interior — The Cimmerian — Halcyone — Dell' Inferno — The Dell House — Devil's Cellar, &c. — Styx — An extraordinary scene — Heathenism, degrading tendencies of — An explosion — A ruined castle — Maun Tor, or the Shivering Mountain — Blue John mine — The new creature — Scenery, ... 54

CHAPTER V.
NORTON.

Norton House — View of Sheffield — Felicity — St. Paul's experience compared — A supposition — Rest for the weary — Chantrey, ... 76

CHAPTER VI.
CHESTERFIELD.

The call to preach — Hastens to Chesterfield — A great outpouring of the Holy Spirit — Charming weather — The pilgrim habit — The revival unopposed — The stolen march — Great success — Joy, ... 80

1*

CHAPTER VII.
PROGRESS OF THE REVIVAL IN CHESTERFIELD.

A successful Sabbath — The Gospel, as developed in a revival — Divinity of Christ — Forgiving sins — An amazed population, ... 84

CHAPTER VIII.
THE LADY ASTROLOGIAN.

A question — The reply — Stars above us every way — The wandering moon — The conjectural sciences — Future events — The Scriptures — Promises and providences — Prayer and Chaldean lore — Assyrian and English skies — The Bible — A light for the wilderness — An oasis, ... 88

CHAPTER IX.
SOLITUDE.

Great principles confronted in silence — Daniel — Jacob — The voices of solitude — Effects upon the soul — The contrast — Revival activities — Sentiment of Herbert, . . 99

CHAPTER X.
PENCILLINGS OF THE REVIVAL IN CHESTERFIELD.

A great move — Effects of truth — A deputation — Singular dream — A comparison — Prophets among the wicked — Their error — The wise architect, ... 93

CHAPTER XI.
PREPARING TO LEAVE CHESTERFIELD.

A great work of God — Statistics, ... 98

CHAPTER XII.
WALKS ABOUT CHESTERFIELD.

Favorite walks — The ducking stool — The town — The old parish church — The crooked spire — Antiquarian controversy — A sonnet — Always awry — The canonized architect — Monuments and inscriptions in the church — The honest lawyer — The witty epitaph — Dedication hymn — Inside of religion — Self-educated, . . 100

CHAPTER XIII.
DONCASTER.

A day of salvation — An agreeable town — An eclipse of the moon — Progress of the shadow — Appearance — Sublimity — The Lunarians and our earth — A supposition — Astronomy — Longevity — Sentiments of Josephus — The moon in her beauty, ... 107

CHAPTER XIV.
A GREAT OUTPOURING OF THE SPIRIT IN DONCASTER.

The town shaken — Showers of blessings — A motley group — A character — A diamond in the rough — A deputation to Christ — The Gospel, ... 111

CHAPTER XV.
"AND AS YE GO, PREACH."

A visit to York — Huddersfield — Honley — A hard time — Character of sinners — Diabolical power and economy — Sheepridge — Backslider reclaimed — A revivalist — Macclesfield — A glorious Sabbath, ... 114

CONTENTS.

CHAPTER XVI.

MACCLESFIELD.

Its trade — Cha*r*:er — Court of Piepowder — John Bradshaw — A singular presentiment fulfilled — Cromwell and the council of state — Rev. David Simpson — His timid bishop — Faithful preaching — A friendly mayor — Persecution — A visit to his church — A moving incident — The earthquake — Singular impression — Anecdote of Simpson, ... 117

CHAPTER XVII.

THE WORK OF GOD IN MACCLESFIELD.

Blows of truth — Critics overwhelmed — Happy deaths — Sin unto death — A prepared people — Progress of the revival — *Twenty-six thousand* years pardon — Numbers saved — Leaves for Birmingham, ... 126

CHAPTER XVIII.

THE BEGINNING — IN BIRMINGHAM.

Looking up — The stone and its water-circles — The prophetic STONE — The great image — The common people — Raindrop and sunbeam — A cheering text — Victory is of God, ... 131

CHAPTER XIX.

THE PATH TO VICTORY.

The spirit of warfare — Misty beginnings — Fervent faith — The powers of darkness — Confidence in God — The gathering of the poor — The rich elsewhere — The golden girdle — Betting with Satan — Dear figs — Achan and Judas — A succession — Corresponding estimates — A sad conclusion — A vast design, ... 137

CHAPTER XX.

SATAN ENTRENCHED.

Important questions — Weapons of war needed — Action — The preacher needed — Style, ... 141

CHAPTER XXI.

GLIMPSES OF BIRMINGHAM ; OR, LOOKING DIFFICULTIES IN THE FACE.

The best general — Napoleon and his victories — Nehemiah's mission — A lesson — The state of sinners — Brain-sick — Perilous state — *Baxter's* illustration — Professors — A proverb — Chasing shadows — The golden apple — Satan's rich and Christ's poor — A Grecian sentiment — The contrast — The leveller — A dark ministry — High life, or the parable of the chimneys — Terrors — The Awe-band — Almost Christians — The wickedly witty — Double trouble — Fearful cases — The silken halter — A sweet poison — Statistics of intemperance — Opposition to temperance — Girding on the armor — A bright side — Gales from Calvary, ... 144

CHAPTER XXII.

PULPIT DEFENCES ; OR, FRAGMENTS OF WARFARE.

Hell — Saying of a German lady — Not a proper motive for Christians — Fire and brimstone preaching — Throwing people into convictions — Hell as a means — The cross — Apology defined — A great truth — The crier in the wilderness — Eloquence — The Agami — Plain preaching — The soaring preacher — The pouncing preacher — The gentlemanly preacher — The speculative preacher — The mean nobody preacher — The spoiled child — A lawyer defending his cloth, ... 161

CHAPTER XXIII.
FRAGMENTS FOR HYPERCRITICS.

A soft kernel — A supposition — Hell — A startling difference — Wisdom in swine — Hypocrites — The man of lips — The silver-tongued but strong-hearted — The comet — Sincerity — David's bridle — An honest tongue — Wholesome tongue — A criteria, ... 168

CHAPTER XXIV.
A LESSON ON PREACHING.

The poet and the painter — Their pandemonium and paradise — The great defect — Lesson derived — The painter's gallery — Adam in the bush — Deformities of character — Divine assistance — Human nature — The painter's advice — The single aim, ... 171

CHAPTER XXV.
MORE FRAGMENTS OF WAR.

The German moralist — Blemishes of character, how treated — The queen caricatured, a supposition — Christian stature — A Swiss sentiment — Gospel intolerance — Meroz — Expostulation — A political maxim, ... 177

CHAPTER XXVI.
SPIRITUAL BATTERIES AND WEAPONS OF WAR.

The battle-field — Judas — The last supper — Scene in Gethsemane — The sound of a going forth — The bee and the butterfly — Shells for certain entrenchments — Example, responsible for — The nervous architect — Influence of example — The cloudy pillar — Retribution — Exhortation — Religion diffusive — A law of nature — Confessing Christ — Self-interest — A significant motto — A low principle — The snail with its house on its back — A sore trial, ... 181

CHAPTER XXVII.
HOW TO HAVE A REVIVAL.

A retarding or promoting church — How treated — Courage — Example of Christ — Character of his hearers — Scenes in his ministry — Truth, its mission — The accepted time — An exhortation, ... 193

CHAPTER XXVIII.
THE THEME RESUMED.

A supposition — Christ's style — Fortified guilt — Dreadful artillery — His tears and lamentations over impenitence, ... 202

CHAPTER XXIX.
CHRIST WEEPING OVER JERUSALEM — A SERMON.

Weeping, instances of — Not suppressed by the Hebrews — Gilboa — David's lamentation — Jerusalem sinners — Sympathy for sinners — A cause for tears — A spiritual epidemic — Backsliders — Hope — The rescued Lamb — Floods of mercy — Sinners repenting — A glorious scene, ... 206

CHAPTER XXX.
CHRIST WEEPING OVER JERUSALEM — A SERMON.

Design of preaching — Effective preaching — Intellect reached through the passions — Instances — The obtuse — Unthinking — The well-informed — The wearied —

The disheartened — The standard-bearers — Spiritual tactics — Tears defended — A weeping-time for sinners — Hell a place of weeping — Burns, sentiment of — The pen behind the curtain — Going in debt — Satan's object — An old proverb — A crisis — Three penitents — Impossibilities — Legion — Consequences — The Lord's uttermost — The five smooth stones — Justification by faith — Exhortation, . . . 213

CHAPTER XXXI.

CHRIST WEEPING OVER JERUSALEM — A SERMON.

The compassion of Jesus — Metaphysical divinity — The hallowed contagion — Revealings of the heart — Sustaining a reputation — Style, how influenced — Christ's method — Individual cases — A strong attraction — Objected to — Defended — The panorama in motion — The pleasures of sense — Expensive — Combatted — The Bible within — A Swiss definition of conscience — Searching inquiries — The unawakened sinner — Strange state — Awakening questions — Perilous — Presumption — Damned by mistake — Saying of a French divine — God is not slack, ... 231

CHAPTER XXXII.

CHRIST WEEPING OVER JERUSALEM — A SERMON.

A word to "A finally impenitent" — The delirious patient — Orthodox devils — A significant wish — The sin against the Holy Ghost — Consequences — Hope for a sinner out of hell — The precipice — Final impenitence here — Mercy offered — Dr. Chalmers and the dying sinner — Blue lights — A death-scene — Trembling in hell — A mother's prayers — The preference, ... 246

CHAPTER XXXIII.

SATANIC POLICY.

The Devil's game — Darkness — His cards — An unloved master — The contrast — Sentiment of Pythagoras, ... 262

CHAPTER XXXIV.

THE PATIENCE AND PROVIDENCE OF GOD.

Abused — Wilful sin — The wilfully blind — Iron, cold or hot — A rough part of the road — A rod and honey — Contrary wheels — A precious text, ... 266

CHAPTER XXXV.

IN THE FURNACE.

Manner of the seizure — Sudden death deprecated — St. Paul's strait — The young recruit — The two tombstones — Feebleness — Buckling on the armor — A wish — Past experience — God's jewelry — The broken mirror — Good omens — Spanish proverb — Carle-hemp, ... 271

CHAPTER XXXVI.

RETURN TO THE BATTLE-STRIFE. — SOUL-SAVING MINISTRY.

An encouraging physician — Gold in the fire — Truth and the sinner — Cuts like a sword — Serpent-like — Health — Seneca's man — The inner man — A noble purpose — Job's leviathan — Parody — The true succession, ... 277

CHAPTER XXXVII.

PERSONAL EXPERIENCE AND PENCILLINGS ABOUT PREACHING.

Christmas day — A Grecian memento — New converts — Solitariness — Two musical strings — The lame take the prey — Salt for sores — Progress of the revival — Sanctified fright — The contrary — Weapons of war — A sermon characterized — A solid square — Disordered order, ... 283

CHAPTER XXXVIII.

THE NEW YEAR.—THE PROPHESYING TRUMP.

Farewell and hail — Watch-night — The bitter before the sweet — Providence — Exodus - Light for the soul — A hard time — Trembling sinner — A crisis — Hot iron Hotter fires — Louder blasts — Call for the trumpet — Tokens of God — His arrows — Battle signal — Whirlwinds — Sling-stones — Notes of victory — Pentecost — New wine — Precious stones — The beauty of God — Whirlwinds of the south, ... 289

CHAPTER XXXIX.

AN EXPERIMENT REJECTED.

Devil — Pleasing preaching — Genteel efforts — A whisper for a thunder — Gideon's three hundred — Obstinate violence — Devil-arousing preaching — Shoulder of an earthquake — Robert Bolton — Sinner-awakening preaching, ... 296

CHAPTER XL.

RENEWAL OF THE COVENANT AND PROGRESS OF THE REVIVAL.

Covenant service — A moving season — Revival joy — Onward for victory — Wonderful displays of mercy — Newspaper notices — Multitudes saved, ... 301

CHAPTER XLI.

NOTES OF CORRESPONDENCE AND PRIVATE REFLECTIONS.

"A field officer " — Sheffield and Chesterfield reported — Smooth preaching — Afterthoughts — Success of the year — Safeguards of zeal — Jesus — Heaven — Sanctification — Wesley's opinion — Islington chapel — Great success — Remarkable conversion, ... 307

CHAPTER XLII.

DISPASSIONATE PREACHING.

A proviso — Goldsmith's comparison — Erasmus on moving to purpose — Dean Swift on preaching — Manner — The test — War and violence — Rock-breaking — The resolve, ... 314

CHAPTER XLIII.

MORE PENCILLINGS OF THE REVIVAL IN BIRMINGHAM.

Revival preaching — Truth, power of — Heaven — Hell studies — Providential interposition — Faith and purity — Victory — New converts — Invitation card — Blessings in hurricanes, ... 319

CHAPTER XLIV.

A MEMENTO.

Beating the air — Lightness before sermon — Tea-table influences — The great effect — A resolve — A slack soul — The tight bow-string — Fearful possibilities — A throne of power — Alone with God — Outpouring of the Spirit, ... 325

CHAPTER XLV.

GLIMPSES OF THE REVIVALS AND PRINCIPLES OF ACTION.

Sanctification — Truth in the head — Cain's offering — Heavy ordnance — Progress of the work — A great melting — Tinselled preaching — Believing — Satan's hope — Reminiscences — Sacrament — Playing with truth — Motives — Dealings with sinners — Christ sweet — A scene in Wesley chapel — The judgment, ... 331

CONTENTS.

CHAPTER XLVI.
SANCTIFYING AND AWAKENING TRUTH.

A great promise — A mine — Curious hearers — Thoughts on dress — A predicament — Believing — The lark — Vocal spark — A query — A great day — Death of a backslider — Last knocks — Life-giving truth — Holiness — Deep things — A newspaper notice — Extraordinary conversions, ... 339

CHAPTER XLVII.
GOOD NEWS — HOW TO BELIEVE FOR A CLEAN HEART.

Private experience — Extent of the revival — Dull scythe — Tinsel — Inequality of style — Olympus — Conjectural ability — Life not circular — Waller s letter — Difficulties stated — Light increasing — Last to give way — Prophecy and promise — Out of the fog — Salvation, ... 348

CHAPTER XLVIII.
JOURNAL CONTINUED.

An anchor-hold — Accountability — The dial-plate — The moving flame — Love feast — Holy alliance — Opponent in pamphlet — Introduction — Fans the flame, . . . 353

CHAPTER XLIX.
CHEERFULNESS AND COURAGE REQUIRED.

Sadness — A Swiss remark — Cheerfulness necessary — Napoleon's officer — World's opinion — The sinner hit — Saying of Erasmus — The madman's idea — Law and Gospel, ... 364

CHAPTER L.
PEACE OR WAR.

Natural weapons — Animals and men — The new creature — Armor — Mischief — The rub — Nurse of peace — War secures peace — The fenced city — Secret of war — Alternatives — Aggression — Controversy declined — Undebatable things — A tame devil — Selfish preacher — Crafty politician — Dagon — Self-conquest — Violence — Truth a loadstone — A great move, ... 367

CHAPTER LI.
EXTRACTS FROM THE JOURNAL.

Birthday — Watch-night — Circumlocution — Retribution — A hard time — A great day — Zeal and health — Decision and holiness, ... 377

CHAPTER LII.
MORE NOTES OF THE REVIVAL.

Opposition — True Methodists — Fair-weather sailors — The inheritance — A paradox — Wesley's visit — Art of war — Spiritual batteries — Weeping sinners — Definition of a Christian — Dejection — Errand for God, ... 380

CHAPTER LIII.
MISTAKING THE PATH.

Early experience — Satan's snare — Out of the path — Sorrows — Salvation, . . 389

CHAPTER LIV.

LINES IN PLEASANT PLACES.

Sparkbrook House — Walking-place — The *swans* — The surprise — Warwick castle — Wooden legs — Saying of Bellarmine — The difference — Image of religion — First principles — A diluted gospel — Eternity and revivals — Ordinary effort, ... 394

CHAPTER LV.

INCIDENTS OF THE REVIVAL.

Sabbath-breaker saved — Shop closed — A Roman Catholic converted — Justification by faith — Another Romanist converted — An apprentice — Post-office clerk, advice to, ... 399

CHAPTER LVI.

PERSECUTION.

Newspapers — Of the pen and the hand — Chips of the cross — The persecuted wife — Husband converted — Sabbath at Bradley — Returns to Birmingham — Tea meetings — Statistics of the revival, ... 404

CHAPTER LVII.

CONCLUSION.

Resolutions — Striking account of the revival — Wonderful displays of mercy — Closing Remarks — Glorying in the Lord — Farewell — Note, ... 409

SHOWERS OF BLESSING.

CHAPTER I.

TRIUMPHS OF GRACE.

"And as ye go, preach." — MATT. 10 : 7.

IN the year 1845, Mr. Caughey received an invitation to visit *Birmingham*, England, for the purpose of promoting the work of God in that populous town. Having laid the subject before the Lord, and waiting before him for *guidance*, he concluded the *providential cloud* moved in that direction.

We thought it well to apprize the *reader* of this at the commencement of the volume; for it is to that scene of his labors, his footsteps appear to be tending in the following excursions to various towns to preach the Gospel,— a record of which will be found in several chapters immediately following.

The reader may rest fully assured that those chapters will conduct him to scenes in Birmingham of no ordinary interest. There Mr. Caughey spent several months in the great work of saving souls, and with *amazing success*.

Bearing this in mind, the reader will trace the footsteps of our evangelist through his various previous excursions with all the deeper interest, knowing that his path is leading him to a scene of *toil, battle* and *victory*, which he himself little anticipated; where *truth* and *error*,— "the *arms* of *God Almighty*, and his *Enemy*,"— met in severe combat, and with astonishing results.

In the mean time, the introductory chapters alluded to will be found full of *interesting matter*, and *success* in the awakening and conversion of sinners.

Mr. Caughey's health had been much affected by his extraordinary labors in *Huddersfield, York*, &c., and it became necessary he should excursionize for the benefit of his health, while it allowed him opportunities to call sinners to repentance, — *the ruling passion of his soul.* Some account of his excursions we present to the reader, gathered from his Journal and Letters, which, we trust, will be interesting and profitable.

Eighteen hundred and forty-five is rushing away into eternity, like its predecessors. It will not do for me to sit still! Time is flying, and poor sinners are dying, and eternity has its *terrible revealings.* O, it will not do for me to sit still! Another consideration is my *health.* It has been much shaken; but it recovers more speedily, sometimes, in *motion*, than in a state of *inaction.* My mind is *happier*, and that has a good influence on the health; besides, change of *air*, and change of *scene* and *employment*, have a most favorable influence upon soul and body.

We had a great work of God in *Huddersfield*, where thousands were saved in pardon and purity; * and we had a great work in *York*, also; but my *health* suffered. It

---

* See volume "*Earnest Christianity Illustrated.*"

is *better*, however, and I hope, by keeping myself in *motion*, and exercising *prudence*, it may become better still.

In company with brother *David Greenbury*, I visited Goole, in *Lincolnshire*, the other day;—*David* praising God all the way, and with always a choice word in readiness for the ear and conscience of fellow-travellers, regarding *the life of faith*, and *life or death* in the eternity beyond,—himself all life, and peace, and joy! David is

" A man of *cheerful yesterdays*,
And *confident to-morrows.*"

He has an *adjective* for every day of the week,—*triumphant* Sabbaths, *glorious* Mondays, *happy* Tuesdays, &c., &c.,—running over them all in a twinkling, like a musician on his *gamut*, the loftiest note ending with the Sabbath, and a shout of "*Glory, hallelujah!*"

We had a large assembly in the afternoon, to whom I preached with sweet liberty;—the Lord was among the people indeed;—after which, we took tea with about five hundred people in the Philosophical Hall. The congregation was much larger at night, the chapel being literally crammed, aisles and all. Before I ascended the pulpit, a brother informed me that a *local preacher*, who had been present in the afternoon meeting, had died suddenly. He left the chapel, walked a short distance, became faint, reclined, and in a few moments found himself

"——————— in the gap
Between the life that is, and that which is to come,
Awaiting judgment;"

when those standing by, exclaimed, "He is dead!" Yes, he had passed over Jordan at the narrowest place,—"*absent from the body, present with the Lord."* O, what a change! The announcement had a very solemn effect upon the congregation. Little did I think, I remarked, when addressing you this afternoon, that there sat one among you who would be my Lord's guest, and "*sup with him*" tonight in Paradise. The audience seemed electrified. O, how awfully glorious to behold that great mass of human beings waving to and fro, like a forest in a gale, — spread over aisles, gallery stairs, pulpit stairs, — every available space above and below crammed to the utmost capacity of the chapel! This prepared them for my text and sermon, which had a great effect upon sinners; of whom many were "*the slain of the Lord,*" — *twenty-five* of whom found mercy, and *nine* purity of heart.

From Goole, David and I hastened to *Armin*, where I preached *twice*, and had a few saved. We were entertained at the mansion of Edward Thompson, Esq.,— David's home when in these parts. Thence we hastened to Huddersfield, where I preached to a noble congregation in *Buxton Road Chapel*, in behalf of a small, favorite *school*, which needed funds; obtained for them fifty-eight pounds, or nearly three hundred dollars; but, better than money, we had over *thirty* souls converted to Christ before we parted. Hallelujah!

Well, David Greenbury is a character; — like his namesake in the Scriptures, seldom without a psalm or a hymn in his mouth. How he *sings!* — *everywhere, tirelessly,* like those above; as if his *heaven* is everywhere, which is really the case,— sings

" As if he wished the firmament of heaven
Should listen, and give back to him the voice
Of his triumphant constancy and love."

After taking an affectionate leave of David, I hastened up to *London* by railway, in company with *Joseph Webb*, Esq. We rode all night, during which I worked hard upon an index for my *fourth volume* of Letters; but about daybreak sleep quite overcame me, and I sank down on the floor of the car and slept.

And now here I am in *Sheffield.* We spent only a couple of days in *London.* This is a precious spot to me; memorable, as being the scene of one of the greatest victories my Lord Jesus ever achieved by my ministry; where, in something less than *four months,* upwards of *three thousand* persons professed to obtain the *forgiveness* of sins, and nearly *fifteen hundred* sanctifying grace!

I do realize the sentiment of that *Scottish* divine, who said, "Sweet are the spots where *Immanuel* has ever shown his glorious power in the conviction and conversion of sinners. The *world* loves to muse on the scenes where *battles* were fought and *victories* won. Should not we love the spots where our great *Captain* has won his amazing victories? Is not the conversion of a soul more worthy to be spoken of than the taking of *Acre?*" Let Matt. 16: 26, set its *seal* upon the *sentiment,* and upon my heart for ever and ever. Amen.

A year has passed away since that great work of God, but the *glory and power* of God have not passed away. They are still revealed among the assemblies of his people in *Sheffield;*—no *reäction.* Blessed be Jesus for that work of *holiness* which accompanied the revival! Much of the *permanence* is traceable to that. I preached twice yesterday in Brunswick Chapel. We had a *high day* in the courts of our God; *seventy-six* souls were justified, of whom *thirty-five* were from the world; *thirty-three* persons besides, obtained *purity of heart.* — Matt. 5: 8. Total, *one hundred and nine;* — so report the *secretaries*, and they registered with conscientious care, having conversed individually with each subject of divine mercy and goodness. All *glory be to God* on high, and on the earth *peace* and *good will.* Amen.

Pondering upon that couplet of an old poet; — felt I could honestly appropriate it:

> " My armor is my honest thought,
> And simple truth my highest aim."

But, — a poor *captive* of my Lord, wandering to and fro, swayed hither and thither, like the *tides* of the sea, attracted by his love, but having no certain dwelling-place; yet welcome everywhere, and in no place more than in Shirley House, near Sheffield, — still a *loneliness* and a *weariness* will creep over me; and a *home*, like other men, and *domestic comforts*, excite *sighs* which are sternly *suppressed.* And so girding on the armor again, and buckling it tight about me, "fly on the prey, and seize the prize;" and shout the victory won through the blood of the Lamb, and the word of our testimony!

But on these accounts I need more religion than other men, differently circumstanced. It is a great point of victory, I find, to have power over one's *own will;* or, rather, to let the *will* of God rule it. As good Richard Baxter says, the *will* is to rule the faculties, and *God* is to rule the *will!* — that if ever God is dethroned from thence, it is *self* that does it, and seats itself in his place, and so *self* rules the will, or the *will* rules self. In either case, he shows it is to have a *fool* for one's master; it is to be at the choice and disposal of a fool and an enemy, and to be in such hands as would certainly undo us. But he would have the *will* of God in our will and faculties, as the *first wheel* in the clock, by which all the *lesser wheels* are moved. That is a rousing thought, that a will that is not dependent upon God's will, is an *idol,* usurping the prerogative of God! We have a *will* to do something or other continually, but it is of the first consequence one should know what it is that commands the will, — *God* or *self ; holiness* or *depravity ; Christ* or the *Devil.*

O, but I do *know* and *feel* that the Lord God rules this *will* of mine ! — the *will* of God is the *first wheel,* and that sets all the *lesser wheels* agoing. But my soul is *weak* in itself, — " weaker than a bruised reed ; " and unless *grace* and *purity* are bestowed from moment to moment, there is no standing. Lord, help me, and keep me thine forever! Amen.

CHAPTER II.

SHEFFIELD.

IN consequence of heavy demands made upon my time by a large number of correspondents, and the many engagements necessarily connected with a *great revival*, I have been hindered, till now, from giving you the desired information respecting this interesting town. As the result of the same *hindrances*, my sketch must, even now, be brief; indeed, the very *meagre materials* which the history of the town offers rather incline me to this.

Sheffield is the great metropolis of English cutlery and other hardware manufactories. It has been distinguished, I believe, from the earliest periods of its history, for this department of human ingenuity and industry. Iron *arrow-heads*, and a particular sort of *weapon-knife*, were articles which employed the artisans of Sheffield, in very early times, long before the use of fire-arms became general. An abundance of minerals, *coal*, and *iron-stone*, in the neighborhood, indicated the destiny of Sheffield, as if by a decree of Providence itself; the *locality being so peculiarly adapted to the processes of metallic manufactories;* — to which may be added, several important streams of water, advantageous for *grinding* purposes.

And to what wondrous perfection have they carried the art of *metallic transformations!* I was thinking, to-day, were *Tubal-Cain* to revisit the earth, and wend his way to

Sheffield, it would surprise him to behold the *progress* of his favorite art since his day! — Gen. 4 : 22.

Mrs. *Sigourney* has ingeniously woven into verse the "*fierce ore meltings, transmutations,*" and many curious things which are wrought out by "*hard hammerings,*" on this "*the world's anvil,*" with as much ease as if they had been but "*threads of silky filaments.*" Speaking of her visit to Sheffield, she says :

> " Many a curious thing
> Was shown us, too, at Sheffield ; ornaments,
> And thousand-bladed knives, and fairy tools
> For ladies' fingers, when the thread they lead
> Through finest lawn ; and silver richly chased
> To make the festal board so beautiful,
> That unawares the tempted matron's hand
> Invades her husband's purse.
>
> But as for me,
> Though the whole art was patiently explained,
> From the first piling of the earthly ore,
> In its dark ovens, to its pouring forth
> With brilliant scintillations, in the form
> Of liquid steel ; or its last lustrous face,
> And finest network ; yet I 'm fain to say,
> The manufacturing interest would find
> In me a poor interpreter. I doubt
> My own capacity to comprehend
> Such transmutations, and confess with shame
> Their processes do strike my simple mind
> Like necromancy. And I felt no joy
> Among the crucibles and cutlery,
> Compared to that, which on the breezy heights
> Met me at every change, or, mid the walks
> Of the *botanic garden*, freshly sprang
> From every flower."

We visited, a few days since, the botanical and horticultural gardens, to which the closing lines of the above allude, and were highly delighted with the place. These gardens comprise about eighteen acres, extending over a gentle declivity, embellished tastefully with flowery parterres, agreeable walks, with plantations and shrubberies on either hand. Here and there we noticed some choice plants from foreign climes. The conservatories are more than one hundred yards long, ornamented with Corinthian pillars, and filled with a choice assortment of all kinds of valuable plants. The principal entrance to the gardens is an elegant Ionic structure, differing little from a similar construction at the temple of *Ilyssus*, at Athens. The second and lower entrance is in the style of a Swiss cottage.

Sheffield is pleasantly situated near the conflux of the rivers Don and Sheaf, and spreads itself along the uneven slopes of gently swelling hills, which rise above the town till they are gradually overtopped by other hills of considerable magnitude.

I was particularly struck, when walking through the town, with a succession of beautiful views of the neighboring landscape. I do not remember any other town so peculiarly privileged. There is scarcely a street, indeed, of any importance, that does not afford a pleasing glimpse of verdant hills, enriched by trees and tracts of woodland, in which are nestled the pretty mansions of *wealthy citizens;* many of whom have "*made their fortunes* in the Sheffield trade," but who love their native town too well, and are too well aware of its pleasant and healthy situation, to leave it and spend their fortunes elsewhere.

Such *views* as I have been speaking of must, however, always be taken *to windward;* especially when there is wind sufficient to waft the clouds of smoke. Or, to be more poetical (for I am now in a town "immortalized by the presence of poets,"— to be more poetical, then), the view must be taken when the wind "*lifts a fold of the inky cloak,*" Sheffield's most fashionable and most popular garment, and throws it over, not the nakedness of the land, but over some of the noblest forms of adorned nature; otherwise the stranger is left to the dictations of his own imaginings. But the scenery is not sufficiently stupendous to impart those impressions of "*romantic grandeur,*" to which a vague and dusky medium, such as this, is so peculiarly favorable. *Rural beauty*, set off by a particularly happy amphitheatrical arrangement of hills, which make a near approach to the *picturesque*, is, perhaps, the leading characteristic of Sheffield scenery.

Nature is really beautiful around Sheffield, but she is too frequently veiled; and I have been offended with Sheffield sometimes on that account. It seems as if the *old town* indulged in fits of jealousy, and was determined to conceal her lovely features, beaming out, as they often do, from the embrace of guardian hills. To one who has been long accustomed to the transparent atmosphere which is drawn over American scenery, such an intervention is far from being pleasing; particularly, too, when he is aware that England, when she has "fair play," presents as lovely a face to the eye of a beholder, as any country in this round world. It is right to say, however, that there are seasons, in the absence of the *smoky mood*, when Nature, in the vicinity of Sheffield, stands forth to the view of her admirers in unveiled loveliness.

In every direction around the town the visitor is treated with a variety of beautiful views:

"The woodland, waving o'er the landscape's pride;
The mansions, scattered o'er its sloping side;
The cornfields, yellow with autumnal wealth;
The meadows, verdant with the hues of health;

"The lifeless walls, that intersect the fields;
The quick-thorn hedge, which now its fragrance yields;
Yon *neighboring town, capped with its cloud of smoke;*
The ceaseless sound with which the calm is broke."

The rivers, streams, and reservoirs, which supply grinding-wheels and forges, are pretty objects. Those busy wheels and tiny cataracts, situated as they are in retired dells and shady groves, rather increase than lessen the power of that pleasing calm which belongs to deep solitude. In the ravine of the Rivelin, the eye is cheered with a succession of small transparent lakes,—rather artificial reservoirs of pure water, for the benefit of the town,—resembling so many crystal mirrors, where dame Nature may look down and ee *herself as others see her.* The country, indeed, for many miles around, is rich in all those objects which beautify a landscape. It is remarkably well wooded; hills and valleys are in a high state of cultivation.

Sheffield, geographically considered, holds a position somewhat central between *Hull, Huddersfield, Leeds, York, Manchester, Liverpool, Nottingham,* and *Birmingham.*

The parish church is a rectangular Gothic fabric, surmounted by a lofty spire. The site is at once central and commanding. It contains several *ancient* monuments. None of them, I believe, possess greater interest than some *modern* productions. I mean those which have emanated from the chisel of the celebrated Chantrey; one, especially, "*the eldest born of his chisel,*" a bust of a clergyman, is considered, by citizen and stranger, as the glory of the edifice.

St. Paul's church has a Grecian aspect. A bust of one of its former ministers, by Chantrey, adorns the interior, and is the principal object of attraction to the admirers of the arts. You will not, I presume, deem it desirable I should enumerate and describe all the churches of the Establishment in this town, or those of other denominations. Those belonging to the Wesleyan Methodists will be the most interesting to you, as they are connected with the present scene of my labors.

Norfolk-street Chapel is the oldest place of worship among the Wesleyans, having been built in 1780. *Carver-street Chapel* is a plain, commodious edifice, erected in 1804. It contains an elegant mural monument, to the memory of the late Mr. Henry Longden, with whose Memoirs, you will remember, we were so much pleased and profited. His name in Sheffield, and, indeed, in almost all parts of England, is as *ointment poured forth*. I have formed a most agreeable acquaintance with his son and biographer. His health is, at present, extremely delicate; *but he inherits his father's talents and piety, with his name*, and enters, so far as health will allow, *"heart and soul"* into the revival. With himself and Mrs. Longden, and their excellent family, I have formed an acquaintance that will, I trust, be perpetuated above.

Ebenezer Chapel, a *pseudo*-Gothic structure, surmounted by a tower (a strange appendix, by the way, for an English Wesleyan Chapel), was erected in 1823. It is a neat building. Here I commenced my labors in Sheffield. *Bridge-houses Chapel* is a substantial building. The *Park Chapel* I have not yet seen.

Brunswick Chapel is *my favorite*. It is really a handsome edifice, with a noble Doric portico. In no other chapel, throughout my travels in this country, have I preached with so much ease and satisfaction, and, perhaps, I may add, SUCCESS. It accommodates about two thousand hearers.

Of the various *"literary edifices"* of Sheffield I can say little more than what relates to their architecture. My time is so completely engrossed, that I cannot command even an hour to obtain additional information.

The *Wesleyan Proprietary Grammar School** presents an extensive and lofty front. Its porticos are of the Corinthian order. It is, when viewed from a distance, altogether a noble and beautiful structure. As there is some probability of your paying Sheffield a visit, it is best, perhaps, not to be too lavish of my praise. The columns of the portico, in front of the college, never satisfy my eye upon a nearer approach. I know you will demand my reason; and my knowledge of your architectural taste and acquirements renders me somewhat shy of assigning it. But I suppose we should not find fault unless we can tell "*the why and the wherefore;*" and that is not always easy or safe; especially for one who makes no pretensions to *connoisseurship* in architecture.

Well, then, I shall venture to say, the columns of the portico are too slender; their diameters do not appear proportionate to their altitude. The intercolumniations seem too large, and appear to fall into the manner of the Ἀραιοστυλος (*Arœostylos*) arrangement; a style that strikes me as being unfavorable to columnar effect, unless the shafts of the columns are proportionate in thickness to the distances by which they are separated. There is that in the *space* or *air* which is interposed between the columns. which apparently lessens their real thickness, and should, therefore, be provided for by adjusting the proportions of the columns to the quantity of air interposed between them. I only write from mere impression, and not from any pre-

* Now *Wesley College.*

cise acquaintance with the rules which belong to the several styles of intercolumniation in architecture. However highly we are pleased with *utility*, there is that in our nature which relishes *beauty*, in architecture. The eye is ever seeking for it, is disappointed at not finding it, or in beholding anything to mar it. The accomplished architect, I may also add, is ever awake to those proportions which satisfy and please.

With these slight exceptions, this edifice takes its place with the handsomest scholastic institutions I have seen in England. The interior arrangements are admirable. The literary departments are conducted with singular ability. The *Rev. John Manners*, the first master, is a clergyman of the Church of England. He is a most agreeable gentleman, possessing qualities of the first order as a teacher; and is a devoted Christian. With him I have also formed an agreeable acquaintance, which, I trust, will last forever. The institution, I understand, occupies a high place in public estimation. Methodist parents send their *boys* to be educated here, from various parts of England, with a *confidence*, which must be a great relief to a parent's heart, that their moral and religious welfare will be as conscientiously guarded as when under the parental roof.

The edifice was erected at an expense to the proprietors of more than ten thousand pounds. The pleasure grounds, comprising about six acres, cost between four and five thousand pounds sterling, in addition.

A short distance below the Wesleyan College stands the Collegiate School. The edifice is upon a much smaller scale, with little more than half the pleasure grounds. But the situation is agreeable, and the style of architecture, *Tudor Gothic*, is peculiarly pleasing. Near to these institutions, on the gentle slopes of the opposite hill, with the vale of *Sharrow* interposed, is the *General Cemetery*. It is a favorite walking-place of mine, in some of my particular moods of mind, as it is but a short distance from Shirley House. The entrance lodge is of the Grecian Doric order. There are two ranges of catacombs; the lowest is surmounted by a terrace in front, over the unprotected verge of which one may step as easily as into eternity. The uppermost range has a parapet and balustrades. The chapel is a handsome structure, with a stately portico of fluted Doric columns. The minister's house is on a still higher elevation. It is a substantial mansion; its Egyptian character has given it a sort of *gloomy elegance*. There are several good monuments; and the grounds, about six acres, are tastefully disposed.

A few days since, in company with two of my fellow-laborers in the revival, *Mr. Unwin* and *Mr. Jepson*, I visited the *Cholera Mount*, another cemetery; *but its gates are closed to all but the* LIVING. A law was enacted during the prevalence of the *cholera*, in 1832, which required *the separate interment of its victims.*

Mr. Montgomery has immortalized the place in a short poem:

> " Yet many a mourner weeps her fallen state,
> In many a home by these left desolate.
> Humanity again asks, ' Who are these?
> And what their crime?' *They fell by one disease*
> Not by the Proteus maladies that strike
> Man into nothingness, not twice alike;
> But when they knocked for entrance at the tomb,
> Their fathers' bones refused to make them room;
> Recoiling NATURE from their presence fled,
> As though a thunderbolt had smote them dead;
> Their cries pursued her with a thrilling plea,
> ' Give us a little earth for charity;'
> She lingered, listened, all her bosom yearned,

Through every vein the mother's pulse returned ;
Then, as she halted on this hill, she threw
Her mantle wide, and loose her tresses flew :
'Live,' to the slain, she cried, 'my children live !
This for an heritage to you I give ;
Had death consumed you by a common lot,
You, with the multitudes had been forgot,
Now through an age of ages shall ye not.' "

I know you will be pleased with the above extract. It was new to me, and peculiarly interesting, having walked over the spot. The poem, I understand, was written during this dreadful visitation in Sheffield. The place where the cholera victims repose is no longer an object of terror, but rather of *mournful reminiscence*, to the inhabitants of Sheffield. None, indeed, would presume to open a grave, or bury there; but there is no risk in visiting the place. Upwards of *four hundred* persons repose here; and their resting-places are not likely to be disturbed for many generations to come, unless Sheffield is made to take the cup of trembling once more, in a similar visitation.

All that *Mr. Montgomery* has claimed for the unfortunate dead, in the poem to which I have referred, has been accorded by the generous people of Sheffield. It is tastefully planted with flourishing trees. *"Perennial daisies,"* and other flowers, begem its emerald verdure. The little birds sing sweetly over their graves, and *"the shrill skylark builds her annual nest* upon their lowly bed." The dew-drops of the morning bespangle the green grass; the moonbeams throw their sweetest influences upon them; the planets seem to look down upon them and bless them; and sometimes "the rainbow throws its sudden arch across their tomb." Trees, likely to become the growth of centuries, wave their branches in the healthy breeze; — "a forest landmark on the mountain head; — a sepulchral eminence,"

— all that the poet desired, it is likely to be till the end of time; — and then how shall the dead arise? How many were ready to die, *fully fitted for heaven?* How many *unprepared?* Alas! even these solitary *four hundred,* should they not be disturbed till the judgment day, will doubtless then present the usual contrasts of character, — saint and sinner, — which we see in every-day life. *But in what proportion? Such as we see in the streets of Sheffield daily?* Alas! then, — but the day will declare it.

In the centre of the grounds stands a monument, — a sort of tapering triangular structure, surmounted by a cross:

> "That all who here sin's bitter wages see,
> May on this mount remember Calvary."

I may just remark that I had the pleasure of dining with Mr. Montgomery * at the mansion of Mr. Jones, at Broomgrove, a few days since. Enjoyed a very pleasing interview. You desire "a short description of his personal appearance." I cannot improve upon the following: "The poet continues to reside at Sheffield, — esteemed, admired, and beloved; a man of purer mind, or more unsuspected integrity, does not exist. He is an honor to the profession of letters; and, by the upright and unimpeachable tenor of his life, even more than by his writings, a persuasive and convincing advocate of religion. In his personal appearance, Montgomery is rather below than above the middle stature; his countenance is peculiarly bland and tranquil, and, but for the occasional sparkling of a clear gray eye, it could scarcely be described as expressive. Those who can distinguish 'the *fine gold* from the sounding brass' of poetry, must place the name of James Montgomery high in the list of British poets; and

---

* Since died.

those who consider that the chiefest duty of such is to promote the cause of religion, virtue, and humanity, must acknowledge in him one of their most zealous and efficient advocates." Perhaps I may never have another opportunity of spending an hour with this eminent person. How transporting the prospect of *an eternity* with "*the excellent of the earth*" — in *heaven!*

I have noticed numerous public buildings, *hospitals, dispensaries, banks*, etc., a particular description of which would afford you but little interest. The hall of the *Cutlers' Company* would please you; it is an elegant Grecian structure, with a Corinthian portico, supporting a triangular pediment, in the tympanum of which are the Cutlers' arms, in bold relief. I did not visit the interior.

I am glad the account of my visits to *Chatsworth, Haddon Hall*, and *Castleton Caverns*, afforded you, and your "select circle," so much pleasure. Since then, I have enjoyed another excursion, in a different direction, in company with my host and hostess, Mr. and Mrs. Greaves, and a few select friends, to *Warncliff*, one of the wildest glens I have seen for many a year:

" Crags, knolls, and mounds confusedly hurled,
The fragments of an earlier world!"

The savage aspect of the place, the singular positions and shapes of the huge fragments of rocks, and the wild manner in which they have been hurled, one upon another, tell of some tremendous concussions as having occurred in this glen, — perhaps beyond the periods of English history. I write as a *stranger*, not having seen any work which affords satisfactory information upon the subject:

" 'T would seem those iron times had reached this glen,
When giants played at hewing mountain blocks,

So bold and strange the profile of the rocks,
Whose huge fantastic figures frown above."

The *Sheffield trade* is, generally, prosperous at present, but it has had great *fluctuations*, and is still subject to them, from a variety of causes. I was particularly struck, the other day, with the following bold sentiments of a native of this town: "No p.ace has suffered more from the *vicissitudes of trade* than Sheffield. The American war produced a state of considerable depression; and the town had only just recovered from the effects of that abortive effort to establish the principle of taxation, without representation, when the wars of the French revolution came to plunge its inhabitants in still deeper distress. The frame of society, throughout the world, was disordered by this long and exhausting contest; and peace itself, when it returned, did not bring prosperity in its train. In order to force a market, the spirit of competition among the manufacturers was carried to such an extent, that they relinquished the fair profits of their trade; the consequence was, an undue depression in the wages of the artisans, and the introduction of the pernicious practice of paying wages in goods instead of money. Many of the workmen, in consequence, became themselves pauper manufacturers, and wholesale dealers in hardware, which they sold, not for what the articles were worth, but for what they would fetch,— not unfrequently at thirty, forty, and even fifty per cent. below the regular prices. The glut of cutlery thus became excessive. The parish was burdened with a host of half-famished claimants, and the poor's rates were so heavy that many of the contributors to those rates reduced their establishments to the lowest possible standard, and took up their residence in the neighboring townships, where the parochial imposts were less oppressive. These evils, like most others in trade, carried in them their own remedy; in time, the quantity of goods manufactured became better adjusted to the extent of the demand; the rate of wages was advanced; money was paid to the workmen instead of goods; and Sheffield began to return slowly, but certainly, to a state of prosperity, which it continued to enjoy till the *great commercial panic* of 1837, which was brought about chiefly by the over-speculations of the three preceding years, and from the baneful effects of which Sheffield, like other manufacturing towns of this kingdom, has not yet recovered; though it has suffered, perhaps, less than Manchester, and many other places. This long depression of our trade and commerce has created much *popular discontent*, from which sprung *Chartism*,—a political faction which threatened the overthrow of the national institutions as now established; but, happily, the *Chartist conspiracy* to take and sack this town was frustrated by the vigilance of the magistrates and police, on the night of January 11th, 1840, when Samuel Holbery, the chief leader of the insurrection, was apprehended in his house, in Eyre-lane, where a quantity of hand grenades, and other combustibles, were found. Some of the insurgents, however, mustered with pikes, etc., in various parts of the suburbs, and, entering the town at midnight, wounded several watch-men, but were soon dispersed by the military and the police, who took a number of prisoners, several of whom were sentenced to various periods of imprisonment at the ensuing York assizes. There seems to be a want of confidence between *masters* and *workmen*, which is a source of *much uneasiness*. This has given rise to *secret combinations* among the workmen, the nature of which I do not understand; but the effect of which is to *awe* and *coerce;* and *some villanous and successful attempts have been made to blow up premises.* This is to be regretted. The *Shef-*

field wares are indeed popular in all parts of the civilized world; yet this circumstance does not insure the *perpetuity* of its trade. Men of capital may be tempted to turn their attention elsewhere, and establish themselves in other towns. The *cutlery* trade is the birthright of Sheffield, and to divert it anywhere else would be *ruinous* to the town. It is to be hoped that *the parties concerned* will come to a better understanding, and no longer persist in bringing about a catastrophe which posterity must deplore, and which would be fatal to their own interests. Perhaps the late great revival of religion, and which is still progressing so sweetly, *may contribute largely to a better state of things*. It surely will, so far as it shall spread among the masses of the population. A revival of pure religion is a *public benefit;* it is a presage of *future prosperity* to the town so honored. *Sheffield*, I trust, will not be an exception."

CHAPTER III.

HADDON HALL AND CHATSWORTH

IN the last chapter MR. CAUGHEY alluded to a visit he made to *Haddon Hall* and *Chatsworth*. We extract his account of the visit, from one of his letters.

On the 10th inst., in company with a party of my Sheffield friends, I visited an old baronial edifice in Derbyshire, named Haddon Hall. The day was charming. Our route lay through a rich and fertile region, with the exception of a few miles, which extended across the wild moors of Derbyshire. These moors present a ridge of considerable elevation, and extend many miles. They are covered with heath and bilberry, presenting a singular contrast to the noble and finely diversified landscape on either side. Having passed the moors, we traversed a picturesque and cheerful country, which improved in beauty all the way to *Bakewell*. This town is pleasantly situated on a hill-side, overlooking the river *Wye*, about two miles from its influx into the river Derwent. Turning suddenly to the left, we proceeded down the lovely vale of Haddon, southward, when, suddenly, the *towers, turrets, and embattled parapets* of *Haddon Hall* burst upon our vision, presenting a picture of singular beauty and interest,—a charming subject for the pencil. As we approached, its architectural detail gradually unfolded Light clouds, careering along the sky, involved the venerable pile now in shadow, and the next moment in sunshine. Lofty trees, full of years, but covered with luxuriant foliage, waved their branches around it. The hill, which rises abruptly from the knoll upon which it is built, is covered with a dark grove of "*massive trees.*" A background so imposing, throws out into fine relief all parts of the edifice. Fifteen or twenty minutes after we caught the first glimpse, we crossed the Wye, and were wandering outside the walls.

I should have informed you that, though uninhabited, it is in a fine state of preservation, and, at a distance, has all the appearance of being the busy residence of wealth and grandeur. The gloomy and solemn silence which pervades it, as one approaches, soon banishes the illusion. The old tower which surmounts the gateway, and which, in the days of Haddon's glory, evidently formed the principal entrance, is very ancient. Historians agree that it had its origin prior to the Conquest. Indeed, every part of this noble fabric has the appearance of having stood the storms of many centuries. There is little in its *history* that would interest you. During a succession of centuries it was the residence of the rich and the great. Mirth and gladness long resounded through its halls, and many thousands have been regaled at its festive board. The descendants of one family (the Vernons) occupied it about four hundred years; "during which," says an historian, "it was invariably regarded, not only as the seat of feudal splendor, but of the most sumptuous and munificent hospitality." It is now the property of the Duke of Rutland, and has been deserted about one hundred years.

The duke has left a servant in charge of the place, with permission to conduct visitors through it. As these baronial residences are so famous in English story, and as this is the most complete of any in the kingdom, remaining, " after a sort," as it was in the days of yore, untouched by the hand of modern improvement, I felt no small desire to inspect the interior. We readily obtained admittance, and were conducted through the various apartments.

> "The postern low,
> And threshold, worn with tread of many feet,
> Receive us silently. How grim and gray
> Yon tall, steep fortalice above us towers!
> Its narrow apertures, like arrow-slits,
> Jealous of heaven's sweet air; its dreary rooms
> Floored with rough stones; its uncouth passages
> Cut in thick walls, bespeak those iron times
> Of despotism, when o'er the mountain-surge
> Rode the fierce sea-king, and the robber hedged
> The chieftain in his moat."

Several of the rooms are hung round with loose tapestry, which afford one a fine idea of the manner in which castles, now in ruins, were furnished in ancient times, as, also, specimens of the taste and comforts of other generations. This tapestry appears to have been as essential to comfort as for ornament. The uncovered walls are of the coarsest masonry, and the doors of the best rooms of the rudest workmanship; but these deformities are delicately concealed by, what a writer terms, "*the cumbrous magnificence of tapestry.*"

It would require more time than I can command at present, to give you a detailed plan of the interior. The number of *apartments* really surprises one; they are indicative, certainly, of a very large household. It is recorded, that, in addition to a numerous family, with, usually, a vast number of visitors, no less than seven score servants were maintained and lodged within it. The walls are massive, and, where there is no tapestry, the apartments are exceedingly comfortless and gloomy. With the exception of the kitchen, the cellar, dining-hall, and the gallery, and a few select rooms, we may say, in the language of one, "The whole is a discordant mass of small and uncomfortable apartments crowded together without order." How very striking the contrast between the order, neatness, and air of comfort, observable in the interior arrangements of American and modern English mansions, and that which is presented at Haddon Hall!

The chapel forms a part of the south and west fronts of Haddon, enriched with painted windows. Upon the stained glass of one we noticed the date, "Millesimo ccccxxvii." [1427.] A witty visitor, some time ago, remarked, that from the very limited capacity of the chapel, when compared with the large scale upon which other parts of the noble pile was laid out, it appeared that the good people of former ages, however much room they required to manage their temporal affairs, contrived to arrange the accommodations for the transaction of their spiritual concerns within very modest dimensions. The pulpit, desk, and several of the pews remain. When peeping around, and peering into every nook and corner, we found, in a little lobby of the chapel, the remains of an old clock; possibly the very same that reproved the prolixity or lengthened zeal of the preacher, at the very time he was receiving the commendations of the spirits that inhabit eternity. The works of the clock, in a state of decay, through very age, and eaten with rust, had fallen down into a rusty, mouldering heap. Thus, Old Time, "the august inheritance of all mankind," marches on, while "Time's sentinel," which measured out the moments, minutes, and hours of other centuries, and sounded the "warning knell" of their departure to other generations, lies *silent, motionless*, and *meaningless*, covered with rust, dust, and cobwebs. A fine subject this for a poet. Come, now, try your genius, and send me "*the results*" by the next steamer

In the central gateway, between the upper and lower courts, we were shown a *relic* of great antiquity, — a Roman altar. It was discovered in the meadows, a short distance from Haddon. The workmanship is uncouth. It contains an inscription, but the letters are so injured and effaced by *time and careless usage*, we tried in vain to decipher them. Through the kindness of a friend, I have seen several transcriptions, differing somewhat. That from Camden, the historian, I judge to be most correct, as it was copied at a date much earlier than any of the others, when the characters could, doubtless, be more easily and correctly deciphered.

DEO
MARTI
BRACIACÆ
OSITIUS
CACCILIAN
PREFECT
TRO
V. S.

As Mr. * * * is a professed antiquarian, this inscription may, perhaps, suggest a train of thought which he may turn to some account in his future "articles" for the press.

The *dining hall*, with its elevated platform, where sat "the lord of the castle, at the head of his household and guests, and the gallery at the end appropriated to mirth and minstrelsy," on festive occasions, is still, though solitary and desolate, imposing. On the wainscot we observed a singular fastening, large enough to admit the wrist of a man's hand; the tradition of which was a subject of merriment to the party. It was designed as a method of punishment, it seems, for trivial *offences*, as also to enforce certain laws, enacted by the servants themselves, with regard to each other. He that refused to drink his horn of ale, or neglected to perform properly the duties of his office, had his hand locked into this "*keep*," a little above his head, when abundance of cold water was poured down the sleeve of his doublet. Rather a hazardous affair to be a tee-totaller in those days!

After inspecting some ancient pictures and furniture, armorial crests, carvings in wood, &c., the ladies of our party treated us to an excellent dinner, "on the premises;" after which, we rode forward to Chatsworth Castle, the residence of the Duke of Devonshire. I can hardly tell you why, but it is seldom I have felt emotions so singularly pensive and melancholy, as when walking in and around Haddon Hall. It was not, indeed, until we stood in a little flower-garden,—once "the gem of Haddon," now "neglected and forlorn,"—that I recognized the *solitariness* of my feelings in full. *Mrs. Sigourney* must have had feelings somewhat similar, as she penned, it seems, the following lines on the same spot:

> " 'T is passing strange!
> Dwell life and death in loving company?
> Why bloom those flowers, with none to inhale their sweets?
> Who trim yon beds so neatly, and remove
> Each withered leaf, and keep each straggling bough
> In beautiful obedience?
>
> — Come they back,
> They of the by-gone days, when none are near,
> And with their spirit-eyes inspect the flowers
> That once they loved? Toil they in shadowy ranks
> 'Mid these deserted bowers, then flit away?
> They seem but just to have set the goblet down
> As for a moment, yet return no more.
> The chair, the board, the couch of state, are here,
> And we, the intrusive step are fain to check,
> As though we pressed upon their privacy.
> Whose privacy? *The dead?* A riddle all!
> And we ourselves are riddles.

> While we cling
> Still to our crumbling hold, so soon to fall
> And be forgotten, in that yawning gulf
> That whelms all past, all present, all to come,
> O, grant us wisdom, Father of the soul,
> To gain a changeless heritage with thee!"

It is Dr. Johnson, I think, who observes, and properly too, that whatever withdraws us from the power of our senses; whatever makes the past, the distant, or the future, predominate over the present, advances us in the dignity of thinking beings; and he deprecates, both for himself and friends, the *rigidity of that philosophy* which would conduct us unmoved over any ground which has been dignified by wisdom, bravery, or virtue; — that the man is little to be envied whose *patriotism* would not gain force upon the plains of *Marathon*, or whose *piety* would not grow warmer among the ruins of *Iona*. Haddon Hall, unless I am mistaken, lays claim to no such stirring recollections. It possesses an interest of its own, — not, I should judge, emanating so much from historical reminiscences, as from its *great antiquity*, and its *utter loneliness*. Though identified with the present, as well as the past; though occupying still the "site of its youth," and permitted still to lift its turreted head in sunshine and glory, invested with the foliage of many trees, and graced by a charming modification of scenery, itself the noblest object in the picture; although it bears the mark of a foreigner, like myself, yet it claims affinity with the mansions that are. A contemporary with the present generation, as it was with those generations which have passed the flood, who now dwell under other skies, "on those eternal shores," yet it is *isolated, lonely* and *ruinous*, and seems rather to hold communion with the dead than the living; pleading *haughtily* (perhaps this is too *harsh* a word), but

4*

mournfully, and, rough as its features are, *feelingly* for glories gone by, and which are never to return; as if claiming "*a sigh to the memory*" of the good and the bad, the virtuous and the vicious, the beautiful and the ungraceful, the religious and the irreligious, the humble and the proud, the pensive and the gay, the learned, the intellectual, and the illiterate, the happy and the unhappy, the courageous and the pusillanimous, the Christian and the infidel, who sojourned within its walls.

When passing down the vale, with the head instinctively turned toward the desolate pile, my eyes lingered long upon its crumbling battlements, with emotions hallowed and tender; something akin to what one feels sometimes when recalling the memories of the *faded past;* "like the memory of joys that are past, pleasant and mournful to the soul."

"Forsaken stood the hall,
Worms ate the floor, the tap'stry fled the walls;
No fire the kitchen's cheerful grate displayed;
No cheerful light the long-closed sash conveyed;
The crawling worm, that turns a summer fly,
Here spun his shroud, and laid him up to die
The winter death. Upon the bed of state,
The bat, shrill shrieking, wooed his flickering mate.

* * * * * *

The air was thick, and in the upper gloom
The bat — or *something in its shape* — was winging.
And on the wall, as chilly as a tomb,
The death's-head moth was clinging.

* * * * * *

The floor was redolent of mould and must;
The fungus in the rotten seams had quickened,
While, on the oaken table, coats of dust
Perennially had thickened.

* * * * * *

The subtle spider, that from overhead
Hung like a spy on human guilt and error
Suddenly turned, and up its slender thread
Ran with a nimble terror."

* * * * * *

The above is a gloomy picture, and strangely out of harmony with the eloquent and majestic exterior of Haddon, and the verdant beauty of surrounding nature. * * * *
Still I carried out the propensities of my nature, *gazing back upon the past;* the lovely meadows, and cheerful uplands, dotted or fringed with trees; the devious windings of the busy, sparkling Wye; the groves of Haddon, with the ever-varying features of the romantic and venerable pile, — a view changeable through shade and sunshine, and singularly dependent upon the various turnings of the road which led us away from a picture so enchanting. Arriving at length at a *decisive* bend of the highway, Haddon Hall disappeared from my eyes,— *perhaps forever;* but it has left an impression upon my heart, with a series of beautiful images, not speedily to be erased or forgotten. One said: "There are three things we should constantly keep in view,— What we *once were*, what we *now are*, and what we *shall be* hereafter." Every Christian, I thought, should cheer his heart by a contemplation of that "deed of settlement" drawn out for us by St. Peter: *"Begotten us again unto a living hope,— to an inheritance incorruptible, and undefiled, and that fadeth not away, reserved in heaven for you, who are kept by the power of God, through faith unto salvation."* Give me that estate, then, and that mansion, which cannot be wasted or spoiled by invasion; of which war cannot deprive me; which law cannot win from me, nor debt mortgage, nor power wring from me; which cannot be defiled by sin, or sink to decay and ruin by *time,*

storm, or *human caprice;* of which death cannot disinherit me; which must increase in value throughout the lapse of eternal ages; and, in the possession of which, by the will of God, eternity shall confirm me. Hallelujah! Amen! Eternity claimed our thoughts; — the probable destinies too of the multitudes who, in by-gone ages, gladdened those halls we had just left, and who, like ourselves, for the last time, glanced a farewell to "turret, battlement and tower." Hopes of possibly meeting my own friends upon earth, but *surely* in heaven, though now separated by the mighty ocean, — in that bright world where *ruin* and *death* are words unknown, and where "farewells are heard never,"— animated my pensive spirit, as we entered the cheerful grounds of Chatsworth Park. And what a park! — it covers an area, it is said, of eleven miles. The afternoon was one rarely excelled for loveliness.

> "I've heard the humid skies did ever weep
> In merry England, and a blink of joy
> From their blue eyes was like a pearl of price.
> Mine own indeed are sunnier, yet at times
> There comes a day so exquisitely fair,
> That, with its radiance and its rarity,
> It makes the senses giddy.
>   Such an one
> Illumined Chatsworth, when we saw it first,
> Set like a gem against the hanging woods
> That formed its background. Herds of graceful deer,
> Pampered, perchance, until they half forget
> Their native fleetness, o'er the ample parks
> Roamed at their pleasure. From the tower that crests
> The eastern hill, a floating banner swayed
> With the light breezes, while a drooping ash,
> Of foliage rich, stood lonely near the gates,
> Like the presiding genius of the place,
> Unique and beautiful. Their silver jet
> The sparkling fountains o'er the freshened lawns

Threw fitfully, and, gleaming here and there,
The tenant-statues with their marble life
Peopled the shades.
    But wondering most we marked
A princely labyrinth of plants and flowers,
All palace-lodged,* and breathing forth their sweets
On an undying summer's balmy breast.
And well might wealth expend itself for you,
Flowers, glorious flowers! that dwelt in Eden's bound,
Yet sinned not, fell not, and whose silent speech
Is of a better paradise, where ye,
Catching the essence of the deathless soul,
Shall never fade."

We spent an agreeable hour in walking through the palace. The generosity displayed by English noblemen, in allowing the public free access to their splendid mansions, cannot be too much admired. Every room is thrown open. A servant is ready to conduct every party which arrives, and seems emulous to gratify the visitors to the full extent of their wishes. The rules which visitors are required to observe seem to be very few; — none which impose any painful and unnecessary restraint, or to which any person of politeness and good breeding could possibly object. The succession of rooms through which we were conducted presented a wonderful contrast to those of old Haddon, — *spacious, lofty* and *elegant*. The dazzling splendor of the furniture, the rich decorations of the ceilings, and even of the walls of the staircases, where the talents of a *Verrio*, a *Laguerre*, and others, are displayed in, at least, splendor of coloring and design (though the gods and goddesses — allegorical personages, and mortals like ourselves — are mingled together with little regard to order, and are not at all remarkable for taste or *decency*), are yet truly magnifi-

---

* The Conservatory.

cent. The great variety of carving in wood, dead game, flowers and shells, encompassed with appropriate ornaments, — the work of one *Gibbons*, an artist once celebrated in this country, — appeared exquisitely beautiful, and so *natural* as to take one's senses by surprise, to find them only wood. The immense collection of paintings, — *portrait, history* and *landscape*, — by the first masters in Europe; the numerous ornaments and curiosities, products of British and foreign art, laid out in magnificent profusion; the library, filled with the works of almost all ages and climes, — were all, and more, than the fame of the justly celebrated " Palace of the Peak " had led us to expect.

A short distance from the palace stands the *conservatory*, — a splendid object; the largest of the kind, we were informed, in the world. The genius of the duke is now exerting itself in a series of improvements around this conservatory, which, when completed, must have a grand effect. He seems determined upon carrying the "capabilities of the place " to the highest possible perfection. His rock-work, upon an extensive scale, water-works, and accompaniments, must render the place a scene of " fairy enchantment."

> " Great princes have great playthings. Some have played
>   At hewing mountains into men, and some
>   At building human wonders mountain high."

A path from the conservatory directed our steps along the margin of a small lake, which seemed to serve the green slopes and surrounding trees as a transparent mirror. A slight bubbling in the centre attracted our attention, out of which arose suddenly a connected column of water, which continued to ascend to the suprising height of seventy or eighty feet, played beautifully for a few moments, and then gradually shortened to the height of ten feet, when it came down with a splash and disappeared. A short walk brought us to another sheet of water, clear as crystal, where an aged man managed a secret spring, which surprised us with another column, of a similar height to the former, but somewhat varied in its motions, white as the ocean's foam, brilliant and beautiful. I dare not trust myself with an attempt to describe the appearance of the falling particles of water illumined by the sunshine, the reflected radiance upon the foliage of the trees, and the verdant margin of the water, with all the poetic ideas they inspired, lest you should suspect me as having exchanged my sober and favorite authors in theology for the contaminating and fictitious visions of the novelist.

> " 'T was beautiful to stand and watch
> The fountain's crystal turn to gems;
> And from the sky such colors catch,
> As if 't were raining diadems."

Chatsworth for several years afforded a shelter to unhappy *Hobbes*, the infidel. In one of the rooms of the palace, which we had no curiosity to see, he smoked his twelve pipes of tobacco every afternoon, and, in the midst of its appropriate and offensive fume, he "*belched out upon paper*" his more *offensive and dangerous sentiments against Christianity;* which, but for the interposition of the Almighty, would have spread themselves over these kingdoms, if not over the whole world, like a smoke from the bottomless pit. As it was, his writings injured many. The Earl of Rochester, and other English noblemen, not a few, were ruined by them. "*I hate,*" was the *surly motto* of this unfortunate man; and its poisonous venom mingled with the spirit of his every attack upon all that is holy, just and good, in the religion of the Son of God. The ways of

Providence are mysterious. This man was suffered to remain upon the earth to the advanced age of *ninety-two*, tormented with fears, for which sceptics were by no means able to account, but which preyed perpetually upon his wretched mind:

"In sleep,
In sickness, haunting him with dire suspicions
Of something in himself that would not die.'

Such fearful visitations, although they rendered his life miserable, were mercifully designed, no doubt, to alarm his conscience, to restrain his pen; yes! and to save his soul. The sequel of his melancholy history shows their inefficiency. With an *infatuation*, for which the pious and learned men of his age found it as difficult to account, as the sceptics for his humiliating fears, he continued to cling to infidelity while he wielded his weapons, as he could, against Christianity. Of him it might be said truly:

" The infidel has shot his bolts away,
Till, his exhausted quiver yielding none,
He gleans the blunted shafts that have recoiled,
And aims them at the shield of truth again."

Death, it is said, he would never allow to be a subject of conversation in his presence. Reflections of the most tormenting character seemed to be associated with the idea. An unaccountable terror seized him, if his candle went out in the night. He did not die at Chatsworth; but his last hours were the most melancholy imaginable. "Where are you going, sir?" inquired one of his friends. "I am taking a leap in the dark," replied the dying man. In the "dark!" What! and does the light of your philosophy afford you no aid in such a trying hour as this? Ah! no; it may *bewilder and terrify*, but it is insufficient to assure and comfort the departing soul. Infidel philosophy, — if *philosophy* that may be called, which *"puts darkness for light, and light for darkness"* (Isaiah 5: 20), presents only *darkness for light*, in that hour, in which, above all other hours, the soul demands light the most clear and satisfactory. *"I am taking a leap in the dark!"* Ay! and *into* the dark! A *"leap!"* — no, that is a motion quite too rapid for an infidel. Such characters are not usually so *courageous*. The last sensible words the dying Hobbes was heard to utter, after being told he could live no longer, were, "I shall be glad, then, to find a hole to *creep* out of the world at."

In whatever direction we strayed through "the grounds of Chatsworth," we were cheered with a perpetual succession of new and interesting objects. The "*exuberance of wealth*" has introduced a variety of *petty defects*, which appeared to me to detract from that simplicity, unity, and majesty of nature, for which Chatsworth is so deservedly famous. The truth is, so extremely beautiful is nature, in this earthly paradise, that any attempt to improve it, unless by the hand of the most delicate and exquisite taste, is but to deform; — like applying *rouge* to the face of a perfect beauty, or adding colors to the blooming flowers in our gardens. Chatsworth reminds one of Tasso's description of *Isolla Bella:*

> " Here a new world of joy surrounds our path ;
> With spreading shade, the trees and evergreens
> Burst into gladdening life ; the fountain's play
> Sheds sweet refreshment upon all around ; the boughs
> Move quivering in the gentle breeze of morn,
> And flowers uprising from their beds, with eyes
> Of infant sweetness, seem to smile on us.
> The gardener now unroofs the winter-house,
> And gives the citrons to the balmy air.

> The blue expanse of heaven rests overhead,
> Whilst the far mountains, in the horizon's verge,
> Shake off their wintry coverlet of snows."

The picture, beautiful as it is, is not complete, unless we add the lines of an English poet to those of the Italian,— to which I would add a *gem*, to which, were the poet alive, he would not, perhaps, object:

> "And streams, as if created for his use,
> Pursue the track of his directing wand,
> Sinuous or straight, now rapid and now slow,
> Now murmuring soft, now roaring in cascades,—
> Even as he bids! The enraptured owner smiles.
> 'Tis finished, and yet, finished as it seems,
> Still wants a grace, the loveliest it could show,—
> A WIFE."

After enjoying a walk of considerable length, through the park, we returned to the hotel to tea, after which we set out for Sheffield. When crossing the *Derbyshire Moors*, on our return, we noticed abundance of game, with their young, now well grown, enjoying themselves midst the *bilberry* and *heath*, which afford them both food and shelter.

But what a pensive, *solitary stillness* presides over these "wild, unpeopled hills!"

> "That seldom hear a voice save that of heaven;
> They seem alone beneath the boundless sky."

They look imposing when seen from afar. Distance lends them a singular enchantment; softens down their rude features into soft harmonious masses, and invests with rich purple, poetry-inspiring *tint*, as they sweep away in graceful and long-continued outlines; but, ah me! when one is in the midst of them, as in life-scenes, *poetry* gives place to stern, stubborn, rugged *reality!*

And, speaking of *poetry*, what an interest does that divine art fling over scenes and places however wild and barren! Mrs. *Sigourney* passed over these *Moors* a few years ago, after visiting *Sheffield*. Among her "recorded impressions" of *Sheffield* and its vicinities is the following touching story:

> "There stood a cottage, near a spreading moor,
> Just where its heathery blackness melted down
> Into a mellower hue. Fast by its side
> Nestled the wheat-stalk, firmly bound and shaped
> Even like another roof-tree, witnessing
> Fair harvest and good husbandry. Some sheep
> Roamed eastwards o'er the common, nibbling close
> The scanty blade, while toward the setting sun
> A hillock stretched, o'ershadowed by a growth
> Of newly-planted trees. 'T would seem the abode
> Of rural plenty and content. Yet here
> A desolate sorrow dwelt, such as doth wring
> Plain, honest hearts, when what had long been twined
> With every fibre is dissected out.
> Beneath the shelter of those lowly eaves
> An only daughter made the parents glad
> With her unfolding beauties. Day by day
> She gathered sweetness on her lonely stem,
> The lily of the moorlands. They, with thoughts
> Upon their humble tasks, how best to save
> Their little gains, or make that little more,
> Scarce knew that she was beautiful; yet felt
> Strange thrall upon their spirits when she spoke
> So musical, or from some storied page
> Beguiled their evening hour.
>   And when the sire
> Descanted long, as farmers sometimes will,
> Upon the promise of his crops, and how
> The neighbors envied that his corn should be
> Higher than theirs, and how the man, who hoped
> Surely to thrive, must leave his bed betimes,
> Or of her golden cheese the mother told,
> She with a filial and serene regard

Would seem to listen, her young heart away
'Mid other things.
    For, in her lonely room,
She had companions that they knew not of—
Books that reveal the sources of the soul,
Deep meditations, high imaginings,
And ofttimes, when the cottage lamp was out,
She sat communing with them, while the moon
Looked through her narrow casement fitfully.
Hence grew her brow so spiritual, and her cheek
Pale with the purity of thought, that gleamed
Around her from above.
    The buxom youth,
Nursed at the ploughshare, wondering eyed her charms,
Or of her aspen gracefulness of form
Spoke slightingly. Yet when they saw the fields
Her father tilled were clad with ripening grain,
And knew he had no other heir beside,
They, with unwonted wealth of Sunday clothes,
And huge red nosegays, flaunting in their hands,
Were fain to woo her. And they marvelled much
How the sweet fairy, with such quiet air
Of mild indifference, and with truthful words
Kind, yet determinate, withdrew herself
To chosen solitude, intent to keep
A maiden's freedom.
    But in lonely walks,
What time the early violets richly blent
Their trembling colors with the vernal green,
A student boy, who dwelt among the hills,
Taught her of love. There rose an ancient tree,
The glory of their rustic garden's bound,
Around whose rough circumference of trunk
A garden seat was wreathed; and there they sat,
Watching gray-vested twilight, as she bore
Such gifts of tender and half-uttered thought
As lovers prize. When the thin-blossomed furze
Gave out its autumn sweetness, and the walls
Of that low cot with the red-berried ash
Kindled in pride, they parted: he to toil
Amid his college tasks, and she to weep.

The precious scrolls, that with his ardent heart
So faithfully were tinged, unceasing sought
Her hand, and o'er their varied lines to pore
Amid his absence, was her chief delight.

— At length they came not. She, with sleepless eye,
And lip that every morn more bloodless grew,
Demanded them in vain. And then the tongue
Of a hoarse gossip told her, he was *dead —
Drowned in the deep, and dead.*
                    Her young heart died
Away at those dread sounds. Her upraised eye
Grew large and wild, and never closed again.
' Hark, hark ! he calleth, I must hence away,'
She murmured oft, but faint and fainter still
Nor other word she spoke.
                    And so she died ;
And now that lonely cottage on the moor
Hath no sweet visitant of earthly hope,
To cheer its toiling inmates. Habit-led
They sow, and reap, and spread the daily board,
And steep their bread in tears.
                    God grant them grace
To take this chastisement, like those who win
A more enduring mansion, from the blast
That leaveth house and home so desolate ! "

From an eminence on the moors we obtained a noble prospect of the extensive, hilly, and well-wooded vale in which Sheffield reposes, — apparently at the extremity. The scene was everywhere varied and full of beauty. A rich tone of coloring from the setting sun spread itself over all objects. Our party were all happy in the love of God, and rejoiced in prospect of that glorious hour, when, like Moses on Pisgah, we should, from *" the ridge that separates two worlds,"* behold our heavenly Canaan, and, like him, enter immediately upon the enjoyment of our eternal inheritance.

5*

CHAPTER IV.

CASTLETON AND PEAK'S HOLE CAVERN.

BEFORE entering upon those *extraordinary manifestations* of the grace and power of GOD, for which the ministry of *Mr. Caughey* has been so remarkably distinguished, we invite the *reader* to an excursion with him into *Derbyshire*, — to behold other scenes of *beauty*, of *solemn sublimity*, and *grandeur*, — the *work* of the same Almighty God, to whom are *known all his works, from the beginning of the world.* — Acts 15 : 18.

We copy from the letters of Mr. Caughey.

In company with a party of Sheffield friends, I enjoyed, the other day, an agreeable excursion into *Derbyshire*, as far as *Castleton*. In the language of a native of Sheffield, "We bade adieu to the *sooty majesty* of Sheffield, and the thick atmosphere in which it was enveloped, for the purpose of participating the pleasure of another ramble among the heathy hills of Derbyshire, and inhaling the fresh breezes which play upon their summits." With the exception of a salute from a tremendous shower of rain, which met us at the base of the wild moors, to which I alluded in my last letter, and another as we approached Castleton, we had a lovely day, and were blessed with such a succession of charming rural scenery as I have seldom seen excelled. There is a good carriage road over the moors. From their summits, at various points of elevation, we surveyed a finely disposed and variegated landscape, with a great abundance of *woodland*, quite equal, in this respect, to extensive tracts of country in America; while,

> " On either hand the knolls and swells
> Were crimson with the heather bells."

Descending from this wild range of hills, our route lay through a highly cultivated country, picturesque and cheerful. We passed along the verge of a valley, in which Hathersage is seated, and through which meanders the river *Derwent*. If the scenery was not *sublime*, it was really *exquisitely beautiful*. But I must be excused the "*particular description*" you require, as, at the time, I took no notes of the numberless objects that chained our admiration; and I feel unable now to give you a just idea of this lovely specimen of English scenery.

We did not alight at *Hathersage*, else I could have related an incident that would have greatly interested the *boys*, who were so much amused, you remember, with the story of " *Robin Hood ;*" namely, that I had visited the tomb of his celebrated follower, " *Little John.*" Tradition says, he was buried in the church-yard of this village. A grave of gigantic dimensions is still pointed out as the spot where his ashes repose. The house, too, in which he died, is said to be still in existence, close by. I fear they will scarcely pardon my indifference, for we could not spare time to see it; but you will please to inform them that a kind gentleman of Sheffield, and his family, who are *ruralizing* at Hathersage, or near it, have given me an invitation to spend a day with them. Should I do so, they may expect ' *particulars in full ;*" but, should they become impatient, you may cool their ardor a little by saying, that a worthy historian has thrown the village story into "the swamp of doubt;" so that the tradition is at such a discount at present as greatly to embarrass the eloquence of some antiquarian adventurers.

From Hathersage, we proceeded through Hope Dale to Castleton, six miles, where we arrived in the midst of a tremendous storm of thunder and lightning and rain; reminding us of Him of whom an old English poet speaks, —

> "That sendeth thundering claps
> Like terrors out of hell,
> That man may know a God there is,
> That in the heavens doth dwell."

After the storm, which lasted nearly an hour, the sun came out in brilliancy. We left the hotel, and sallied forth in quest of the celebrated *Peak's Hole Cavern*. Suddenly, on turning a corner, the rocky projections which overhung the entrance met our view; masses of rocks, craggy and menacing, and blackened with the storms of centuries, towered on high. A few steps, and the eye measured the vast dimensions of the mouth of this stupendous cavern. The heavy masses of unsupported rock, which form the sweep of a depressed *natural arch*, and which rises high into the precipice; the ribs and layers of rock lining the sides and roof of a *spacious vestibule*, one hundred feet wide, three hundred long, and forty high; the dubious twilight that pervades it, and which fades imperceptibly into deeper gloom, and at length into utter darkness, as the eye attempts to image a sort of perspective, present a *scene* of such extraordinary wildness, if not sublimity, as inspires the mind with feelings of a powerful character. The ladies of our party substituting *shawls* for bonnets, and the gentlemen crowned with low white hats, prepared for the occasion, — each with candle in hand, — we bade farewell to *day*, following our guide along a rude path, in a winding direction, which became more and more awful, as the feeble light from advancing tapers rendered the scene more palpable and visible, reminding one of *Homer's* description of the abodes of the *Cimmerians* :

> " The gloomy race, in subterraneous cells,
> Among surrounding shades and darkness dwells ;
> Hid in the unwholesome covert of the night,
> They shun the approaches of the cheerful light :
> The sun ne'er visits their obscure retreats,
> Nor when he runs his course, nor when he sets.
> Unhappy mortals ! ——— "

It must have been some such dark caverns as this, we thought, which afforded the heathen such a variety of gloomy and frightful imagery when describing the abodes and deeds of their gods. The cavern of *Somnus*, if I recollect right, was located somewhere in the country of the *Cimmerians*. Iris, by the command of Juno, arrayed in a "*brilliant robe*," and seated upon "*the glowing curve of a radiant arch of many colors*," descended, upon a special mission, into the cavern of Somnus. Her visit was represented as one of mercy. It was to require the god of the place to put an end to the sorrows of the unfortunate *Halcyone*, who had long been imploring the gods for the speedy and safe return of her husband from a long voyage which he had undertaken. Though a lady of fortune, and living in a splendid palace, with her own hands she prepared a superb garment to present to him on his return. This event became the one all-absorbing feeling of her heart. Daily did she visit the temples of the gods, offering rich and costly gifts at their shrines and altars, to induce them to interpose their protection, and hasten him home. Alas! she was a *widow*, and she knew it not. Her husband lay at the bottom of the deep and troubled sea. "Hope deferred maketh the heart sick." The time expired when he had promised to return. She became more and more importunate. The altar of Juno was honored and enriched by the disconsolate *Halcyone*. The goddess resolved, in great compassion, to put an end to prayers and anxieties, which must forever be unavailing; for even the gods of the heathen were supposed to hear prayer, and to honor those who honored them. Iris was sent down from heaven with an order to *Somnus*, the god of sleep, to show Halcyone, in a dream, that her husband, Ceyx, was "*numbered with the dead in shipwreck.*" Iris reached the cavern, and walked onward, as we did through Peak's Hole. The radiant robes of this goddess illumined the swarms of dreams which crowded the place, but she pushed their unsubstantial forms aside with her hands, and threaded her way through the cavern, till she arrived in the presence of the god of sleep. She found him stretched upon "*a bed of ebony, hung with black curtains,*" enjoying a comfortable nap. Dreams, numerous as the stars of heaven, or sands by the seaside, surrounded his bed, in all sorts of shadowy forms, over whom the goddess noticed three chiefs, *Morpheus*, *Phobetor*, and *Phantasus*, sons of Somnus;—all were awaiting the orders of the drowsy god "*with regard to embassies*" to mortals. But how striking their description of the cavern itself! They represented it as a place into which no sunbeam had ever entered, no chink or cranny had, from *periods* immemorial, admitted a single ray of light into this shadowy abode, sufficient to distinguish day from night. No crowing of cocks, no barking of dogs, no cackling of geese, nor any other sounds inimical to sleep, had ever disturbed the silence and death-like tranquility of the place. There were indeed certain gurglings of the *river of oblivion;* but the rippling of its gentle waves over the smooth pebbles of its channel, only whispered peace, and contributed to lull the mind into the most profound repose. Poppies and other narcotic plants grew at the entrance in great quantities. From these the hand of *Night* extracted *soporific* juices, which she always scatters around her when she exercises her soft enchantments upon the eyelids and senses of mortals.

Somnus, in obedience to the command of Juno, despatched Morpheus to inform the unhappy *Halcyone* of the untimely death of her husband; and Iris, endangered by the "*stupefactive vapors*" of the cavern, made a hasty retreat, and reäscended into heaven. Morpheus finding Halcyone asleep, transformed himself into the form and likeness of Ceyx, and appeared before her imagination in a dream; but *pale, cold* and *deathly, hair wet, water dripping from* his beard! He leaned over her, pronounced her name, — "Dear Halcyone!"—and wept bitterly, while he told her, "*You are a widow!* I am no longer numbered with the living;— your Ceyx is no more. The ship in which I sailed was overtaken by a storm;—a whirlwind from the mouth of Auster,* shook our vessel to pieces, and we were all swallowed up by the reckless, insatiable waves of the sea. Your name, dear Halcyone! was uttered amidst the remorseless roar of billows, and it formed the last faltering accents of your Ceyx, when he sank in the deep. My spirit is now

---

* The *South-wind god;* — each of the winds of the cardinal points was under the command of a particular god, according to heathen mythology. Sacrifices were frequently offered them, to obtain their favor, or to appease their anger or fury

wandering to and fro, awaiting the consolation of funeral ceremonies, and the tears of the object of its faithful affections, ere it descends to the realms of Pluto." Halcyone awoke with a scream, which aroused her attendants. She searched the room, but in vain, for it was but a dream, and Ceyx was not there. She left the palace in a state of distraction, and ran to the place, close by, where she parted with her husband, and where he stepped aboard the ship that was never to return. Wild with woe, from a rock she gazed forth upon the waves. She saw a dark object among the billows — it approached nearer and nearer. The waves bore their charge to the shore — it was a "*dead body.*" Support Halcyone! the *corse* of her husband rolls at her feet! * * * This is an affecting picture. It was thus the refined and polished heathen accounted for dreams — especially those of a remarkable or supernatural character.

Do excuse this long digression. I have related, it is true, nothing new, as your classic reading has long since made you familiar with this and other mythological fables, and "*deeds and doings*" of these imaginary divinities of the ancients. But it is Monday, and my head is in a state of such confusion, after the efforts of yesterday, that I am unfit for anything else; and it has afforded me a few minutes' amusement, which I hope you will not deem unbecoming. Modern literature is not averse to mythological allusions; indeed, some of our own poets, as well as the poetry of those we denominate *classics*, are scarcely intelligible, without a knowledge of the mythology of the ancients.

But, to return to the exploring party in Peak's Hole Cavern,— *not altogether a classical name*, but no matter; onward and onward we went, into deep and total darkness; as if descending into the *Erebus* of *Pluto*, "*where reign monotonous gloom and ever-during silence;*" if not into

Tartarus, his second hell. But no Tityus greeted our vision, tormented by a devouring vulture; nor a Tantalus, nor a Sisyphus; — a fit place, one would imagine, for unhappy *Tantalus*, as the presence of *rills* and *fountains of water, high as the lips*, would have *taunted* and *punished* him sufficiently for the affront he offered the gods at the celebrated feast. Did Dives discover " *the location of the water*," think you, when " *he cried and said, Father Abraham, send Lazarus, that he may dip the tip of his finger in water, and cool my tongue; for I am tormented in this flame*"?—Luke 15: 24. Pardon me for introducing this *scriptural fact*, surrounded by the fabled characters of heathen mythology, and the fancies of Italian poetry; but Dante, you remember, in his *Dell' Inferno*, represents the soul of one in hell, tormented by thirst, greatly aggravated by a recollection of the *rivulets and streams* of his native regions, with which he was so familiar in his lifetime, and crying to the passers by:

> " O ! you," he cried, " that without pain (though why,
> I know not) pass through this unhappy world,
> Hear and mark well the sorrow of Adamo ;
> Living, I had whatever my heart could wish,
> And now, alas ! I lack a drop of water.
> The murmuring rivulets down the verdant hills
> Of Cassentino, flowing into Arno,
> Which keep their little channels moist and cool,
> Are ever in mine eyes ; and not in vain,
> For their sweet images inflame my thirst
> More than the malady that shrinks my visage.
> The rigid justice, which torments me here,
> Even from the place that I committed sin,
> Draws means to mock and multiply my groans "

Sisyphus, too, might have had his punishment here, as there is no lack of steep rocks, up which, in the darkness of eternal night, he might continue to roll enormous stones forever, without the possibility of getting one of them to the summit. The thought, however, struck us that, had the insulted *Latona* chosen this place for the punishment of *Tityus*, she could not have found a chamber sufficiently large in which to punish the giant, as he covers a space of *nine acres* of ground. Such a difficulty, however, in the estimation of a heathen, would not have been too formidable for the power of *Latona's* children —*Apollo* and *Diana*. *Ixion*, too, as a punishment for his vanity, in boasting of his successful addresses to the *cloud-formed Juno*, to the great injury of Jupiter, might have been subjected here, with little ingenuity, to the *dizzy and uneasy whirl of an ever-turning wheel*. And the Danaides, inhabitants also of the realms of Pluto, could have been accommodated with a "*prison of adamant*," and plenty of water; if not enough to fill a *bottomless barrel*, yet sufficient to afford them perpetual employment in these doleful regions. A "*classical thinker*," seated aloft upon one of those gloomy crags, for which this cavern is remarkable, might, at the expense of our party, have treated himself to a variety of such fabulous illustrations. Our ladies, indeed, were not so numerous as the family of the Danaides; and, perhaps, his admiration of the fair sex might have inclined him to spare them a comparison with the forty-nine unhappy daughters of the king of Argos; yet, the appearance of the "*rough remainder*" of our sex was well calculated to afford him a theme for some of "the *worst imaginings*," connected with his characters in the realms of Pluto. I am sure, dear sir, this part of my letter will greatly interest the youthful branches of your family. But if they are inclined to smile at the *simplicity* of the heathen, to whose mythology I have been alluding, you must remind them that, if they have a more *consistent, sublime*, and *elevated* faith, they owe it to that *Bible*, which many American infidels attempt to despise.

Continuing our subterranean tour, we passed through a variety of spacious halls and chambers, some of which our guide named,— *The Bell House, Roger Raine's House, the Chancel, the Devil's Cellar, the Half-way House, Great Tom of Lincoln*, &c., &c. Portions of the roof, with pretty *spars* and stalactites, were successively revealed by the fitful gleams of our lights, and sometimes shone with beautiful splendor. A number of small rivulets crossed our path at intervals, which, considering the darkness and uncertainty of their *origin, depth,* and *destination,* did not produce an agreeable sensation. Their gentle and *silvery ripples,* as they passed over their pebbly bottom, whispered *uneasy apprehensions, instead of tranquil repose.* So far from lulling the mind into *"an oblivious insensibility"* of danger, like the murmuring sounds of the waters of *oblivion,* they rather rendered the mind more sensitive to the possibility of a *"false step"* and its *consequences;* suggesting the idea of deep pits and chasms, into which, had we tumbled, as did the *priest of Diana,* related in his story to the weeping Egeria, we feared there would have been no waters of Phlegethon in which to have *"washed to their healing,"* our lacerated limbs; nor a miraculous escape, through the means of a *"covering of cloud,"* by the benevolence of her *ladyship, Diana,* to hide our exit from his majesty, Pluto; nor the prospect of being honored with the significant title, *Virbius,*— that is, *twice a man.*

As vision became more accustomed to the gloom of the place, objects were perceived with greater distinctness and satisfaction. At length we arrived at *"the river Styx,"* so named by our guide; a dark sheet of water, three or four feet in depth, overhung by dismal rocks; but, unlike its infernal namesake, in heathen fable, which encircles and flows nine times around hell,* it only extends, we were told, thirteen or fourteen yards. Perhaps they meant, it is only navigable thus far. It doubtless has an outlet through which it passes, and, after many meanderings through the bosom of the mountain, gains the light of day, and plays and sparkles in the sunbeams, a crystal stream; — as if to illustrate that beautiful thought of a late writer: "Here our *minds* are like *springs*, lying coldly and darkly in their native bed; but who can calculate their depth and fulness when the rock of mortality is smitten, and the refulgent stream of intellect gushes forth to roll and sparkle in the light of heaven?" Well, we stood upon the banks of the *Styx*. A boat there was, but no ferryman; or, to be more classical, no *Charon*. "Where is the son of Erebus and Nox?" All was silent and death-like. It was not an unclassical thought, in our guide, to detain us on the gloomy shores a few minutes; as if to remind the visitors of the *disabilities* of those who had not been honored with *funeral rites*. The souls of such were doomed to wander one hundred years along the gloomy shores of Styx ere they were allowed to enter the boat of Charon; or, to put us in mind of the *ferriage*, or, more properly *passport*, which every *living visitor* to the lower regions had to present, ere he was ferried over the Stygian lake. A good apology for the absence, silence, and tardiness of old Charon, is found in the fact that, centuries ago, he was imprisoned one whole year, because, against his own will and judgment, he ferried Hercules over without a passport. Indeed, the ancients always placed a piece of money *under the tongue of the*

---

* The ancients said it was named *Styx*, in honor of a celebrated heroine of that name, who, with her three daughters, according to their mythology, assisted *Jupiter* in his war against the *Titans*.

deceased, as a fee for Charon. I could not avoid the pleasing reflection, that this, and many other fabulous representations of the invisible world, of which the ancients were so fond, prove how deeply they were impressed with the belief of the soul's immortality, and of a future state of rewards and punishments. I do not remember meeting, in their writings, with any sentiment which indicates that they entertained the most distant hope of the resurrection of the body. They believed, however, that an exposure of the corpse to the elements, or the leaving it to perish without proper funeral ceremonies, would have an influence upon the soul in the eternal world. The story of Charon and his boat originated, I believe, with the ancient Egyptians, who always pronounced sentence upon their dead. In order to this, the body was conveyed across a lake, in a boat. When disembarked, it was judged and sentenced, according to its actions. If good, it was honored with a splendid burial; if bad, it was left unnoticed, to waste away and perish in the open air. To the judgment of the gods in the invisible world, they left that which they could not reach — *the soul.* Thank God for the Bible! for its *doctrines*, as well as its precepts. How *simple*, how *grand!* How *rational*, how *sublime!* How *glorious*, how *terrific!* "Here a lamb may wade," said a good man, "and here an elephant may swim;" it is a depth suitable to every intellect. "Other writings," said another, "may make us *wise to admiration*, but the Scriptures only can make us *wise unto salvation*." Clouds and darkness must have ever rested upon eternity, deeper than all the "*murky vapors*," which, in a heathen's estimation, settled down upon the boundary river of Pluto's domains, had we been left without the light of *revelation*. Through life, and in our dying moments, we can with safety repose upon its declarations.

A watchword from our guide was reëchoed lustily from the opposite shores by Charon. A couple of us entered the little boat in faith. We were ordered to lie down flat in the straw, candle in hand, and off we went, we knew not whither; till suddenly we were underneath an arch of rock, which just allowed our boat to pass; thus, "*two by two*," we were ferried over, through the "muscular power" of Charon, exerted at the end of a rope. The shores upon which we landed were quite as bleak as those we left. Hence, we saw nothing of the *Elysii Campi*, said to be on that side of Styx; — nor "*singing of birds, nor pleasant streams, nor evergreen bowers, nor delightful meadows,*" nor any other mortals but ourselves; — nothing but blackness and darkness, which our lights rendered more *palpable* and oppressive, as if we had arrived at that awful spot mentioned by the poet, and from which, a *poet* only could have won "*an idea of sublimity:*"

> "Whose battlements look o'er into *the vale
> Of non-existence* — *nothing's strange abode*

But a truce to fables; we are in an *English cavern;* certainly one of the most imposing I have ever, in the entire course of my travels, visited. We proceeded onward, through a variety of windings and narrow apertures, till we arrived at the extremity of the cavern, — a distance, from where we lost sight of day, of between two and three thousand feet, and at a very great depth below the summit of the mountain. The longer we remained, objects could be perceived with more and more distinctness. On our return, we paused beneath a vast gulf, which shot upward to what seemed to us an immeasurable distance. Suddenly a numerous array of blue lights and torches kindled and blazed upward through the vast profound, which illumined an ex tensive portion of this magnificent vault. The hitherto dark vacuity seemed instantly full of curious objects, of whose existence we had no conception a few moments before; rugged projections, bold and curiously-formed crags, columns, arches, domes, — *nature's own masonry*, — rather, the wonderful workmanship of an Almighty hand; lofty recesses, ornamented with spars and stalactites, which sparkled with various lustres. The entire cavern is composed of a limestone strata, with a mixture of marine exuviæ, and gemmed in many places with these pretty formations. But *the eye is never satisfied with seeing;* there were altitudes to which vision could not reach; *unexplored* portions above and beyond, filled with deep darkness, which bade defiance to the glare of lights; literally, " *The light shined* in the *darkness,* and the darkness comprehended it not;" that is, *received it not.* — John 1: 5. A solemn illustration this, we thought, of the *darkness,* ignorance, folly, superstition, wickedness, and consequent wretchedness, which have so long settled down like the gloom of the bottomless pit upon vast portions of our race. "The *blue lights and torches*" of heathen sages have for ages glared heavenward through the *gloom profound,* but only to cast a few fitful gleams upon the murky shades in their proximity. "Clouds, alas! and darkness, rested upon" all beyond. The light of *nature* and *providence* has been as ineffectual as the light of *reason* and *conscience.* The Jewish religion was the *lamp* of the world; it cast a cold and feeble light upon the gloom which overspread all nations, but was inefficient to penetrate it; *the darkness received it not;* it neither understood nor profited by it. These lights, all of them, were but as *lights shining in a dark place,* — as our lights in this *cavern,*—awfully illustrative of our world, and of every sinner's heart, "*until the day dawn, and the day-star,* φωσφορος, *the* LIGHT-BRINGER, *arise in your hearts*" (2 Peter 1 : 19); till a voice from heaven, which shall be heard ana felt, says to every nation, "*Rise and shine, for thy light is come, and the glory of the* LORD *is risen upon thee.*"

These lights and torches, which glimmer through this cavern, do but excite our curiosity, without satisfying it; they scatter their fitful gleams about, but do not illuminate the gulf. A long continuation of such *artificial light* must blacken what it proposes to brighten. These spars and other crystallized formations must, in course of time, become sooted over, till their brilliancy has totally disappeared. No one will deny that nature, providence, reason and conscience, have sent forth emanations of light; but only sufficient to *alarm* the human mind, to *arouse its powers*, to *start energies, propose problems*, and *state difficulties;* but this light offered no terms of peace or reconciliation, answered no questions, solved no problems, and settled no difficulties; it only bewildered and terrified the understanding of man. The human powers, by their fearful and corrupt workings, absorbed a more deathly taint from surrounding gloom, became encrusted in deeper ignorance, and blackened with grosser vices. Nature may retain within herself, in this cavern, a method of self-purification. These pretty mineral productions may possibly cleanse themselves periodically from the effects of the smoke; or they may possess properties capable of *neutralizing* the effects of such sooty exhalations. Human nature inherits no such power of *self-purification.* It has become *worse and worse, blacker, and more degraded, and brutish,* as century has succeeded to century. Look at the ancient Greeks and Romans. In them we see *unassisted human nature,* — I mean, *unas-*

sisted by a divine revelation, — in its brightest polish ; intellect at its largest grasp ; arts and sciences, — *philosophy, eloquence, sculpture, painting, poetry,* — at their highest noon. "There is no elastic energy," says one, "in a heathen mind, no recuperative power to bring it back to God, no well-spring of life to purify the soul. The heathen are, of themselves, making no advances towards the truth, or towards a better system of religion. They make no progress towards civilization, intelligence, liberty. The effect of time is only to deepen the darkness, and to drive the heathen further from God. They only adore more shapeless blocks ; they bow before worse-looking idols ; they worship less elegant and more polluted temples. The idols of the heathen are not constructed with half the skill and taste with which they were two thousand years ago, nor are their temples built with such exquisite art. No idol of the heathen world could now be compared with the statue of Minerva, at Athens ;* no temple can be likened to the Parthenon ; no sentiment, originated now in China, India, or Africa, equals in sublimity or purity the views of Socrates. The heathen world is becoming worse and worse ; more degenerate, more abominable, more pitiable, from age to age ; darker, and more debased, till the space which divides the human race from the brute has become reduced to the narrowest possible dimensions, consistently with preserving that distinction at all."

The *day* which now shines over Castleton could illumine this cavern in a moment, could it be introduced. This may never be, unless by the spasms of an earthquake, *hitherto unknown to these parts*, unless we suppose this natural wonder was occasioned by some such convulsions in nature.

* Or the Apollo at Rome.

This darkness may have a lease of the place, extending to the latest period of time; when the blaze of the last day shall burst into all these subterraneous passages; when *darkness*, like SINNERS, must fly *before* it, and cry in vain for rocks and mountains to hide it from the face of the pursuing and consuming enemy. — Rev. 6: 12—17. But a day has dawned, a Gospel day, which shall never know a close. The *Sun of Righteousness has arisen* upon our world, *with healing in his wings*. Portion after portion of our globe shall become illuminated by his rays, until the whole world shall be filled with the light of the glory of God. That *natural sun*, which is now showering down his rays upon England, were we *above ground* to see it, will survive all the moral and intellectual darkness which disgraces our race; even that which exists in the innermost recesses of those dark places of the earth which are the habitations of cruelty. There is not a single nation within the circuit and visitations of his rays, that shall not be enlightened, cheered and warmed, by the glorious beams of the *Sun of Righteousness*. Hallelujah! The Lord God omnipotent reigneth! Amen!

But I have detained you quite too long in this gloomy and solitary abode. Highly entertained with our *underground excursion*, we emerged into open day. One of our party, who did not accompany us into the cavern, informed us there had been another storm of thunder and lightning; but we heard nothing of it; besides, we had something of the kind of our own. Our guide detained us half an hour for the purpose of "*charging a rock with powder;*" the explosion was succeeded by thousands of echoes from above, beneath, running far and wide through chasms and crannies, extending into other caverns yet unvisited by the foot of man. As the distance increased, the echoes became soft and sweet, resembling the ripple of waves, or "rain coming down like music," fainter and more distant still, till they seemed to fall by solitary drops into the profundity of some capacious and far-away reservoir. How great the change, when once more in "*open day*"! (but not greater than the infidel emerging from the caverns of infidelity, into the light and sunshine of Gospel day) — the sun shining through a glorious sky, reminding us of those fine lines of a poet who sang the honors of *Christianity*:

> " From ostentation as from weakness free,
> It stands, like the cerulean arch we see,
> Majestic in its own simplicity."

After dinner, we ascended a steep hill, behind the village of Castleton, upon which stands an old dilapidated castle; a venerable ruin, and hoary with years. It stands upon the verge of a rocky precipice, almost directly over the cavern I have been describing. This is the ancient " Castle of the Peak." Some consider the structure Norman; others assert it was a place of royal residence during the government of the Saxons. Descending from this eminence, we walked on in the direction of *Mam Tor, the shivering mountain*, considered, in these parts, as one of the seven wonders of the *Peak of Derbyshire*. It is an immense hill, one thousand three hundred feet above the level of the valley. It bears some resemblance to Mount Ida, which overlooks Troy, U. S., with a similar broken front; as if a mighty avalanche had but lately come away from the top, bringing with it to the very base, the fifth part of the mountain. This *eruptive side* has a singular appearance; it is composed of a sort of *flaky substance*, which decomposes in the winter, by the action of frost, and is continually coming off. The decomposition during winter is said to be rapid; and it is kept up during the year, by the action of the sun's rays, wind, rain, and by the various changes of the atmosphere. The descent of these small particles gives the mountain a *shivering aspect;* but the inhabitants affirm that a *rumbling sound* is frequently heard to proceed from the bowels of the mountain. Sometimes it sends forth a *rushing noise,* like a river running over its pebbly bed. Notwithstanding these perpetual dilapidations, the oldest inhabitant, I understand, is not able to perceive any diminution in the size of the mountain. Here is another "*subject*" for your speculating mind. Your philosophy, of course, discards the old notions of the *spirit, genius,* or *genii,* of the mountain; but, were this mountain on classic ground, it would stand, unquestionably, connected with the transformation and punishment of some of the gods or goddesses of antiquity. The ancients, you will recollect, accounted for the convulsions and eruptions of Mount Ætna by the incarceration, within its burning caverns, of the giant *Typhœus* or *Typhon,* by the offended gods. A thunderbolt from the hand of Jupiter left him sprawling beneath the island of Sicily, his feet reaching to the utmost verge of the island, while his arms and shoulders ran beneath an extensive territory. His head was supposed to be directly underneath Ætna. From his mouth and nostrils proceeded flames, vapor, and smoke. The rivers of lava were but the product of an emetic; and those tremendous convulsions, which shook and terrified the country around, were but his gigantic efforts to disengage himself from the ponderous weight under which he groaned. This allusion will make the foundation for a classical story for the boys, which you know so well how to improve.

Leaving the shivering mountain on the right, we ascended an eminence to the left, and arrived at the *Blue John Mine.*

The entrance has nothing of the *picturesque* which characterizes Peak's Hole; it is quite concealed and covered by a little house on the brow of a gentle hill. Our guide, having furnished us with lighted candles, led the way through a small door in the apartment, not unlike the entrance to an humble cellar. Through a series of rugged steps, hewn in the limestone rock, we descended nearly five hundred feet. The passages and rooms through which we passed, some of which are spacious, were brilliant with spars of various shapes and splendors. We paused for a few minutes in one apartment of uncommon dimensions, where the company, forming a circle in the centre, sang very sweetly:

> " From all that dwell below the skies
> Let the Creator's praise arise;
> Let the Redeemer's name be sung
> Through every land by every tongue."

My "*observations* and reflections" in the Peak's Hole Cavern have been spun out to such a length as to preclude a minute description of these subterranean abodes. After remaining an hour or two, encompassed by "*blackness of darkness,*" we emerged once more into "*open day.*" How great the change! How like the circumstances of the *new convert* (I thought), when just emerging out of the gloomy cavern of *dark and despairing repentance*, — having been, perhaps, there for weeks; and "*those awful syllables, hell, death, and sin,*" forever "ringing a tempest" in his ears; "*a dark importance*" saddening every hour of his dreary existence! While "conscience writes a doomsday sentence on his heart," there is "*a pale procession*" of many sins, marching onward to meet him at the bar of God. There is, however, an outlet of mercy. By the light of the cross it is revealed: "Behold the Lamb of

God, that taketh away the sins of the world!" The outlet is in this direction, and in no other. *Repenting and believing*, he hails it from afar, and presses forward, "with vengeance at his heels," into life, liberty, and glorious day.

After tea we set out for Sheffield. The evening was one of the loveliest. As we passed down the vale, the eye was charmed by a variety of agreeable objects. Castleton, seated amid quiet and sweet seclusion, in the bosom of the mountains, was gradually retiring from view, while our vision ranged up the cultivated valley, and swept along the rugged sides of the mountains, some of which were reposing in deep shadow, others were radiant with the rays of the declining sun. An immense cloud, of a peculiar brown color, stood over Mam Tor, casting a shadowy tinge, to a proportionate length, down the mountain. The village church, at length, the ruin above, Mam Tor, and all the guardian hills of Castleton, disappeared from our sight, and we pursued our way homeward over a succession of hills and dales, where nature has been by no means niggardly in the bestowment of her favors.

Our company separated a few miles from Sheffield, when I rode on to Dronfield with the family of the Rev. David Clark, minister of the Independent church of that village. I spent the night at his house. Next day, visited the school connected with this chapel, and was much gratified with the exercises of the children, and gave them a short address. The village church is ancient. We spent an agreeable hour in the interior,

> "Reading the mural tablets of the dead,
> Or poring o'er the dimly-sculptured names
> Upon its sunken pavement."

Returned to Sheffield in the afternoon, and preached to a large congregation at night. The revival is still advancing in power. As I intend to forward you, by the next steamer, a full account of the work of God, I shall bring this long letter to "*an abrupt* close." Farewell!

CHAPTER V.

NORTON HOUSE.

YESTERDAY I arrived here, — *Norton House*, the residence of *Thomas B. Holy*, Esq. It is a fine, venerable, *baronial-like* mansion, partly covered with ivy, venerable in aspect, and "*beautiful for situation.*" Brother *Unwin* accompanied me from *Sheffield*. We had a lovely ride. The neighborhood of Sheffield is famed for its *rural beauty*, which is seen to great advantage in ascending the hills of *Norton*. The points of observation are so numerous and advantageous, that one may post himself upon many a "*speculative height*," as Cowper terms them, and view, exulting, "a spacious map of hills, with valley interposed between." The hills, "swelling and undulating to and fro," are enlivened with green fields, tufted with trees, and fringed with foliage. Groves and thickets spread themselves over the sides and summits of gentle eminences, and nod upon the neighboring steeps. *Guilty*, or *cold* and *dejected*, must that heart be, that is not *warmed*, *cheered*, and *elevated*, by a scene so innocent, so diversified, so lovely! Few landscapes, in fact, can vie with it in beauty and fertility, or afford richer materials for the rural pencil:

"——— Soft declivities, tufted hills,
With view of waters turning busy mills."

Nor should Sheffield be overlooked in the distance:

"Whose fragrant air is yon thick smoke,
Which shrouds it like a mourning cloak."

And now *adieu*, once more, beloved Sheffield! I have added a few more *pleasant days*, and *successful efforts* to bring sinners to God, to the many such-like days I have spent, within thee. *Farewell!* I love thee though thy *mantle of smoke* is drawn so closely around thee! My heart is with thee; for where one's *treasure* is, *there will the heart be also!* — my *spiritual children* are within thy walls. Peace be unto *thee* and *them*, and to the *friends* I leave behind.

And now, with what *comforts*, *elegancies*, and *mercies*, am I *surrounded!* — many of them such as *Cicero* labelled, "*Circumstantial pieces of felicity!*" O, how kindly has the Lord provided for me in my *weaknesses*, during my travels in this and other lands! — *hiding-places*, as well as *resting-places* for the poor, weary, disabled *Evangelist*, or *Revivalist*, as I am called, — which all Christ's ministers should be; — with *persecutions* sometimes, — what St. Paul named *outside fightings*, and *inside fears*, — "*Without were fightings, within were fears; — our flesh had no rest, but we were troubled on every side;*" — a little brush of such things now and again, but wisely *proportioned*, by my Lord and Master, to my strength; — but he soon kindles my *soul* again, into a *pillar of fire*, travelling through the *wilderness of unsaved sinners!*

Had St. Paul been favored with such a resting-place as this, how he would have enjoyed it, when he wrote to his brethren in Christ at *Corinth*, "*Now ye are full, now ye are rich; ye have reigned as kings without us; and would to God ye did reign, that we also might reign with you. For I think that God hath set forth us the apos-*

tles last, as it were appointed to death: for we are made a spectacle unto the world, and to angels, and to men;" then followed a list of his *grievances* and sufferings; — that he and his fellow *apostles* were called *fools* and *weak,—* were *defamed* and *persecuted,*— *labored* and *worked* with their *own hands*, that they might preach the *Gospel* without charge; yet for all that they were *reviled*, and counted the *filth* and *off-scouring* of all things, — were *buffeted*, did suffer both *hunger* and *thirst*, ay, and *nakedness*, and had *no certain dwelling-place.* — 1 Cor. 4: 8, 13. O, my Lord and my God, I may well be *ashamed* here! —

"I blush in all things to abound."

How long would *St. Paul* have been contented here? — Only till he felt the *stirrings* of the *gift divine!* — till he felt the *fire* begin to *burn within*, — till the word of the Lord became as *fire* in his *bones*, as with the prophet *Jeremiah* of old! Ah me! thus it will be with *me* before long; then the *paradise* of *Norton House* would turn into a *wilderness*, haunted with the still small voice, " *What doest thou here, Elijah?*" Ah, my Lord! But he permits a *rest,* — he who said to his wearied disciples, " Come ye yourselves apart into a desert place, and *rest a while.*" "*Rest* is necessary for those who *labor,*" says *Dr. Clarke;* "and a *zealous* preacher of the Gospel will as often stand in need of it as a *galley* slave." But Jesus called them into a *desert place;* and lo, I rest a while in an *Eden!*

Norton is the birthplace of the celebrated sculptor, *Chantrey;* one of the greatest artists England has produced. There is a *monument* to his memory, in the old church close by, of plain white marble, enriched with a *medallion* likeness of the artist. His remains repose a few yards from the church, encompassed by an iron palisading. A short time before his death he came down from *London* to choose his place of sepulture. In doing so he remarked to the aged clergyman, "But I do not intend you to bury me;" but he did so, shortly after!

CHAPTER VI.

CHESTERFIELD.

EXTRACTS FROM THE JOURNAL.

Chesterfield, Derbyshire, October 27, 1845.—After a few days I became *restless* at Norton, and longed for *action.* This *call to preach* is an *intrusive* thing;—like the *conscience* of *Shakspeare's* hero, it *"mutinies* in a man's bosom, and fills one full of *obstacles."* The *reflection* of what *might* have been done in *rescuing souls* from Satan, while one has been *loitering*, becomes annoying, and weighs *heavy ;*—the *call* lies heavy on the heart, when one is out of *action.* But, O, how *light* and pleasant amid the *battle* for *Christ* and *souls !* Well, I hastened away to this town on Saturday, and gave battle against the Devil and all his works, yesterday. The Lord of hosts was with us indeed, *" as an armed man, and a mighty one ;"* to *kill* and make *alive,* to *rend* and to *bind up,* to *wound* and to *heal.* There were *forty-two* sinners converted from the world; and *twenty-seven* church-members justified; and *twenty-three* believers sought and found full salvation. *Total,* during the day, *ninety-two* saved. Of these, a dozen were *backsliders. Surely the fields are already white unto the harvest !*

A pleasing letter from the Rev. D. Walton, the superintendant of Wesleyan Methodism in the city of York. He tells me the revival is still progressing, and that no Sabbath has passed since I left without souls being saved. That was a noble work in York, during those three or four months I spent in that city, when over *nine hundred* were converted from the world; *three hundred* members of the Wesleyan and other churches were saved, and *between seven and eight hundred* believers were sanctified. Memorable months to me.

Oct. 29. — *Chesterfield* must be the battle-ground some time longer. *Crowds* upon *crowds* listen to the *word;* and scores and scores are slain and saved by it. The scenes are becoming sublimely awful. My *joy*, in beholding these displays of the power of God, is mingled with an adoring awe. The human soul is a fearful thing, when aroused to a sense of its danger. To behold the *tears*, and hearken to the bitter cries and wails, of despairing sinners, pierced by the word of God, and torn by their own consciences, gives one some idea of St. Paul's meaning, when he says, " *The word of God is quick and powerful, and sharper than any two-edged sword, piercing to the dividing asunder of soul and spirit, and of the joints and marrow, and is a discerner of the thoughts and intents of the heart.*" — Heb. 4 : 12. Extraordinary language that. Such is that *living* and *powerful* word when preached with the Holy Ghost sent down from heaven. It then penetrates the *heart*, as a sword does the body; reaching the inmost recesses of the mind, as the sword the *marrow* of the bones, and conveys *life or death* to him who receives it.

Oct. 31. — The *weather* is charming. Although busy with the *pen*, when not in the pulpit, I find time to enjoy it in solitary rambles two or three hours a day. There is a little rural lane, which runs through the fields, near the house of Mr Savage (where I am entertained), where I enjoy delightful walks. The air is so pure, and the quiet is so deep and unbroken. O, what sweet, deep *peace*, and *purity* of heart and thought, I enjoy there! What heavenward *aspirations!* What freedom from *care!* What communion with the *past*, and with God, who knows it all! What a *pilgrim-like* looking forwards and upwards, in that quiet lane! And then at night, to willing crowds, preaching Jesus, and life and salvation through his name:

> "The business pursue, he hath made me to do,
> And rejoice that I ever was born."

Nov. 1. — The *work of God* here, like a river, deepens and widens as it proceeds, and with increased rapidity and power. There seems to be little or no opposition as yet. It is as if it had *stolen* a march on Satan, and fallen upon his kingdom before he was prepared to cope with it. The people have been taken by *surprise*, and neither sinners nor Satan seem to know how to resist it. It is not the first time I have seen it thus; may it not be the last! About *one hundred and fifty* souls converted since Sabbath morning last, and many sanctified. Now hath the word of the Lord free course, and is glorified of all. This is the Lord's doings, and marvellous in the eyes of all his people hereabouts.

And O, what charming weather! What heavenly afternoons! What splendid sunsets!

> "How cheerful, through her shortening day,
> Is *Autumn* in her weeds of yellow!"

And, then, one's own sweet, deep peace of heart and gladness. I cannot believe with him who said:

"Joy is the portion of the skies,
Beneath them, all is care."

No! no! *Faith*, and *Hope*, and gentle *Love*, Prometheus-like, seize upon this portion of the skies — steal this celestial fire, wherewith to inspire and animate my poor needy heart, cheering the exile wonderfully!

CHAPTER VII.

PROGRESS OF THE REVIVAL IN CHESTERFIELD.

Mr. Caughey, speaking of the work in this place, says:

The Lord did great things among us yesterday (Sabbath); *ninety-seven* souls found mercy, of whom *fifty-seven* were from the *world;* and *twenty-six* professed entire sanctification. Of those justified, *seventeen* were backsliders. Yesterday was a day long to be remembered in *Chesterfield;* such as has not been seen here since it was a town. Hallelujah! O, what amaze and sweet surprise filled my soul! Such scenes as we beheld yesterday seem really necessary to make one realize the *real grandeur* and *omnipotent power* there is in the Gospel. And of all the *evidences* our world affords, that Jesus Christ, the Son of God, lives and reigns equal with the Father over the universe, these scenes of power and mercy seemed to me to be the greatest. To tell a poor, miserable sinner that Jesus Christ *hath power upon earth to forgive his sins;* to have him *believe* this, so as to risk his *all* for time and for eternity upon it; then to see how instantly his *sorrow* is turned into *joy*, his *darkness* into day, and not in one or two cases merely, but *scores* and scores of instances in a few short hours, the *evidence* of the *truth* of that *mighty fact* becomes overwhelming.

When Jesus said to the *paralytic* man, "*Be of good*

cheer; *thy sins be forgiven thee*," the bystanders said within themselves, "*Why doth he thus speak blasphemies? Who can forgive sins but God alone?*" This unuttered sentiment was a universal sentiment, wide as the world of man. It was not limited to the breast of a Jewish scribe, but claimed the empire of a *universal instinct*. And never had Jesus a better opportunity to do it reverence, and to confirm it forever, than at that moment; never a time more *favorable* or more *suitable* to *disabuse* the public mind of the *suspicion* of his *acting* the *very God*, and usurping the throne and prerogative of the supreme Jehovah. But did he seize so suitable an opportunity to do so? No; for it is recorded, "But he, *knowing their thoughts*, said, Why do ye think *evil* in your hearts? For which is easier to say, *Thy sins be forgiven*, or to say, *Arise and walk? But that ye may know the Son of man hath power upon earth to forgive sins* [he saith to the paralytic], Arise, take up thy couch, and go to thy house;" thus confirming the dread impression which his words, "*Thy sins be forgiven thee*," had conveyed. "*Who can forgive sins but God alone?*" Thus, as one finely observes, "forestalling the functions of the last day, he remitted the claims of justice on a sinful being, erased his guilt from the book of God, changed the relations of an accountable creature to the supreme Governor, and, in effect, asserted that he possessed the power of taking from the inmost soul the sting of conscious guilt; while, by declaring that he retained this power, though he was then the *Son of man upon earth*, he carries our thoughts to the state whence he had descended, and reminds us that no distance from his throne above, no depth of humiliation to which he might condescend, can deprive him of his right to pardon; that as it is exclusively, so it is inalienably divine; and that he is therefore free to use it as God, though for a time he may choose to rank as the Son of man.

"Preceding prophets, jealous for the divine honor, had scrupulously guarded against the remotest suspicion that they spake in their own name; they distinctly confessed their delegated capacity, and perpetually appealed to the authority which sent them. But Jesus, we have seen, without any modification or reserve, employed the language of supreme personal authority. He did not, indeed, in any way impart the impression of an interest, or even an existence, detached from the Father. The authority by which he spoke, though expressly his own, was, by identity of nature, the authority of the Father also. As often as he exercised the functions of the legislator, he placed himself, if I may say so, on a level, and in a line, with the eternal throne; so that its glory fell directly upon him, and by him was again reflected back, mingled with the lustre of his own greatness. While he stood forth distinctly in his own personality, and addressed us in his own name, he stood in so perfect a conjunction with the Deity, and so far within the borders of the encircling light, that his voice came with the authority of an oracle from the central glory. 'Glorify thy Son, that thy Son also may glorify thee. I am in the Father, and the Father is in me. No man knoweth the Father but the Son, neither knoweth any man the Son but the Father. Whatsoever things the Father doeth, these also doeth the Son likewise. He that hath seen me hath seen the Father also. I and my Father are one.'

"But of all his displays of authority, his forgiveness of sin is immeasurably the greatest. This, according to human conceptions, is the highest and uttermost prerogative of the Supreme. It is to ascend a throne above the lawgiver, and to silence his voice, and suspend his functions, for a *reason* paramount to all law, and more comprehensive. It is to overrule the claims of justice, and, stopping it in its full career towards the sinner, to exhibit a reason for mercy, to which justice bows with reverence, and before which it retires. Law, the dictate of infinite wisdom, is the rule by which man is to act towards God; but forgiveness is a dispensation, a reason, issuing from a deeper recess of his mysterious nature, and by which he chooses to act towards us. But this prerogative, essentially divine, this high and incommunicable right, Jesus exercised, and vindicated his competence to do so." And so he did yesterday, blessed be his name! Nearly *one hundred* sinners, saved by grace, were enabled to "set to their seal" that *Jesus Christ hath power upon earth* to forgive sins. Hallelujah to God and the Lamb!

The population are in a state of *amaze*. This amazing work of God has evidently taken them by *surprise*. They seem as if stunned. *Sinners* know not what to say. Those who understand the Gospel ask for no *explanations* or *apologies*, and they get none; only more and more of the same *great truths* which have been thundering so at the door of their hearts, followed by the animating cry of

"*Behold, behold the Lamb!*"

CHAPTER VIII.

AN ASTROLOGIAN LADY.

Nov. 3d. — Have been requested by a romantic lady, some distance off, to give her my views of "*the* science of astrology;" — seems anxious to know whether I belong to the family of him, who,

> " Among the heavens his eye can see
> *Trace of things that are to be.*"

Or, forgetting all that has been said in England, *pro* and *con*, about the *apostolical succession*, whether I have the honor to be in the noble *succession* of the *Chaldean shepherds*, who once "beneath the concave of the unclouded skies," read in the stars "the *decrees* and *resolutions* of the gods." My reply, I fear, will neither be considered gallant nor satisfactory; — that I never meddle with the *stars*, only to *admire* them, — leaving them, usually, to take care of themselves; being much of the same mind of him who said,

> " I 'd rather have no hand with the *stars;*
> They 're above us all every way."

Although, with Milton, I am fond of beholding

> " ——————— the *wandering* moon,
> Riding near her highest noon,

> Like one that has been led astray
> Through the heavens' wide, pathless way ;
> And oft as her head she bowed,
> Stooping through a fleecy cloud."

Adding, I am not fond of the *conjectural sciences*, although they have their *fascinations*, doubtless. The stars may have their *effects* and *influences* upon this *fine weather*, for aught we know ; but that *future events* may be foretold by their *situation* and *aspects*, I leave those to demonstrate who have time to consult attentively the book and volume of the sky. The *Scriptures* are safer guides than the *constellations ;* the *promises* of God, than the *stars* of the astrologist. The *light* of *passing providences* is better to go by than the *light* of *passing stars ; safer*, besides, unless one covets the fate of him who, when gazing at a *star* tumbled into a ditch. *Sincere prayer* to "the *Father of lights*, with whom there is *no variableness, neither shadow of turning*" (James 1 : 17), is safer and better than the closest attention to the lore of the Chaldean shepherds, or any of their *successors*. I am not averse to "*celestial observations,*" but there is a *volume* more *reliable* than that which *astrologists* consult — the Holy Bible ; the *promises* and *intimations* of which are unaffected by *clouds ;* and seeing that the *steady, serene, unclouded skies* of the *Assyrian* sages have not been vouchsafed to *Old England*, I may be pardoned for clinging so closely to a volume designed to be "*a lamp unto my feet, and a light unto my path*" (Ps. 119 : 105), through this *wilderness world ;* in which, doubtless, there is an *Oasis*, or an *Eden*, which has *survived the fall* for most travellers through it ; but the light of the *Bible* is better than the light of the *stars*, to make the *discovery*.

8*

CHAPTER IX.

A GLIMPSE OF PRIVATE EXPERIENCE.

Nov. 3. Afternoon. — *Solitude!* It makes the *head clearer*, and the *heart better!* — where one may learn more and more of *God*, of *self*, and *men*, — "at proper angle I take my stand to see them better;" and then in public come out and tell them all that passed before me, — all I *saw* and all I *felt*. A great place is *solitude* to study *self*, and all that lies deep in the depths within; "*deep calling unto deep*," — *voices* never heard amidst the din of outer existence. "I was left *alone*, and saw this great vision," says Daniel. *Great things* and *great principles* must be confronted in silence and solitude. There, they must be *discovered, conversed* with, *wrestled* with, 'midst the thoughts, as *Jacob* with the *angel*, and *conquered*, until they speak, and tell their secrets, and give their blessing. Then out and confront, and *conquer*. For he that, as an intellectual prince, thus prevails in secret, will prevail with men also. He has mastered *himself* and his *theme*, and he will master *opponents* also.

It is amidst the solitudes of *nature*, and the solitudes of *thought*, where one encounters other voices, — the voice of God, and the *voices of eternity*. And thought rolls upon thought, as the waves against the shore, — unbidden, deep, awful, — over the solemn silence of the soul. There, sometimes, the *soul* resigns herself with the Will and Reason, into the arms of a profound *stillness*, passive and waiting "on some heavenly impulse!" And there, and from thence, the soul travels into "*heavenly places*," or down the steeps of solid darkness, through brazen gates, through perdition's woes. Thus she gathers fresh strength, and vivid perceptions, and mastery over what escapes her in the *crowd*. The *crowd!* My mind relaxes in the crowd, and loses its elasticity, its independence, and the mastery. Thought *dilutes* in the crowd, or escapes, as the parents missed *Jesus* in the crowd, and sought for him there in vain.

It is in silence and solitude my *soul finds* herself, *possesses* herself, and joins herself to God, and learns the meaning of Jesus, "*In your patience possess ye your souls.*" There she narrowly scans and weighs her *difficulties*, learns how to master them, and walks up and down the mount of God, 'midst stones of fire! Or, like *King Lemuel's* model wife, "*she girdeth her loins with strength, and strengtheneth her arms; her candle goeth not out by night; strength and honor are her clothing, and she shall rejoice in time to come; she openeth her mouth with wisdom, and in her tongue is the law of kindness; she looketh well to the ways of her household, and eateth not the bread of idleness; her clothing is silk and purple; her price is above rubies; the heart of her husband doth safely trust in her, so that he shall have no need of spoil; he is known in the gates, when he sitteth among the elders of the land; she will do him good, and not evil, all the days of her life.*" — Prcv., 31st chapter. It is thus with the soul of a minister that understands how to improve *solitude*, in gathering *strength*, and *energy*, and *material*, for the great battle-strife of soul-saving.

The activities of *revival life* are *preservatives* from the evils of an inglorious and lazy *mysticism*; while the *experiences* gathered in retirement fit the soul for its public conflicts, and repair "the *wear* and *tare*," sustained in the great battle for Christ and souls. The soul comes forth out of her solitudes, realizing the truth of Herbert's sentiment:

>Softness, and peace, and joy, and love, and bliss,
>Exalted manna ; gladness of the best ;
>Heaven in ordinary ; soul well drest,
>The land of spices ; *something understood* "

CHAPTER X.

EXTRACTS FROM JOURNAL, CONTINUED.

Nov. 5th. — There were *thirty-nine* saved last night. A great *move* among the people. The cries of penitent sinners like the wailings of hell; only full of the hopes of *mercy*, — a thing unknown in hell. Sinners *fly* or *fall* beneath the strange power which so mysteriously assails their feelings. When the Gospel becomes "*the power of God unto salvation*," who can stand before it?

Yesterday, a deputation from *Macclesfield* waited upon me, — Messrs. *Bowers, Brocklehurst, Hooley, Braddock*, and *Collier*, requesting me to visit that town. I postponed a reply till this morning, that we might have time to consider and pray over the matter. They called again, and I agreed to visit them on my way to *Birmingham*, the latter part of the present month.

A singular little incident occurred this morning, with regard to these brethren. Yesterday, on arriving in town, they inquired for lodgings, and, preferring a private boarding-place to a hotel, were directed to the house of a Quaker lady. She replied she could accommodate but *four* of them; so they lodged there. When taking leave of their hostess to-day, she burst into *tears*, and said, "I cannot let you go without telling you that I saw you all *five*, the night before you came, in a *dream;* and when I awoke, I told my two daughters that I had seen *five men*, and that they would come to our house. To which they replied, 'Go to sleep, mother, it is only a dream.' I repeated my dream when I arose, and again at the breakfast-table, and said, 'They will come to-day.' The day passed on; three o'clock arrived, and my daughters said: 'Well, mother, your five men have not come!' Very soon after, I saw you all pass by our house, and I called my daughters, and said, 'There they are! Those are the men I saw in my dream; and they will come to our house.'" Remarkable! — an indication, perhaps, they were sent of God. I shall visit Macclesfield with courage. The Lord has his "hidden ones," and his "*little ones*," and "the secret of the Lord" is with them. "Shall I hide from Abraham that thing which I do?" It is by this and that little incident, the Lord shows them, that *small* as they are in their own estimation, and in the estimation of the world, they are *great* in his sight, and *loved* and *prized*.

I was struck with that sweet remark of one, to-day, that, as the *stars* are scattered over the sky, and not gathered into one *luminary*, so *Christians* are not all gathered into one place, or *church*, but scattered over the world in the churches, as the *stars* in the firmament of heaven. That, as *city lamps* are planted here and there, up and down the streets of the city, to relieve and enlighten its darkness, and not collected and gathered into *one*, so *believers*, who are "the lights of the world," are not all planted to shine in *one church*, but are planted, by *divine wisdom*, wide apart over the earth, to *enlighten*, enliven, and bless the world. And though the *wicked*, like city *thieves*, could very well dispense with these *lights*, yet they cannot, or dare not, *blow them out!* That Christians are compared to *salt* by our Lord,— to salt the earth, and preserve it from *corruption;* but as, when a man *salts down meat*, he does not cast down the salt in a lump, but scatters it all over the meat, so Christians, whom our Lord calls "*the salt of the earth,*" are not huddled all together in one place, but scattered over all the earth, to preserve it from destruction. Adding, that a *sower* does not drop his seed by *handfuls*, nor in *heaps*, but scatters it broadcast over the field; so " the field is the world," as Christ says, and the righteous are "*the good seed*" wherewith he *soweth* it; not dropping them all down together in one place, but scattering them broadcast over *the field of the world,* turning the *wilderness* into a *fruitful field*, and the *desert* into the garden of the Lord. Those sweet lines occur :

> " Scattered o'er all the earth they lie,
> Till thou collect them with thine eye ;
> Draw by the music of thy name,
> And charm into a beauteous frame.
>
> " The gates of hell cannot prevail ;
> The church on earth can never fail : —
> Ah ! join me to thy *secret ones !*
> Ah ! gather all the living stones ! "

Nov. 6. — Over *forty* found mercy last night, and *seven* full salvation.

> "The heavens are big with rain."

O, what a "teeming shower" is this ! and such multitudes, — *thirsty multitudes*, — to draw its life-giving torrents !

What a pity to leave such a work ! And yet my *engagements* elsewhere must *sever* me from it soon. May these new converts stand fast in their glorious liberty. The wicked are beginning already to prophesy their *downfall,* assigning this, that, and the other reason, but they forget the *mighty God.* They have not studied Rom. 14 : 4.- — "Who art thou that judgest another man's servant? to his own master he *standeth* or *falleth.* *Yea, he shall be holden up; for God is able to make him stand.*" Nor are they well versed upon the nature of the *foundations* of Christian character;—that, if some build upon the *sand,* others *dig deep,* and lay their foundations on the *Rock of Ages.* But they know not this Rock, nor the guarantee for stability a *conversion* has which is founded upon it, no matter how unfavorably circumstanced! Brother *Savage,* my host, is a practical *builder* and architect. He told me, to-day, that many years ago he was employed to erect a large *mill,* upon a very *treacherous soil,* being of an *alluvium* nature, upon the banks of a river, subject to frequent *overflows,* one of which occurred during the progress of the work.

The *mill* was to sustain massive and powerful *machinery;* which, after immense labor and care with the foundations, was *completed,* all but the great *chimney,* which was the greatest difficulty, in the estimation of those who pretended to know all about it. It was intended to be *thirty-five* yards high, and it was asserted that such a *quicksand bottom* could never sustain such a structure, suffering from the *vibrations* of machinery in full operation. But, said Brother S., "I took care to *dig deep,* in search of a foundation; but, to my sorrow, the deeper I went, the softer became the bottom. But I had my plans, and spared no pains, deeply aware of my responsibility. At a given point of depth I lowered great stones, from *three to six tons* weight, pile upon pile of them, leaving to them and the law of gravitation to find or make a solid bottom, and my success was complete. Upon these I built my chimney. Many were the speculations in town, that the chimney would not stand, when the mill went into operation. But the *fires* were kindled, the smoke ascended in columns, the machinery started, the ground shook, but it had no effect upon any part of the structure. *All stood firm,* and still stands *firm ;* but the secret of the stability lay in the foundations of the whole. Once, indeed, the chimney was struck by *lightning,* but it only knocked a few bricks off the top, but did not overthrow it. The *prophecies* were all *falsified,* thanks to my excellent foundations!"

And it is upon a similar principle we hope for the *stability* of these new converts. We have taken much pains with their *foundations* in a *sound regeneration ;* for, that is to the soul what a *good and sound foundation* is to an *edifice.* Outward circumstances are the *data* from which the *Sanballats* and *Tobiahs* draw their *inferences* and *conclusions;* Neh. 4 : 1, 3 ; — a *drunken,* careless, or opposing *husband ;* a *gay* and *trifling wife ;* an *ungodly father,* or a *careless mother ;* an irreligious, or worldly, or *fashionable family,* and wicked neighbors, and past profligate associates. O, what mighty arguments are these against the stability of those but newly found in Christ ; But such prophets little know what a *powerful pledge* of future faithfulness and stability has been *embedded* in their genuine conversion and regeneration !

CHAPTER XI.

PREPARING TO LEAVE CHESTERFIELD

THIRTEEN happy, busy days have I spent in this town, and now I am about to bid it farewell, perhaps forever. An hour or two's work at the pen, and then I am off for *Doncaster*. The work of God burst forth in glory and in grandeur the first *Sabbath day*, and it has advanced with amazing swiftness ever since. *Thirteen days* only, and over *five hundred* persons have professed to find peace with God, through our Lord *Jesus Christ!* — *three hundred and sixty-nine* of whom were from the world, and about *one hundred and thirty-seven* believers were *entirely sanctified.* — 1 Thess. 4 : 23, 24.

The following table, furnished by the *secretary*, shows the results of each day :

Date, 1845.	Day.	Justified.				Sanctified.	Total each day.
		Out of the World.	Members of Society.	From other Societies	Backsliders reclaimed.		
Oct. 26.	Sunday, ..	42	27	4	12	23	108
" 27.	Monday, ..	19	5	5	2	3	34
" 28.	Tuesday, ..	22	7	2	6	11	48
" 29.	Wednesday,.	18	5	2	3	7	35
" 30.	Thursday, .	31	5	3	4	7	50
" 31.	Friday, ...	29	4	5	7	11	56
Nov. 1.	Saturday, .	9	1	4	2	2	18
" 2.	Sunday, ..	57	10	13	17	26	123
" 3.	Monday, ..	21	1	3	4	1	30
" 4.	Tuesday, ..	20	3	6	10	33	72
" 5.	Wednesday,.	26	5	3	4	7	45
" 6.	Thursday, .	43	4	5	14	5	71
" 7.	Friday, ...	32	4	6	3	1	46
		369	81	61	88	137	786

The subjects of this work of grace were conversed with, and judiciously advised; their names also, and places of residence, carefully registered, and the *pathway* of pastors and leaders accurately mapped out, for their future *visitations*.

O, how much might be done to prevent those painful *reäctions* which sometimes follow a work of God like this, were the subjects of divine mercy properly *cared for*, *looked after*, *sought out*, and *built up* in their most holy faith!

Many of these trophies of mercy were from the neighborhoods around, but a large number have united with the Wesleyan church.

It seems a pity to leave such a work as this. The town is *moved* and *shaken;* and multitudes more might be converted to God. But my appointments are out before me. leading me on to *Birmingham*, and I cannot stay. But the work need not *stop*, — shall not, I hope. To God be all the glory!

I was hospitably entertained at the house of *Mr. Savage*. He and his excellent *wife* are deeply devoted to God; — a precious family. The Lord reward them for evermore!

CHAPTER XII.

PENCILLINGS ABOUT CHESTERFIELD.

As to my "*Notes* and *Observations*, in [my] walks about Chesterfield," I have made but few of the sort you inquire after; have had but little time for that purpose; besides, my love for the *smiling fields, green lanes,* and *quiet paths,* quite neutralized the *attractions* of the *town.* However, such as I have they are at your service.

First, then, — and, were there any "*scolds*" in the *circle* to which I write, I would be inclined to an *apology* for my *first note;* which not being necessary, I would apologize, if possible, for the *barbarity* or *illiberality* of "the lords of creation," were it not that the law of the *oppressive usage* is traceable to "the times" of *Queen Elizabeth,* "of glorious memory." I refer to the use of the "Ducking Stool" for women who were as strong advocates for "the *freedom of speech,*" as we are in our day for the freedom of the press!— for I am now on the path to "a piece of water" where once stood the *Ducking Stool,* remembered by some of "the oldest inhabitants" of *Chesterfield,* but which had gone out of use before their day.

Now, is your curiosity, ladies, sufficiently excited? Well, then, the *Ducking Stool* was intended as a punishment for "*scolds, unquiet,* and *brawling women!*" That is what 't was for. It consisted of a post set up in a pond, across which was a transverse beam, turning on a swivel, with a *chair* at one end, in which they placed the *scold*, and, turning the chair and its occupant to the water, *dipped* both as often as the virulence of the *distemper* required, until *quite subdued*. Well, ladies, "*Women's Rights*" are better understood in our times, and in Chesterfield; for the *Ducking Stool*, —

> " That stool the dread of every scolding *quean*," —

has quite disappeared, but whether the same may be said of all the scolds of *Chesterfield*, I shall not undertake to decide, or whether the punishment answered the purpose intended; but you may criticize at your leisure the following opinions of a poet of 1780:

> " Down in the deep the stool descends,
> But here, at first, we miss our ends;
> She mounts again and rages more,
> Than ever vixen did before.
> So throwing water on the fire
> Will make it burn up but the higher;
> If so, my friends, pray let her take
> A second turn into the lake;
> And rather than your patient lose,
> Thrice and again repeat the dose;
> No brawling wives, no furious wenches,
> No fire so hot but water quenches."

Chesterfield is pleasantly situated upon a gentle elevation, in the beautiful vale of *Scarsdale*, at the confluence of two little rivers, named the *Hipper*, more classically, *Ibber*, which meant to *ebb* and to *flow*, from its sudden rising and falling, I suppose, not from the *pulsations* of the ocean, but the clouds that burst in the mountainous districts of *Holymoor*-side. The name of the other river is the *Rother*, anciently *Yr Odar;* that is, the *boundary*, the most southern point in the country of the ancient *Brigantes:*

> "—— Bowery Scarsdale loves and boasts
> The purple distance of her Alpine views,
> While *Rother*, loveliest vagrant, roves below."

The town itself stands upon an extensive *coal-field;* *iron-stone* also abounds in the neighborhood, of which some use is made, but not to the extent which *Providence* would seem to invite. There are also fine beds of *potter's clay*, and clay for making *brick;* but the inhabitants seem to prefer to work in *silk*, and *bobbin-net lace, hosiery, ginghams, ropes, sacks, cotton-wick*, and *leather*.

The *architecture* of the town is not attractive; irregularly built, and chiefly of brick.

The old *parish church* is the chief object of attraction; built nobody knows when,—some suppose in the early part of the thirteenth century; but a stone over the south entrance dates A. D. 1037. It is a venerable structure, and one never tires looking at it; seems as if pleading eloquently for the gloomy or glorious past.

But its *crooked spire* is the chief object of interest to strangers, and the *glory* of *Chesterfield* in the estimation of many of the inhabitants. It is, indeed, a singular object, viewed in any direction, aspiring like a mammoth *screw* between two and three hundred feet high. Viewed in one or two directions, its *crookedness* would be taken as an *optical deception*, owing to its *twisted* or *screw-like* appearance; but, viewed in other directions, it is unmistakably *crooked*, — a peculiarity which excited considerable controversy in past ages. However, it has been ascertained to lean *six feet* towards the south; yet, as one walks eastward or westward, it assumes a perpendicular appearance, — yet it leans *four feet* westward, which is soon perceived by a slight deviation in one's footsteps. An architect once ascended the spire to the "*crow hole,*" and ascertained that it leaned *southward eight feet;* but he got *frightened!*

When the spire was erected is not known, or whether perpendicular at first, or *crooked.* Advocates on both sides of the question have been numerous, "as generation has succeeded to generation," and century after century fled away! One thing is certain, it is built of *wood,* and covered with *lead,* put on in a *spiral* manner over *fluting* or *volutes,* that run up also in a *twisted* direction. Some *antiquarians* suppose it was constructed thus crooked by some ingenious architect; others that it was built perpendicular, and afterwards *warped* by the *sun,* or struck by *lightning.* But, as *oblivion* has swallowed up every fragment of *tradition* concerning it, each has claimed a valid right to his own opinion. It is certainly a *curious affair*, and impresses beholders differently, as an *ornament* or a *deformity.* A witty poet speaks of it thus:

> "Whichever way you turn your eye,
> It always seems to be awry;
> Pray, can you tell the reason why?—
> The only reason known of weight,
> Is that the thing was never straight.
> Nor know the people where to go
> To find the man to make it so;
> Since none can furnish such a plan,
> Except a perfect *upright* man:—
> So that the spire, 't is very plain,
> For ages crooked must remain
> And, while it stands, must ever be
> An emblem of deformity."

It is remarkable that *wood-work* so situated, and in so moist a climate, could last so from "time immemorial;" so as to outstand all records regarding its construction.

Architects have examined it from time to time, and *reported* as to its solidity; but so *contradictory* have been their reports, that one is tempted to suspect it has exerted a kind of *witchery* over their feelings or judgment; some declaring its timbers rotten, drawn, disjointed, and liable to fall at any moment, with contemptuous criticisms on its *carpenter-work*; others, in "after years," reported its wood-work "*firm and good*," supported by a *basis* so constructed, and the *strapping* of the spire so ingeniously fitted, that it is "morally impossible it should ever fall, until the *base* itself gave way; that there is not the slightest *bearing* from the shoulders, tenons, dovetails, or any other joint whatever; which convinced them that it had never given way in the least since the first day it was erected, else it had fallen down instantaneously; and that the rising sun a century hence would illumine the *crooked spire of Chesterfield!*" Honor to the ancient architect, whoever he was! Had the old church remained Roman Catholic, the Pope would probably have *canonized* it by this time, though as ignorant of its destination in eternity as the Athenians were of "*the Unknown God*," to whom they erected an altar! Indeed, I saw the remnants of an *old bridge* in France, a few months since, which once spanned the *Rhone*, the architect of which was *canonized* by *Pope Nicholas* the Fifth, who decided that "the bridge was raised by the inspiration of the Holy Ghost;" and the dead architect won the title of *Saint Benedict!*

The *monuments* in this old church of *Chesterfield* are ancient and numerous, and the *inscriptions* interesting;— some of which commence thus:

"*DEO OPT: MAX: ET POSTERITATI SACRUM;*"

That is, "*Sacred to God, the best and greatest, and to Posterity.*"

Another offers these agreeable lines:

> "O poore house of clay, now empty here thou lies,
> When all the furniture is gone to Paradise:
> Angels has conueyede to Heauean thy jewell mind,
> And nothing but the cabinet left behind."

The tomb of a *lawyer* bears the following, — worthy the attention of our young friend, so soon to sit with those of "subtle look, amid their parchments, weaving sophistries for *court* to meet at mid-day:"

> "A tender husband and a friend sincere,
> Consign'd to earth, implores the silent tear.
> Learn'd in the laws, he never warp'd their sense,
> To shelter vice, or injure innocence:
> But, firm to truth, by no mean interest mov'd,
> To all dispens'd that justice which he lov'd:
> Virtue oppress'd, he taught her rights to know,
> And guilt detected, fear'd the coming blow.
> Thus humbly useful, and without offence,
> He fill'd the circle mark'd by Providence,
> His age completing what his youth began,
> The noblest work of GOD, an honest man."

There is something that struck me as *quaintly witty* in the following inscription over the dust of an excellent lady, the namesake of *Martha* of old, — a wife and mother:

> "We boast no vertues, and we beg no tears:
> O Reader; if thou hast but Eyes and Ears,
> It is anough: But tell me; Why
> Thou com'st to gaze? Is it to pry
>   Into our Cost, or borrow
>   A Copy of our Sorrow?
>   Or dost thou come
>   To learn to dye,
> Not knowing whom to practise by?
>   If this be thy desire,
>   Then draw thee one step nigher;

> Here lies a precedent ; a rarer,
> Earth never shewed, nor Heaven a fairer.
> She was, — But room forbids to tell thee what ;
> Summ all perfection up and she was that."

The *Establishment* has another fine new church in this town.

There is much *wickedness* in Chesterfield; but there are many *pious* people therein, — such as resemble an *eminent divine, two hundred* years ago, who was born in this town, of whom it was said, "*He was a man of prayer, and well acquainted with the inside of religion!*" It was further remarked of him, that, "What some might reckon a reflection upon him was, in the judgment of wise men, his great honor, — that he acquired his learning without being beholden to any *university.*' Well, *adieu* Chesterfield! The *pilgrim* must be off to another part of the vineyard of the Lord!

CHAPTER XIII.

DONCASTER.

EXTRACTS FROM JOURNAL.

Nov. 8. — I arrived here this evening, accompanied by Brother *Unwin*, and several *Sheffield* brethren, who have come over to *Doncaster* for "a *field-day*," as they call it; that is, to *sing* and *pray*, and *exhort* and *agonize*, for the conversion of sinners, and the sanctification of believers, from daylight in the morning till midnight, as the Lord may lead them on to victory. *Noble men!* the true *heroes* of my Lord! And what can stand before these *flames of fire!* I received a hearty *English* welcome to the mansion of Mr. *Wilton*.

Monday morning, Nov. 10. — Yesterday was a day of salvation. Many saved. There is a glorious prospect.

Nov. 11. — A great move last night.

Nov. 12. — *Salvation!* O, how great! What can withstand the *Gospel*, when it becomes the *power* of God? Rom. 1 : 16.

Nov. 13. — The word runs like a fire. Hallelujah! I like *Doncaster;* an agreeable town, surrounded by a fine agricultural country; an old town of *West Yorkshire*. *Methodists* numerous, *hearty*, of the *right stamp*,— rife with the spirit of Wesley and the old Methodists, in *soul-saving!*

Nov. 14. — One o'clock in the morning; observing an

eclipse of the moon. The shadow of the earth has been progressing sensibly over her surface, till all that is left *unobscured* of that beautiful moon which arose a few hours since, in full-orbed majesty, is the small segment of a circle

* * * * * *

Nature seems to *mourn*, and to grow *sadder* and *sadder*. The moon is of a *dusky copperish color*, supposed by some to be her *native light*, but more likely the *effects* of the scattered *beams* of the sun *refracted* by our earth's *atmosphere*, and by it *bent* into the *earth's shadow upon the moon*, revealing her form and outline in this dusky grandeur.

* * * * * *

And now a slight mist seems to arise and veils that bright speck in a sort of *nebulous aureola*, which has a solemn and impressive effect.

The *shadow* begins to retire, and that luminous speck increases sensibly. My soul adores the great Author of this sublime phenomena,— these amazing motions and aspects of the heavenly bodies. What sublime sensations does such a spectacle inspire! How wondrous the *laws* which govern these motions,— these orbs of immensity, and our *earth*, in harmony with the rest, although so full of *rebellion* against Him, the mighty Creator and Governor of all!

Is the *moon* inhabited? If so, how does our earth appear to the *Lunarians? Magnificent*, doubtless; that is, if it really is what astronomers say it is, a *moon* to the *moon;* and appearing *twelve* or *thirteen* times larger to them, than the moon does to us; and, of course, affords to them twelve or thirteen times more light; — our earth, in fact, the *largest body* within the range of their vision, and progressing through the heavens with a motion *thirteen* times *quicker* than the moon to us, but, like the moon, *waxing* and *waning* regularly.

But is it possible that a scene so *magnificent* has no *spectators* in that moon to behold it? If as ignorant and proud as we are, they may possibly be vain enough to suppose that our earth is for no other purpose than to cheer and enlighten *them*. Could we *telegraph* them, we might be disposed to *humble* them a little upon that point! But, in doing so, we ought to be honest enough to confess we have been quite as vain *ourselves*. Ah! if the moon has inhabitants, they are holier, *happier*, and *wiser* than we, doubtless.

Astronomy is a darling science to me. It would make me an *enthusiast*, had I time to study it. It always inspires me with *sublime* emotions.

Time, however, has been allotted me for other *purposes*. I know what they are, and must attend to them. The Ruler of the universe *calls* and *qualifies* others, doubtless, to this study, that they may show forth his glory. *Josephus* accounts for the *longevity* of the antediluvians, that it was so ordered of God, that they might have time to study, to some perfection, the geometrical and astronomical sciences; that "the period of the grand year," which, among the Jews, consisted of *six hundred years*, was an era it was necessary they should *live to see*, in order to lay a proper basis for those sciences. That "grand year is still a sublime idea in astronomy; it implies, according to some, the period necessary to bring the *sun* and moon exactly into the same positions which they occupied in the beginning of the creation; a period which most of the learned, I believe, suppose to perfect the *solar year* and *lunar month* more exactly than any other.

It comforts my heart to anticipate a period, in my coming *eternity*, when I shall perfectly understand what is now so *sublimely mysterious* to my present limited faculties. And may remember, with corresponding emotions, the time of my ignorance, when gazing at an eclipse of the moon, from the window of a house in Doncaster, England. And if associated with that, there shall stand another fact, "the grand year" of my ministry, when my call to preach the Gospel received its most signal verification, and that this and the next year were comprised therein, it would add a yet *brighter illumination* to the past, and inspire still *sublimer emotions.*

* * * * * *

Towards morning, the moon regained all her splendor, and more, apparently; for, with what *surprising beauty* she did shine! Like the Christian, after emerging from the shades of unsuccessful temptations, it seemed as if the moon was celebrating her triumph over that envious shadow, which had cast over her fair face a gloom so humiliating.

CHAPTER XIV.

THE REVIVAL IN DONCASTER.

MR. CAUGHEY, writing from *York*, on the 15th of November, observes :

I spent *six* days in Doncaster ; — busy days they were, I assure you ; — days of glory and of victory. My soul stood in a sort of amaze at the work, — its *swiftness*, — its *greatness*. The whole town seemed to be moved. But so rapid and overwhelming was the visitation, sinners had little time for *exchanging thoughts* upon the subject, and less for *combination*. Clouds of mercy gathered over the place at once, and burst forth and came down in "*showers of blessing*" upon the people. — Ezek. 34 : 26. "*The Lord was there*," — Ezek. 48 : 35, — *there* in majesty and in power, and hardly anything was found that could stand before *Him* and his *truth*. There was no *mistaking* of the nature and reality of his *glorious presence*. Angels and disembodied spirits seemed as if filling all the air, — as if rejoicing in

> "The growing empire of their King."

But, alas ! my engagements would not allow a longer stay. Is it right to throw out ahead of me *appointments* that must be met, whether the *Providence* of God says "*stay here*," or not ? O, how hard it was to tear myself away from such a work, — from such *awakened masses* of sinners, which may possibly relapse into the former state of spiritual death! But leave them I *must*, and leave them I did.

The secretary, at Doncaster, reports the number saved, during those six days, thus: — *three hundred and fifty-six* cases of *justification*, and *one hundred and thirty-seven* souls *sanctified*. Total, *four hundred and ninety three*. The last night I spent there, not less than *one hundred and fifty* souls professed to find *pardon* or *purity*.

The people came in from many miles around. One among the converts, on that last night of "the feast," created a *sensation*, at least in my mind, as I attentively observed him. I queried whether England could present such another, although he was surrounded by a motley group, some of which the Devil had evidently been using very badly! But this man was of an amazing height, — *rough, muscular, uncouth,* and in *clothes* as badly *torn* as his *conscience! — weather-worn,* and *weather-torn,* and *battered,* — one of Zechariah's "*Oaks of Bashan!*" — as if ready with *long arms* to grapple unceremoniously with anything a storm might fling in their way; — reminding one of *Shakspeare's* character,—"a fellow by the hand of nature *marked, quoted,* and signed to do;"— as if *circumstances*, with a hand of iron, had made him what he was. *Wordsworth's* Peter Bell might have been his brother, whose picture the poet drew so *graphically*:

> "There was a *hardness* in his *cheek*,
> There was a *hardness* in his *eye*,
> As if the man had set his face,
> In many a solitary place,
> Against the wind and open sky!"

A *diamond in the rough*, this man may possibly be. If so, he will not be long in Christ's hands, if faithful, before he shall shine with *sparkling* splendor in the bosom of the church. What a pity Satan has had him so long! I stood and looked at him, standing head and shoulders above the tallest, and above a motley group, some of whom the Devil had been using as bad, probably, as himself; — for what a *scene*, surely, that was; and what a variety of character! But among such materials, the Gospel of Jesus Christ is in its glory; and would seem to speak aloud to bystanders, as Jesus did to the deputation sent by John to inquire whether he was the Christ that should come, or were they to look for another. Jesus raised his head, and, pausing from his *miracles* of mercy, said: "Go your way, and tell John what things ye have *seen* and *heard;* how that the *blind see*, the *lame walk*, the *lepers are cleansed*, the *deaf hear*, the *dead are raised*, to *the poor the Gospel is preached.* And blessed is he, whosoever shall not be *offended* in me;"— *offended*, that is *stumbled* at the expenditure of my wisdom, benevolence, and power, upon such miserable objects as these! — Offended! stumbled! O, why should it be so, blessed Jesus? Such exhibitions of thy mercy, such proof of thy Messiahship, ought never to have been a cause of *stumbling* to those who beheld them! — no, nor such scenes as we witnessed in Doncaster. And multitudes there were, in Doncaster, who desired no more convincing evidence than that they witnessed, on that parting night, that *the Gospel is the power of God unto salvation to every one that believeth!* — Rom. 1: 16.

CHAPTER XV.

EXTRACTS FROM JOURNAL.

"AND AS YE GO, *preach.*"

York, Nov. 17. — I preached yesterday forenoon in the *Centenary Chapel* in behalf of the *Wesleyan Missions.* In the afternoon, the Rev. Mr. Cornuck preached a stirring sermon for the same cause, after which we held a *prayer-meeting;* and *ten* souls were saved. At night, in the same chapel, to nearly *three thousand* people, I opened and applied that awful text, spoken by the supposed ghost of Samuel the prophet, to *Saul,* King of Israel: " *Why hast thou disquieted me to bring me up? — seeing the Lord is departed from thee, and is become thine enemy?*" — 1 Sam. 28: 15, 16. Had an awful time; and *nineteen* were saved, before the service closed.

Nov. 19. — Attended the *missionary meeting* on Monday night, and gave an address. Preached last night to a fine congregation; a few were saved.

Huddersfield, Nov. 24. — Yesterday, I preached twice here; *fifty* saved. The *new converts* of the great revival, *nine or ten months since,* are doing well, generally, — standing fast in glorious liberty, full of energy and activity. Surely that was a great work! — over *eighteen hundred* souls justified, and between *seven* and *eight hundred* sanctified in, *five months.** This visit seems to have fanned

* See volume "*Earnest Christianity Illustrated.*"

the flame anew, and given the *new converts* a fresh impulse along the heavenly road!

Nov. 28. — At *Honley*, ——— a hard time; sinners hard and defiant. *Devils* of a peculiar order have *charge* of that district; would require a *siege* to rout them. They maintain a strange sort of feeling; and, here and there, head and shoulders above others in sin, are "champions cased in adamant."

A hard class of infernal spirits have charge of sinners up and down that valley, and over those hills; I know it and have felt it; and Satan is their *general.*

"On earth the usurper reigns;"

and hereabouts especially; for his *baneful power* is felt in some places more than in others. Satan had his *seat* in *Pergamos* once. "I know thy works, and where thou dwellest, *even where Satan's seat is.*" — Rev. 2 : 13. His *throne* was there, and there he *reigned* over his obedient subjects. He has but a small cause in Pergamos now, and not much of a cause *here*, comparatively; but he holds the position with a tenacity which bespeaks great principles, in Satanic estimation. *What we know not now, we shall know hereafter.* His *infernal battalions* are widely extended, and advantageously stationed. They have their *districts.* Their *dispositions* are varied, I sometimes think, as are the depraved human beings they have in charge!

O, what a valley of *dry bones* is within sight! A place that calls for Ezekiel's "*four winds.*" — Ezek. 37 : 9.

Well, I was *defeated.* Never mind! I may yet have my revenge of a *month's* cannonading hereabouts, against the works of darkness.

Nov. 29. — At *Sheepridge*, near Huddersfield, last night, to a people of a very different spirit. Edward Brook, Esq., the great Yorkshire revivalist, resides in their midst,— a host in himself. We had a real "set-to" for souls, he helping me, with the Lord; several were saved; and one *backslider* literally *roared* aloud, through the *bitterness* of his heart; but his *tones* changed before the meeting closed, for the Lord had pitied him, and shown him mercy.

It does me good to meet with such a spiritual *warrior* as Mr. Brook. He is a noble soul, and understands well *satanic tactics* in every part of Yorkshire, and knows how to *cope* with them, with that "rough and ready" talent of his; nor has he ever to go in search of his armor for a skirmish or battle with the Devil's troops. God bless him!

Macclesfield, Dec. 1. — Arrived here on Saturday, 29th ult., by railway, and next day made an *onslaught* on the works of darkness, the Lord helping, and before *midnight* there were *one hundred* souls saved, in *pardon* and *purity*. The proportion from the *world* I have not yet learned.

Dec. 2. — There were *twenty-five* saved last night. A noble beginning.

CHAPTER XVI.

PENCILLINGS IN MACCLESFIELD.

I LIKE *Macclesfield*. It is an agreeable, thriving town, the *metropolis* of the English silk-trade, "for growing and manufacture of silk, *winding silk*, and *twist-making*," the *staple* of the town for ages. There are, of course, many mills.

The town *charter* dates May 29, 1261. The charter, however, under which the present corporation acts, was granted by Charles II. I was amused with one of its privileges, — "*The Court of Piepowder*"! A court for the semi-annual *fairs*, for the immediate redress of *disturbances* committed at them, and to redress the *grievances* of the buyers and sellers.

But why call it the *Piepowder* Court? It seems to be derived from two *French* words, — *pie*, a *foot*, and *poudré*, *dusty* — the *Dusty-foot* Court, signifying that the *dusty-footed* folks, who had come from afar to the fair, were the *patronizers* of this court, *befooled*, doubtless, in many cases, by strong drink. One at my elbow, doubts the definition, and thinks it stands for *Pied Puldereaux* — a *pedler*. Well, no matter, the *pedler*, is a *dusty-foot!* and whether it was good or ill to him, it saved him from "*the law's delays*," if not from "*the insolence of office ;*" and that was something.

A few miles from town, is the birthplace of the celebrated

John Bradshaw; he who presided in the *high court* of justice, on the trial of Charles I. He received most of his education at *Macclesfield*, and seems to have had a *presentiment*, of some sort, of notoriety in coming life, as he perpetrated the following *stanza* upon a tombstone, between two and three centuries ago:

> " My brother Henry must heir the land,
> My brother Frank must be at his command;
> Whilst I, poor Jack, will do that
> That all the world shall wonder at."

True enough, and so he did! The tragical death of Charles I. was sufficient for that. But he stopped not there. A warm *republican* in his principles, he hated all sorts of usurpation, and, beholding it in *Cromwell*, " he opposed him to the teeth." *Cromwell*, on the day he dissolved " the *Long Parliament*," went direct to break up the *Council of State*, addressing them thus:

" If you, gentlemen, are met here as private persons, you shall not be disturbed; but if as a Council of State, this is no place for you, since you cannot but know what was done in the house in the morning; so, take notice that the Parliament is dissolved." To this Bradshaw boldly replied, " Sir, we have heard what you did at the house in the morning, and before many hours all England will hear it. But, sir, you are mistaken, to think that Parliament is dissolved; for, no power under heaven can dissolve them but themselves; therefore, take you notice of that."

Cromwell afterwards said, " I did it in spite of the objections of honest Bradshaw, the president." Bradshaw, from henceforth, lost the friendship of the Protector; but he divided the *notoriety* with him afterwards, by sharing with him one of the *three* angles of *Tyburn*. *Cromwell* had one,— that is, the *head* of Cromwell,— *Bradshaw* the other, and *Ireton* the third. They were raised from their graves, and thus promoted after the restoration. The three *famous heads* drew all eyes towards Westminster Hall, where they frightened away the birds for some time!

And here, in Macclesfield, preached and died that great and good man, the Rev. *David Simpson,* author of " Simpson's Plea for Religion; " a powerful antidote against infidelity.

He was a famous divine, of the English church, contemporary with the *Wesleys;* a bold and unsparing opponent of all *ungodliness,* one of the brightest ornaments of the established church; but his faithful, uncompromising preaching brought upon him great *persecution;* first at *Buckingham,* where his *extemporaneous style* was pronounced an *innovation,* and was made a *plea* for raising a *storm* about his ears; but the truth was, his preaching had raised a *storm* in their *consciences!* The bishop listened to their appeal, and was weak enough to sign the paper for his removal; but the bishop, knowing the irreproachable character of the man, had the *candor* and *conscience* to say, " Mr. *Simpson,* if you are determined to *do your duty* as a clergyman ought to do, you must everywhere expect to meet with *opposition.*" And yet he yielded to the popular clamor, and removed the faithful watchman!

In the year 1773, he arrived in *Macclesfield,* the place designed for him, doubtless, by the Head of the Church. " I never withheld any *truth,* either from *fear,* or with a desire to obtain the *favor* of any man," was one of his sayings.

In this spirit, he opened his commission in *Macclesfield,* and in this spirit, he continued to preach the Gospel. The truth, it was said, fell *like sparks of fire* upon the *con-*

sciences of his hearers; especially upon those, " the nigh minded *sensualists* in the town," who would attend church on the *Sabbath*, although immersed in the *grossest profligacy* through the *week*. To these, his preaching became intolerable, and set them " casting about " how they might get rid of him. They *spurned* the preacher, and stigmatized his doctrine with the hated epithet of " *Methodism;* " and so the fire of opposition increased.

The idea of having to endure this sort of preaching, became *insupportable*. *Profligates* and *formalists* were in arms. The man of God never *flinched*, but poured into their ranks the *burning truths* of God.

At this crisis, occurred an event which let loose the storm of war. Sir William Meredith came to hear him. The *baronet* was *notoriously licentious*. The preacher announced his text: " *Marriage* is honorable in all, and the bed undefiled; but *whoremongers* and *adulterers* God will judge." The sermon exploded like a *bomb-shell* around the ears of the noble baronet, and kindred spirits. " It is extremely *ill-bred*," exclaimed one party. " *Public taste, good manners*, and *common decency*, are outraged," said another party. " Such *puritanical* stuff is not to be endured," vociferated another. " No *gentleman* or lady can be safe in hearing this *puritanical parson*," exclaimed a fourth class. And now the storm of opposition began to rage in earnest. " This *moralist* must be silenced." The bishop was appealed to, under the insinuation that he had sent them a *Methodist preacher*, instead of a proper *clergyman*. The bishop yielded to the clamor, and suspended him. But he refused to be silenced thus; and went out among the neighboring villages, as a flame of fire, preaching in private houses, and calling sinners to repentance everywhere. All the pulpits of the Establishment were closed against him; but he heeded it not, and kept on preaching, declaring the whole counsel of God to the people; and Christ was with him.

The head of the church interfered. That bishop was removed, and another appointed, who did not oppose Mr. S. His enemies were on the alert, and tried to work upon the new bishop, with the old charge,— "The man is a Methodist; and his preaching is turning the people into Methodists." Mr. Simpson thought proper to address the bishop also, which he did thus:

"My method is to preach the great truths, and doctrines and precepts of the Gospel, in as plain, and earnest, and affectionate a manner as I am able. Persons of different ranks, persuasions, and characters, come to hear. Some hereby have been convinced of the error of their ways, see their guilt, and become seriously concerned about their situation. The change is soon discovered; they meet with one or another, who invites them to attend the preachings and meetings among the Methodists, and hence their number is increased to a considerable degree. This is the truth; I own the fact; I have often thought of it; but I confess myself unequal to the difficulty. What would your lordship advise?"

A friendly mayor came into office at this time, and immediately asserted a right, invested in him, to reïnstate Mr. Simpson in the parish! While the *bishop* was pondering, Providence was planning. A wealthy gentleman, Mr. *Roe*, offered to build Mr. Simpson a church in another part of the town, which he did in a very short time; and it was dedicated on Christmas Day, 1775. Here Mr. Simpson stood up for God, without fear, and preached the whole Gospel, with the Holy Ghost sent down from heaven. Multitudes crowded to his ministry. His *eloquence*, it is said, was pure and commanding, and poured forth like a flowing stream.

The *Methodists* loved and honored him. He often seated himself under their ministry, and listened to the Gospel from them with the greatest delight. To the youth of Macclesfield, his *ministry* was greatly blessed; especially to the *operatives*, of both sexes, in the *silk-mills*. To the *young woman* he would say, "Your *character* is like *glass;* if once injured, it can never be restored;" and the *effects* of his teaching were felt to be a blessing to the entire population. Although *forty and six years* have passed away, since that good pastor was laid in the *tomb*, his name in Macclesfield is still *as ointment poured forth*.

To-day, I visited his church, in company with a few *brethren*, ascended the pulpit, and looked around; and thought, where are "*the crowding thousands*" who hung upon those lips of eloquence and power? And where

> "That *eye of lightning*, and that *soul of fire*,
> Which thronging thousands crowded to admire?"

In the *dust*, in the *spirit land!* Hushed in death was that fine *voice*, which illustrated, with all the resources of genius, and force of intellectual energy, those eternal truths of God, which awakened and converted men! He, and all those *multitudes*, gone,— gone into the world of spirits,— *illustrating*, in life and in death, that panoramic view of them, by a great poet of the same age:

> "Opening the map of God's extensive plan,
> We find a little *isle, this life of man;*
> Eternity's unknown expanse appears
> Circling around and limiting his years.
> The *busy race*, examine and explore
> Each creek and cavern of the dangerous shore.

> With care collect what in their eyes excels,
> Some shining pebbles, and some weeds and shells;
> Th is laden, dream that they are rich and great,
> And happiest he that groans beneath his weight;
> The waves o'ertake them in their serious play,
> And every hour sweeps multitudes away!
> They shriek and sink, survivors start and weep,
> Pursue their sport, and follow to the deep.
> A few forsake the throng; with lifted eyes
> Ask *wealth of Heaven*, and gain a *real prize*,
> *Truth, wisdom, grace,* and *peace* like that above,
> Sealed with his signet, whom they serve and love.
> Scorned by the rest, with patient hope they wait
> A kind release from their imperfect state,
> And, unregretted, are soon snatched away
> From scenes of sorrow into glorious day."

I admire those lines; — a faithful picture of our times as well. Of the *latter class, Mr. Simpson* had very many seals to his ministry.

And there is the same "communion rail," where the faithful followers of the *Lamb* so often knelt to receive the sacred emblems of his broken body and shed blood; where he and Mr. Wesley administered the sacrament to *thirteen hundred* persons, many of them Methodists, — for they had not the ordinance in their own chapels then, — when that little incident occurred, of which Mr. Wesley speaks in his Journal: "March 29.— [Being Good Friday] I came to Macclesfield just time enough to assist Mr. Simpson in the laborious service of the day. I preached for him morning and afternoon; and we administered the sacrament to about *thirteen hundred persons.* While we were administering, I heard a low, soft, solemn sound, just like the Æolian harp. It continued five or six minutes, and so affected many, that they could not refrain from tears. It then gradually died away. Strange that no other organist (that I know) should think of this. In the evening," adds Mr. Wesley,

"I preached at our room. Here was that *harmony* which *art* cannot imitate."

And there, at that *communion table*, stood Mr. Simpson, at the dread moment when this church was rocked to and fro by the heavings of an *earthquake*, and before him the terrified congregation endeavoring to escape, while he tried to allay their fears; and here, in this pulpit, he preached his famous *Earthquake Sermon!*

A little incident occurred to me, when descending from the pulpit of this church, which strangely affected me; — a strange sensation and singular awe crept over me when halfway down, as if a spirit awaited me at the bottom, — the spirit of the departed *Simpson*. I reached the lower step as if *enchained*, so to speak, by a mysterious influence; — felt his *spirit* was at my right hand, between me and the altar, which is behind the pulpit. I stood still, as before a *presence*, — a *power*, — a *living thing*, — an *invisible intelligence*, — as if it would speak aloud to me; — when these words *thrilled my inmost* soul: "*Save souls! win souls! He that winneth souls is wise!*" It was all inaudible, — invisible. But how irresistible the conviction of a *presence*, — speaking to me, — from which I broke away at length, feeling God *is in this place, and I knew it not. It is God's own house and heaven's gate.* I quietly moved on as if from *the spirit of the place.* Well, if it was but an *hallucination*, it quickened my spirit, and my preaching received a fresh impulse and a keener edge. What we know not now, we shall know hereafter, when we meet the soul of *Simpson* in the *upper sanctuary.* Perhaps, many of the children and grandchildren of his former hearers, are soon to be converted to God. In looking over the *Memoirs* of Mr. Simpson, I met with the following incident, which I give in his own words: "When I was yet a boy, and undesigned for the ministry, either by my parents or from inclination, one Sunday evening, while I was reading prayers in my father's family, suddenly a voice, or something like a voice, called aloud within me, yet so as not to be perceived by any of the persons kneeling around me, 'YOU MUST GO AND BE INSTRUCTED FOR THE MINISTRY.' The voice, or whatever it might be, was so exceedingly quick and powerful, that it was with difficulty I could proceed to the end of the prayer. As soon, however, as the prayer was ended, I made request to my father to let me be trained up for the ministry. I told him all I knew of the circumstances. He, of course, denied my request, thinking it was some whim I had got into my head, which would go off again when I had slept upon it. But the voice — or what shall I call it? — gave me no rest night or day for three weeks; when my ever dear, honored and indulgent father gave way to my wishes, and put me in a train of study to qualify me for the University."

CHAPTER XVII.

THE WORK OF GOD IN MACCLESFIELD.

Dec. 3. — A great time last night. *The blows of truth* fell thick and fast, and brought many to their knees with a cry for mercy. *Fifty* saved. The *critics* had no time to "stand from under;" they had no *warning*, and came *down* with the rest. It is not best to stand too much upon *preliminaries;* gives them too much time to get ready; they guess what is coming, and the preacher, like

"Entellus, *wastes his forces on the wind.*"

That, I do not like, and so fall upon them *suddenly*. We have a few *whimpers* about "*extravagance,*" &c., but the next onset of truth levels the whimperers to the ground, where they cry outright for mercy!

* * * * * *

Dined a few miles from town, in company with Mr. S., whose wife, a pious lady, and a *Wesleyan*, died very happy some time since. She had been confined to her room but a few days, when the call for her departure to heaven came suddenly, and found her, like "*the wise virgins,*" ready. — Matt. 25 : 1. She was sitting in her chair when *Death* came, — when the *chariot* of heaven arrived. She sat a few moments, absorbed in thought, as if adjusting her spiritual armor; then arose and walked across the room to her bed, repeating that fine stanza as she went:

"Jesus, in thy great name I go
To conquer death — my final foe!
And when I quit this cumbrous clay,
And soar on angels' wings away,
My soul the second death defies,
And reigns eternal in the skies."

She then quietly lay down upon the bed, like a *warrior* seeking rest, after having driven the enemy from the field; and then uttered, faintly, but in an adoring attitude, —

"I will
Clap my glad wings and soar away,
And mingle with the blaze of day,"

and sweetly fell asleep in Jesus, and was escorted to heaven. "*Our people die well*," said Dr. *Newton*. They do, blessed be God, who giveth them the victory through Jesus Christ our Lord!

The death of this Christian lady reminded me of another, who died here in Mr. Wesley's time. "I rode on to *Macclesfield*," says Mr. Wesley. "Here I heard an agreeable account of Mrs. R——, who was in the society at London from a child; but, after she was married to a rich man, durst not own a poor, despised people. Last year she broke through, and came to see me. A few words, which I then spake, never left her, not even in the trying hour, during the illness, which came a few months after. All her conversation was then in heaven; till, feeling her strength was quite exhausted, she said, with a smile, 'Death, thou art welcome!' and resigned her spirit." Ah! perhaps, had she *walked in the light* after her marriage with the rich man, her *pilgrimage* might have been longer, and more honorable, and her reward in heaven greater.

Much depends upon what degree of the light and influences of the Holy Spirit we sin against. St. John says, "*There is a sin unto death;*" sometimes the death of the body only, while the soul is saved. However, Mrs. S. was one of those who walked closely with the Lord before her family and his people. She did not refuse her influence for Christ, although surrounded with *affluence*. Her work was done.

What a work God has begun here! I have come among a *prepared people*. These godly ministers, *Harris* and *Clay*, have prepared the way of the Lord; and so have others before them. I love to preach where such devoted men as *David Simpson*, and others, walked, and toiled, and fought the great battle of *truth* for God, and sowed the seed for a future harvest, and sent up many *prayers*, answers to which are, doubtless, constantly descending, to their great joy, where they are enthroned on high, among *the "spirits of* just men made perfect." It seems as if their *spirits* are sometimes *present*,—as if they hover around and over us, observing with delight the successive answers to their long-recorded prayers; and as if they helped *to shout the harvest home!*

Besides, the *history* of such great souls is so familiar to those they left behind them, and to their children,—of which their fathers have told them, showing to their children the wonderful works which God wrought in their day, by the ministry of his servants, and the *manner of it* (Psalms 78: 3),—that they are not taken by *surprise* when the Head of the Church repeats his miracles of mercy under a *modern ministry*. They are not *offended*, or *stumbled* at this or that *extraordinary movement;* at me, for instance, when the Bible is clasped to my breast, by something akin to an irresistible impulse, or lifted clear over head, like a *battle-axe*, "contrary to the rules of rhetorical gesture;"

for, who of all the children of Macclesfield, would say a word against that, seeing that *Simpson*, the beloved of their fathers, often held the Bible aloft in his right hand, to the no small peril of breaking their *heads* below, by missing his hold of the Bible above! and who, contrary to all rules of pulpit propriety, on seeing an old woman fast asleep while he was preaching, did actually seize upon the pulpit *cushion*, and flung it at her drowsy head, quite interrupting her nap for that afternoon, and, I dare say, ever after in that place!

However, there is no need of *cushion-flinging* just now in *Macclesfield;* for they are all "*wide awake.*" Old men and women, young men and maidens, and children, all hearing for *everlasting life!* Not less than *one hundred souls* have professed salvation since last night; of these, thirty are cases of full salvation; but *seventy*, within a few hours, are the trophies of pardoning mercy; not such *pardons* as those inscribed upon a *brass plate* in the wall of the parish church, close by, granted, by the Pope of Rome, to a *woman* and her *seven children*, placed there, when *Romanism* was the religion of England, and that their church. The inscription reads thus:

"The pardon for saying V paternostors, and
V aves, and a crede, is XXVI thousand years,
and XXVI days of pardon."

Not such, these *seventy pardons*, granted those *seventy distressed penitents*, from the Lord God, through repentance and faith in our Lord Jesus Christ:

"A pardon written with his blood,
The favor and the peace of God;"

not with the appended *nonsense* of "*twenty-six thou-*

sand years, and *twenty-six days;*" no, no! but forever and ever, if *faithful until death!* — Rev. 2: 10.

Birmingham, Dec. 5. — Had a tender parting with the friends at Macclesfield. The *scene* was indeed *amazing* the last night; the glory of the Lord filled his temple. The *cries of the wounded*, and the *shouts* of the *healed*, were heard afar off. During those six glorious days I spent in *Macclesfield*, the secretary reported some *two hundred and sixty souls justified*, and *one hundred and forty sanctified*. Total, *four hundred souls* in six days! All glory be to Christ! He doeth the work. "He touches the *mountains*, and they smoke — the *hills*, and they melt;" and earth and her sons tremble, and fall before the mighty God of Jacob!

I was hospitably entertained at the house of *Mr. Bowers*, Mill-street. May the *smiles* of Jesus be the *sunshine* of his dwelling-place evermore. Amen.

The *Rev. Mr. Harris*, superintendent, and the *Rev. Mr. Clay*, his amiable and excellent colleague, showed me much kindness, and did all they could to render my visit agreeable to me, and *profitable* to the people.

Arriving at *Birmingham*, I was met at the depot by the *Rev. Alexander Bell*, superintendent and *chairman* of the district, who gave me a hearty welcome, and escorted me to *Sparkbrook House*, the noble mansion of *John Wright*, Esq. where I felt myself instantly and perfectly at *home*.

CHAPTER XVIII.

BIRMINGHAM.

PREPARING FOR THE CONFLICT.

WE have now introduced the reader into the principal scene of Mr. Caughey's labors, — where he labored several months; and where his ministry was greatly blessed to multitudes of souls. The following, from his pen, will afford a glimpse of his feelings and prospects; — a good illustration of a soul encouraging and strengthening itself in God.

It was thought proper I should open my commission in *Newton Row Chapel.* I have preached there a few times with some success; feeling very *small* and *humble*, and attracting but little notice. What of that? A *stone* is a small affair, compared with the mass of water into which it *falls;* nevertheless how wide the circles which it forms in the water, and ever widening! Besides, the higher the stone ascends *heavenwards*, the more decided its effect in forming *circles.*

The exhortation to myself, is, Arise, my soul! Ascend — climb — soar heavenward unto God, with all thy affections and powers, that the force of thy descent upon the vast mass of mind around thee may be felt in circling waves of sanctified power and influence, even from centre to circumference.

Be of good cheer. O my soul! Thou art indeed but a small,

insignificant particle flung upon the brink of this great population; but what of that? If thou art a fragment of that *prophetic Stone*, mentioned by *Daniel*, which was *cut out of the mountain without* hands, and destined to fill the whole earth; then may *thy influence*, through Christ that living *Stone*, fill all *Birmingham*, for his glory in the salvation of sinners!

Rouse thee, then, my soul! If thou dost claim kindred with that Stone, expect to feel thyself possessed of some of its *momentum* and *diffusiveness* ; — a *momentum*, to break down *opposing .influences*, and to overturn "the great image" of Birmingham idolatry, — of *gold*, and *silver*, *brass, iron* and *clay* ;— DIFFUSIVENESS, of *light, life, love* and *power*, radiating throughout all this mass of minds, bringing *life* out of *death, purity* out of *putridity, light* out of *darkness, love* out of *enmity, strength* out of *weakness;* causing the *weak* things of this world, as Paul hints, to confound and bring to naught the things that are *mighty*. Amen!

The great *image* may be considered *civilly* ; and what if the will of God should have it, that this *impetus* of thine shall smite its *iron and clayey feet* first, — the *poorer classes* in the satanic confederation? For, mark, when the *little stone* cut out without hands, in *Nebuchadnezzar's* dream, smote the image upon its *feet* that were of *iron and clay*, down came the whole image,— *legs of iron, belly and thighs of brass, breast and arms of silver*, and *head of fine gold*, — all came down together when the *feet* gave way; — then commenced the *threshing*, till all this heterogeneous mass of metal was broken in pieces, and became like unto the *chaff of the summer threshing-floor*. — Dan. 2. Lord Jesus, bring me in contact with "*the common people*," — the *poorer classes*, first; — it was they who heard thee *gladly*, when upon earth. — Mark 12 : 37. *Christ Jesus*, the Heaven-commissioned *Stone*, came in contact successively with those four great empires of the earth,— the *Chaldean*, the *Medo-Persian*, the *Macedonian*, or *Greek*, and the *Roman*,— and made them *like the chaff of the summer threshing-floor*. Commission a poor *worm*, O Jesus, and he, too, will thresh the *empires of sinful confederations* in Birmingham,— *metallic Birmingham*,— this *great worker* in gold, silver, copper, brass and iron, and clay. Amen! And then shall rise, from the materials of this *moral rebellion*, a structure of converted and *sanctified mind*, indestructible and eternal!

* * * * * * *

There is a *danger*, I am aware, of one's *conscious insignificancy* and *unworthiness* and *weakness*, bringing on a *timidity*, an *enfeebling solitariness*. If it was not able in past years to detain me in the *shade*, or to bind me down in the solitudes of an *inglorious ease*, why allow it to *prostrate* me *now* on the rough edge of one of my most glorious battles? Down, *unbelief!* Be exalted, *faith* in God!

* * * * * * *

I like that thought of a poet, who pictures a solitary *raindrop* tarrying in the *cloud*, discouraged by the apparent impossibility of a thing so insignificant as itself to *water the thirsty earth*, which was calling loudly to the heavens for rain (Hosea 2 : 21—23); and the soliloquy of the humble *sunbeam*, lingering in the sun, considering the idea that it could create *day*, or disperse the *gloom* which had overspread the whole hemisphere, preposterous. But the *raindrop* took courage at length, and rushed down courageously on its mission of mercy; and it soon found that thousands and thousands more of *drops* followed, and that heaven and earth were being shaken by *thunder* and *lightning* and *wind*, with a *teeming shower* over all the thirsty land, bidding every *dying* thing *live*, and it *lived* and praised the Lord! The *sunbeam* also, thinking better of the matter, concluded to try what it could do. Trusting firmly in the aid of its great parent, the sun, down it came also, on its *errand of love;* the sun saw it, and rejoiced at a benevolence so like his own, and despatched to its aid millions of other sunbeams, filling the whole hemisphere with sunshine, and a most *magnificent* day, calling out of doors everything that loved the sun, causing heaven and earth to rejoice in each other's smiles; when only *bats* and *owls* were left to mourn the absence of their beloved darkness, and to hate the light and the sunshine.

Here, then, my "far-away friends," you have a fragment of my philosophy, which I have "set down" as much for my own *encouragement*, as for your *curiosity* or *information*.

How often have I heard the spirit of those words sounding in my spiritual ear, *Be not afraid, but speak, and hold not thy peace, for I am with thee; for I have much people in this city!* — Acts 18: 9. And the *raindrop* is speaking to me, and the *sunbeam*, that *mine* is the more glorious mission, — as *heaven* exceeds earth, as *eternity* outweighs time, as the *soul* is more valuable than the body; — the *salvation* of which being at the top of all salvation.

I have two sermons on Rom. 1 : 16 — "*For I am not ashamed of the Gospel of Christ, for it is the power of God unto salvation*, to every one that believeth; to the Jew first, and also to the Greek." What! *timid* and *doubtful* in possession of such a power as this — after penning such sentiments as those sermons contain — after such *deductions* and inferences? Never. If they are mere *theory*, and unfit for practical purposes, — for such hoped-for victorious *onslaughts* upon the ranks of wickedness, — why, then, "Away with them," saith my soul, "and take thy pen and write something more consistent with fact, *practical fact*, and *common sense.*" Nay, my soul! but thou knowest the contrary. "*What I have* written, I have written," said *Pontius Pilate*, regarding the *inscription* over the head of Jesus on the cross. So say I. Let me abide by it, then, nor betray, nor crucify the Gospel, as Pilate did its divine Author; *but play the man* in the management of this Heaven-appointed *artillery*, push *principles* to the utmost, *make full proof of thy ministry*, as Paul exhorted Timothy.

Theory! theory! Ye friends of Jesus! was that it? — to confide in mere theory, without regard to the *full proof* in *practical effects?* Was that my own notion in the sermons referred to? — as the Spanish poet has it,

"——————— to *confide*
In *painted words, the eloquence of pride*"?

God forbid! Nay, I was *sincere!* — the design was *practical*. Then *practical be it!* I am not ashamed of the Gospel, nor of any one of those sentiments penned in those sermons! No! But I see a *struggle* before me, — an agony of conflict. But "Victory is of the Lord!" So exclaimed a *Jewish* warrior of old, on the eve of battle, when, with a handful of men, he was about to cope with *one hundred and twenty thousand men*, headed by *thirty two elephants*, and *horses many thousands*, and hundreds of chariots of war. The battle commenced with the *thunder shout* of the few against the many, "Victory is of the Lord!" and the swords flew around like lightning, nor did the sun descend under the arches of the west, before the Lord gave the few the victory. "Victory is of the Lord!" That is my motto.

A few *trophies* already. But, O, this *skirmishing* is harder than the conflict of the decisive battle!

CHAPTER XIX.

THE PATH TO VICTORY — COUNTER-ATTRACTIONS.

How true the following *sentiments* of a poet! I like them; they do me good; there is a *spirit* in them which seems to say, "*Press forward!*" They thrill me after the manner of the warriors of old, who, when they heard the Gospel read, instinctively put their hand to their sword. My *weapons* are not carnal, but spiritual; but to the lines:

" Every *beginning* is shrouded in a *mist*, those vague ideas beyond,
And the traveller setteth on his journey, oppressed with many thoughts,
Balancing his hopes and fears, and looking for some order in the chaos, —
Some secret path between the cliffs that seem to bar his way:
So he commenceth at a clue, unravelling its tangled skeins,
And boldly speedeth on to thread the labyrinth before him.
Then, as he gropeth in the darkness, light is attendant on his steps,
He walketh straight in fervent faith, and difficulties vanish at his presence;
The very flashing of his sword scattereth his shadowy foes;
Confident and sanguine of success, he goeth forth conquering and to conquer."

Thus, I have found frequently, that when there is anything great and noble to be effected, especially against the empire of darkness, why *darkness* is sure to be encountered at first. Indeed, that proves, or illustrates our Lord's expression, and that of Paul, "*The power of darkness;*" and St.

John's, also, "*And his kingdom was full of darkness.*" — Rev. 16 : 10. We *feel* this darkness as "the Captain of our salvation" leads us on ; for, like the darkness that was in *Egypt*, it is *a darkness that may be felt*. How often have I *experienced* this ! and yet I am not hardened nor fortified altogether against its influence. *Philosophy* and *experience* often fail me for a little, in time of need ; but even this may be overruled for good ; as the less confidence in *self*, the more room is left for confidence in God, unless when the devil and unbelief beat the soul down to the ground, so that it cannot *look up*.

The *poor* are gathering around me in considerable numbers, and seem truly in earnest to enter into the kingdom of God. The *rich* have something else to do at present. They have not yet *recognized* me or the work as worthy of any particular attention. They are *looking* in quite a *different direction ;* — *trade* for some, which a poet calls, "the *golden girdle* of the globe ;" and as *Agabus* took Paul's girdle and *bound* his own *hands* and *feet* therewith, and *prophesied*, that so the Jews at Jerusalem would bind the man who owned that girdle ; so does the devil bind many a poor, busy, prosperous sinner with that "*golden girdle* of the globe," *trade*, and delivers him finally into the hand of death bound ; a sad *prelude* to the announcement and fulfilment of that dreadful sentence of the Eternal Judge, "*Bind* him *hand* and *foot*, and take him away, and cast him into *outer* darkness ; there shall be *weeping* and *gnashing of teeth.*" — Matt. 22 : 13. This must be *beaten* into their *ears*, when I *obtain their ears*, which will not be long, I hope ; for their attention must be turned in *this direction* somehow.

Gain ! what a magnet is that for others ! *Gain* at the *soul's expense ;* "*betting* with the devil, and *staking* their souls for a *rifle,*" observes a shrewd man. The man we read of, who threw *coin* at a fig-tree for the sake of the fruit, was a *wise man,* when compared with these, who throw away their souls for the sake of some perishable good. *Dear figs,* those, when *silver* pieces were flung and lost in bringing them down; and *dear* the fruits of sin, if the eternal soul must be the price! Such are "*fools in folio,*" and worse off than fools in yonder Lunatic Asylum.

The *wedge of gold,* and the *Babylonish garment* were more glorious in the eyes of *Achan,* than *victory* with Israel in the field, and his own inheritance in the land of promise. He bartered one for the other, and, like many since his day, inherited neither, poor man! — a *heap of stones,* only. Alas! the Achan family became not extinct in him. Would that it had! Whatever may have become of the "*apostolic succession,*" here is a succession that has never yet failed. For less gain than Achan acquired, how many *betray* the cause of God, and their own souls! Nor need one wonder much at all this, seeing that one of our Lord's own companions betrayed him for *thirty pieces* of silver. With *Judas,* as an instance, we are not to *marvel* that men are blind enough to barter away their own souls, in the devil's market, for a small consideration.

I was thinking, to-day, that never did any man esteem *Christ highly,* who esteemed his *own soul lightly;* and never did any man *estimate* his own soul *properly,* and, at the same time, *Christ lightly,* or held the **Gospel** in *low estimation,* or scorned the efforts of zeal and benevolence in saving souls from perdition.

A *high* valuation of *Christ,* and a *low* valuation of the *Gospel,* are *anomalies.* A high esteem of the Gospel, and a low estimate of one's own *soul,* is a *paradox,* — that is, a *contradiction;* equally so, is a high regard for one's own salvation, and a low disregard for the salvation of others. But who does not know that *hypocrisy* and self-deception bring forth a brood of strange *monstrosities?* *Prejudice* and *selfishness*, likewise, are the father and mother of a strange brood of *inconsistencies*, like Milton's *Sin* and *Death* at the gates of Hell; nor need we go there to find them.

Thus it is, when men, *dead in trespasses and in sins*, are left to themselves even in this world. The first chapter of *Romans* proves this.—Rom. 1: 21, 32. And thus has it been ever since, through all generations of men; at every point of time, these *eighteen hundred years*, good men have been forced to exclaim, with good old *Richard Baxter*, "But now I perceive the *devil* will be the *devil*, and *mankind* will be born *blind*, *sensual* and *malignant*, till there be a new heaven and earth, in which dwelleth righteousness." But still, I like better the idea of the *wit* of whom *Hannah More* speaks, who said, "*To mend the world's a vast design.*" To be sure it is; and a *noble* design, and *glorious*, although one should fail in the attempt!

CHAPTER XX.

SATAN ENTRENCHED.

1ST. You desire to know what are our "prospects" here of a revival; "the difficulties to be encountered;" and "by what course of action" we propose to "succeed." Well, my *friend*, I could write much upon these questions, for I assure you my heart is full. But, if I tell you all 1 know, and all I fear, and all I feel, you will suspect me again of "looking through smoked glass;" or, through those "*spectacles*" which you say the devil is "ever ready to clap upon the nose of the melancholy, or disheartened." Well, the thing is not among the impossibles; but I am not *naturally* given to melancholy, neither am I disheartened, but I have a habit of *looking difficulties* in the face; and have you any objections to that? The ancients, you remember, used to say, "One pair of *eyes* is worth a hundred pair of *spectacles.*" It only requires one to use his own eyes to see how strongly Satan has fortified himself in Birmingham; not, indeed, by the civil law, as in *Italy* or even in *France*, but by the laws of depravity, his most faithful ally.

2d. Nor do I think it is *detrimental* to faith, altogether, to have as full view as can be obtained, of what must be encountered in order to success. It prompts faith to *rely* upon the *Holy Ghost alone*, and to cry to God for those *weapons of war* and *divine artillery*, necessary to insure the victory; not "tilting with straws," but slashing right and left with "*the sword of the Lord and of Gideon;*" not a *painted* sword, but the *real sword;* not a *painted fire*, but the *real fire* from above; — it is *that* that *cuts* to the dividing asunder of soul and spirit, and the joints and marrow of the sinner, *wounding the heart*, and dividing the *sinews* which bind him to his sins; and this is the *fire* that *warms* and *burns*. It is not the *Aurora Borealis*, which the folks in the *Shetland Islands* call "*the merry dancers*," which neither shatter nor strike the proud, gnarled, defiant *oaks;* but the real living *lightning* of the *thunder cloud!*

It is not a *pomp of words* that is wanted in Birmingham, I assure you, but *action*. As *Hannibal* said to his army, as "the battle trembled to begin," — "It is not *words* that we want, but *action;*" and so *action* was the order of the day, till *victory* spread her wings over the field at the close of the day.

3d. The *preacher* that will prevail in *Birmingham*, I perceive, needs to be a *moving pillar* of fire, and not a *floating iceberg;* not a style which one denominates "*a polished* mediocrity," as free from *blemish* as from *energy*, but the "*rough and ready*" sort of preaching, the *out-of-the-way* style (to use an idea of Rowland Hill), *to catch those who are out of the way;* "the *slap-dash*" kind of preaching, as one named it; that style which *Luther* said made the *best preacher* for the common people. "He who speaks in the *meanest, lowest, humblest,* and most *simple* style." I have often thought of that; besides, "the common people" are the bulk of our hearers in every place. And was not this the reason that *the common people* heard our Lord *gladly?* — Mark 12: 37; because he preached to their *capacity* and *circumstances*.

Ah, it is not such preaching as "*inflating an idea or frothing a sentiment,*" that will *reach the heart*, although it may *catch the head;* but words and sentiments like *drawn swords,* — not decorated, nor muffled, nor encumbered with *ornament*, but the *naked blade* of truth ; then, no objection to the German poet's fancy :

"The hilt of precious gold,
The blade of shining steel."

But give me the *blade of shining steel*, whether its *hilt* be of precious gold, or *vulgar iron.*

CHAPTER XXI.

GLIMPSES OF BIRMINGHAM; OR, LOOKING DIFFICULTIES
IN THE FACE.

My pen had free scope at *Haddon Hall, Chatsworth, Sheffield, Macclesfield,* &c.; but here in *Birmingham* — what shall I say? I have no heart to attempt such descriptions. Not but there is much to admire in Birmingham. I like the town; it contains much which, under other circumstances, would inspire my pen; — have traversed it in various directions with pleasure; — have paused from *weightier thoughts* to mark the classic taste of its people, not merely in some of the public edifices, — the *Town Hall*, for instance, great in design, and beautiful in architecture, but even the *entrances* to private dwellings are studies! — houses, otherwise quite unassuming, have their portals graced by the modest *Doric*, or the elegant *Ionic* pillar, with its appropriate volute, or the rich *Corinthian*, with its acanthus, — and so *generally*, too! — but especially the *creative genius* of its *artisans* exhibited in their manufactures. But, alas! *the moral condition* of the *masses* around, — the great conflict upon which I have entered, — the *vast* and *far-reaching consequences of success or failure!* Ah! these thoughts leave *room* nor *heart* for little else. But how well has *Mrs. Sigourney* sketched, at least the "*strange creativeness*" of Birmingham genius and talent. — thus:

"'T is something to be called
The 'toyshop of a continent,' by one
Whose voice was fame. And yet a name like this
Hath not been lightly earned. Hard hammerings
And fierce ore-meltings, 'mid a heat that threats
To vitrify the stones, have wrought it out,
On the world's anvil.
             Ponderous enginery,
And sparkling smithies, and a pallid throng,
Who toil, and drink, and die, do service here;
And countless are the forms their force creates,
From the dire weapon, sworn to deeds of blood,
That sweeps, with sharp report, man's life away,
To the slight box, from whence the spinster takes
Her creature-comfort, or the slighter orb
Of treble-gilt, which the pleased school-boy finds
On his new suit, counting the shining rows
With latent vanity.
       *   *   *   *   *   *   *
             Here, too, were fabrics rich,
That taste might covet, cabinet and screen,
Table and tray, with pearly shell inlaid,
And bright with tints of landscape or of flower.
Here glass in crystal elegance essays
To emulate the diamond, and we saw
The flaming fount from whence its glories came,
And how the glowing cylinder expands
Into those broad and polished plates that deck
The abodes of princes."

But, alas! other transmutations and creations have attracted my attention — those of DEPRAVITY; for *Satan* has stretched his "iron hand" across the gulf of hell, — to *rule*, to *grapple*, or in *league* with *Birmingham*. O, what shall I say? How describe the *works* of this old *sorcerer* of perdition?

1. I was thinking, to-day, that he is considered the best general in a campaign, who best understands the *tactics* of the *enemy*,—his strength, plans, fortifications, &c.,—and has

instructed himself well as to the geography of the country through which he must pass, *where* he is likely to meet the foe ; and who has the tact or genius to choose the best and most advantageous *position* for his troops. *Valor* will serve him little, if lacking in these, and such like qualifications. *Napoleon Bonaparte* spent whole nights, *compasses* in hand, 'midst maps, planning a single campaign. And nobody doubts that it is to *that fact*, as well as to the valor of his army, that his *extraordinary success* and *victories* may be ascribed.

2. I was thinking, to-day, of *Nehemiah* the prophet, who, on arriving at Jerusalem, with a heart overflowing with patriotism and religion, resolved *to revive the stones out of the rubbish*, and to *rebuild the walls* of the desolated city of his fathers. He says: "I came to *Jerusalem*, and was there *three days;* and I arose in the night, I and some few men with me; neither told I any man what my God had put in my heart to do at Jerusalem." *Secrecy* and *expedition.* These were the life of his undertaking. "And I went out by *night* by the gate of the valley, even before the *dragon-well*, and to the dung-port, and viewed the walls of Jerusalem, which were broken down, and the gates thereof were consumed with fire. Then I went on to the gate of the fountain," &c., &c. And so he took the circuit of the city, and through the *darkness* looked *difficulties* in the face ; observed the *compass* of the walls, and their dilapidated condition, in order to make proper provision for such a great and perilous undertaking; for there were many *enemies without*, and *untrustworthy persons within* Jerusalem.

This *night-view* of the desolate city, rendered matters to Nehemiah very gloomy and discouraging, doubtless. Nothing the worse for that. The *desolation* and the *darkness* well reminded him of coming difficulties and perils, — *magnified* them, perhaps; — a wholesome *ordeal* to his faith — served, it may be, to make his trials lighter when they came, because anticipated and prepared for. The more *discouraging* the aspect of things, the more resolute became his dependence upon the God of his fathers.

3. There is a *lesson* for my heart in all this; and something to excite and enlist the prayers of my *special friends* for divine aid. We have spiritual foes to encounter, here in Birmingham, more *malignant* than those who surrounded *Nehemiah:*

> " Are *secret, sworn, invisible,*
> With hate and malice inextinguishable."

And *thousands* of poor sinners, of all sorts, under their control, — some of whom are *brain-sick*, to use an odd term of one; *so sick up there*, as to think there is *no life to come for man*, because he has no immortal soul to partake of it! And others are *profoundly asleep*, and, at the same time, "*wide awake;*" — which was called, in old times, the *Devil's charm*, in rendering men "*Dormire Deo, et mundo vigilare*," — *asleep to God, and awake to the world!* — who "think aloud," what some sinners dare hardly own to themselves in secret, that *sin* is better than *grace*, and the *pleasures of sin* here are better than [possibly a blank] eternal happiness hereafter.

These *sleepers* must be *awakened*. Their being asleep does not lessen their *peril*, but increases it rather. There is a *moral*, as well as a *literal truth* in what *Baxter* said a long while ago, that, when the *coachman* is asleep, the horses may miss their way, and possibly break his neck or their own; when the *watchman* sleeps, the *thief* may steal at pleasure, and fire the premises if he will; and, if the *pilot* at the helm drops asleep, likely as not the ship will visit the rocks of destruction; so, when *reason* is laid asleep, and out of the way, what may not *appetite* do? and what may not *passion* do? and what may not *temptations* do with the soul? A *wise man*, when he is *asleep*, has as little use of his wisdom as a *fool;* a *learned man*, when he is *asleep*, can hardly dispute with an *unlearned* man that is awake; a *strong and valiant man*, though skilful in the use of *weapons*, is scarcely able, in his sleep, to deal with the *weakest* child that is awake. The soul has *powers*, but they are asleep, till *consideration* awakens them, and sets them to work. How little better is a *man for being a man*, if, having reason, he makes no use of it when needed! The *keenest sword*, or the *greatest cannon* are useless against an enemy, if they lie by neglected. Reason, conscience, hell, what are these to deter a man from sin, who never thinks of them? Ah! the *truth* of these remarks is seen everywhere in *Birmingham!*

4. Birmingham presents another class, who well sustain that charge, preferred against such characters ages ago, "who *commend* God and *godliness* with their *words*, and *condemn* them in their *lives;* afford them the highest position in their *mouths*, and degrade them to the lowest estimation in their *hearts;* give them the *first place* in their *prayers* and *professions*, and the last place in their *lives* and *labors.*" Never a truer people to the old Latin proverb, " *Use God*, but *enjoy the creatures.*" These must have their mouths stopped, or a transfer made from the *mouth*, to the heart, — from the *prayers and professions*, to the *life and the labor!* The proverb must be *reversed*, or they are *ruined*, — *enjoy God* and *use the creatures!* That is it. O, what a conflict with such, ere these *transfers* are made, ere this *victory* has been achieved!

4. And many are grasping at what a shrewd man calls *nonentities;* hunting *butterflies* at best, or chasing shadows, and *embracing phantoms;* as *Ixion* embraced a *cloud* for *Juno,* and found himself whirled about amid the vapors of disappointment; or, like *Apollo,* as the Grecians feigned, who hugged a *laurel-tree* in mistake for *Daphne,* — such their idea of their sensual gods; and thus, if the *deities* mistake, why may not men? As the *gods,* such were their *worshippers!*

What was *fable* at *Athens,* is *fact* in *Birmingham,* so far as *sinners* are concerned; and by many who admit the *holiness* of God, but who, alas! reject his command, "*Be ye holy, for I the Lord your God am holy;*" as strong in *inference* that holy they should be, as it is authoritative in *command;* but, alas! as one remarked, *holiness* is so hateful and grievous a thing to them, that they will venture upon hell to avoid it.

5. And here are *scramblers* by the thousand for "the *golden apple,*" even along the brink of hell; and every day one and another of them drops off and falls where *flames* await them; the devil all the while keeping the *apple* moving along the perilous edge; and though the *scramblers* are dropping off continually into the gulf beneath, the others "bate not a jot of heart or hope," but press forward for the prize, to perish in like manner.

These *scramblers* must be *awakened,* if possible, to behold and struggle for a *nobler prize.* A thankless task at first, but, O, what *gratitude* is felt by such, if one is but successful! This is an *encouragement.* O, for a *voice* and power from Heaven, to awaken them from their *infatuation!* By the help of Him who reigns, I have tried, and am trying; and who shall say I shall not see these *eager multitudes* struggling as earnestly for "the golden apple" of salvation and eternal life, along the King's highway of holiness?

6. And there are *professors* of religion, who, if not among the infatuated *scramblers* for the world, honor greatly those who are such. If St. James were here, he would have to shout once more in the ears of such, "Hearken, my beloved brethren, Hath not God chosen the *poor of this world*, rich in faith, and heirs of the kingdom which he hath promised to them that love him?"— James 2: 1, 5. Solomon made good use of his eyes and his understanding, when he said, "*Servants* on horseback, and *princes* as servants upon the earth."— Eccles. 10: 7. *Christ's poor* are the *real* princes of the land; and the *devil's rich*, though they ride upon horses, or in splendid chariots, are but *servants* and *captives*, driven to and fro like their restless master. Besides, the *soul* ought to be the true prince, and the *body* but its *servant*, as the old *Grecian* philosophers maintained: "The *soul is the man, the body is but its servant.*" Alas! we see every day how the *body*, with its fleshly appetites, is made the prince, and the *royal soul* dragged down to be its *servant*.

A *true revival* reverses all this. The *saints* of God are the *true princes*,—of *blood royal*,—as good old *Charles Mather*, of *Belper*, says; but they are frequently bound down to the humble drudgery of life, and are oftenest found in the abodes of poverty and want, while the servants of the devil ride upon the high places of the earth. But, as I noticed the fire in the grate, the other morning, the small coal at the *bottom* kindled first, and, when all in a red glow, they set fire to the *large coal* above; so it is in a revival: the *Lord's poor*, and the devil's poor, are the small coal· when these are enkindled by the *Gospel* into a flame of love to God, they are sure to send up the *flames of salvation* to the *devil's rich folks.*

And thus, as the *revival* spreads, the *soul*, in *hundreds* and in *thousands*, becomes the acknowledged *prince*, and the body, what it should be, its obedient servant.

7. And there are others in *high life*, of whom a shrewd observer of men spake a parable, — of *chimneys*, which, though the highest part of buildings, are not the *cleanest* nor the *sweetest*, but *scorched* with fire, and suffocated with smoke.

O, but I should like to throw some *Gospel fire* into these chimneys, and burn them out ! — or, to alter the figure, to blow in their ears a few trumpet-like blasts, after the manner of good *Richard Baxter:* "The *inexorable leveller* is ready at your backs to convince you by irresistible argument that *dust you are, and to dust* you shall return. Heaven should be as desirable, and hell as terrible, to you as to others. No man will fear you after death; much less will Christ be afraid to judge you. — Luke 19: 27. In the hour of his own temptation, he condemned the kingdoms of the world and the glory of them; how inconsiderable, then, are all your present advantages, to procure his future approbation ! Let not uncertain riches be your trust. Look out upon earth and upon eternity. As you stand on *higher ground* than others, it is meet that you should see further, and behold more clearly the difference between things temporal and things eternal." *Loud blasts* these ! Ah, but many are sitting under a *dark* or *heavy* ministry, and if Baxter were alive now, he would still have to complain that it is always dark where "*glow-worms* shine, and where *rotten posts* do seem a fire ! "

8. And there are others whose *positions* in life are *lower*, yet have their *portion in this life*, and cling to it, although

God offers them a *better*. Their hands are so full of the world, they cannot receive the better portion, which *death* would not take from them. A peculiar class these, and require a peculiar method of address, and *plain dealing* withal.

Both these classes stand *high* in *Birmingham;* and my fear is, I can do little more than *look up* and *pity* them, — certainly not to *envy* them; rather with him of old, "I had rather twenty times look up at them that are so exalted, than stand with them and have *the terror of looking down.*" Alas for them, they are as truly dead to God, as she of whom the apostle spake, who *lived in pleasure*, and was *dead while she lived!* Or, as Seneca said, "The *carcass* is as truly dead that is *embalmed*, as that which is dragged to the grave with hooks." They are as dead to God as the devil's poor, who are poor and wicked, although *embalmed*, so to speak, with human riches. O, for a power to awake these dead!

9. Another class, "the lovers of *pleasure* more than God,"— who are passing through life as through a *dream*, and through their shadowy employments as a tale that is told; but the *true business*, the *one errand*, but for which they had never seen the sun, is neglected, — to *glorify God here*, and to *enjoy him hereafter;* spiritual life and eternal life, to enjoy which, and to prepare for which, the *present life* was bestowed. But the design of God is either *spurned* or trifled away, and eternity bartered for time; the joys of the saints in glory, and the miseries of the lost in hell, are nothing but subjects for *pleasantries* among these *merry-makers;* they would even *pun* upon that "*puritanical supposition*," — "as many thousands of years as there are *sands* on the sea-shore, or *spires of grass* on the whole earth, or *hairs* on the heads of all

the men in the world, yet when these are past, the *joy of the saints*, and *the torments of the wicked*, are as far from an end as ever they were;"—a soul-arousing supposition to every man who is not profoundly asleep in sin.

Alas! let these *merry ones* hold on thus to the end, and they will wish, as many times as there are *stars* in the firmament of heaven, either that God had never given them life, or that they had laid the *true end of life* to heart. "Forced at last," as one said, who is now in his grave,— "forced at last to justify the *wisdom* of the *godly*, and the *self-denying*, and wishing, with *many fruitless groans*, they had been *imitated*." The world is full of illustrations how men's minds *change*, as they are bidding farewell to life;—change with their *state;* but not the *Gospel* change, alas! but a change which *extorts* these most striking of all *acknowledgments*.

And, yet, not one in *one hundred*, perhaps, of these pleasure-takers intend to die so miserably. They will stare at me when I tell them such is the *fate* that awaits them, and yet press onward to it, with a "God forbid!"— reminding one of the illustration of a celebrated divine, "If you see a man cutting his own throat, and you ask him, 'What are you doing, man? Will you kill yourself?' and he answers you, 'No, God forbid! I have no such meaning, I will hope better;' would you think this would save his life?—or that his *hopes* and *meanings* would prove him the wiser man?" And then he went on to show that thus and thus is the conduct of those who are hoping all will be safe with them at last, while they are destroying their souls,—sowing the seeds of misery, the harvest of which will be eternal.

10. And here are the *thoughtless*, and the *God-defying*,

and the *Christ-despising* O, how are these to be reached? Can a whisper do what requires a *thunder?* "Knowing the *terrors* of the Lord, we *persuade men*," says Paul. The terrors of the Lord are in his own *threatenings* and *declarations.* The tongue of man never spoke it plainer, than do the *Scriptures,* that these are on the *brink of hell,* — *within a few steps of everlasting fire.* "*Fear him who, after he has killed, hath power to cast into hell,*" said Jesus. The ancients used to call the fear of God the *awe-band* of the soul. Our Lord sought to bind this *awe-band* upon the timid souls of his disciples; but go it must upon each of these giddy ones, or they will be destroyed; when another *awe-band* is called for, with a "*Bind him hand and foot,* and cast him into *outer darkness,* where there is weeping and gnashing of teeth." Their *attention* must be arrested, and held long enough to make a sufficient impression to awaken them; then, and not till then, shall they hear as for life. "But who is *sufficient* for these things?" exclaimed an apostle. Let my *sufficiency be of thee, O Lord my God!*

11. And some there are, like Agrippa of old, "*Almost* thou persuadest me to be a Christian;" and, dying thus, they will be *almost saved,*— *almost* escaped the damnation of hell. The *almost repenting,* and the *almost believing,* have *terrifying* scriptures recorded against them; "They stand dodging and halving with God, without entirely giving themselves to him," as one remarked, who considered such in as great peril of hell as the *drunkard* or the *whoremonger,* though their *torment* may not be so great. These must be *carried,* and *borne down* by the truth, and broken.

12. And Birmingham, I perceive, has its *quota* of *witty sinners,*—"the wickedly witty," as one named them,—who

will sooner or later be compelled to say with him who is lying in the grave, "It is time for us to be *serious*, when we are so near the place where all are serious; for there are no *jesters* in hell!" A great thought that. These too, must be *reached*.

13. Others there are to be dealt with, who have long been *daubed* with *untempered* mortar, as the prophet speaks; and, as one of old observed, their *spiritual wounds* have only been *skinned* over, and they must be *opened* and *probed* anew;—a *double pain* must now be endured. Some of these, to use an idea of David, have had their spiritual *bones broken* and *put out of joint*, and never were *soundly set*;—must have the double sorrow of being *stretched* and set anew; a thorough, radical change of heart and reversion of the soul's *tendencies*; a *real conversion* to God. These spiritual cripples must be healed, or they will be cripples for ever and ever.

14. And, along in front of Zion's ramparts, are to be seen miserable souls, occupying a territory of their own; "full of *wounds* and *bruises* and *putrefying sores*," as the prophet Isaiah speaks;—who have learned the dreadful art (to use a thought of a German divine) of wrenching from their bleeding bosoms the *arrows* of *eternal truth*, and healing the wounds, or trying to do so, with the deadly salve of *wilful deception*, or worldly lust.

They are seen stalking around Zion, *Hercules-like*, in proof armor, all but the *heel* of *conscience*, which still finds it "*hard to kick against the pricks;*" and *hell-fire*, by their own confession, flashing continually in their faces from the ramparts, and grumbling that the *Gospel*, as *Micaiah* to *Ahab*, *never prophesies good concerning them, but evil.*—1 Kings 12: 8.

Some of these linger, because they cannot help it. They

struggle hard to get away, but God has put them in *chains*, so to speak; they are under *the chains of truth*, which, though they do not *convert*, they *gall* and *discommode*. While others (to use a terrible idea of one) have had *sentence* passed upon them, and the *rope*, as it were, about their neck, standing at the very gates of hell.

Alas! here is a scene to *move* this soul of mine, and to stimulate it to action, if by any means I may save some. — 1 Cor. 9: 22.

15. Again and again have I scanned the ground occupied by "the *well-to-do*" sinners of Birmingham, the votaries of *pleasure*, which one called "a *silken halter*, a *flattering devil*, that kills while it embraces;" which *Plato*, I remember, called "*The devil's bait* for *soul-catching*;" the *innocent pleasure*, if it draw the heart away from God, as well as those that are *perditionable*, which bear the insignia of the devil on their front.

16. *Another class*, and they occupy ground of their own, and they are not a few, who are swallowing daily *the sweet poison of error*, in the form of *scepticism* or infidelity; a satanic invention, which *Ignatius*, my friend may recollect, considered a *spiritual drunkenness*, or going to *hell* on a *drunken opinion*, as others around us, of *bar-room* notoriety, are *reeling* thitherward upon a *drunken life*.

17. *Drunkenness!* — a drunken life; — never a town better supplied with means to sustain that sort of thing, than *Birmingham;* where every *thirtieth* house is occupied either in the *sale* or *manufacture* of intoxicating drinks; and every such house, it has been estimated, is supported by *one hundred and thirty seven* of the population, taking into the account men, women and children; where there are not less than *five hundred and fifty-seven* public houses and *dram-shops*, and besides, *five hundred and fifty-one*

ale-shops; and to sustain these, there are *fifteen wholesale spirit-dealers,* and *one hundred and thirty-three maltsters;* the number of *distillers* I have not learned. The last *three classes* should have been mentioned first, perhaps, as they are the chief men in this work of ruin, although they so often boast they have no *drunkards* about them. But, as Dr. *Fisk* asked, are they not the *chief men,* — the very *mainsprings* of the business? Do they not stand at the *head* of this fiery fountain? Do they not command the gateway of this mighty flood? Do they not stand, as it were, at the bulk-head, and hoist the gates of this river of fire, which spreads its streams all around, burning up every green thing, — the *retailers* only doing their *drudgery?* Have they not a large share in the *profits* also? — and shall they not have a large share in *accounting* for the *consequences* before the tribunal of the God of heaven and earth, whose law is, "Thou shalt not kill," which includes every injury to human life? How much less accountable than the *infatuated victim,* who throws himself upon the bosom of the burning torrent, and is borne down by it into the gulf of woe! I have not quoted Dr. Fisk's sentiments accurately, as I write from memory; but that is the substance.

And what are the *fruits* of these busy laborers in the cause of human ruin? I do not inquire after their *gains,* but the *destruction* they produce annually! It is supposed that over *four hundred* persons are killed in Birmingham every year by these drinks. During the last year, *thirteen hundred* persons were brought before the magistrates for *drunkenness.* To this add *forty thousand sterling,* which the *town* pays annually as *poor levies;* and it has been clearly ascertained that *three fourths* of the *paupers* were made such by intoxicating drinks. But these liquor-sellers are notified annually to appear for a renewal of license, and the *tax-payers* have to *foot the bill of consequences*, to the item of *two hundred thousand dollars a year*, to say nothing of *legal expenses* in criminal prosecutions, *police, jail,* and other extraordinaries.

18. And, while upon this sad theme, I may add a surprising fact; — that so many *professors* of *religion* here, and *ministers*, think it their duty to oppose the *advocates of temperance ;* — indeed, they scout and laugh at the *reformation*, under a plea that its *advocates* are not so *wise in sentiment*, or *discreet in language*, as they might be. But, instead of denying themselves of some small liberties among the *decanters* at table, and throwing their influence on the side of *total abstainers*, so as to be able to correct such *errors* (which by the way are very few), they rather set their faces against the whole thing.

What the feelings and views of the present *Wesleyan ministers* are, upon the subject, I have not learned; but such are the barriers raised against the temperance movement in past years, I doubt whether I would be allowed to deliver a *temperance* lecture in any Wesleyan chapel in town.*

However, *lecture* I shall somewhere in Birmingham. I have identified myself with the English *tee-totalers*, and shall strike a blow for the cause at the first opportunity. The friends of temperance are on the alert. May God speed the *right!* and the *right*, I know, is on their side.

Judge also, if you can, the *influences* and effects of these things upon *public morals* and religion.

I have said nothing about *theatres*, and *gambling houses;* nor of *Sabbath-breaking*, and *profanity;* but enough to

---

* It is presumed that the subject of temperance is looked upon now in a more favorable light in Birmingham, than at the time Mr. C. visited that town. — *Editor.*

prove to you, and to my own soul, that if we are to have a great revival in *Birmingham*, the effort to bring it about will be no "children's play," but the *efforts* of men in downright earnest to overturn the empire of darkness.

Men are wanting like those of old, of whom it was said, they *turned the world upside down* (Acts 17: 6); for I am sure it is wrong side up in Birmingham!

The *weapons* of our warfare must be real weapons, our artillery, real artillery, — mighty, through God, to accomplish all the purposes of his will.

Paul, who preached on *Mars-hill*, is needed here. *Paul* is *dead;* but Jesus Christ lives and reigns. He offers me his strength; bids me take hold of it, and prevail, and promises to *stand by me*. I have the same Gospel to preach that Paul preached, and the same *Holy Spirit* to give it *overcoming power*. O, to be armed for the *battle*,

"With *stubborn patience* as with triple steel"!

Ah, poet! I like St. Paul's advice better, "Take unto you the *whole armor of God*, that ye may be able to withstand in the evil day;"— and again, in the same chapter, "*Put on the whole armor of God, that ye may be able to stand against the wiles of the devil*," — the *Goliath* in the field, who is the great *centre and rallying point* of all the evils to be encountered.

Let me improve upon that hint of a poet, "Set thyself about it, as the sea about the earth, lashing at it day and night," the *power* of God helping. Rouse thee, O my soul! "like to a *spirit* in its tomb at rising, rending the stones, and crying '*Resurrection*'!" though at my heels, as Milton hinted,

"All hell should rise with *blackest insurrection*."

He who exclaimed, "What a *map of hell* is the greatest part of the earth!" felt something as I do at this crisis in my ministry.

19. I have only given you, and myself, a view of the *darkest side of the picture.* There is a *bright side* to it; and it is every day becoming brighter. No day passes without a *few sinners* being converted, and some *believers sanctified.* To add to my encouragement, I am becoming acquainted daily with many godly persons,— "*the excellent of the earth,*" — full of life and zeal, who are ready to *push the battle to the gate,* and to shout the victory! Bless thou the Lord, O my soul! The gales of grace are evidently blowing from Calvary. The *tide* of corrupt nature is against us; but the *wind* is in our favor; — not an unfrequent occurrence in *spiritual seamanship.*

The sailor does not care much for the *adverse tide,* if the *wind* is favorable, and there is plenty of it, with *sea-room.* The Holy Spirit's *influences* are frequently compared to *wind,* in the Scriptures, *blowing* where it listeth. O, for *more* of that *divine influence* to stem this *adverse tide,* even a gale! — and, by what I can infer from the spirit of the *Wesleyan ministry* here, there seems every disposition favorable to allowing me *sea-room* plenty.

CHAPTER XXII.

PULPIT DEFENCES; OR, FRAGMENTS OF WARFARE.

1. To one who objects to the *matter* and *manner* of the preacher :

A lady in *Germany*, some time since, remarked to one in conversation, "*Damnation* is a *joyless*, and therefore an *incorrect idea.*" There is *logic* for you! It is doubtful if *you* would go so far as that; but you consider *hell* an "*unsuitable motive* for Christians." Thus, had you and the German lady your *wills* and *tastes* gratified, that little "vulgar *monosyllable*" would never be heard in the Christian pulpit at all; *you* would deny it to the *Christian ear*, and she would prohibit it from *all ears;* so you would have fine, quiet times for everybody.

Let us dismiss the *German's* notion, and deal with *yours* for a little while. Did our Lord think with you, do you suppose? Why, then, did he say to his own much-loved disciples, "*And fear not them which kill the body, but are not able to kill the soul : but rather fear him which is able to destroy both soul and body in hell*"?—Matt. 10 : 28. Do you perceive the nature of the *motive?* It is unmistakable. Are you *wiser* than Christ? Which is the safest to follow, *your opinion*, or *Christ's example?* Dispute with my Master on the subject. Do you question his wisdom? You would not insinuate, surely, that you understand the nature and wants of Christians better than He!

Your ideas of "fire and brimstone preaching" are well enough, had nothing else been preached; mark that. But *Christ* was preached, — *Calvary* at a distance, however, and Sinai and Hell nigh at hand. But *Calvary* drew nearer as the people began to *feel* they had need of everything which the *Sufferer* endured for them there. Did you not notice that?

Are you not aware that it is the doctrine of Hell that throws a *grandeur* over the scenes of Calvary? And can you be ignorant of another fact, that no man denying a hell ever properly appreciated the *sufferings* endured on *Calvary?* Need I also remind you that it is not the *matches*, nor the *brimstone*, that sustains a *fire* when kindled, but the *fuel;* and that the "flinging about of fire and brimstone" would effect nothing, were it not for the *fuel* which the *consciences* of the people supply? Perhaps you overlooked these things. O, my dear friend, try to *understand yourself*, and the great doctrines you profess to believe and venerate!

My plan is, *first*, to show men their *sins;* secondly, their *danger;* thirdly, the remedy. To throw them into *conviction* for sin is my first aim; then into an awful sense of *peril;* then, if successful, *Christ* is set forth *crucified* for them. In attempting the first, I show the nature and extent of God's *law*, and *compare character*. It is the *straight edge* that shows a crooked or uneven surface! Then comes the *broad-axe* [of truth], and the chips fly; and, if the timber had sense, it might cry for mercy! If my second plan cannot succeed, then *everlasting burnings* for fruitless trees come next. — Matt. 3: 10. And, if nothing will do but that, I must excursionize through perdition for sights and for arguments; then, to use the ideas of an eminent divine, I unbar the iron gates of hell, and lead them, through solid darkness, to the worm that never dies, and to the fire that shall never be quenched; and to show him those apostate angels fast bound in eternal chains; and the souls of wicked men overwhelmed with torment and despair; and to open his ears to hear their cries, which never ascend but to return again in forlorn echoes, which make the deep itself groan, and which add to the *horrors of perdition*, and which *accent* them terribly.

This sort of infernal *panorama* is as varied as the *vistas* and *glimpses* of hell, which the Scriptures afford us, assisted by all that *reason* and *conscience* are well able to suggest.

Close to this hell, I usually plant the *cross*, with this inscription: "God so loved the world as to give his only begotten Son, that whosoever *believeth* in him should not *perish*, but have *everlasting life*." And yet another: "God hath not *appointed* us to *wrath*, but to obtain *salvation*, through our Lord Jesus Christ." And yet another: "*Christ* is the *end of the law* for *righteousness*, to every one that *believeth*." And yet another Scripture: "Believe in the Lord Jesus Christ, and thou shalt be saved;" assuring my *distressed* and *alarmed hearers* that, what was sufficient for the salvation of the trembling *jailer of Philippi*, is sufficient to save the best and the worst among all the trembling multitude! Then follow signs and wonders among the people. Hallelujah!

2. A few words to another:

Apologies I usually avoid in the pulpit, — so liable are they to be mixed up with the *exhalations* of *vanity*, and a *fishing for praise*, — or doing so well under such unfavorable circumstances. I said, *usually*, for sometimes occasions occur when they are absolutely called for; not so much in the sense of an *excuse*, perhaps, as a *reason*, or *defence*, after the manner of the old writers, who penned their "*Apology for the Bible*," or "*An Apology for Religion.*"

Have you never heard of that saying of one, who stood high in the church? "He, who lets another sin, and holds his peace, is a *manslayer*. When men declare their sin like *Sodom*, it is the *preacher's* duty to lift up his voice like a *trumpet*." Who has a word to say against this? Must I *except yourself?*

What was the command of God to the prophet of old? Hear it: "*Cry aloud, spare not:* lift up thy voice like a *trumpet*, and show *my people* their *transgression*, and the *house of Jacob* their *sins.*"— Isaiah 58: 1. Can that be wrong which God commends or commands?

It was only the other day, I was reminded by one that, all the name, *John the Baptist* could give himself, was "*Vox Clamantis*,— the voice of a *crier*. *Ego vox clamantis in deserto*,— the voice of a *crier* in the wilderness." Ah, sir! whoever you may be, I readily admit, such *crying voices*, such *trumpet-like blasts*, as you have heard lately, "sound more like *war* than peace;" and that the grace, the dignity, and elegance of *elocution* often suffer by what you name "*noisy vociferation;*" nevertheless, the *voice* must keep on *crying* amid the wilderness of *Birmingham follies*, and *Zion's inconsistencies*, "*Prepare the way of the Lord;* make his paths straight." My poor voice has not sufficient compass to resemble much

> " The *trumpet's* loud clangor,
> Exciting to arms;"

though it may stir up and remind your conscience of *the war between God and you*,— as that singular bird, the

Agami of South America, stirs the *hearts* of those who have been in the *wars*, by its trumpet-like noises! — rather, by its slender imitation of the *trumpet* which leads the battalion to the *charge!* It is called the *trumpeter!*

Well, sir, "trumpet-voice" be it; if it *shocks* you, it does not *mock* you with what St. Paul called "*an uncertain sound.*" For, although it has come from *afar*, and has been blown under *other skies*, and in *far-distant battle-fields*, it has no *barbarian* sound that you cannot understand! You know its meaning well, however "wild and barbarous" its notes. Its sounds have neither been *uncertain* nor *meaningless*, nor without *signification*. Your *conscience* understands it well without an *interpreter!* England has *ambassadors* sent to her from afar, which need an *interpreter*. The *stranger*, whether he is an ambassador sent by Christ or not, needs *no interpreter*, nor lexicon, nor dictionary, in order to be understood. All present will be witness to that; and do, I pray, *note* that down on the credit side of "the balance-sheet," if you think it worthy.

A good man observed that some *ministers* soar aloft like the eagle; but so high above the *capacities* of the people that it is evident they soar more to be *admired*, than to be understood; — to drop the figure, that they would rather *shine* than *burn*. Why did he not keep to his figure, and say, they would rather *soar* than *pounce?*

It is not the *soaring* and the *shining* some find fault with, but the *burning* and the *pouncing*. A preacher may *soar* as high as the moon, and out of sight, and out of light, if he please, and it will be pronounced *sublime;* but, if he comes down, for a *pounce* on the conscience, he has lost his dignity. and is *vulgar!* — a terrible anticipation to some preachers!

If he ascend toward heaven like a *rocket*, and fills all the sky with the *coruscations* of his wit and genius, he is a *magnificent* preacher; but, if he come down upon the *conscience* in a shower of fire, — a shower of the *sparks* of *truth*, so as *burn* and *alarm* it, — what then? He is ' *manifestly mad*, who would hear him." He is both " a fine gentleman, and a fine preacher," who, when " stepping down from the moon," where, to the really spiritual, " he has been soaring in search of his wits," he is "too much of the gentleman," on his descent, to act as if he had a search-warrant from heaven for the *consciences* of his admirers!

He may have as many "mild thunders, and glowing clouds, and traversing coruscations, and shooting stars," as he will; but he must shoot no *arrows* at the consciences of his hearers.

Let him, if he please, and as often as he shall please, soar into the *altitudes* of speculation, number the stars, and call them by their names, and " pierce through infinite in search of God; " if he turn not in the *other direction*,— if he have good sense and politeness enough to avoid the *profundities of depravity*, and from calling *sins by their proper names*, nor illustrate what the ancients called "the *inquisitive hand* of a *piercing ministry*,"— a very *troublesome* part of *oratory*, which they will not hesitate to call a *vulgarity*. Nor will they refuse him the liberty, sometimes, to be "*terrible as an army with banners*," while he is "*bright as the sun, and fair as the moon*," if he conduct himself gentlemanly amid the *terrors* of his oratory; that is, if he refrain from *particularizing sins*, and *individualizing character*, and *daguerreanizing* persons, so that everybody knows them. An *unpardonable* offence, that!

But it is time to conclude. It is well if the person I have been addressing is not *like a spoiled child*, that has been *humored* too much,—has had *its own* way more than was good for it! His strong *prejudices*, as to "pulpit style," may have had too much control of the *pulpit*, hitherto, so far as to have *the word of God bound*, reversing St. Paul's note of victory, "*But the word of God is not bound!*" Nor is it *now*, thanks be unto God! But the spoiled child *cries* when *crossed*. Never mind! he will feel better by and by, I hope.

Did you notice the *Scripture lesson* for this evening,— Luke 11? That hearer must have felt pretty bad, and much concerned for the credit of his cloth, when he exclaimed, in the midst of our Lord's discourse, "*Master, thus saying, thou reproachest us also.*" Who did he mean by "*us*"? His brother *lawyers!* Jesus had just joined the *Scribes* with the *Pharisees*, and compared them to *concealed graves*, overgrown with grass, or something else, over or into which the unsuspecting passenger might *stumble* to his *hurt*. The hearer felt himself and those of his profession *aggrieved*. "*Master*," &c., "thy general rebukes of the *Scribes and Pharisees* bear hard upon us *lawyers*, also." Poor man! he had better been still! Jesus turned round upon him and them, uttering three terrible *woes*, which must have come down upon their awakened consciences like so many *lightning strokes!*

CHAPTER XXIII.

FRAGMENTS FOR HYPERCRITICS.

My language may be "*hard*" at times, but, sir, with a *soft heart*, I hope. As Luther remarked of himself, "The *shell* may be hard, but the *kernel* is soft." If you could have the views I have sometimes, they would melt your heart too, and make "your language astound," also.

Perhaps you may not have read that remark of the excellent Flavel, that if the sinner could see the present and future misery of the *damned*, and the great and terrible *wrath of God* that is coming upon his own soul fast as the wings of time can bring it, such a *view* would either *bring him to Christ*, or *drive him out of his wits!* What think you of that? Which is safest, to have these views *now*, or not till the gates of eternity are just opening to receive you? To use the idea of one who is now in the world of spirits,— is it not better to go into hell by *contemplation*, than to go into it by *condemnation?* What think you of the *prophecy* of some, "If he go on at this rate, he will drive not a few of our citizens out of their senses"? But are not many of them *out of their senses* already, *living* and *sinning* as they do? O, that our God would use my *violence* to drive people back again into their proper senses, and to Christ! How many of you can say "*Amen*" to that?

To have *hell* for a home, and *devils* for companions, is

enough to frighten any sinner, who has the use of his reason. The very *swine* themselves, in the time of our Lord, chose rather to *drown* in the depths of the lake, than to live in the companionship of devils. The lost in hell would choose *strangling*, were it possible, rather than to endure it. To sinners, who are mad in sin, is the thing *tolerable*.

2. I am not fond of the epithet "*hypocrite;*" nevertheless, it is easily borne, when one knows its *inapplicability*. It is possible, I admit, for "a preacher's *lips* to be at variance with his *heart*, and to have his *tongue* outstrip his *experience*." But a very well read person delivered himself more entertainingly thus: "A blazing *comet* is no *star*. The *Hebrews* called a great talker '*a man of lips*,' — the true definition of a hypocrite, I fancy! — the *lips* being the most *active*, and the *honestest* part of him. The hypocrite's *tongue* may be *silver*, but his *heart stone*, and under his tongue, as the Psalmist says, '*mischief* and *vanity*.'" What think you of that? *Ingenious*, is it not? Sinners love *sin and folly* so well, that they bring themselves to think everybody else must do the same; and, when they speak the contrary, they suspect them as *hypocrites!* An easy matter that, but not so easy to *prove*. Nevertheless, I like the idea of a "*comet*," for it is no hypocrite! It imitates no star that burns, and has an orbit of its own; — answers some great purpose in the universe of God, as well as the *fixed star*.

Jesus Christ may have *comets* in his *church*, as well as in the *sky; evangelists* as well as *pastors*. Both may answer wise purposes in the economy of salvation.

The orbit of an *evangelist*, like that of a *comet*, may be *eccentric, mysterious, unaccountable*, yet he may answer some very important designs in the salvation of sinners.

He may be "a man of *lips*," and a man of *heart* too, and

an *honest* one; — his *heart* may be as active and as honest as his *lips*, and may go as fast and as far as his *tongue*, in its *experiences!*

An *honest tongue* may be under the control of an *honest heart;* though some think the *tongue* in question would be the better for *David's bridle* (Ps. 39: 1); for they say, though it has no *bone* in it, it *breaks bones,*— *hearts* they mean; and some call it a "*flail,*" and others "a sharp instrument having teeth." But *allowance* for figures may be claimed, as you Birmingham folks work in the *coarser*, finer, and *precious metals!* Would to God my *tongue* was more than all they say of it, in *reproving sin!* — only, I will have it, and insist upon the fact, that my poor *heart* is certainly as sincere and honest as my tongue. Allow that, and say what else you please!

Continue to *hear*, and to *yield*, as scores of you have been doing lately, and you will find Solomon's definition to be true even now, where he compares "a *wholesome tongue*" to "*a tree of life*"! — Prov. 15: 4. It may prove itself thus to thousands, through the mercy of our God, before the owner thereof leaves Birmingham.

The *tree* is known by its *fruit*, was a maxim of my Lord. It is not of *thorns* men gather grapes, nor of *thistles* do they gather *figs;* nor will a *good tree* bring forth *evil fruit.* By such criteria, let the *tongue* in question and its *owner* be judged. Look around you, and behold already the *effects* of this preached Gospel upon many of your fellow-townsmen!

CHAPTER XXIV.

A LESSON ON PREACHING.

A FRAGMENT TO OFFENDED HEARERS.

I ONCE received a lesson on *preaching*, which has been of some use to me, — on the necessity of selecting a proper *background* (to use a painter's phrase) either for the *principal propositions*, or *leading characters*, to be represented in the discourse; — so to arrange all the *peculiarities* of the *background*, that they may not be superior to these, but *subordinate*.

The lesson was conveyed in a *critique* of some writer, on the poetry of *Milton*, and the painting of Martin; — their distinguishing characteristics.

Milton, it was observed, made all his *Pandemonium* a *background* for his *Satan;* and all his *Paradise* a *background* for his *Adam* and *Eve;* — that is, the *background* for each was but a succession of *minor accessories*, designed not to *eclipse*, but to *set off* and give greater *effect* to the *principal figure* or *character*.

Martin, who *illustrated* Milton, made, on the contrary, his *background*, with his *accessories*, more *prominent* than his heroes ; — that any one may see how his *Pandemonium*, with its succession of lofty *pillars*, and *endless colonnades*, prodigies of architecture, and amazing candelabra, sink into insignificance the principal figure, the *Chief of*

Hell, his *Satanic majesty;* and that a similar defect is evident in his *Paradise,* where *variety* in excess of beauty quite eclipses what every one perceives should have been the glory of his Eden, — *Adam* and *Eve!*

My reflections were, that many an otherwise excellent sermon has a *similar defect;* too prominent a display of *minor accessories,*— what painters consider only as *secondary,* — merely *ornamental,* and in such *excess* as to be detrimental to the principal *doctrine, feature, moral,* or *character* to be represented; — a background *"frothed with sentiment"* and *glittering* with thoughts and *pomp* of words, and labored efforts of oratory, — *sonorous trifles,* and *prodigies of oratorical creations,* quite *eclipsing* that *which should have stood out, in bold and commanding relief, above all else* in the *background or foreground,* winning all eyes, and making its own mark on the judgment, the imagination, or the conscience; — standing out there, like the *Devil* in Milton's Pandemonium, or Adam and Eve in Paradise!

O, but it is sad, when an audience loses sight of the *chief figure,* lost in the admiration of the *grandeur of the preacher's imagination,* and the *creations* of *his genius!* — but, alas! the *character,* may be, which ought to have stood out prominently, to be *arraigned, tried* and *convicted,* has escaped, like a *thief* in the crowd, greatly to the relief of more than one interested party.

Suppose, again, a higher and nobler *personage,* whom such a preacher delighteth to honor — alas for him! whether *human* or *divine,* he will be almost *smothered* amidst the flowers of oratory! — like some portraits I noticed some time since in the famous gallery in Florence (Italy), set apart for the portraits of old painters; where the accessories in the picture, background and foreground, are more interesting and attractive, frequently, than the *portrait* itself; here and there a *face* of the *sterner sex* peeping ludicrously out of a *bouquet* of flowers, or an *arbor of roses*, — a lesson for the florist, or botanist, — while the poor head seems to say, 'Am I not in a pretty fix?" And that is all you see or know of him whom the painter would hold forth for your *reprehension* or *admiration*.

Well, as I said in the beginning, the lesson was of advantage to me. When I wish this or that *character* to work conviction, or create a *sensation*, I always take care to subdue my background, ay, and *foreground*, — sometimes to the stern rigidity and sterile dampness of your *Derbyshire moors*, — making him stand forth 'midst his *desolations* like Milton's Satan in his Pandemonium; as if he were ready to cry out with Shakspeare's hero,

"You know the character to be your brother's."

Hazardous work that for the daring, self-denying, conscientious preacher. Let him never dare to do it without counting the cost!

Had the *background* and the *foreground* of the discourse in question been more prominent and *florid*, — you know what I mean, — the *character* represented would have been less offensive and disturbing to your *neighbors* and to *yourself*; but certainly less *convincing*, to say nothing more. The *portraits* were too much in *relief*; the *accessories* in the background and around too sparse for *concealment*. The *leaves* of the trees were not thick enough to conceal *Adam*, when the voice of the Lord God, in the cool of the day, called, "Adam, where art thou?" Poor Adam, thou hast no background *dense* enough to conceal thee from him who calleth thee! "I heard thy voice in the garden, and

I was afraid, because I was naked, and I hid myself;" but only for a moment or two, Adam! Alas! a power had hold of thee, and set thee forth in mournful and terrible *relief.* To angelic spectators, and God, all other material objects in Eden sunk into insignificance.

And was it not somewhat so on the night in question? With what fearful significance did those characters stand forth! The pen of a *Milton*, or the pencil of a *Morton*, would have been powerless to have cast them into *insignificance* when the preacher sat down! The *character* and *walk* of one; the *wavering inconstancies*, and *eccentric deviations* of another; the *spiritual palsy* of a third, and the *distorted features* in the character of a backslider were clearly seen! And yet, be it known to yourself, my friend, and to all who were *troubled* on that occasion, I was not "retailing the *gossip* of neighbors," but facts that were known to a *higher power*. Do you understand me?

But enough; — my love to all of you, with an assurance that the time of *healing* has come; and of *finer features* and a *fairer complexion* to the *sin-deformed*, as well as the *sin-defiled.*

Better be *angry* with yourselves, than at the stranger; especially, if it result in *amendment* of life and a happier state of mind. Let this occur, and present annoyances are nothing. It is easier for some to win *hearts* than *souls*. The harder *task* be mine to win *souls* to Christ; hearts for myself, I care little about, unless my Lord has first sealed them his forever.

The Sun of righteousness hath arisen upon my soul with healing in his wings. I dwell under his *constant shining*. The spiritual state of *Birmingham* has been laid open to my *vision*. Many more *sad pictures* have been *daguerreotyped* upon my imagination, to be finished and exhibited for the conviction of the originals, when He pleaseth who hath called me to be faithful.

*   *   *   *   *

Glad you perceive I am "no *copyist*," although you suspect an attentive ear to "gossip," in the details of character. Beware of unjust suspicions. Little time have I had for gossip, or listening to *tattlers*, since my arrival in town. But I walk with God, and have a tolerably correct idea of the state of things. It is the Lord who teaches my *hands to war and my fingers to fight.*

Perhaps you have never thought closely upon what God said to the prophet *Ezekiel :* " *Thou shalt hear the word at my mouth, and warn them from me.*" There is much in that intimation, is there not? Information from that source, as to the *delineation of human character*, is more reliable than the *sources* you suspect. Tell me, may not our God speak sometimes now in the ears of his *chosen* ones? Why not? Is there not a necessity for it, frequently? If so, could he not tell me more about the state of affairs, than all the *tattlers* in town put together? Ah, my friend, take care ! it is possible to be

" *Inspired* beyond the *guess* of folly."

Human nature is a study, — a life's study. There are *mysteries* in its *operations*, as in its *structure*. I study it as well as my *Bible*. What I learn in both, I *teach ;* more, indeed, than some uneasy consciences are willing to bear, — *yours*, for instance.

Do you remember the advice of a celebrated *painter*, to one who was ambitious of excelling in the art? " Be *desperately individual* in your studies from *nature ;* in your perfect compositions, be as general as you please." I like the idea, ' be desperately individual;'" it is the great secret of effective preaching. "And they which *heard* it, being *convicted* by their *own conscience*, went out one by one, beginning at the *eldest*, even unto the *last*," till Jesus had only *one* of a congregation left. — John 8: 9.

It was said of one, he was *desperately national;* — too *general* that, for effective speaking, either in politics or religion. "Desperately personal" was an epithet applied to one, — but he was never *insultingly so*, never; but he had the most exquisite taste and judgment in the selection of his *colors*, and in laying them on, till the *portrait* of the character was complete, and true to nature as the original.

The *singular* is better than the *plural*. It is the *single aim* of old Humphrey's *rifle-barrel*, instead of the scattering *blunderbuss;* — that was Nathan's idea, when he said to David, "*Thou art the man.*" But *David* did not get out of *humor*, like some, but moaned out, "*I have sinned against the Lord;*" and for that, the Lord pardoned his iniquity

CHAPTER XXV.

MORE FRAGMENTS OF WAR.

*   *   *   *   *

No! I profess no *microscopic vision* in detecting "the *defects* of Christians;" nor but little of that talent once imputed to a German moralist,—that he could *analyze the strata of society*, as with a *microscope*, and, if he detected a few *scratches* in the crystallization, he forgot the *large outlines* which solicited his inspection.

Now, I happen to be a plain man, and a plain, *common-sense* preacher. If the *scratches* upon the fair crystallizations of Christian character be slight, and not too deep to be *mortal*, or, to effect materially the value of the material in the estimation of the *world*, God forbid I should apply a *microscope!* A knowledge of my own infirmities and short-comings would forbid it! Scratches that require such *microscopic inspection* had better be left to the judgment of an all-seeing God; and not laid open to the *sneers* of the ungodly.

God only is able to judge in some cases; and his judgment is just. He cannot *err* in his estimate of human character. Instead of the *microscope*, my hand would rather busy itself in adjusting the *veil* of charity, and arranging the *drapery* of concealment; or turning the scratches into the shade.

But when the scratches are deep enough to be *damaging*

to the *material*, and damning the owner of such a character, and injurious to the work of God; give me the microscope, hammer, *powder*, and *crowbar*, or *what you will; shatter* it, and *batter* it, and *remove* it out of the way, that sinners may not stumble over it into hell.

Is it not declared that Christians are *predestinated* " to be *conformed* to the *image* of his *Son* " ? That is, we are to be like him,— *inwardly* in our souls, and *outwardly* in our moral character. And, again, that, " as we have borne the *image* of the *earthy*," — that is, the *first Adam*,— " we shall also bear the *image* of the *heavenly*," — that is, the *second Adam*, the Lord from heaven! But let it be a *correct* image, not a *caricature* — not a ridiculous resemblance!

Who would not *resent* it to have a *wife*, a husband, brother, friend, sister, or parent, *caricatured?* Or, suppose some artist should caricature the queen — representing her in the complexion of a *negress*, or deformed; minus an eye or a limb, or scarred in feature, or leprous, or in some ridiculous attitude or gesture, with a sufficiency of *lineament* for recognition; and, as if that was not enough, " *Victoria* " is legible beneath; and, not content with having it suspended in his *studio*, he must exhibit it in the window of some print-shop, while he himself goes on to multiply copies; how long before public indignation would be aroused? Who would insure his exhibition window or his person from harm? And what are *Christians* but the living images of *Christ*, exhibited for the world to look at? But, suppose there are those who, in their own characters and persons, thus *caricature* our *Lord Jesus Christ*, can we stand and look on, and say nothing? Were B—— to do so, in the case supposed, his loyalty to the queen might well be *suspected*. Were we to do so, our loyalty to Jesus Christ would lie open to suspicion. Would it not?

St. Paul speaks about Christians, that they should all come into "the *unity of the faith*, and of the *knowledge of the Son of God*, unto a *perfect man*, unto the measure of the stature of the fulness of Christ."—Ephes. 4: 13. Dr. *Adam Clarke* lamented in his day that many *preachers*, and multitudes of professing people, were studious to find out how many imperfections and infidelities, and how much inward sinfulness, is consistent with a *safe state* in religion; and that how few, very few, were bringing out the fair Gospel standard, to try the height of the members of the church; whether they were fit for the heavenly army; whether their stature was such as to qualify them for the ranks of the church militant; that the *measure of the stature of the fulness* was seldom seen; but the *measure of the stature of littleness, dwarfishness*, and *emptiness*, was often exhibited. Alas! the lamentation is no less called for in our times!

* * * * * *

What you say is all very well, and *plausible* enough; but you have left the difficulty quite untouched. My assertion was this: "You are every moment exerting an influence *for* or *against* this revival." Not one point of my argument have you meddled with; you had substantial *reasons*, doubtless; you might have offended your *conscience!* Mr. Wesley says, "We are every moment *pleasing* or *displeasing* to God." I insist upon the application of his sentiment to you and others, with regard to this work of God. Is not Matt. 12: 30, much to the point? "He that is not *with me* is *against me;* and he that *gathereth not with me scattereth abroad.*" Now, if my sentiment was "intolerant," what think you of that?

A divine, in Switzerland, commenting upon the above decision of our Lord, remarked: "This is the Gospel, with all its *intolerance;* for the intolerance of the Gospel is to consider every man an *enemy* who is not a *friend."* The angel of the Lord, according to your principles, was *intolerant*, when he cried, "*Curse ye Meroz, curse ye bitterly the inhabitants thereof; because they came not to the help of the Lord, to the help of the Lord against the mighty."* — Judges 5 : 23.

Am I preaching any other Gospel than did Christ and his Apostles? How much do the *effects* differ, so far as they are made to appear? Look around you, and consider, for I may now venture to ask you to do so. Free your mind from *prejudice;* behold and judge!

We are struggling hard for the victory. Why should you stand *aloof?* Why not identify *yourself* with us and with the work? At this season of the year, certain *affairs* may be *pressing*, and demanding your attention. I am not to judge in such matters. To your own master you stand or fall. But, when *present*, why stand aloof at a *crisis* like this? as if you are doubtful of the right, or question the *propriety* of this pushing the Gospel to its proper results, in the awakening and conversion of sinners; or, as if you doubted the possibility of the victory which we are struggling so hard to win. The conduct of *yourself*, and of some others, is hardly the thing at *this crisis*. It is more *distressing* than if we knew you to be positive *enemies*.

A *political writer* holds the sentiment, that there are occasions when a lukewarm friend, who will not put himself the least out of his way, who will make no *exertion*, who will run no *risk*, is more *distasteful than an enemy!* What think you of that? Have you never had any such trials in *politics?* Has it not a point of application in matters of religion? You would think so, I am confident, did you occupy my position.

CHAPTER XXVI.

SPIRITUAL BATTERIES AND WEAPONS OF WAR.

It is said the scenes upon a *battle-field* after the victory are most *impressive*. To say nothing of the dead and the dying, — for that is *horrible* beyond imagination, — but to behold the spectacle of broken swords, &c., and fragments of artillery, and balls over the field, lying scattered like hail, deeply moves the spectator, while it impresses him with some idea of the terrible nature of the conflict just decided. We gather up the following "*fragments of war.*" They tell their own story, and will, we hope, be interesting relics of this and that scene in a great spiritual battle for Christ — truth — *souls!*

*   *   *   *   *

Judas was too harsh a term in that discourse, perhaps; and yet I feel disinclined to any *apology* for using it. The *application* was somewhat severe. But, convince me if you can that *Jesus Christ* and his *cause* are not *betrayed* now in various ways by his professed followers, — I will not say I shall *reconsider* the matter, but a most humble apology shall be forthcoming.

Ah, my friend, this refusing to confess Christ before men, — this being ashamed to follow him in the way of the *cross*, — weighs heavily with me, because it is so severely reprimanded in the *New Testament*.

One said, "Peter became half a Judas; for the *denier* was but little better than the *betrayer* of Christ." How would you set about to cope with that? *Ambrose*, I remember, gave this definition: "To *deny* is to *betray*." Beware! O, beware of *denying* Christ the benefit of whatever *influence* any of you may have, at such a crisis as the present! Behold the few, how they battle for him! How boldly they stand by the *truth*, in its onset against *error*, sin and Satan! O, beware of betraying, that is, *denying*, *Christ* before his enemies, who are saying, "Ah, so would we have it! It is as we expected! This one and that have no confidence in the movement." If the *tongue*, by unguarded expressions, license such conclusions among opponents of the work, it is even worse than the *silence* of a do-nothing testimony.

Be assured of one thing; so long as Jesus is *wounded* variously in the house of his friends, and *betrayed*, the epithet "*Judas*" is never likely to fall into disuse.

Let none whom it does not concern be displeased; but let us consider *Judas* as he appears among our Lord's disciples How many *searching sermons* and touching *appeals*, from the lips of his Lord and Master, saluted his ears! And what stupendous *miracles* did he witness, but all in vain! He betrayed him, — betrayed him with a kiss!

And tell me, is it not possible that some among his disciples in the nineteenth century exhibit a similar experience, a similar character, so far as *circumstances will allow*? Need I draw a parallel? O, no! You understand me. Sermons are preached, and appeals are made, and "*showers of blessing*" descend; but with results similar to rain descending upon a *dead tree*, which grows not, but decays and rots all the faster for the rain and the sunshine.

And tell me, further, is it not possible, like *Judas*, to *kiss* Christ and his cause with our *professions*, and then to kiss and *betray* him in our *lives*, through the instigation of some *bribe* or other from Satan? — and to do so in the face of the strongest and tenderest *obligations?*

O, but it does grieve me to speak so! and let me relieve myself and you, by pouring all our emotions upon that notorious *Judas* himself, who *has gone to his own place*, wherever that place may be. Suppose my words this night could reach his ear, how terribly would *eternity* reverberate them! O, ungrateful Judas! how couldst thou bid those hard-hearted soldiers bind those *hands*, which a few hours ago had so kindly washed thy *feet*, and which lately fed thee at his table with his chosen ones, — thy Lord, who honored thee with tokens of his friendship and confidence, by making thee his *treasurer* and *almoner?* Dost thou wonder now, that, on that doleful night, when thou didst take with him his last supper, he used the word *"me"* with such *tender emphasis*, — " *Behold the hand of him that betrayeth* ME *is* with me on the table"? O, what a "world of meaning" was conveyed in that little pronoun *me!* " It is *me*, not you, my disciples, the owner of that hand is about to betray; and yet, your *interests*, your *peace*, your *safety*, are all involved in his act. And, *Peter*, Satan desires to have you also, that he may sift you as wheat; but it is *me* he would betray, who has never done him any *wrong*, but, on the contrary, continued *good*, ever since he became my disciple. And yet, remaining my disciple, or numbered among my disciples, he is about to go out and betray me to my enemies." O, Judas!

Judas! didst thou not comprehend this, and more than all this, in that little word "ME," as it came from his blessed lips in the soft and mournful tones of that ever-to-be-remembered voice? And was there nothing, in all this, to move thee out of thy foul purpose?

No, no! We see thee stalking forward in front of that troop of soldiers, 'midst the gloom of *night*,— a fit time for such a deed of darkness,— such a *breach of friendship*, to say nothing more.

And thou didst say, "Hail, Master," and *kissed* him; — so much *honey* on thy lips, *Judas*, and such *poison* in thy *heart!* And Jesus said to thee in return, "*Judas, betrayest thou* the Son of man with a kiss?" Ah, was there nothing in this to touch thy heart? Every word is big with the tenderest reproach; every word a *sigh*, as it were. "*Judas — betrayest — thou?*" O, it was full of that tender soliloquy of the Psalmist, as if it had been penned for the occasion: "For it was not an enemy that reproached me; then could I have borne it: neither was it he that hated me, that did magnify himself against me; then would I have hid myself from him; but it was *thou!* — and with a *kiss*, a symbol so significant and endearing; this the signal of thy treachery." O, Judas, how couldst thou stand up under all this? How able to contain thyself? How avoid falling down at his feet, content to die in his stead? Did not thy conscience smite thee? Were not thy sympathies ready to overpower thee?— while every word from the lips of thy Lord was but a *sob* over betrayed friendship; enough, one would think, to make the night grow darker, — enough to awaken the sympathy of the surrounding rocks, and to make the trees in the garden to tremble, and cry out, —

> " Judas ! dost thou betray him with a kiss ?
> Dost thou find hell about those lips, and miss
> Of life just at the gates of bliss ?
> O, what has ever equalled this !
> Earth, hell and conscience hiss,
> For black ingratitude it is, —
> Was ever grief like His ? "

Brethren, what thoughts are those which have been flitting over your minds ? What other than these, — that it is a *marvellous* thing *Judas* could ever have had a *successor ;* one professing to know Jesus, and honored with his *friendship*, and many tokens of his love, and then *betray* him, — yes, as far as circumstances allow,—*betray* him in his *cause*, before sinful men, and for a less advantage than Satan tempted *Judas*. And to think there are many such in our day, is a *sad thought*. * * * * But let us pray for such *wrong-doers ;* not forgetting to consider ourselves, lest we also should be *tempted* to the same. Save us, save us, O thou *Lover of souls !* Keep us, O keep us, and let not Satan pluck us out of thine hand ! Hear us, O hear us, and mark the purposes and confiding sentiments of hundreds of loyal-beating hearts now present, saying,

> " Light of the world, thy beams I bless !
> On thee, bright Sun of righteousness,
>   My faith hath fixed its eye ;
> Guided by thee, through all I go,
> Nor fear the ruin spread below,
>   For thou art always nigh.
>
> ' Ten thousand snares my path beset ;
> Yet will I, Lord, the work complete,
>   Which thou to me hast given ;
> Regardless of the pains I feel,
> Close by the gates of death and hell,
>   I urge my way to heaven.

> " Still will I strive, and labor still,
> With humble zeal, to do thy will,
> And trust in thy defence:
> My soul into thy hands I give;
> And, if he can obtain thy leave,
> Let Satan pluck me thence!"

* * * * * * *

Let those who have *eyes* to see, use them, and those who have *ears* to hear, hearken!

Behold *the signs of the times!* What meaneth this gathering of the people together? — *this sound of a going forth in the tops of the mulberry trees?* — 2 Sam. 5: 24. Is it not time to bestir ourselves? Know you not that the Lord God is in our midst? — that the *Captain of* our salvation has gone out before us to smite the Philistines, as of old? — but mark, to smite and to heal, — to rend and to bind up, — to kill and to make alive. Hallelujah!

Here we have all sorts of people, filling up a significant space between "*the painful saint*" and "*the lazy notionist.*" Alas for the *latter!* — what uses or abuses do they make of what they hear! — I could say much, but forbear. We must pity and *pray* for them, for we see their day approaching; when they shall "*beg in harvest and have nothing,*" because they misimproved their season, their day of grace. But allow an *illustration.*

Last summer, at *York*, along came a *busy bee*, and after it a *wanton butterfly.* Both seemed attracted to the same *flower*, and alighted. Both were busy for a while. The *bee* hummed and worked; the *butterfly gayly* but noiselessly spread and contracted its wings, 'midst fragrance and sunshine, in a sort of busy idleness. The *sunny hour* passed away, and so did the bee, bearing off to its *hive* its burden of precious sweets. The *butterfly* had painted its wings, and amused itself, but moved off too, as the sun went down under a cloud. But how is it *now* with the bee and the butterfly? — now that the *storms* of the closing year are howling over the landscape? The *bee* is snugly housed in its home, 'midst a paradise of sweets, regardless of the *storms* and desolations outside. Where is the *butterfly?* It crept into a *hole* and *died!*

But such is the difference between the *active Christian* and "*the lazy notionist,*" whether in the church or out of it, — who gathers none of the *honey of grace*, brings nothing to the *hive;* — amuses himself with our preaching, paints the wings of his fancy, does no good, gets no good; — O what misery in the end! *Hobbes* was not the last who said, "I want a *hole* to creep out of the world at," — to creep into hell at, he should have said! — just such *chilling* scenes do the death-beds of some of these *butterflies* exhibit. But not unfrequently it is otherwise; — the striking acknowledgment to the necessity of a *change of heart* is oftener *appended*, in *tears*, and regrets, and supplications for mercy.

But the *faithful Christian*, like the *busy bee*, bids farewell to the *winter storms* of time and death, and enters into rest, — into the *Paradise* promised him on the cross; — takes wing, as good old Richard Baxter said, *takes wing* and *flies to God*, and *walks in heaven*, and *talks with saints and angels*, — Hallelujah! — and there enjoys his heavenly treasure, and tastes the sweet rewards of a well-spent life. Blessed be God!

* * * * * * *

1. *We are all responsible for the consequences of our example; especially* so in times of a *revival*, when many are awakened, and inquire, "*What shall we do?*"

There is trouble in the camp. *Truth* is mighty. It is searching the *foundations* of Zion. Professors are awake;

some are tremb ing for their foundations, — like an architect in Liverpool, during the *Dedication*, who kept moving about, in a profuse perspiration, examining the foundation and walls, whether they were able to sustain the crowd within. It did him good. He was ever after careful about the *foundations* of such structures. It is doing *professors* good; but it will be of eternal benefit to some of you who hear.

But it was about *example* I proposed to speak; and let *one* who is especially interested, listen. I have no time for circumlocution. There is an *unconscious influence* which some exert, and for evil; and there is a *conscious influence*. Both are bad; but the last is the *worst* for him who exerts it; because he *knows* what he is doing, and his *responsibility* is ten-fold. Therefore, lay to heart what I am about to say. If you do not, it will only increase your responsibility, for God will hold you *accountable;* and he will be *stricter* with you *for what you did know*, than for what you *did not know;* although I believe we shall be accountable at the *day of judgment* for what we *might have known*, as well as for what we *did know*. This is a conscience-awakening truth, but I have no time to *enlarge* upon it; you may hear of it again.

Ponder what I am going to say. Consider your *position* in life, — in the church of God, also. *Reflect*. Your elevation above many renders you *influential* for or against this work of God.

Forget not that what you do and say, others will *imitate*. As you move, they will move. Such is human nature. There is no use to deny it. It is a fact. You will know it as a fact in the Great Day. You have a *circle of influence;* everybody has, but some more than others. But your circle is wide; and your example is telling upon them. This is *undeniable*. Facts prove it; but I forbear.

But is it *right* for you, or *safe* for them, to pursue your present course? Is it helpful to the cause of God? Does it tend to the conversion of your family, to *move* and to *converse* as you do? *Silence, inaction* is bad, but audible expression is worse; the meaning of the former can only be *guessed* at, the latter is plain and *unmistakable*. O, can it be right? Let *conscience* answer.

The Israelites moved in the wilderness, when the *cloud* moved. How *influential* was the pillar of cloud, then, by night as well as by day! Suppose, had it been possible, that *Satan* had got control of that cloud, — would it not have led Israel all wrong, and brought disorder and ruin upon the camp?

Do you shrink from the *comparison?* You need not. It illustrates a fact. Good men and bad men are compared to *clouds* in Scripture. St. Jude compares some professors, if not *ministers*, to "*clouds without water,*" deceptive in appearance, and *unrefreshing* to the thirsty earth. St. Peter compared some to "*clouds carried with a tempest, to whom the mist of darkness is reserved for ever and ever;*" and adds, that "many shall *follow* their *pernicious ways;* by reason of whom the way of truth shall be evil spoken of." — 2 Peter 2 : 2, 17. There is *influence* for you! but it is "*pernicious,*" — that was the word selected by the Holy Ghost. How *expressive!* Look at the results. the ways of evil are thronged, — "*many shall follow,*" &c., "the way of *truth*" is "evil spoken of" by others. Thus, circle moves circle, and who can tell where the influence shall *terminate?* In the mean time *truth suffers*, and *souls perish*.

Beware, I conjure you! The eye of God is upon you.

Persist, and it may be to your sorrow. The adventure may be to your *hurt*. The order of his providence may change concerning you. He may *punish* you, and *try* you as by fire. Ponder what one has said upon the subject, — ponder it well. "If he advance not now, he may receive such a *backcast* as he may hardly ever recover, but come limping behind, and go halting to the grave." You would not like that. But it is happening continually. The world is full of such *limping* convicts. Resolve not to become one of that *disabled gang*, — that *mournful procession.*

Be wise in time. Provoke not God to make you an *example*. *Persist* in the example you have been giving, and he may make *you* an example, and bring you a *blow* from which you may never recover.

O, cry to God that your secret *backslidings* may be healed! Think of what you have admitted. Make haste. Fly for your life. "Agree with thine *adversary* quickly whilst thou art in the way with him." Read the rest. — Matt. 5 : 25. It is as if Jesus himself was sounding that *trumpet* in your ear. There is mercy. Come! Come to Jesus. Get out of the way of sinners. The *famine* is at an end. Stand not in the gate to prevent. Care not for the "*order*" of things, in this or that, if so be your own soul is fed with the bread of life; if so be your heart rejoices in this great salvation. Let my words enter your ears, and sink down into your heart. Do they? Is there a cry within? Or must yours be the fate of that noble lord of Samaria, who was trodden down and perished in the streets, amidst the shouts of salvation? — 2 Kings 7 : 20. Hear, for the time to come, as well as for the present.

2. *A word for another:*

True religion is *diffusive*. This is its insuperable quality the world over as *heat* from fire; as *light* from a sunbeam; as *fragrance* from the rose. True religion is *diffusive*. It always has been, always will be so; and so is yours, if you have got the real thing, — that which will save your soul at last.

The *possession* of religion, and a desire for its *diffusion*, go together. Now, mark that fact. Examine yourself by that fact; you cannot help wishing that others should enjoy it, and that will *prompt* you to do or say something to effect it. It was this which caused the blood of *martyrs* to redden the earth!

Religion is too valuable to lack *diffusiveness*. Consider. is not everything valuable to man diffusive? The sky, the atmosphere, light, sunshine, grass, grain, herbs, trees; flowers, water, thunder, lightning, wind, and rain; the sun and moon, and stars, electricity, attraction, gravitation, the nerves in your body, and the blood in your veins, and the eyes in your head? — the *diffusiveness* of all, or any of these, being equal to their importance.

But how much more religion! — in the world and in the soul! Wide as the world of man is that command, "to preach the Gospel to every creature." A *fig* for any man's religion who is indifferent to that command; and a fig for all he possesses of it, if it is unaccompanied by any desire to diffuse it among his kindred and neighbors!

Think of that command of Jesus Christ, "Let *your light* so shine before men, that they may see your good works, and glorify your Father which is in heaven." A fine illustration that of the diffusiveness of *religion ;* it is *light*, and we are commanded to *let* it *shine*, — as much as to say, it will *shine* if you will *let it*, for its nature is to shine! But let it "*so shine*" as to effect something; and let it shine *timely* and *convincingly*, in your *good works ;* and a good *work* certainly it is to *confess Christ* before men, and to coöperate with others for the salvation of the *hell exposed.*

Hear what our Lord says: "Whosoever, therefore, shall confess me before men, him will I confess also before my Father which is in heaven. But whosoever shall *deny* me before men, him will I also deny before my Father which is in heaven."—Matt. 10 : 32, 33. This is *decisive* enough, surely,—sufficient, one would think, to make men tremble under certain circumstances! And does it not show how deeply interesting are such things to Jesus Christ?

Let me, therefore, beseech you, count it not a mere "hobby" of mine, "intended for effect, and for the accumulation of popularity," but rather an *uncompromising principle* in the religion and government of the Son of God.

Receive the *conviction*, then, that you must let your *light shine*, and *so shine* as to meet the approbation of Him who judgeth, as well as of those who behold it; convincing them that you enjoy it, and that they may glorify God in your behalf.

Consider: the *sun* in the sky, a *city* upon a hill, and a *candle* in a candlestick, were our Lord's *figures* upon this subject. When the *sun* shines, and when the *city* is seen, and the *candle* fills all the room with light, the *existence* of the thing is *unquestionable.* It is thus our Lord would have our light to shine, that men may see it, and glorify our *Father* which is in heaven, who is the author of it. Do you understand me?

Would it not seem as if he intended that illustration in Matt. 5 : 15, for *you?*— where he speaks of lighting a *candle*, and putting it under a *bushel*, instead of on a *candlestick*, "*that it may give light unto all that are in the house!*"

St. Paul *flashes* forth his *signal* among the churches, thus: "Among whom ye *shine* as *lights* in the world." — Phil. 2: 15. In what did he consider this *shining* to consist? Read the answer in that and the following verse: "*Blameless* and *harmless, the sons of God, without rebuke,* in the midst of a crooked and perverse nation, holding forth the word of life." Depend upon it, such needed no such rebukes as the *stranger* has been sounding in your ears!

As to "*self-seeking,*" consider how the apostle follows up such pointed injunctions: "*That I may rejoice in the day of Christ, that I have not run in vain neither labored in vain.*" — verse 16. Here he confesses to "*self-interest,*" and is not ashamed of it! But you see how *gently*, as if by *rays of light*, he twists, as a three-fold cord, *Christ's honor, their duty,* and *his own interests together!*

Remember the motto of your own celebrated *John Smith*, of precious memory: "*Obtain* more of God, and *diffuse* more of God." Who of you will adopt it as *your* own, and act upon it from this hour, and become our fellow-helpers in this great struggle for souls? O, come one, come all of you, and be our *companions* in *tribulation*, if need be, and in *the kingdom and patience of Jesus Christ!* — Rev. 1: 9.

Let all who are of this mind *come*, — come seek a baptism of the Holy Ghost, and of fire, — buckle on the Christian armor, and join the *fight* for Christ and souls!

Do not, I conjure you, wait until *victory* or *defeat* is no more *doubtful.* To alter the figure, wait not to ascertain whether this tide of salvation has got to its *flood mark*, its *highest water mark*, to be followed by a *painful ebb ;* or whether it is likely to rise much higher in *popular favor* and *success*, even to the *high-water mark* of Pentecostal times!

Ah! how much of this sort of thing have I witnessed elsewhere, among certain classes of "the *élite* of Methodism," — lending the *effort* no countenance until they were able to *ascertain* in which direction the *popular tide* was likely to *set;* their *empty pews* a subject of *remark*, of *surmise*, of *inference;* making only "a civil visit" on the Sabbath, as if to let the public see they were alive and well, but too well *educated and refined* to appear among "the vulgar throng" in the week time, to be carried away by *novelties* and *innovations;* continuing this *policy* until reports of strange things reached their ears, — that some of "the first families of the place" were in attendance, night after night, and one and another and another of them *converted*, and active for God; and the evidence becoming unmistakable that the whole thing was *popular*, and likely to succeed beyond all expectation! O, but how quickly their *policy changed then!* Their *pews* no more *deserted*, week-day or Sabbath, fair weather or foul; there they were, wreathed in smiles, and full of the spirit of *patronage*, when the revival could go on well enough without them; provoking the *shrewd* or *rude* remark of an observer, — of a *snail*, with its *house* upon its back, putting out its *horns*, trying if the way is clear, and plucking them back on the least intimation of *risk;* but, at length, when all is *sunshine and safety*, surrendering its sensitive person to all the advantages of the occasion; — a *disrespectful comparison*, which might have well been avoided, had they honored Christ and his cause when the *revival* was weak and small, — an outcast, as it were, like the infant Jesus in the manger!

O, how much of this sort of thing have I seen in my

time! The *snail* with the *house* on its back, and its *feelers* out! — the *credit* of the family, for *taste* and *refinement* and *discernment* to be cared for, whatever may become of the *cause of Jesus Christ!* — that, in case of a *failure*, they might receive credit for *discernment* and *decision of character*. Ah me! *snails* were *unclean* things, and *forbidden* by the Jewish law! Nor should we forget that "*the fearful*" are classed with "*the unclean*" and "*the unbelieving*," in Rev. 21: 8, which are to have their final portion in regions not to be coveted by any man in his senses, be his *house* high or low.

Let none present be *offended*. At this early stage of the work, it is well to tell you these things, "*Lest Satan should get an advantage, for we are not ignorant of his devices.*" — 2 Cor. 2: 11. Lest he should get an advantage of any of *you* by this sort of *mean device;* and, at length, either render you *ridiculous*, or do serious injury to your *souls* and families; lest, also, he should *retard the work*, and render our effort *hard* and *discouraging*.

It has been remarked, already, I have had some painful experience of these things elsewhere; and would to God I could say, with a clear conscience, a somewhat similar spirit has never been exhibited among my brethren in the ministry in some parts of *Christendom*.

For example: "The stranger" arrived, heralded by some notoriety as to *success* in other parts; *expectation* had been on the tip-toe for some time; now it is about to be gratified. The *plain man* makes his appearance in the pulpit, and preaches a *plain Gospel sermon*. There is a hope he will do better after the fatigue of his journey is over. Sermon succeeds to sermon, but there is nothing great or eloquent, — plain home truth, that is all, with but little *unction* — *curiosity* has grieved the Spirit; there is nothing that *promises* much influence with "*the public mind;*"— the *Spirit* is grieved at this looking unto man, instead of *looking unto Jesus;* and the poor stranger is *shorn of his strength;* he is *down*, and cannot get up, and no influential hand is extended heartily to help him up. The people are looking to man, instead of to God; — much *talk* and little *prayer*, low criticisms and comparisons in certain quarters, and *unbelief* on the fearful increase.

The *stranger* feels it all; cries to God; comes before them with honest tears, but cannot *rise*. Thus matters proceed. He would fain retreat, but dare not. *Hopes* in *God*, but is *greatly humbled*. The *ministers* of the place look on, — pray if asked; they are determined not to lay a straw in "the brother's way;" but they will not throw themselves into the work, and *succor* him earnestly in the conflict; will not ally their strength with his, for *victory* in the onset. "No; the people would not be content with the *ordinary ministrations*, but called loudly for the *extraordinary*. Now they have it, and let them make the best of it; the *responsibility* is not *ours*, but *the brother's*. If he succeed, we shall be glad of it; if it turns out a *failure*, it will do our people good; make them value their *own ministry* the more. It will teach them a lesson. We shall look on, — must not *absent* ourselves; that would be to come in for a share of the blame in case of a failure. We shall help, occasionally, as the brother may direct; but he must be led to understand that the *meeting* is entirely under his own control, and that the *responsibility* is his." The stranger feels and sees how matters stand; finds himself in a hard spot, but knows not how to complain; *weeps* and *sighs* and *groans* in secret; puts forth·Herculean efforts in public; but feels there are *hindrances, drawbacks, weakness and death*, somewhere. — cannot tell where;

likes to be *charitable;* must appear *charitable;* but something is wrong, and *victory* a problem. Thus he proceeds with the *wasting* and killing effort; sinks and rises again, flounders and recovers; now and then, in spite of *hell* and difficulties, gains a slight advantage, and a few souls saved, but for which his heart would break;— the Holy Ghost all the while beholding "*an accursed thing in the camp*," a *contrary spirit*, a policy;— the *heavens brass* again, and *the earth*, the *hearts* of *men, iron,—discouragement* all around.

What is to be done? He "winds up" with as good grace as possible, and disappears; or *girds on the armor, lighter than ever*, and, sword of truth in hand, rushes upon opposing powers!—rushes upon the *church* and upon the *world*, with the cry of "Victory or death!"—rushes upon *opposing influences*, at the risk of *health and life*, till the *power of God* comes down and sweeps away the opposition *like chaff before the wind ;* and the work of *soul-saving* advances with a power that astonishes earth and hell !

Ah! how much of all this have I encountered hitherto; and, perhaps, might say, with him in *The Lay of the Last Poet:*

"And what I felt, I oft shall feel again,
Thou first, last, best, great Giver, Lord!"

CHAPTER XXVII.

A RETARDING OR PROMOTING CHURCH; OR, HOW TO HAVE A REVIVAL.

A FEW words before my text. And let those whom it may concern, *listen* and *ponder*.

1. It is written, *Judgment must begin at the house of God.* Where Jesus Christ has a church, it is either in a state to *retard* or *promote* his work of salvation among sinners. None, I fancy, will disagree with me here.

Now, a *Christ-sent preacher* will look well to this, and will very soon discover the *retarding* or *promoting* state of the church. He must address himself to that state;— must *cope* with it in the former, or *lead it on to victory*, if in the latter state, or he will *fail* in his duty, and have no *revival*. For it is vain to expect any remarkable work of God in any church, so long as its spirit and character are *antagonistic* to the will and work of Christ, and the full designs of the Gospel.

2. But there are, usually, in every church, some *living members*, although there may be many dead. These he should *recognize, cherish, encourage,* and lead forth to do battle for the King of kings. But the *membership* who are of another spirit, should have a different treatment;— *caustic*, to eat away "the proud flesh" gathered upon their spiritual wounds, or a vigorous application of the *lancet* or the *knife;* or an *emetic* which will eject from the foul

stomach of the soul, certain satanic deposits, of no very agreeable nature; — and let the *spiritual physician* beware *of a bespattering!* But if he *lack courage* for these things, he is certainly not *the man* for the *times*, for the *place*, for the people. He had better *retire*, that God may send another, of a *stronger heart*, and more *unflinching* purpose You understand me.

3. Judge of my ministry among you, then, by these *simple, common-sense rules*. If your *consciences declare* for them, then *reason* and *infer* accordingly. Look at our *efforts* through *this glass*. It is *transparent;* look through it, and decide, all of you, whether there is not a *cause*, — whether this *pointed faithfulness* is, as some insinuate, "contrary to the meek and lowly mind that was in Christ." But is it so? — anything at *variance* with his *example*, when *circumstances demanded*, — when, as an eminent divine remarks, "He walked as an *incarnate conscience* through a guilty land; and its people trembled at the rebukes of his sacred presence; when the voice of Him, who was '*meek and lowly in heart*,' uttered forth the hoarse and exasperated accents of divine wrath, in a manner more terrible than the recollections of *Sinai*. But how was it possible that even mercy itself could visit a scene like that which he traversed, and maintain a style of unmingled tenderness? Accordingly, there were occasions when, surveying the proud, hypocritical, and guilty throngs which crowded his path, he clothed himself with zeal as with a garment, and, with a consuming jealousy for the insulted majesty of God, 'took them into his lips, and smote them with the sword of his mouth.' Witness the cleansing of the temple. Intent on gain, the Jews had converted the holy place into a scene of sacrilegious traffic; they had turned the ancient and solemn Passover itself to profit;

they bartered deep in the blood of human souls; they worshipped Mammon in his Father's house. But, 'suddenly coming to his temple,' he flamed around its hallowed walls, 'like a refiner's fire,' and, with the tones of injured and insulted Deity, rained on their consciences such strokes of terrible dismay, that they eagerly sought refuge from his holy indignation in flight, leaving him the Lord and sole possessor of the sanctuary." What think you of scenes like these?

Consider: Do you suppose, were Christ to appear suddenly, and walk forth visibly among his churches in Birmingham, he would differ much from his old style of address?

4. Hearken unto me, all of you; but, O remember, that it is a *sinner like yourselves* who thus speaks to you,— though, to the glory of his grace, I must acknowledge his mercy and goodness, in styling myself a *sinner saved by grace*, and laboring with all my strength to have you saved also. Hearken! Jesus is no more *visibly* present. The heavens have received him until the times of the *restitution* of all things. But he has left TRUTH upon the earth. What to do?—to stand still and do nothing? Nay, verily. What then? To walk forth among the guilty throngs of earth, *like himself*, as an *incarnate conscience*. Is that all? What, and not enter the house of God? Nay, nay! But it enters his sacred temple. It flames around its hallowed walls, "*like a refiner's fire;*" vindicating, in tones of terrible power, the insulted majesty of Him who is Lord also of the temple; and raining upon trembling *consciences*, that which comes down with the force and effectiveness of the nimble and piercing *lightnings* of heaven.

This is all I have time to say at present. Expect something additional, *to-morrow evening*, previous to the text.

In the mean time, hearken to my *message* for to-night: "*Behold, now is the accepted time; behold, now is the day of salvation.*" — 2 Cor. 6: 2. We may say of this text, as one of the fathers said of a *martyr* : — to name a man a *martyr* is to commend him sufficiently. So to name this text, is to commend it sufficiently to all who have *ears* to hear the will and counsel of God; to all who have *hearts* to feel, that the day, the hour of salvation has come; that if you prove it not so, the *blame* must lie upon *yourselves*, not with God. The text is a witness.

The question as to *time* is settled; and that is an important point with some, — the *time* to be saved. They *hope* and *intend* to be saved some time or other, but somehow the *right time* has not arrived. My text says *it has;* it earnestly demands *attention :* "Behold, *now* is the *accepted time;* behold, *now* is the *day of salvation.*" But the *halting, unbelieving* sinner will not believe it. He thinks, or acts as if he thought, there must be some *mistake* about it. My text *repels* the insinuation; and I repel it, and conjure all such to beware how they provoke the displeasure of the Holy Ghost, who speaks therein. Beware, lest he take away *your time* altogether, seeing you reject *his time*. That will be a *terrible* affair; for, O how it will enhance and terribly accent your misery, the recollection that you had an *accepted time and day of salvation,* which you *spurned* or *neglected!*

CHAPTER XXVIII.

HOW TO HAVE A REVIVAL, CONTINUED.

1. ARE you willing I should resume the *theme* of my *introduction*, last night? You know I intimated an intention to return to it.

2. Well, then, allow the inquiry once more, Were Christ to appear visibly among the *churches* in Birmingham, what *style of preaching*, suppose ye, would he adopt? Would it differ materially from that which characterized it, when last among men?

Hear what one said of it: "Finding himself surrounded in the temple by a large assemblage of Jewish doctors, scribes, and lawyers, and Pharisees, — the very element and essence of the nation's guilt, — he assailed and demolished the enormous fabric of sanctimonious hypocrisy which their laborious impiety had reared, and, with the fidelity and fearlessness of the king of martyrs, denounced and delivered his final protest against the pride and the power which upheld it. They had occasionally heard his fearful comminations before, and trembled for their security, for every word was a weapon; but now, having regularly invested and approached their fortified guilt, he opened on them the dreadful artillery of his divine malediction. An occasional flash had before apprized them that a storm might be near; but now, having collected together all the materials of tempest into one black and fearful mass and having awed them to silence, as nature is hushed when awaiting a crisis, he discharged its tremendous contents, in one volleyed and prolonged explosion, on their guilty and unsheltered heads. He arraigned them, as though he had already ascended the seat of doom, and laid open all the sepulchral recesses of their iniquity, as though he read from the book of God's remembrance. Hypocrisy was unable to conceal itself in the clouds of incense which it offered. The proud, the covetous, the intolerant, he confounded and covered with the shame of detection and conscious guilt. As they came up for judgment, in succession, he fulminated against them the woes and imprecations of his wrath, 'the wrath of the Lamb,' in tones anticipating those of their final sentence." How *awfully terrible* the utterances of those woes! — as the *seven thunders* heard by *John* in *Patmos*. But what they uttered none of us know, for John was forbidden to write. But those *thunders* of Jesus, — seven or eight of them, — which he launched forth against the workers of iniquity, have been recorded. — Matt. twenty-third chapter. Each began with a "woe;" and followed by *facts*, the *reverberations* of which, within the surrounding consciences, were sufficient, one would think, to make devils themselves tremble; but the last volley was the climax: " *Ye serpents, ye generation of vipers, how can ye escape the damnation of hell?*" The leading and chief reason why he thundered out these eight *woes*, he stated himself in full, in the utterance of the first woe, — " *For ye shut up the kingdom of heaven against men: for ye neither go in yourselves, neither suffer ye them that are entering to go in.* " This was his charge, and it gave *tone*, and *energy*, and *terribleness*, to all the thundering *woes* that followed.

But a *shower* follows a *thunder-storm*, usually. Were there no *tears*, think ye, when he *bewailed* the coming desolation of that city and people thus? "*O Jerusalem, Jerusalem, thou that killest the prophets, and stonest them which are sent unto thee, how often would I have gathered thy children together, even as a hen gathereth her chickens under her wings, and ye would not! Behold your house is left unto you desolate.*" It was but a day or two before, he had a *weeping time* over that city,— when, it is said, "He beheld the city and *wept over it*," and then lifted up his voice in lamentation over its coming calamities, which he foresaw, saying, "If thou hadst known, even thou, at least in this thy day, the things which belong unto thy peace! but now they are hidden from thine eyes." Then followed the character of their calamities, and the manner of their utter ruin.

And do you think he had no *tears* on this occasion, when he lifted up his voice in the hearing of surrounding multitudes, and in such *mournful* and *deprecatory accents*, and with such *inimitable pathos*, he cried bewailingly, "*O Jerusalem! Jerusalem!*" Can I *repeat* them without *tears?* Can you *hear* them without tears? But consider the lamentation was uttered over those, who, two or three days afterwards, imbrued their hands in his blood! O unparalleled *love! O unparalleled impenitence!*

But, hearken! even then, at that moment, after all the *woes* he had denounced against them, he was ready to throw his protecting wings of mercy and power over them, and forgive them all;— *but they would not;* — their obstinacy and impenitency were unconquerable.

Suppose Jesus, in the same *mysterious majesty* and *disguise*, were to appear among us now, and *thunder* out as justly merited woes in Birmingham,— what then? How would he and his *woes* be received? Would there be no *perversity*, *impenitency*, and *rebellion*, manifested, think ye?

And now, in view of all this, can you find fault with the *stranger?* — with the alarming truths he has been compelled to sound in your ears since his arrival?

CHAPTER XXIX.

CHRIST WEEPING OVER JERUSALEM — A SERMON.

"And when he was come near, he beheld the city, and wept over it, saying, If thou hadst known, even thou, at least in this thy day, the things that belong unto thy peace! But now they are hid from thine eyes." — Luke 19: 41, 42.

1. THERE is much said about *weeping* in the Scriptures. *Abraham wept* over the death of *Sarah*, his wife. *Joseph* wept when he recognized his brethren, from whom he had been so long separated; but he sought how he might conceal his *tears*. *King Hezekiah* "*wept sore*" when he was sick, and the Lord's message by Isaiah had sounded in his ears, "*Thus saith the Lord, Set thine house in order, for thou shalt die, and not live.*" *David* wept freely on several occasions.

2. We do not wonder at such *weeping*. The *occasion* demanded it. *Nature* had its way, and *tears* their course. Among the *Hebrews*, it was not considered *unmanly*, or a sign of *weakness*, to *weep*; it was not looked upon as an evidence of want of *courage*, or *self-possession*, or *greatness of soul*, to weep when there was a *cause* for it; but rather an evidence of the presence of these manly and noble virtues. Therefore, they did not *repress* their *tears*, as if ashamed of them, in times of bereavement and sorrow.

3. But when we behold Jesus drawing near to *Jerusalem*, and *weeping* over *it*, — ah! but there is something

in that scene exceedingly *touching*. But more of this by and by.

I was reading, to-day, David's pathetic lamentation over the death of *Saul* and *Jonathan*, upon the mountains of *Gilboa*. How *touchingly eloquent* it is! — 2 Sam. 1: 17—27. That passage thrilled me. "The beauty of Israel is slain upon thy high places; how are the mighty fallen! I am distressed for thee, my brother *Jonathan ;* very *pleasant* hast thou been unto me; thy *love* to me was wonderful, passing the love of women." No wonder his *distress* at their untimely end was so poignant, and his *excess of grief* so great, as that "every word was *swollen* with a *sigh*, or *broken* with a *sob*," so endearing were the recollections of their *friendship*, especially that of *Jonathan !*

Had Jerusalem sinners been so endeared to *Jesus*, his tears and lamentations over them would not so surprise and move us. But they were on the point of cruelly imbruing their hands in his blood. More of this hereafter. But how are we to view sinners around us?—as the *friends* and *lovers* of Jesus ? — as really and truly *our friends?* How can we *think* so, when they repel his truth, hate it, scorn it, and force us into agonies, and cries and tears, night after night, for their salvation? — as far from the *love* which should win tears, on mere human principles, as the devil from the beauty and holiness of an unfallen angel !

And shall we *weep* over them, as Jesus did over Jerusalem sinners? Yes, we shall, and to-night, too ! But where are we to find *motives ?* What is it that shall open the fountains in our heads, and cover our cheeks with tears ? I answer : some such views as Jesus had. 1. That the things which belong to their *peace* are *hidden* from their *eyes*. 2. An intense desire it were otherwise. 3. The terrible calamities which await every one of them. 4. The willingness of Jesus to rescue and save them all, were their eyes but open to *facts* which would surely awaken and alarm, and bring them to repentance.

3. And why should we be *ashamed* to *weep*, even if to-night the sight of our eyes affects our hearts? Why should not *we* weep over *sinners* in our day, if *Jesus* wept over sinners in his day? Should *our* cheeks be dry, when *his* were wet? But Jesus, we see, wept over his *enemies*. If *we* weep, it is over *relatives* and *fellow-townsmen*, who have no intention of *harming* us; who would *fight* for us, were any one to attempt to *molest* or *injure* us. Ay, but alas! alas! we must not forget that they are at *enmity with God*, and, perhaps, on account of the *truth*, are not well *pleased* with us; what they must cost us, by their perversity, labor, sorrow, and tears, before their *conversion*.

4. Nevertheless, *tears* are called for now over *sin-slain* and *devil-deceived* sinners and *backsliders*; for, in this age, in which the *falling sickness* is an epidemic, when so many have *fallen from God*, lamentation and tears are surely not uncalled for.

5. We behold their *peril* now. Nor should devils nor men be surprised at our *emotions*, or our *tears*. Weep! yes! let us weep more and more, for we have *backsliders* among us! "*How are the mighty fallen!*" exclaimed David, over the gory bodies of his *friends* on Gilboa. "How are the *mighty* fallen!" exclaim we over those who were once mighty in prayer and praise, — "*the beauty of Israel!*"— fallen, and fallen *so low*, and in *peril* of falling *lower* yet, even where *flames* attend their *final fall!* Hearken! "Is it nothing to you, all ye that pass by? Behold, and see if there be any sorrow like unto my sorrow," — or any *cause* of sorrow greater than this, — to behold that melancholy procession of poor backsliders, now in the

devil's *chain-gang!* How are the mighty fallen! O, what shall I say more? From what a *height* of *felicity* fallen! To what a depth of misery! As the *apples* are the glory of the *tree*, so were these once the glory of the church. But, now, alas, they are but *windfalls*, as one named them, — windfalls in the devil's mouth. But there is hope of them, as he has not yet run down with them into hell. O, there is hope, although their case may be as desperate as the little *lamb*, which *David* rescued alive out of the fangs of the brindled *lion*, and his grim associate, the *bear*. There is hope yet; let us, therefore, *weep* and *pray*, and *pray* and *weep;* for He, in whom we trust, is stronger than the devouring enemy.

6. Notice, again, that *requiem* or *dirge* of *David,* over a fallen *monarch,* — that touching line,

"*Ye daughters of Israel, weep over Saul.*"

But, O, let me say, ye daughters of Israel, weep over the *sinner;* weep over him, and cry unto God for him besides. It was in vain that the daughters of Israel wept over the gory corpse of their much-loved monarch; for they could not *weep* his soul back from eternity to reänimate that body, nor, by their tears, heal those cruel wounds. But your *tears* may recall the quickening Spirit of God; may bring nigh that precious *blood* of the Lamb, which cleanses, closes, and heals every wound that sin has made.

O, let your sighs, your sobs, your tears, your cries unto God, witness to the *sinner* your deep distress for the peril of his soul, and prove to Heaven, how sincerely you commiserate his condition. Think of *Jesus* weeping over Jerusalem, sobbing, as he wept, "*If thou hadst known, even thou;*"— so let us all weep over the coming perdition of the

18*

poor sinner, to which he is being hurried on by that stern march of Time,

> "That knows not the weight of sleep or weariness, —
> On, still on, he rushes and forever!"

And, like the *heavens*, the other day, which poured down their *rain as tears* upon that *funeral procession* as it passed on, so let us weep, and shower with our tears the mournful procession which is conducting yonder poor sinner to his last, long, dreamy home, in hell.

O, who can tell, but *He* may pass by, who met that *tearful procession* at the gates of *Nain;*—who may say to *us*, as he said to that *bereaved widow*, as she moved along with that *bier* that bore the corpse of her *only son*,—moved along, bowed down with *sorrow*, and bathed in *tears*,—"*Weep not!*"—may touch the *bier*, as at the gates of *Nain*, and cause the bearers to *stand still;*—may speak to that *corpse-like soul*, as he did to the corpse of the widow's son, "*Young man, arise!*"—may deliver him to a weeping *church*, and to a weeping *mother*, alive and saved, as he of *Nain;*—while *fear* comes upon all who ought to fear, and God is glorified of all, saying, "*God hath visited his people!*"

Amen! Hallelujah! *Look up, ye weeping saints!* Look up, thou *weeping mother!* The Lord Jesus Christ is approaching! He is near at hand, who shall say, "Weep not!" Behold, he has come! See! Look yonder! He stands by the side of that sinner. Hearken! He *speaks* to him! There is *life* in his features,—life in his *reason*,—life in his *understanding*,—life in his *conscience!*—a *tear-drop in his eye*, on his cheek! See! he would wipe it off; but another comes, stealing, as if forbidden. Jesus has spoken to him, "Young man, *arise!*" This is the effect of the voice of Jesus! Look! expect! *signs, wonders, miracles* of mercy to-night, by the wondrous power of Jesus! He who can open the sinner's *eyes* to *see the things which belong to his peace,* is doing so now, not in that one case, yonder, but in *many.* *Wonderful!* Stir up thy strength, O, Jesus, and save the *many!* for that is as easy to save the *few.* The ocean wave that pushes shore-ward, covers scores and hundreds of pebbles and rocks, as well as one or a few; so can this *broad wave* of thy mercy and power, O, thou *Ocean* of love, that is sweeping over this congregation!

Look up! I call upon you all to look up through your tears, and behold what is going on! — the *uplifted* hand for mercy!—the *upturned eye!*—the returning love-glances of an ever-merciful Jesus! Yes! he who *wept* on the heights over Jerusalem, but wept in vain,— and has long wept over these poor sinners in vain,— *he weeps,* and *loves them still* — and more than ever, seeing they are now giving him *tear for tear, sigh for sigh, sob for sob;* while he says to each, "*I am thy salvation.*" Hallelujah! shout, ye sons of the morning! Let every golden harp in heaven be vocal. Let the transporting name of a *victorious Jesus* fill heaven with acclamations! *The time to favor Zion has come.* Many a mother shall rejoice! many a *widow!* for He who had *compassion* on her of *Nain,* whose sorrow was very *bitter,* has compassion on *them!* — He who said to her, "Weep not," — and no one had *reasons* for saying so, such as he could show, and did show in that hour, that moment. The *dead son,* became a *living son,* a *speaking son,* in the arms of his mother. What did he say, I wonder? O, ye praying, weeping *mothers* in Israel, you, whose *dead sons* are about to be made alive, know ye not what their language shall be, when next you meet? — *prayer* and *praise* and glory! "Your son that was *dead,* is alive again, was lost, and is found!" Ay! see, your daughters are in tears also! "Mother! mother! your daughter, that was dead, is alive again, was lost and is found." Let every heart among you leap for joy! Let all present recognize something of that for which *Jesus* wept and sighed in vain over Jerusalem, saying, "If thou hadst known, even thou, at least in this thy day, the things which belong unto thy peace." Let all present recognize what comes of having the *eyes* of the people *opened* to *behold the things which belong unto their peace.*

I intended to say more, but can proceed no further. Let us cry unto God, that he may proceed with this work of mercy and power, so gloriously commenced. And to the Father, and to the Son, and to the Holy Ghost, be all the glory, world without end. Amen and Amen!

CHAPTER XXX.

CHRIST WEEPING OVER JERUSALEM — A SERMON.

"*And when he was come near, he beheld the city, and wept over it, saying, If thou hadst known, even thou, at least in this thy day, the things which belong unto thy peace! but now they are hid from thine eyes.*" — Luke 19 : 41, 42.

1. THE *grand design* of all preaching should be to *make people good*, and to *keep them good*. To accomplish the first, they must be *awakened* and *converted* to Christ; next, *built up* in *faith and holiness*.

2. The secret of *effective preaching* lies much in its *appropriateness*, or being *adapted* to the *state* and *circumstances* of the people. It is on this account, I refer so frequently to events, which occur among us, for or against the success of the truth preached.

3. It will not, I hope, be considered a *departure* from this principle, or from the spirit of my *text*, if I drop a few words just here in the ear of a *hearer*. — "One who believes in the *enlightening* of the *intellect*, before *appealing* to the *passions*." And yet, sir, those who have had much *experience* in these things, often find that the intellect has to be reached through the medium of the *passions;* that is, the *light* intended for the *darkened understanding*, must be carried through the *avenue of the passions;* and so *brilliant* must it be, and so *penetrating*, and accompanied withal by such an array of *reflective imagery*, as to arouse the

passions, the *emotions*,— those allied to *hope* and *fear*, especially,— *awaking, rousing*, and *melting* them; *disordering, terrifying, gladdening*, constraining, overpowering, into one general outcry for mercy, or burst of triumphant praise, thanksgiving, and adoration, to the King of kings, and Lord of lords. O, that it may be so, once again, to-night!

Now, observe: we often find it necessary to approach *certain classes* of mind thus, before we can gain the *attention* of the *understanding*, or the *conscience*, and to hold them *steady*, and *long enough* to receive the *requisite impression;* thus, for instance, the *obtuse*, the *unthinking*, the *well-informed*, the *wearied*, and the *disheartened*. 1st. The *obtuse*, that is, the *dull*, the *stupid*, the *insensible*, against which the *truth* beats but in vain, so *impressionless* are they. 2d. The *unthinking*, that is, the thoughtless, the gay, the frivolous; *heedless* persons, whose *attention* it is impossible to *fix* until their *feelings* are awakened. 3d. The *well-informed*, who know much, and feel little; who, if assailed directly through the *understanding*, are left just as we found them, *cold, passionless*, and *inactive*. These are the *Thermopylæ* of our congregation; and they cannot be readily taken by a *direct assault* without much loss of time and strength, and risk of failure; so difficult is it to surprise them into a surrender by some *truth* they know not, for they seem to know everything,— much less, by the truth they *know*, and by which they have been assailed for so many tedious years!

What is to be done with these, whose *heads* are clear as *angels* or *devils*, as to the *theory* of religion, but whose *hearts* are cold and senseless? To make them *feel* what they *know* is the desideratum. But that is seldom accomplished, I think, by an exclusive address to the understanding; but they may give way under the power of a *surprise:* If one can find "*the secret path*," to use a phrase of Rollin, when describing the taking of *Thermopylæ*, the *understanding* and the *knowledge there* may be reached through the *pathway* of their *emotions*, or *passions*, if you like the term better; so that what is *believed* in the *head* is *felt* in the *heart;* then we have *action! — repentance*, and the "*God be merciful to me a sinner!*" and "*Heal my soul, for it hath sinned against thee,—save Lord, or I perish!*" with *tears* and *earnest cries*, and *faith*, and such like, as the Gospel sanctions, with signs and wonders following.

And there are, 4th, the *wearied* and the *disheartened*, the poor *discouraged penitent*, who *believes everything* (he thinks), and yet *feels nothing;* — poor soul! — there is a *secret path* to his soul, and I give myself no rest until I have discovered it. Besides, *believers* and *standard-bearers*, and bearers of burdens, often get *tired*, physically and mentally, through excessive toil.

In such cases, I change my mode of conducting the *siege*, or *attack*, and rush upon the *outworks* and *inner works* of the EMOTIONS and PASSIONS, by a suitable *address*. When these *give way*, and are carried, I never halt, but thunder, in an instant, before the *citadel* of the understanding, which seldom holds out long when the *passions* have been carried. When the *citadel* surrenders, *the day is ours*, and the banner of Emanuel waves over the captured sinner, and the city of *Mansoul*, as *Bunyan* named it, is in the possession of the Lord of glory!

There, sir! perhaps you may find in these remarks more " philosophy " than " rant; "— *common sense*, where you suspected *nonsense!* These are some of our *spiritual tactics*, in the conquest of souls. Nor do we wish them to remain secret. We care not, if they were *placarded* all over the town; for, whether the people *understand* us or not, we are determined they shall *feel* what they profess to believe!

If we had "a weeping time" last night, it was not so much on our own account as that of others, who are persisting to trample *under foot the Son of God, and doing despite unto the Spirit of grace.* — Heb. 10 : 29. We *wept*, and did not *Jesus weep?* Hearken: "And when he was come near, he beheld the city, and *wept over it*, saying, If thou hadst known, even thou," &c. But *we* wept over sinners returning home to God. Our eyes were *wet*, because the eyes of so many were opened to see *the things which belong unto their peace.* If our *tears* were but the evidence of "mental imbecility," bring the same charge against Him who taught us to weep over undone sinners by his own example.

> "Did Christ o'er sinners weep,
> And shall our cheeks be dry?"

We are not, therefore, ashamed of our tears. Let the *North American Indian* despise the *tear-drop* in the eye of a brother *warrior;* and let that warrior seek to repress the tear that would follow, if nature has its course; and let a whole tribe exclaim at once, "It is old-womanish to weep." *Pagans* may so talk, but we are *Christians*, the followers of Him who sought not to hide or suppress his tears, as he *lamented* a city doomed to destruction!

If Jesus *wept* over Jerusalem, when he beheld a *cloud of wrath* gathering over it, — *wrath and ruin* irretrievable, *temporal, spiritual, eternal,* — why, O, why, should not we weep? I repeat it, *why* should not we *weep* to behold the mouths of the *grave* and of hell preparing to open and to engulph so many of you; and the catastrophe so nigh at hand? Instead of *repressing* our tears, should we not rather say with the prophet *Jeremiah*, " O, that my *head were waters*, and mine *eyes a fountain of tears*, that I might weep day and night for the slain of the daughter of my people"? And if sinners will despise, and sin on, we can only resolve with *Jeremiah* again : "*But if ye will not hear it, my soul shall weep in secret places for your pride, and mine eyes shall weep sore and run down with tears.*" There is *sympathy* for you! But who of us, or who that has ever read the writings and history of *Jeremiah* the prophet, would charge him with *weak-mindedness?*

We are the followers of "*The Man of Sorrows.*" Like him we are "*acquainted with grief.*" From his own lips we learn that, unless you are *born again*, you cannot *see* or *enter* the kingdom of heaven. — John 3 : 3, 5. And, had he added, you shall never, in that case, see or enter *hell*, perhaps our eyes could remain as *dry* as any of you who hear me this evening. But, alas! *exclusion* from heaven implies *incarceration* in hell, — " the *fire* that never shall be quenched, — the *worm* that never dieth, — the *weeping*, and *wailing*, and *gnashing of teeth*, in *outer darkness*; — and the *horrors* of *everlasting punishment*, — *eternal damnation*, — the *fire* prepared for the devil and his angels," as the *alternative* of exclusion from heaven, were too frequently on his lips for us to doubt where your *final landing-place* is to be! Hearken!

> " Did Christ o'er sinners weep,
> And shall our cheeks be dry?
> Let floods of penitential grief
> Burst forth from every eye.
>
> " The Son of God in tears
> The wond'ring angels see ;
> Be thou astonished, O, my soul,
> He shed those tears for thee!

> "He wept that we might weep;
> Each sin demands a tear;
> In heaven alone no sin is found,
> And there's no weeping there"

Ah! poor sinner! *We* have the *weeping* part now but YOUR *weeping time* is coming, but with this difference, *ours* is limited to *time*, *yours* has an *eternity* appended. The promise to us is, that *God shall wipe away all tears from our eyes* in heaven. — Rev. 7 : 17. Neither *sorrow*, nor *cause* of sorrow, nor *tears*, nor *cause* of tears, shall afflict us there any more forever; for the days of our mourning shall be ended in heaven.

But, alas for you who may drop into hell! — for *sorrow* and the *cause* of sorrow, *tears* and the *cause* of tears, must coëxist with your eternity; — your *mourning* and the *cause* of mourning shall never, never end. Why, then, should we not *weep* over you, in view of your sad future? Why should we not *weep*, seeing there is yet *hope* of your *salvation*,— that you may begin and weep as freely for *yourselves*, as *we* do for you? There is *hope*, and we *weep*. No wonder *tears* are wiped away in heaven, when *hope* for the wilfully damned is gone, and gone forever!

Hearken, all of you, to what Jesus says on this subject: "Woe unto you that *laugh* now; for ye shall *mourn and weep*." But he had just said to his *disciples*, "Blessed are ye that *weep now;* for ye shall *laugh*." So, then, this is *our* weeping time. Yours is to come. May it be *now*, also!

4. Nor can I withhold a word of *warning* and *expostulation* from *another*.

Hearken! for the *things* which *belong unto thy peace* are concealed in what I am about to say.

Burns, the poet, seized the *veil* with a determined hand, when he said:

> "O would they stay to calculate
> Th' eternal consequences,
> Or your more dreaded hell to state,
> *Damnation of expenses!*"

There! he almost *rends* the *veil of eternity!* — a *glimpse* of "the *eternal consequences*," — a sudden flash of *eternal penalties*,— "*damnation of expenses.*" The *rub* is there, and you cannot misunderstand him! That "*blue light*" of *Burns*, if you will allow another figure, will burn as a signal of distress and peril for many ages yet to come. It has a double effect. It shows the *peril* of sinners, and how *dear* they must pay for their *sinful pleasures*. It discovers, also, *the things which belong to their peace*,— or, at least, the *necessity* of *feeling after them*,— or indicates the *path* which leads to them. *Saints* above, and saints below, heaven above, and earth beneath, might well *bewail* you, if such *consequences*, such *expenses*, were hidden from your eyes;— for, in such a tempting world as this, it would be about the sure way to incur them. *Forewarned, fore-armed*, was the old maxim.

Do you remember how one of the *martyrs* of old was armed with caution, when before his judges? None being present to *take notes* of what he said, he began to express himself *freely*, perhaps *incautiously*; but, hearing the *scratching* of a *pen* going on paper behind a *curtain*, close by, he became *reserved* and then *silent*. The sound was *disagreeable* at first, but it suggested *caution*, knowing that what was being noted behind the curtain, he was sure to hear from again; and he was afterwards *thankful* for the intimation. The sound of that pen agoing, reminded him well, not to forget the things which belonged to his *peace* in this world, to say nothing of the next. Hearken! Do you understand the application? There is a *recording pen* behind the curtain of time; it records all your actions, and you shall hear from them again. Is it not written, "For God will bring *every work* into judgment, with *every secret thing*, whether it be good or evil" (Eccles. 12: 14); and, in another place, that we *must all appear before the judgment-seat of Christ, that every one may receive the things done in his body, whether they were good or bad;* and again, that every man shall be *rewarded according to his works*, for the *books shall be opened?* Know, then, that the *pen of eternity* is going, that your *accounts* with your Maker are strictly kept. Think of this, when you are *sinning.* Think *now;* be on your *guard.* Remember the *martyr*, and the sound of the hidden pen. Be *reserved*, that is, hold yourself in *check;* impose restraint upon your thoughts, words, and actions. Be assured *the things which belong unto thy peace* are involved therein.

An individual, in a certain place, had a snug little property, and, of course, had good credit with a neighboring merchant, who was willing to let him have all he wanted, *on credit.* But, expecting to "*foot the bill*" incurred there, he was prudent; he *priced the articles*, exercised his *judgment*, and refused much that was offered. He escaped a *snare*, saved himself from ruin, and remained an honest man. Hearken! Give this a similar application as the *martyr* and the *pen:* thus thou shalt have a glimpse, once more, of *the things which belong unto thy peace.* God help thee!

But hearken again, — and let that *thoughtless* one, over yonder, give ear. Not far from this man who had the *snug little property*, there lived something of a *rogue*, who was not encumbered with property, and boasted of it; and if he had not *cash* in his purse, he had always *brass* enough in his face nor did he ever once think that *time* and *personal liberty* were property. But, to be short, he ran in debt wherever he could, for he never intended to *meet the bill;* and, finding himself "sorely *cornered*," he enlarged his steps by a sort of *near cut* to fortune; was tried for a *swindling* transaction, and, in a *disagreeable cell*, he learned to calculate consequences, — "expenses," to use Burns' idea.

Eternity has its *reckonings* also. Your *soul* is your property; it would *bankrupt a world* to buy it *without a swindle.* The *Devil* is the neighboring merchant. His goods and his books are open for you; — excellent credit with him. You may "*run tick*," "*buy upon tick*," to any amount; for he has his eye upon your *soul*, nothing *short* of your soul. He never trades for less, — so much for the soul in every temptation, otherwise no trade. It is the *soul* he wants; all else are but trifles. *Arch-fiend!*

Now, if your eyes are open to the *things which belong to your peace*, you will refuse to "*buy on tick*" from Satan, and so escape the *snare*, and save your soul from perdition. You will become "the *prudent man*," mentioned by Solomon, who *foresaw the evil and did hide himself*, while the "*simple*" sinner, like him over yonder, "*passed on*" and was *punished.* — Prov. 22: 3. *Simple* enough, to believe the Devil and his own heart, — that he might resist the truth, repel the Holy Spirit, and "run tick" with hell, without *consequences.* But, as the Devil foresaw that which the *simple* one *refused to foresee*, Death made an arrest, closed accounts, drew aside the veil of eternity, and posted him off without ceremony to "foot his bill," to pay the *reckoning* in eternity, — "*Damnation of expenses.*" O, Lord, open the eyes of that young man! Reveal unto him the things which belong unto his peace. Thy servant is trying to do so, but O give my humble *illustrations* of this truth both *significancy* and *conscience-awakening* power!

Behold, then, in these respects *the things which belong unto thy peace;* nor think, for a moment, thou canst "*sin cheap,* without paying dear." Alas, alas! The *archangel Gabriel* would fail in computing the *eternal expenses,* the *eternity of costs,* which *sin incurs!*

Nay! *stay,* poor sinner, and hear me out! But if *you* will not, there are scores and hundreds of sinners present, who will. Look out for *Death,* when you get out of doors, for he is on full march to meet you; and the *Devil,* who, according to St. Paul, has "*the power of Death*" (Heb. 2: 14), accompanies him,—that old merchant, that old *broker* in souls, who has been *jewing* you out of your soul, —he is at *Death's* heels, and, as St. John tells us, *Hell* following with him.—Rev. 6: 8. O, *woe* be to you, if you fall into such hands! * * * * That is right; stay and hear me out. A *wise* man changes his mind, says the old proverb; a *fool* never! Now, then, *hear me out;* and may your *knees* reach the *floor* before you get out, and with your *voice* cry for *mercy!* It is coming to that, I think!

Well, thank God, sinner, if it does come to that,—if matters with you come to that *extremity,*—I can tell you, beforehand, it will not be in *vain.* No, indeed! When has it ever been in vain? How can it be if Jesus is waiting—and he is—to receive you at his feet, a weeping *penitent,* as you are? I tell you, plainly, it is coming to that. You cannot remain so long! What is that which so shakes you, body and soul? What but the eternal power of God? What is that which has driven all the blood from your face, and unbidden tears to your eyes? O, what but the *power* of Him, whose *blood* flowed so freely on Calvary for the sins of your soul! Whence that deep distress which almost forces the cry? *"God be merciful to me a sinner"*? O, whence, but from a portion of that *fire*, perhaps, which forced *Jesus* to his knees in the garden; which prostrated him upon the cold ground with a groan of *agony*, — so intense as to make him *sweat blood*, and plenty of it, — the *crimson dew* at every pore increasing until it fell in great drops to the ground; it set all his body a weeping *tears of blood* for you. O, shrink not, then, if it be so, that a portion of that fire consumes upon your conscience; that a cry, which God will not refuse to hear, may rise from your soul to heaven! That *tear* again; — never mind it! it is like *John the Baptist*, a *forerunner* of

"The tears that tell your sins forgiven!"

Those quick *breathings* and *sighs* and *sobs*, so rife among the unsaved and the saved in this assembly; what are they but the forerunner of *sighs* that shall waft our souls to heaven; and *shouts* of praise and adoration to him who once rode in *triumph*, 'midst *hosannas*, over the hills of *Jerusalem*, who hath turned our *captivity*, and sent *salvation*?

5. A few words, in *conclusion*, to "*The hardened penitent,*" and to "*One who mourns because he cannot mourn,*" and to "*A despairing sinner.*"

Difficult cases these, I confess. Indeed, there seems to be a *tincture* of despair in all three! *Impossible*, or *impossibility*, seems a hobby word with their *despondency*. One says, "The impossibility of my salvation lies not so much in my impenitence, as my *hardness;* the Spirit, I fear, has been entirely grieved away." A second says, "I know Christ has pronounced the *mourner* blest; but am I a mourner? Stupid as an ox — it cannot be; it is not possible, on Gospel principles, I can be blessed or saved — no." And, says a third, "His mercy is clean gone forever; he will be gracious to me no more; I can neither reach mercy, nor can mercy reach me; there is an *impossibility* in the way of my being saved."— There! what a *trio* of mistaken souls have we here! And, if it be a fact that they represent numbers of each class, they present a serious barrier against the progress of this work.

Hearken unto me, all of you, and these *impossibles* shall disappear before the *light of truth*, as *darkness* before the light of *day!* — shall *vanish*, to use the idea of a poet, "like a *ghost* before the *sun;* or, like a *doubt* before the *truth of God!*" They are even *now* preparing to vanish away, and may they never return.

Impossible! — but who taught you that naughty word? Not Jesus Christ, I am sure of that; for he says, "*All things are possible to him that believeth.*" If you can but *believe, impossibility* shall vanish away, like a ghost before the sun!

Satan has often tried to introduce that *hard, unbecoming* word among my thoughts, when conflicting with *error, hardness*, and *unbelief*, in efforts for a *revival* of the work of God. But a long time has passed away since my Lord enabled me to give it a bill of *divorce!* When this *unbelief* would seek to reinstate itself into my *revival vocabulary*, or *creed*, my soul takes the *alarm*, and raises a cry to God against it: "Out with it!"— and out it goes, like *Legion*, its brother of old. But I do not always effect an insurance that it will not effect an entrance into some *poor sinners* around me, as *Legion* into the *herd* of old, and set them a galloping down the *steeps* of sin into the *sea of perdition.* But, having got rid of it myself, my soul girds itself with strength, and rushes to the *rescue;*—succeeds often in driving the *fiend* back to his own hell, leaving the poor sinners behind as the *trophies* of salvation! *Jesus* let the herd of swine and the devils go to the bottom of the lake together, without a *countermand!* But his hand is ever ready to rescue the souls for which he *bled and died.*

Impossible! I have banished it from my door!—sorry it has stationed itself before yours;—sorrier still that it has effected a lodgment *within.* But it may be *dislodged* if you are willing to have it so. Mark that!—if you are willing to have it so! Because, if you are in *league* with it, then it will bid me defiance.

Impossible! naughty word! There are more *devils* in it than *syllables! Impossible!* banish it to the hell from whence it came. It belongs to hell. It is the *creed* of the damned. What have *living men* to do with it,—men who *desire salvation?* Let the *damned* have it all to themselves. It belongs to them. It is their *right,* after a life of sin and unbelief. It belongs to them,—it cannot be otherwise with them,—for

> "In that lone land of deep despair
> No Sabbath's heavenly light shall rise,—
> No God regard their bitter prayer,
> No Saviour call them to the skies."

Not so in your case, *O ye prisoners of the Lord!* You are in the land of hope, surrounded by praying people, and, better than all,—

> "Now God invites; how blest the day!
> How sweet the Gospel's charming sound!
> Come, sinners, haste, O haste away,
> While yet a pard'ning God is found!'"

Impossible! Away with it! It destroys hope!—it kills *endeavor* both in minister and mourner. Away with it then! — *Crucify it! crucify it!* for it crucified your Lord and mine. "Impossible!' cried the Jews, — "such a person as this cannot be our promised Messiah. *Away with him! away with him!* Crucify him! crucify him!" Ah, that *cruel*, that obstinate word killed the *Prince of life, the Lord of glory!* and it will *destroy* the whole of you, unless you drive it from you. "*Away with it! away with it! Crucify it! crucify it!*" It will not offend your Lord and mine, if we seize upon this old *cannon* of the *enemy*, and turn it against himself, — discharge it in the face of this *Impossible*, whose name is *Legion!*

Away with it, and turn your ear to St. Paul. Now hearken! " Wherefore he is *able* to *save* them to the *uttermost* that come unto God by him, seeing he ever liveth to make intercession for them."— Heb. 7: 25. Thank God for that word "*Uttermost!*" It is the Heaven-appointed *antagonist* of old *Impossible! Impossible* is, indeed, the great *Goliath*, that has made your hearts, like those of the men of Israel in the plains of *Elah* of old, "*dismayed* and *greatly afraid.*" But this "*Uttermost*" is the *stripling David*, that has rescued many a *lamb* out of the mouth of the *lion* and the *bear;* — this David has come into the camp, and *Impossible*, like Goliath, stalks out with its *challenge*, defying the *mercy and power* of God, and despising all his promises in Jesus. *Uttermost*, with its sling, goes forth to meet this *giant*, and, pausing at a *brook* I will tell you of, stoops down and picks up five *smooth* stones. The *brook* is found in Heb. 6: 17—20, and warbles along thus, telling its own sweet story, as I have heard many a meandering brook, as if relating its history to the shining pebbles in its channel. Hearken! "Wherein God, willing more abundantly to show unto the heirs of promise the *immutability of his counsel*, confirmed it by an oath that *by two immu-*

table things, in which it was *mpossible for God to lie,* we might have *a strong consolation,* who have fled for refuge to lay hold on the *hope* set before us: which *hope* we have as an *anchor* to the soul, both *sure* and *steadfast,* and which entereth into that within the veil; whither the forerunner is for us entered, even *Jesus,* made an high priest forever after the order of *Melchisedec.''* There! that is the *brook,* pure, clear, and sweet as the *crystal stream,* which *John* saw *welling* from under *the throne of God and of the Lamb.* — Rev. 22: 1. Let our hero, *Uttermost,* reach down into this stream, and four out of the five stones are found, before which Satan's *Impossible* cannot stand.

1. The first stone is named *Immutability;* — "*the immutability* of his counsel;" — the composition of which is, "*two immutable* things," — the *promise* and the *oath* of God. *Shout,* ye sons of the morning! Ye men of *Israel,* on this our *Elah's* mountain side, shout! Away with your *fears,* ye despairing ones! — here is a stone of *victory,* — like the *prophetic stone* of the prophet *Zechariah,* which had "*seven eyes,*" to see the *truth,* — to see *error,* — to see the *enemy* on all sides, ready for the advantage in every *difficulty,* in every emergency. This *immutability* against any *impossibility* Satan can bring into the field, any day the Lord our God has made! It is as firm and unchangeable as the hills; but the Devil's *impossibles* in matters of salvation are changeable as the *moon,* — losing their *imp-like* heads, when Jesus enters the field with his "*save-to-the-*UTTERMOST," quicker than those *changing profiles* we saw the other day among the *drifting clouds* of heaven!

2. Look for the *second stone,* which bears the inscription, "*Impossible;*" — the whole composition of which is, "*it was impossible* for God to lie!" And now let Satan and all his *impossibles* fall back before this stone, the constitu-

tion of which is, *the veracity of God!* The mountain adamant is not firmer in texture than this! Ay, this *impossible* against all the impossibles hell has ever issued!

3. The *third stone* for the sling of God's *uttermost*, we may call *Consolation;* the quality of which is "*strong consolation.*" What a *heart-comforting, heart-enlivening, heart-strengthening* quality is this! It inspires *confidence;* it excludes *doubt;* it affords the most powerful argument to *believe.* But what a *heart-breaker* to that satanic *impossibility!*

4. The fourth stone is *Hope;* — "*lay hold on the* HOPE set before us," — the hope of *present* and *eternal salvation,* which the *promise* and *oath* of God secure to those who have *fled* believingly to Christ for *refuge.* O, what a stone of succor is this! — large enough to be the *death* of that fearful *Goliath, Impossible,* and its monument beside. Large enough, at all events, to be as *an* ANCHOR *to the soul, both sure and steadfast,*—*sure* and *safe,* O ye despairing sinners! for its *anchor-hold* is fast in the promise and the oath of God, in Christ Jesus our Lord.

5. But where shall we find the *fifth stone?* Close by, in a *tributary* stream, which comes purling along from Romans 5 : 1. Behold, there it is, shining like a *diamond!* FAITH is its inscription; its substance is, "*Therefore, being justified by* FAITH, *we have peace* with God, through our Lord Jesus Christ." Hearken, O ye despairing ones! for these are the things which belong to your peace. *Hearken,* did I say? nay, but *follow* on after the Lord's *Save-to-the-uttermost,* for by this stone shall victory be given. *Impossibility* shall fall before it, as *Goliath* of old before that Heaven-directed *stone* from the sling of *David.* Behold, it is to be "*justified by faith!*" and if by faith, salvation is no more of works; and if by *faith,* why not now?

Now, then, is the hour, the moment of *salvation*. Where is that *Goliath Impossibility?* Fallen! — has measured his length on Immanuel's ground! Now, then, *Save-to-the-uttermost*, mount his carcass, and off with that *imp*-like head! Here is a sword to do it! " *The things which are* IMPOSSIBLE *to men, are* POSSIBLE *to God.*" — Luke 18:27. And there is a *spear*,— raise the severed head on that before all *Israel;* — this is the spear: "*All things are* POSSIBLE *to him that believeth.*" — Mark 9:23. Shout, ye *men* of *Israel*, shout! Rejoice, ye *despairing sinners*, rejoice! Arise! pursue the Philistine host of doubts and fears, until not one survives. They are routed and fly before you! — now is the day of salvation!

Hallelujah! "*Justified by faith.*" O, what a *power* is that! — the *little stone*, cut out of the mountain without hands, that smote the *image Impossible*, which was so great and terrible! — for it was only an *image* with the Devil in it, — that was what made it so terrible. But it is demolished now, and the day, the victory is ours.

O, bless God, ye hitherto despairing ones, for this *save-unto-the-uttermost*, and for the *five smooth stones* of the brook! That especially, "Therefore, being *justified by faith*, we have *peace with God* through our Lord Jesus Christ." And now, *establish* yourselves in Christ. Hearken! If you have been only *cheered* thus far with the brightening prospect of salvation, for Christ's sake, for your soul's sake, stand no longer there. Come on quickly, and be saved. *The prince of the power of the air* is ready to start up other *images of terror;* rapidly as the winds can roll the *clouds* along, and throng the sky with images, so can he crowd the sky of your souls with images of *terror* or of *sorrow*, as unsubstantial as they!

Hearken unto me! Open wide the eyes of your understanding, that you may see *clearly*, in this your day, the *things which belong* unto your peace.

It is not enough to believe that Christ died for you; — that *alone* cannot *save* you. *Depend* wholly upon Christ. Depend only upon his *merits* and death. Set nothing else before your eyes but Jesus Christ bleeding and dying for your sins. And, when you have gazed long enough upon that, sufficient to inspire a conscious *reliance* upon your part, then look up, and behold a living, reigning, *interceding* Jesus, at the right hand of God, — interceding for you, as your merciful *high priest*, — exalted, also, to be "*a prince* and *a Saviour.*" Rely wholly upon his *mediations* there, and the joy and gladness of a *reigning Saviour* will soon fill your every soul.

Do you understand me? Do you *all* understand me? Away with every *plea* or support besides; *weep, pray, agonize* as much as you please; but you cannot be saved unless you depend entirely upon Christ. A soul undone by sin has only Christ to rest upon; He is the ROCK, and, to borrow an idea of Young, all is *sea* besides, sinks under him, — bestorms, and then devours; but, depending only on Christ, he defies all else, and rejoices in the full assurance of a *present salvation!*

CHAPTER XXXI.

CHRIST WEEPING OVER JERUSALEM — A SERMON.

"*And when he was come near, he beheld the city and wept over it, saying, If thou hadst known, even thou, at least in this thy day, the things which belong unto thy peace! but now they are hidden from thine eyes.*"
— Luke 19 : 41, 42.

1. I LIKE this text, because it shows forth so convincingly the *benevolence* and *compassion* of our Saviour ; his *sympathy* for poor, deluded, rebellious sinners, — a gushing sympathy *unexampled* in the history of our world.

I like it, because it so well defines, so clearly intimates the *economy of God*, as regards the *free-agency* of sinners. I like to think of it after the manner of one who said : "Pitiable, indeed, must be the state of that mind which can find itself at ease to debate a question of metaphysical divinity in the presence of the Redeemer's tears. Yet, there are men whose creed has no place even for his sacred grief; who are actually annoyed at these tears wept over perishing sinners, as at heterodox variance with the divine decrees; who frown at this precious distilment of infinite love as inconsistent with their views of divine inflexibility. There are those who would rather these tears had never been shed, or that the record of this burst of divine compassion should be expunged from the sacred page, than that it should remain as an obstacle to their logical views of the divine purposes. But we linger over it with delight;

we love to remain within the softening influence, the hallowed contagion, of the Redeemer's tears." O, I do love thus to linger within this *softening influence*, — this *hallowed contagion* of our Redeemer's sympathy and tears, — may it be *contagious* to us all!

I like the text for another reason: it so well expresses the feelings of many in this audience, for poor, erring sinners. There is not a sentence or word therein in which the *heart* of Jesus may not be read; and there is not a word or sentence in it in which the *wilful sinner* may not read the emotions of our hearts: "*If thou hadst known, even thou, at least in this thy day, the things which belong unto thy peace! but now they are hidden from thine eyes.*" O, for those *interruptions* of tears, and sobs, which accompanied these utterances by our *Saviour!* But let us proceed.

2. It must be plain to most of you, by this time, that "the stranger" has not been trying to *sustain a reputation* for what is usually termed *sermonizing;* constructing his discourses after some generally approved *model*, in a tasteful and elegant manner; that he has not been preaching as if his *credit*, as a preacher, were at stake, and that must be preserved, whether sinners are saved or damned. No; this sort of thing is of but very small account with him, if so be sinners are converted to God. Nor was it of much account to the *apostles* of Jesus Christ, if we may judge of their sermons by the specimens on record.

3. *Christ* has my *heart*. It is full of *love* to him, and to the *souls* for whom he bled and died. This *love* is usually *general*, extended to all classes of sinners. Then my *style* of preaching is *general*, and my *affections* and *sympathies*, like the *sea*, spread themselves as a tide along all the general shores of mind. But *individual* minds

arrest my love, my sympathies, my zeal; then my *style individualizes* itself, so to speak, and concentrates upon them love, sympathy, zeal, like the *waves* which come with the insetting tide, dashing, lashing, and overflowing those *outstanding rocks*, until they become quite submerged; and then the waves have free course over them, and spread themselves far and wide along the sounding shore.

4. And was it not thus with the preaching of our Lord? He addressed the people by *thousands;* and his promises and threatenings rolled over the general mass, as the *sunshine* or the *thunder* over the population of a city. Nevertheless, he had a word for the *leper*, for blind *Bartimeus*, for weeping *Mary*, a message for *Zaccheus*, a reply for the *Syrophenician* woman, a conversation with *Nicodemus*, a walk with *Jairus*, a word for the young *Ruler*, for *Peter*, for the *Demoniac*, and even for *Judas;* and a *lamentation* and *tears* for *Jerusalem*, although there were many other *persons*, *villages*, and *cities*, which needed his sympathies. But how the *pronouns* spoke for the *individualizing* of his sympathies, and for *Jerusalem* in the lamentation in our text! "If *thou* hadst known, even *thou*, at least in this *thy* day, the things which belong to *thy* peace! but now they are hid from *thine* eyes." And all this interrupted with *sighs*, and *sobs*, and *tears;* for he saw its approaching *desolations*, and its impending ruin; the desolation and utter ruin of its *population* also. "The *chosen ignorance*, and *obstinate perverseness*" of its sinful people, and their *impending doom*, *wrung* his heart, and flooded his cheeks with *tears!*

5. Have you seen nothing of this among us, of late?— our burdened souls *weeping* for, and *pleading* with and for sinful men, who are doomed to hell, and yet may repent and be saved. Thus it has been, *system* or no *system*,

order or *disorder*, — our emotions carrying us over all things, straight to the mark, the heart and conscience of poor sinners!

6. *Individual cases*, you have noticed, strongly *attract* me in the pulpit. I cannot help it. A knowledge of the *facts* of a case, or the sight of my eyes, awakens my emotions, and carries away my feelings; as it would be with you to save a *drowning man*.

Nor do I *regret* this, though there is a *cross* in it; — it is called an *eccentricity* by some, and a *weakness* by others, and *low* and *undignified* by many. Yet it may be the *Lord's order*, therefore no *eccentricity;* it requires both *strength* and *courage*, therefore it is no *weakness;* and it has for its object the *high* and *noble* aim to save a soul *from death*, — to comfort the tempted and the desponding, — and to rescue the *penitent* sinner from the cruel fangs of a devouring despair; therefore it is neither *low* nor *undignified*. I give way to *duty*, to *fact*, or *impression*, and leave my *reputation* where I leave my *soul*, in the hands of Christ. And, if *individual cases* awaken my sympathies more intensely than do the general *mass* of my *hearers*, I have another consolation, — that the sad case of *Jerusalem* affected my Lord more deeply, in that weeping, lamenting hour upon one of her hills, than the case of all the other cities and villages of Israel put together.

7. A *moving panorama* has been before you since my arrival; in which have been delineated many startling things, — "*true to the life*," and you know it; — and among them have been *the things which belong to your peace;* — the *sight* thereof has moved you to *tears and earnest cries;* — has moved *me* also; — has brought hundreds of you to your knees, with cries for mercy, which have not been in vain.

But the *scenes* must be continued; — the *panorama* of *truth* must move on; — the *canvas* of the *future* must continue *unrolling*. There is still a *sound*, as in the prophet Elijah's day, "*a sound of abundance of rain*." The Lord's sign unto David, when going against the *Philistines*, is vouchsafed, after a manner, to us, — "*the sound of a going forth in the tops of the mulberry trees*," and in a *particular direction*; so we must *bestir* ourselves. We have no time to lose. Help me by your *prayers*.

I. Let "*One who is willing, any day, to oppose the pleasures of sense to the glooms of religion,*" give ear!

The *glooms* of religion! Who gave you that information? *glooms!* Satan's *libels*, perhaps! He likes to *libel* Religion. Don't you know it? — to give men *caricature representations* of it, as one said to me in Holland. Think of that!

But what do you mean by "the pleasures of *sense?*" Anything better than a polite way of expressing the pleasures of *sin?* Otherwise, the Christian has as good a right to them as yourself, and, perhaps, partakes of them as largely; — for I believe with the poet,

> " Religion never was designed
> To make our pleasures less."

No, indeed! — *innocent* pleasures, — pleasures that can be taken with a *good conscience*.

If you mean the pleasures of *sin*, why, you and I must *close* (to use a term of *wrestlers*), and grapple for the *right!* Suppose, then, such and such *habits* are *pleasurable*, as doubtless they are to you, because suitable to the *taste* of your *carnal nature:* what then? do they *cost you nothing?* Is there not considerable *expense* attending them?

But that is nothing, I suppose, if *pleasure* is the *remuneration!*

Hearken! Has *conscience* nothing to say? — never *rates* you *alone* by yourself? — never imposes any *tax* upon your enjoyments? — never intimates *eternity?* — nothing of *accountability* after death? — never urges you to *count the cost?* Never stopped to *count the cost?* — never paid any tax to the *feeling within* of *accountability* to your Maker, after death? Think! That *feeling* or principle is as certainly a part of your nature as your *liver*, or the *lungs* in your body. Nay, do not turn away! Look this question fully in the face! It is your *interest* to do so. Has it never caused *conscience* to *recoil* upon you? Have you never seriously *reckoned* with it? Know you not that these pleasures incur a *bill* of *expenses* which must be met in eternity? You may "*run tick*" *here*, but you must "foot the bill" *there*, — that is, *pay costs*, — and costs in eternity are *painful* costs, and eternal in duration; — for we believe, with the *primitive* church, that none *suffer in eternity* but those who *suffer eternally!*

The costs, sir! the *costs!* We cannot allow you to oppose "the pleasures of sense," to "the *glooms* of religion," without opposing the *eternal expenses*,—the "*eternal consequences.*" Or, as Burns has it, to whom we referred the other night,

"*Damnation of expenses!*"

There are some *hotels* where the *tables* are spread *luxuriantly*, and the *accommodations* very fine, but the *reckoning* is heavy! Now, Satan *caters* well for his *guests;* but the *reckoning!* — "Ay! there's the *rub!*" — the *reckoning!* — the *reckoning time!* — by which we mean, eternity! The *expenses!* the *expenses!* the *expenses!*

O, may the word wing its way to your heart, and to every heart in this vast assembly! Keep your seat, sinner, and *hear me out*. It will not cost you near so much as to be forced to "a hearing" in eternity,— in hell, where you will want to tell all the damned, it may be, *how* you came to be damned; for I believe with a minister of the Church of England, who told a London congregation, some time since, that in hell *sin* is its own *biographer*; — that there, too, *thought*, on the wings of *memory*, is searching forever throughout past life, and comparing the *penalty* with the *sins* which caused it! He *closed* upon the sinner, in an awful appeal, — to behold and consider how sweet a *repast* he was providing for himself in eternity.

Sinner, hear me! *Sin* is a dear morsel; and the man who would envy you its pleasures is a *fool*. "*Gold* may be bought too *dear*," was one of the lessons in our *schoolbook;* — and may we not say the same of your boasted pleasures? Would you not say the same, were you to speak right out, this moment, the sentiments of your heart? To be sure you would!

Allow a *question*. Saw you that account of a *soldier* who was tried by *court-martial* in a certain country, and was sentenced to *death*, for the crime of violating a prohibition issued to the army in occupation of the country, that the property of the citizens should be sacred and unmolested? This soldier entered a *vineyard*, and, when in the act of stealing *grapes*, was caught, and tried instantly, and condemned to be *shot*. When led out to the fatal spot where he was to die, he was observed carelessly eating the grapes he had pilfered. One of his comrades, deeply affected, and shocked besides, at his conduct, stepped up to him, and said, "*Comrade*, what do you mean? Why eat those grapes at such a time as this?" The poor fellow instantly replied, "My friend, do not *envy* me my *grapes*, for I shall pay dearly for them; —*I lose my life for them.*" Hearken! Do you anticipate the application?

Consider! What are the pleasures of which you are so enamored? What are they? Have they not been *prohibited* by Him to whom you are *accountable?* What says *conscience?* What speaks that Bible? — I mean the Bible you carry in your breast! — there is a Bible within. What saith it? What is its leading and most prominent text? What but this: "*Accountability after death.*" Is it not so? Is it altogether *silent?* Or have you succeeded in keeping it *closed*, as many do the *visible* Bible? Or have you banished it altogether from your breast, as some have the Bible from their houses? What say you? I doubt it.

But suppose you have; and you are a downright *infidel:* what then? Has it not left its main text behind, "*Accountability to God after death?*" Is it not so? Has it not become an *unowned* creed, — the creed of your heart, though you will not *own it?* Has it not made an impression upon your soul, that you cannot erase? May we not say of that *impression*, what a divine in *Switzerland* said of *conscience*, — that conscience is nothing more nor less than the *indelible imprint* of the hand of God upon the soul? The depravity of man has torn that hand from off the soul; but, on its removal, it left an *impression* behind it, which has resolved itself into a *conscience!* A fine remark that!

Let me still inquire after the *original* text of your *nature*, — or Nature's Bible, — "*Accountability after death.*" What has become of it? Have you denied its *truthfulness?* — *silenced* its intimations? — torn it from off your heart? Have you? With what results? Are you bettered at all? Has it not left an *imprint* behind, as troublesome as your original creed? — an *impression* of coming and *terrible perdition*, as a consequence of what you esteem "the pleasures of sense;" — and the impression thereof as *certain*, — *man, know thyself!* — as *certain* as the impression of *coming death*, left by that *court-martial sentence* upon that *soldier's* mind, — which he felt all the while he was eating those stolen grapes on the way to the place of *execution*, where, poor fellow, he gathered up a dozen *rifle-balls* into his *heart!*

Would to God, you were as *candid* with *us*, and with your *fellow-sinners*, as that condemned soldier! — "My friend, do not envy me my grapes, for I shall pay *dearly* for them; I lose my life for them." — "My friends, do not envy me my *pleasures*, for I shall pay dearly for them; *I lose my soul for them.*" Be candid, then, be candid! The *leper* of old was obliged to give warning to persons approaching, lest they might be smitten with his *leprosy*. "*Unclean! Unclean! Unclean!*" was his cry of warning. Do you *understand* me?

Another question: how does a life of *godliness*, with all its *imagined* "*glooms*," compare with such a life as you are leading? — *inward life*, as well as *outward?* What think you? *Think!* for *God's* sake, — for your *soul's* sake, think! — think, ere it be too late! Think, *when* and *where* thinking may do you good. In *hell* there is *thinking* plenty; but it does them no good, — it only *aggravates* their sorrows, — it only *accents* and *enhances* their misery! This is all I have to say to you, and through you to the class to which you belong. *Therein* you have beheld some of *the things which belong unto your peace*. Consider them well; and may God grant you repentance unto life.

II. The *attention* of "AN UNAWAKENED SINNER" is now requested.

"*Unawakened,*" — what are we to understand by that? *Dr. Scott* defines it to be, "*not roused* from *spiritual slumber* or stupidity." *Sad state*, if your *peril* be what the Scriptures represent it to be. *Strange state*, under present circumstances, when there is so *much* to awaken, and so *many* awakened, and such tokens of a *general* awakening, — so much *noise and stir* of the *truly awakened;* — greater, I imagine, than that which drew the attention of the *blind beggar* on Jericho's highway-side! — which awakened his shrill cry, "*Jesus*, thou son of David, have *mercy* on me!" He was awake *then*, however fast asleep he had been before!

Well, when you are thoroughly *awakened*, should that ever take place in this world, and God grant that it may, your cry may be somewhat similar, and as *loud!* — ay, *loud* as the *cries for mercy* which saluted your ears last night; — unless it may happen that you awaken not until the gates of eternity are just opening to receive you! Then, alas! you may be too weak to make much noise; but your misery and terror may be none the less. May you be awakened to see *the things which belong to your peace*, before that extremity arrives.

Hearken unto me, and consider whether it is not *strange* that you remain "*unawakened*," that is, in a state of *spiritual sleep*, or profound indifference, regarding your soul.

Think a little! Holy Spirit, help this eternity-bound sinner to think a little! My prayer is heard! It shall be so. I have faith you shall be *awakened* this night, whether you will or no. *Jesus* will plead in heaven for you, and the *Holy Ghost* will speak in your conscience, while my poor voice rings through all the chambers of your soul, as surely as it now *rings* through every corner and turn of this crowded house of God.

What shall I say? — *Spirit of God*, help me! — Say! What words more fit than those employed by one who is now in the eternal world? — and the *sinner*, in whose ear they reverberated, is in the world of spirits also.

Hear the words. Let them sink deep into thy heart. They were after this manner: "Think! does a *sleepy soul* beseem your *dangerous* condition? Can you *sleep* with such a load of *sin* upon your soul? Can you *sleep* under the *thundering threatenings* of God? — under the *curse* of his *law*? — with so many wounds in your *conscience*, and *ulcers* in your soul? — with the crawling vipers of *sin* in your nature? If *thorns, toads,* and *adders,* were in your bed, would they not keep you waking? But how much more odious and dangerous a thing is sin! If you had a sick body, sick as Job, could you sleep? An aching *tooth* can keep you awake; and is not the guilt of sin more grievous? If your *body* wants meat, or drink, or covering, that will break your sleep. Is it nothing, then, that your *soul* is destitute of *grace?* A *condemned* man will be easily kept awake; but you, being unregenerate, are condemned already; and yet you sleep; you sleep in *irons;* in the *captivity* of the devil; among the *walking judgments of God;* in a life that is still expecting an end; in a boat that is swiftly carried to eternity; just at the entrance of another world, and that world *hell;* ay, hell it will be, unless grace awake you out of that *hell-inspired* sleep! Going to see the *face of God*, the face of *angels*, or the face of *devils*, and asleep! To be with one or other for ever and ever, and asleep!"

What think you of such questions? How strange a thing, then, that you can remain asleep in sin! Where has *Satan* found a *pillow* soft enough, or so *charmed*, as to maintain *sleep* under *such circumstances?* God himself standing over you; angels watching you; devils waiting upon you; hell moving from beneath, with its flames, to receive and engulph you!

Well might one say, "As wisely might you sleep on the *pinnacle* of a steeple in a *storm*, as be spiritually asleep in such a dangerous position as this. But, if you are asleep," he added, "your *spiritual enemies* are not asleep; — you are asleep in the thickest of your *foes!* — asleep, and the devil rocking your *cradle!*" And for what purpose? To keep you asleep until your eternal interests are all ruined; till, like Judas, you grow into a devil, and then, by permission of Heaven, drive you hence among devils!

Asleep! O, *Christ* awaken you! May the *Holy Ghost* awaken you now! Asleep, like those with the *oil-less* lamps, mentioned in Matt. 25: 5. Awake, O sinful soul, *awake, and Christ shall give thee light!* — Ephes. 5: 14. Awake! arise from the *sleeping* and the *dead* in sin, that you perish not, nor awake in hell, where they have never any more rest, nor sleep, throughout eternity!

Be *assured,* these are the very *things which belong unto thy peace.* O, that I could get nearer unto you! Be it so that you *weep* not when we *weep: Jerusalem* wept not when *Jesus wept;* yet, for all that, he wept on, and bewailed its coming desolations. Jerusalem had no wish but that Jesus might be crucified and die; yet, for all that, he could exclaim, "*If thou hadst known, even thou, at least in this thy day, the things which belong unto thy peace! but now they are hid from thine eyes.*"

III. A *few words to another*, whom I shall name "*A Presumer*," — that is, one who *ventures* his soul upon a *false ground of confidence,* — the *mercy* of God, but living at the same time in *wilful rebellion* against him! — who makes the plea of *Christ's dying,* a reason for *his sinning,* — God's *forbearance* a motive for his *impenitence;* — the exact brother of him, of whom it was said, a long while ago, that, *spider-like,* he sucked *poison* out of the sweet flower of God's *mercy,* — and boldly plucked *death* from the tree of *life,* and through *presumption* went to hell; — yes! went down to hell by the same *ladder* of *Christ's blood,* by which the saints of God ascend into heaven, and by which many a penitent sinner here ascends out of the *horrible pit* and *miry clay* up into the light of day, and the sunshine of God's reconciled countenance! Alas! unfortunate man, he *reversed* the ladder, and stepped down by it into the pit that is *bottomless,* — for, he made the *plea* of Christ's dying, the *cause* of his perishing. St. Paul hints that "*the goodness of God*" should "lead us to *repentance.*" Alas, it only led him to *presumption!* The man *hoped* himself to hell, and was *damned by mistake!*

Hearken! Are you going to hell in the same way? Must one more be added to hell's *wailers,* and that one yourself?

Man! *listen* to me! Nearly *two hundred* years ago one of your English divines appealed to a certain sinner thus: "Verily, if sin had not turned the ungodly part of the world into a *bedlam,* where it is no wonder to see a man out of his wits, people would run out in wonder into the streets, and call to one another, ' Come, and see a man that can trifle and sport away his time as he is going to *eternity,* and is ready to enter another world! Come, and see a man that hath but a few days to win or lose his *soul* forever in, and is playing it away at cards or dice, or wasting it in doing nothing! Come, and see a man that hath hours to spare upon *trifles,* with heaven and hell before his eyes!'"

Did you hear all that? Do you perceive how *applicable* it is to yourself?

Hear what a divine in France said to one of your brethren: "Can you deny that God has *borne* with you? — that you have deserved *punishment?* — that he has *forborne* to punish you? No, you cannot! And *why* has he not? Is it because he *connives* at sin? No; for he *detests* and *hates* it, and *opposes* it everywhere. Is it because he is ignorant of your vices? No; for his eyes pierce the innermost recesses of your soul. Point me to the most *secret stain* of your life, — did that elude his inspection? Nay, verily! no more than any other of your manifold transgressions. *Why*, then, does God *bear* with you? Not, surely, for want of *power* to punish. No, no! He holds the *thunders* in his right hand, the *forked lightnings* in his grasp; at his command hell opens, and the fallen angels wait his *permission* to carry thy soul to his abodes." What says your *conscience* to all this? Can you deny? Dare you treat it with contempt?

But that *French divine* could have well afforded to go further. If God has *forborne* to do this and that, is it not because you have *an Advocate with the Father, Jesus Christ, the righteous?* The *result* has been all that you have experienced of the *long-suffering* and *forbearance* of God, — not "*slackness*," sir! St. Peter spurns that insinuation, and *hurls* the word back upon those that forged it, with these words appended: "— the Lord is *long-suffering, not willing any* should *perish*, but that *all* should come to *repentance*." — 2 Peter 3: 9. There! you have the *secret* why you are out of *hell*. It is a *reprieve* you have had; but if you suppose a *reprieve* is a *pardon*, you and your *reason* have dissolved partnership!

Hearken, and consider, I beseech you! Mark that word

"*repentance*," in the last Scripture quoted; for in that word is comprised much of *those things which belong unto your peace*.

But, alas! if now, in this *your day of grace*, those things are *hidden from your eyes*, as from Jerusalem sinners of old, what more can we do, than, like Jesus on the Mount of *Olives, weep* over you, and *bewail* your coming *miseries*, and say, "If *thou* hadst known, even *thou*, at least in this *thy day*, the *things* which belong unto thy *peace!* but now they are *hidden* from thine eyes"? Let us *pray*.

CHAPTER XXXII.

CHRIST WEEPING OVER JERUSALEM—A SERMON.

"And when he was come near, he beheld the city, and wept over it, saying, If thou hadst known, even thou, at least in this thy day, the things which belong unto thy peace! but now they are hid from thine eyes."— Luke 19 : 41, 42.

1. "*And when he was come near, he beheld the city, and wept over it;* "— as I should, when drawing near to a certain sinner in this audience, who names himself "*One of the finally impenitent, without trembling.*" Ah! if he can so consider himself, without *trembling*, it would ill become me, I think, to consider his deplorable case without *weeping*. What does my *audience* think?

2. Allow me *one observation* just here. It is this: my remarks, my appeals, my cries, my exhortations, my expostulations, perhaps my *tears*, in behalf of that *impenitent one*, this night, will apply more or less to *every impenitent sinner* in this audience; — because, dying as you are, you will just meet as speedy and as sure a damnation, whether you *tremble* or not. Every soul of you, therefore, is interested and involved in what I am going to say; — just as every *city and village* in Israel was involved in *this lamentation,* and those *tears* of Jesus, which accompanied his prediction of the overthrow of *Jerusalem*.

Hearken unto me, therefore, every one of you, while I address *that sinner* in your midst.

3. So, then, you are "*One of the finally impenitent, without trembling.*" And do you glory in that dreadful fact, if it be a *fact?* Is it a matter to be "laughed at," or worthy of self-congratulation? Is it a good reason why you should *trifle* with those who are *weeping* over their *own wretched state,* or with those who would *weep over your coming miseries,* so as to make them your *jest* and your *byword?* If you have sinned away the *grace* of God, have you sinned away your *sense* and *reason* also? — *doffed* the *man,* and, like Judas, become a *devil,* while still an inhabitant of the body? God forbid!

Had you been present the other night, and witnessed a man *delirious* with *fever,* on the brink of death, surrounded by weeping friends, and he laughing at them, and calling them "a parcel of fools," and boasting he was as well and as safe as any of them, — would you not have *pitied* him? would you have wondered that the *tears* of his friends poured down their cheeks like rain? The *application* is so plain, no further remarks are necessary.

4. And you can believe yourself "One of the finally impenitent, without *trembling;*" — so, you have a sturdier intellect than devils, for it is said in the Scriptures, "The *devils* also *believe* and *tremble.*" — James 2 : 19. But *why* do they tremble? Because they *believe. What* do they believe? All that the Scriptures speak about hell and the day of judgment. *Why* do they believe? Because they *see* and *feel* that God is already *fulfilling* his threatenings upon the *damned* in hell; — and, from this fact, they *infer,* they *believe* that the *other threatenings* shall yet have as exact a fulfilment, and they *tremble.*

Are you *wiser* than devils? Well, well, they *tremble* now, because they both *see* and *feel;* but *your trembling time* is to come. When you shall *see* and *feel* what they do, you shall *tremble* also. Would it not be *wiser* in you to tremble *now?* But how can you, if *the things which belong unto your peace are hidden from your eyes?* O, that you may both *see* and *feel* and *tremble*, before you leave this temple of our God!

5. O, that power from on high may be given me in this hour to apply the *steel* of my text to your *conscience*, if yet it be not *too late!* — "And when he was come near, he beheld the city, and *wept* over it, saying, If thou hadst known, even thou, at least in this thy day, the things which belong unto thy peace! but now they are *hid from* thine eyes." I was once struck with the remark of one on this text; he said it was a wish, containing several peculiar *darts.* 1st. Thou *hast known.* 2d. Thou *mightest know now*, if thou *wouldst.* 3d. Thou *dost not know.* Or, thus: 1st. Thou *hast had a day of grace.* 2d. The day of grace has not yet ended in *night.* 3d. Thou hast not *improved* the day of grace. 4th. But thou *mightest* have improved it; — there was nothing to *hinder* thee from improving it, — no *unchangeable decree* to prevent thee; — it has not been thy *fate* but thy folly that has prevented. 5th. But soon it will be forever *too late;* — the hour is nigh at hand when thy day of grace shall be turned into night; — the *measure of thy iniquity* being nearly full; — what more? — he burst into a flood of tears, and wept over the infatuated city.

Allow a question: could you *honestly* deny the applicability of some of these "darts" to yourself?

6. And yet another question. It is this: whether the sinners of *Jerusalem* were not in that fearful hour approaching the crisis of some *terrible sin?* — not so much in the *crucifixion* of him who was now *weeping* over them; no; but against the *Holy Ghost*, and his *closing influences*. This is an important question, just here, and has a *close*

application to the person I am addressing. Hearken to that awful declaration of Him whom you now behold weeping over Jerusalem; — *hearken!* O, that you might *believe*, and *weep*, and *tremble!* — *"Verily, I say unto you, All manner of sin and blasphemy shall be forgiven unto men; but the blasphemy against the Holy Ghost shall not be forgiven unto men. And whosoever speaketh a word against the Son of man, it shall be forgiven him; but whosoever speaketh against the Holy Ghost, it shall not be forgiven him, neither in this world, neither in the world to come."* - - A terrible denunciation, and most solemnly commented upon thus, by a late writer. Hearken to him! " What form of denunciation can be conceived more calculated than this to warn the *trifler* that he is on holy ground, and to bespeak for the whole doctrine of divine influence the reverence of a prostrate soul ? The sin denounced is, probably, *the rejection of the last and greatest evidence of the Messiahship of Christ — the dispensation of the Spirit.* Up to that point of unbelief, the Jews were within the reach of forgiveness. Their blasphemy against Christ, — their rejection of all the evidence arising from his character, his miracles, the testimony of John, and the distinct fulfilment in him of numerous prophecies, — even the act of nailing him to the cross, — all this did not consummate their guilt, and render their condition hopeless. It was, indeed, approaching as near to the *edge of the precipice* as possible, without actually falling over. It was closing their eyes against evidence which ought to have convinced them that Christ was the Messiah; but still there was *further evidence* to be submitted to them, and evidence of a superior kind. The miraculous dispensation of the Holy Spirit, attesting, as it would, his resurrection from the dead, and his exaltation at the right hand of God, and bringing, as it would, the right arm of Omnipotence visibly to certify his claims, was reserved for that closing proof. Till that should be found unavailing, their impenitence could not be pronounced *final*. But should they reject *that* they would be resisting the last proof that would be given that Christ is the Son of God, and the Saviour of sinners; with their own hands, they would have subscribed the sentence which doomed them to perdition; they would have added the final shade of horror to their condition, anticipating 'the blackness of darkness forever.'" Can you think of their case without a *shudder?*

7. How terrible the thought that your *untrembling impenitence* may proceed from a sin like this! Then is it *final* indeed! Alas! alas for thee, if it is so! No longer do *angels* wait with trembling expectation of seeing you at the footstool of mercy a trembling and anxious penitent. No, no! but rather in fearful anticipation of seeing you posted off to hell without ceremony.

And, O, what shall I say more? How can I express it? — but I *must*, and O for a *flood of tears* while I say it, — the weeping and trembling souls of the lost in hell are expecting your speedy arrival, and are hearkening for your final plunge into perdition, and your *cries* filling the vaults of hell with their reverberations.

This is *harsh;* but did not *Jesus* speak of *outer darkness*, and *weeping and wailing and gnashing of teeth?* Did not the voice of *Dives* in hell reach the ears of Abraham in heaven, calling for a drop of water to cool his tongue? Prove that such scenes no longer occur in hell, and I will admit that the cries and *reverberations* of the damned are a fancy.

But you are yet in the *body!* You are not yet in hell. Thanks be unto our God for that! If they have waited in expectation of your damnation, they have waited as yet in vain! You are among your *friends* yet, and not among *fiends*. *Hope* has not departed from my heart, regarding your salvation. The fact of your being *alive* and *here* inspires me with a *trust* that the Holy Spirit has not done knocking at the door of your heart, and while he *knocks* there is hope that the door will yet open, and that you may be saved!

But is this hope *well founded?* If so, with uplifted hands I would thank God, that though you are on *the edge of the precipice*, you have not yet gone over it. *Terrible,* and almost *hopeless,* as that precipice is, you may be saved on its very brink!

8. Do you inquire, "what precipice?" Do you not understand? — that which all but constitutes a sinner a *final impenitent;* — that upon which the sinners of Jerusalem stood when Jesus lifted up his voice and wept; — that *wilful* and *obstinate,* and *invincible resistance* of the *Holy Ghost,* carried to a point beyond which there is no forgiveness; — a rejection of the claims of God, under some overpowering and convincing *illuminations;* — when the demands of the Spirit for *repentance* and *faith* are rejected, not twice nor thrice, but many times, and, at length, *once too much!*

Jerusalem sinners were approaching the *edge of this* precipice, — were as near to it as possible without falling over it, when Jesus "*wept*" over their almost irrecoverable condition.

9. Now you understand me! But it may be thus with *you.* O, that I could weep over you as Jesus did over *Jerusalem sinners!*

10. *Understand me further.* I do not dispute the *orthodoxy* of the title, "One of the finally impenitent, without

trembling." I mean, so far as it regards the *possibility* of such a state of soul in a *living man*. For, did I not believe that *final impenitence* takes place *in this life*, — always *in this* life, — I would turn *Papist*, so far at least as to believe in a *purgatory* after death. But this I reject, and consequently must believe that the dreadful state is consummated here, *in this world;* that the *impenitence* that is *final*, and which damns eternally, occurs in this life, and not after the soul leaves the body. But how *long* before the soul departs, ere its moral state is *final*, — a *moment*, a *month*, or a *year*, — it becomes not man to determine. Such ground is too sacred and awful for *speculative* theology. There is a *last moment*, and a *first*, unquestionably; a *last moment* when the sinner is not "a *final* impenitent," and a *first moment* when he is; and that last moment *belongs to this life;* after that it is *eternity*, and no man can be damned eternally till his *impenitence* has become final. But to decide dogmatically that such a *last moment* is the moment that severs the soul from the body, is *gratuitous*, — that is, *an assertion without proof*, or to *beg the question*.

The question, therefore, remains open; and God alone can decide it. It may take place in the last hour, and it may hours or days previously, for aught that God has revealed to the contrary. It therefore becomes us to be *modest* in our decisions upon such a fearful question; — in the mean time, to keep our eyes open to the *history of facts* among *living* and *dying* sinners. But to abandon this strong position of our Protestant religion is to grant to the *Papacy* all it claims in behalf of its *purgatorial dogma*.

11. Hearken! Aside from your experience, I have no controversy with the *tense* or the *orthodoxy* of your sen-

timent. But, O, I would humbly contest its *truthfulness* with regard to yourself. As the truth of Jesus is in my heart, I believe you may be saved, and *now*. Give way, I beseech you, to the strivings of the Holy Spirit of God. Cry unto God for mercy, and see how soon this snare of the devil will be broken!

Hearken to me! In the name of a *risen Jesus*, I offer you *mercy* through his blood. If you *wish* it; if you *desire* it; if you say, "Would to God it were mine;" if you hate sin, and desire *pardon* above every *boon* here below; then is the Spirit of God with you, to *save*, and secure your salvation!

12. Hearken! Were you stretched on your *death-bed*, and such feelings were *rife* in your heart, I would do the same. And, alas! — and my *heart* sinks, and my tongue *falters* at what I am going to say, — were you *dying*, and not one such *feeling* or *wish* within your *impenitent* breast, I would still whisper in your ear the *promises* of the Gospel. O, I would! I would! I surely would, for I believe with *Dr. Chalmers*, — and my heart *sinks* again, and *lower*, in attempting to repeat his sentiment, and I could weep again over you, — that, to the *last moment* of every man's life, it is the duty of every minister of Christ to urge upon the *dying sinner* the *largeness* and *freeness* of the Gospel; and to assure him that there is not a *deed of wickedness* with which his *faithful memory* now agonizes him, nor one *habit of disobedience* that now clothes the *retrospect* of the *past* in the sad coloring of despair, and which spreads a deeper marble upon the *future*, but what God through Christ will pardon, if he find *faith* and *repentance* in his heart, and a *willingness* to come to Christ; but we may urge this with *every tone of tenderness*, and there may be *truth* in our every utterance; but

it is not to say that our voice will reach him, or make a *resistless way* through the *avenues* of that *heart*, where he has done so much to rear a *defending barrier*, which may now prove to be *impenetrable;* the *truth* of God may fall upon his ear, but the *Spirit* may refuse to accompany it to the heart; an *inveterate blindness* may have long ago gathered upon his soul, that he will neither *receive* the truth nor *love* it, by which a man's heart is softened down into repentance. Thus, while the blood of Christ cleanseth the *believing penitent*, the sin against the Holy Ghost shall not be forgiven, because that with *this sin* and its *consequences* upon him, he *wills not*, he *repents not*, he *believes not,*—*all* of which are necessary in order to receive *pardon*. This, adds the doctor, is the reason that the *word of faith* may fall from the lips of the minister, and the *work of faith* be left undone by the *dying sinner;* and that it is not in the *malefactor's cell*, but in the comfortable *dying* room that *salvation* may be freely offered, and be sadly and sullenly put away. He *wills* not, *repents* not, *believes* not; but without these there can be no *remission of sins;* but with these, *pardon* has never been denied to the *greatest sinners*, nor for *sins* of the *deepest dye.*

13. Have you heard, understood and weighed all this? In this hasty reference to the sentiments of *Dr. Chalmers* on the subject, I have not been able to give you his exact words; but if you wish, you may read his sermon on "*The sin against* the Holy Ghost," one of the most *powerful, convincing* and *alarming* appeals, on that awful subject, which I know of in the English language. And I would say with him, and beat it into the ears of every sinner within the sound of my voice, that, grant that a man has *repentance and faith* in his heart, and we know not a single crime in the whole catalogue of human depravity

that the atoning blood of our Saviour cannot wash away; that there does not sit this night, within the walls of this house, a *desperado* in *vice*, so sunk in the depths of his dark and unnatural depravity, that is not welcome to come to Christ, if he *repent* and believe; nor will he ever find, nor any human being thus furnished, the *crimson inveteracy* of his *manifold offences* beyond the *peace-speaking* and *purifying blood* of the Son of God.

14. But hearken! St. John says, "*There is a sin unto death. I do not say that he shall pray for it; all unrighteousness is sin, and there is a sin not unto death.*" — 1 John 5: 16, 17. What is that but another "*blue light*," thrown up in the moral heavens, *signalizing* a *sin* that is followed by *damnation?* "Another blue light!" exclaims one; "are there others of the same sort?" *To be sure there are!* — the sin against the Holy Ghost, as announced by our Lord, in Matt. 12: 31, 32. And in Mark 3: 28, 29. And, to set the matter out of the way of dispute, that recorded in Heb. 6: 4—8: "*For it is impossible for those who were once enlightened, and have tasted of the heavenly gift, and were made partakers of the Holy Ghost, and have tasted the good word of God, and the powers of the world to come; if they shall fall away, to renew them again to repentance; seeing they crucify to themselves the Son of God afresh, and put him to an open shame. For the earth, which drinketh in the rain that cometh oft upon it, and bringeth forth herbs meet for them by whom it is dressed, receiveth blessing from God: but that which beareth thorns and briars is rejected, and is nigh unto cursing; whose end is to be burned.*" *Tremble,* thou *finally impenitent!* — tremble, if thou canst, at the *burning* that is to come. It is "*the wrath to come!*" "*the wrath to come!*" "*the*

wrath to come!" Tremble in view of it. *Devils tremble.* Are you *stronger* than they? See *yonder.* I behold a *trembler!* Look up, thou penitent sinner! Behold the Lamb of God, that takes away thy sins!

15. Hearken! Behold that *blue light* projected by St. Paul, from Heb. 10: 26, 29: "*For if we sin wilfully after that we have received the knowledge of the truth, there remaineth no more sacrifice for sins, but a certain fearful looking for of judgment, and fiery indignation, which shall devour the adversaries. He that despised Moses' law died without mercy under two or three witnesses: of how much sorer punishment, suppose ye, shall he be thought worthy*"—[O, my God! what *sorer punishment* than to die *without mercy?* Surely we must go into eternity to find it. *Hush,* my soul! repeat clearly *the word of God*] — "*of how much sorer punishment, suppose ye, shall he be thought worthy, who hath trodden under foot the Son of God, and hath counted the blood of the covenant, wherewith he was sanctified, an unholy thing, and* HATH DONE DESPITE TO THE SPIRIT OF GRACE?" Ay, that was the *finishing act* of his depravity, — doing "*despite to the Spirit of grace!*" It was that that *sealed his perdition; wilful sin* against the *Spirit of grace,* and under *superior illumination,* cut off all hope of reconciliation, and *quenched* the *last spark of grace,* and *the last desire of salvation.*

16. And now, tremble at the sight of another, and, perhaps, last *blue light* of warning, O, all ye who can tremble! who are capable of trembling, — whose *mortal sensibilities* may force you to tremble!

Hearken! Upon the bed of *mortal agony* lay the wreck of as sturdy a sinner as this congregation presents, about to die, — and he knew it. His *distress* was very great; more in *mind*, however, than in body. He was urged to pray: — "I pray! I cannot pray. I know *myself*, my inherent *wickedness*. The damning conviction is burned in on my heart, that, should I recover my health, I would fall into the same *courses;* I am quite certain of it. Why, then, appeal to the *invisible?* Why insult Heaven with vain promises of amendment, which I *could never keep*,— would not keep were I to survive? Why play the *hypocrite* here? Why lie to God, when, if there is such a being, I must in all human probability appear before him in *half an hour*, — when no *lie* can serve me?" He *departed* full of *misery*.

17. Sinner, thou that hast styled thyself "One of the finally impenitent, without trembling," I have had *hopes* of your salvation all along; the cry of my heart, amidst all my words, has been, "*If thou hadst known, even thou, at least in this thy day, the things which belong unto thy peace!*" and a hope that *now*, at *last*, those things, *flashing so vividly* before your *intellectual* eyes, may have opened them, so that you could not help *seeing* them, and *feeling* them too. I have done what I could to this end; must close soon. I did intend to have addressed some others, — backsliders and penitents, — but must defer it till another time. Your sad case, with a *hope* of reaching your understanding and conscience, have borne me along.

18. And now, with a drooping heart, *sad, sad* am I to say what I am going to say; but it is the *steel* of my text, and it must be applied, — applied in *hope*, and in full view of Calvary, and of the offered mercy of God in Christ Jesus, if you will but repent and believe. And a *cheering ray* darts into my heart, that, if you will not, there are scores of others who will.

Well, let me proceed with what I was going to say. If

your case be really such as you represent it to be, it will not be long before you are among the *tremblers* of hell. For, if "*the devils believe and tremble,*" I cannot help thinking that all the damned in hell believe and tremble also. If this be so, you can hardly expect to be *exempted*. O, may God in mercy interfere and prevent it! But if you *tremble* not *now* in view of things, your trembling must begin *hereafter;* ay, when "*the cup of trembling*" shall be put into your hands, — "*the cup of his indignation,*" as St. John describes it, — filled with "*the wine of the wrath of God;*" and all around you "*fire and brimstone, and smoke and torment,*" "*the holy angels and the Lamb*" in the far-off distance; and "*no rest*" anywhere (Rev. 14: 9, 10, 11); and, all above, beneath, around, scenes such as a poet attempted to describe. Hear him! Mercy prevent that *catastrophe!* But if it must come to pass, then it must; and when once there, — lost — lost — eternally lost, — and you begin to look around, and behold, —

"Eternal justice! sons
Of God! tell me, if ye can, what then
I saw, what then I heard. Wide was the place,
And deep as wide, and ruinous as deep.
Beneath I saw a lake of burning fire,
With tempest tost perpetually, and still
The waves of fiery darkness 'gainst the rocks
Of dark damnation broke, —
And all around, wind warred with wind, storm howled
To storm, and lightnings, forked lightnings crossed
And thunder answered thunder, muttering sounds
Of sullen wrath; and far as sight could pierce,
Or down descend in caves of hopeless depth,
Through all that dungeon of unfading fire,
I saw miserable beings walk,
Burning continually, yet unconsumed;
Forever wasting, yet enduring still;

Dying perpetually, yet never dead ;
Some wandered lonely in the desert flames,
And some in fell encounter fiercely met,
With curses loud, and blasphemies, that made
The cheek of darkness pale ; and as they fought,
And cursed, and gnashed their teeth, and wished to die,
Their hollow eyes did utter streams of woe.

And there were groans that ended not, and sighs
That always sighed, and tears that ever wept,
And ever fell, but not in Mercy's sight.

  *   *   *   *

And, as I listened, I heard these beings curse
Almighty God, and curse the Lamb, and curse
The Earth, the Resurrection morn, and seek,
And ever vainly seek, for utter death.
And to their everlasting anguish still
The thunders from above responding spoke
These words, which through the caverns of perdition
Forlornly echoing, fell on every ear —
' Ye knew your duty, but ye did it not.'
And back again recoiled a deeper groan.
A deeper groan ! O, what a groan was that !

  *   *   *   *

' Ye knew your duty, but ye did it not.'
Dread words ! that barred excuse, and threw the weight
Of every man's perdition on himself
Directly home.

' Ye knew your duty, but ye did it not.'
These were the words which glowed upon the sword,
Whose wrath burned fearfully behind the cursed,
As they were driven away from God to Tophet.

' Ye knew your duty, but ye did it not.'
These are the words to which the harps of grief
Are strung ; and, to the chorus of the damned,
The rocks of hell repeat them evermore,
Loud echoing through the caverns of despair,
And poured in thunder on the ear of Woe.

  *   *   *   *

And suddenly before my eyes
A wall of fiery adamant sprung up,—
Wall mountainous, tremendous, flaming high
Above all flight of hope.

* * * *

Upon that burning wall,
In horrible emblazonry, were limned
All shapes, all forms, all modes of wretchedness,
And prominent in characters of fire,
Where'er the eye could light, these words you read :
' Who comes this way, behold, and fear to sin.' "

Ay! and high above all that horrible emblazonry, limned upon hell's high and flaming wall, and prominent in characters of fire, are — what more ? — " *a mother's prayers !* " Ay, a mother's prayers ! O God ! touch that heart, and touch it *now ;* — make it tremble now ! — a mother's prayers, prominent in characters of fire ; — more terrible, more horrifying, more distressing to the soul of a *lost son*, than all the shapes, forms and modes of wretchedness prevalent in hell.

O, my soul, hear the word of the Lord ! O, ye sinners, hear ye the words of the Lord ! — Isaiah 33 : 14. " *The sinners in Zion are afraid; fearfulness hath surprised the hypocrites. Who among us shall dwell with the devouring fire ? who among us shall dwell with everlasting burnings?* "

In view of such a terrible perdition awaiting the ungodly, let us *awake to righteousness. Flee from the wrath to come !* " *The smoke of their torment ascendeth up for ever and ever !* " — or hell's " deeper groan," responding to those fearful words, —

" Ye knew your duty, but ye did it not."

There is *mercy* for every one of you, who is disposed to

seek it, by repentance and faith. *Jesus hath died for you*, that you need never taste the bitter pains of eternal death. His atoning *blood* was shed for you. O, then, plead the merits of that blood, and escape that death that never, never dies! May the *Holy Spirit* help you!

CHAPTER XXXIII.

SATANIC POLICY.

In the preceding chapters, some idea may be formed of Mr. Caughey's *public life;* in the succeeding chapters, the reader will have a view of his *private* life. In one, we behold him before his *fellow-men;* in the other, before his *God*, and the *bar of his own conscience;—faithfulness* to his *fellow-men* in the *pulpit*, and *faithfulness* to his own *soul* in *private*,— a necessary discipline to every minister, who desires to *save himself and those who hear him.*

Solomon says, "*As in water face answereth to face, so the heart of man to man;*" so we have no doubt that the earnest *minister* of the Gospel will see much of his own *experience*, in *revival conflicts*, reflected in that of *Mr. Caughey.*

The reader, also, while perusing these pages, will learn something of the *conflicts* which assail a minister, while engaged in promoting a revival, even under very favorable and successful circumstances; and may also judge of what he endures in seasons of *reverse*, or *comparative failure.* He will also, we trust, learn how to *feel* for such, and to sympathize with them in their *arduous* work; — in their great battles for truth and souls.

The reader has already followed Mr. Caughey to Birmingham. He commenced his labors there, in *Newton Row*

Chapel, early in *December*, 1845; and visited in succession, all the Wesleyan chapels in the town, preaching six sermons a week until the following *May*. A glimpse of his *spiritual tactics*, during that time, may be seen in the following items from his journal.

Birmingham, December 5. — Every nation under heaven has its *history*, printed or traditional; and every year adds something thereunto. Every *evangelist*, or *revivalist*, has *his* history; and every *campaign* adds something interesting to its pages. J. C. has his! "*Happy* the *nation* that has *nothing for history*," said a *Frenchman*. Not so, says a *soul-saving* preacher; — *unhappy* for him, if he has nothing for *history!* I like to *note* down events as they occur to myself or others; — to plant my *batteries of truth*, and work them with all the energy God bestows, and mark the *effects*. This is *advantageous* to me in many respects: — can do so much easier, when I stay some time in a place, than during such hasty visits, as to *Chesterfield, Doncaster, Macclesfield*, &c.

December 6. — Throwing light on the *Devil's game* with sinners. He likes to play with them in the *dark;* — one reason, I suppose, why his kingdom is called *darkness*, and his power "*the power of darkness;*" because it is by *darkness* both his kingdom and power exist, and are increased and exercised. But *light* is the antagonist of darkness. Christ's kingdom is a kingdom of light, and his *power* is exerted in and through light. O, for more light! — yet, ever remembering that the preacher, that would effect anything, must *burn* as well as *shine.* — John 5: 35.

Satan conducts his *game* with sinners in the dark, and their *stake* is the *soul;* his *cards* are such as, "Religion is gloomy;—there is no danger now;—be not righteous overmuch, why shouldst thou destroy thyself? — No *need* of all this *ado*, this *stir*, and *fright* ; — God is better than is represented ; — is it not written he is *merciful*, and will not keep his anger forever ? — Leave such gloomy subjects ; — *sin* is better than *sorrow* ; — its *pleasures* are preferable to the *glooms* of religion ; — morality is an easy resource at any time ; — morality is a good enough religion ; — morality you can understand, and not this and this, being born again, and such other mystical problems ; — if those who profess to believe in such things are *safe*, so are you, considering how they live." I need a greater *blaze* of truth to flash over these things.

St. Paul speaks of men being *led captive* by the *Devil* at his will. How few *serve* him because they *love* him ; or would *follow* him, or be *led* by him, through a *fondness* for his *company*, or to have his *favor*, or to dwell in the place of his *captivity* ! — not one, perhaps, in Birmingham. The *foulest* sinner in town expects to give him the slip at some sharp corner, and escape from him forever !

How few of all these active and resisting sinners believe that they have taken up *arms* for the *Devil* ; — that they are fighting for him, and that he is their *general!* Not one. They are only doing the things which please and gratify *themselves* ; and, if it please Satan, it only *happens* so without their intention. Satan knows all this very well ; and does not thank them that he is their master. But this is a part of his policy. He keeps them in the *dark* for this very purpose.

It is not so with *the children of God*. They *serve* God because they *love* him ! They *follow Christ*, and are *led* by him, because they *delight* in his *company ;* and, like the two disciples of old, *their hearts burn* within them, while he opens to them the Scriptures, and talks to them by the way! They desire to share his *heaven*, and are expecting it. They have taken up *arms* for Jesus, and know that he is the *Captain* of their salvation. They *please him*, though it may *displease themselves*. But, when *his pleasure* and *their pleasure* meet, their existence is a paradise! I must return to these things again, and blow a *louder trumpet*. Prov. 3: 17, has half-a-dozen sermons in it, should I follow the lines of thought which it suggests.

Struck with that sentiment of *Pythagoras*, "To *love truth*, and *do good*, are two things which make man *most like God*, and therefore are two of his most excellent gifts." Yes, if they are associated with *holiness!* O, no *gifts* nor *usefulness*, however extensive, can make up for the want of this! No, my Lord! no! O, *make me holy*, and *keep me holy*, through *Jesus Christ, my Lord!* Amen.

23

CHAPTER XXXIV.

THE PATIENCE AND PROVIDENCE OF GOD.

DEC 7th. — Battering down *false hopes;* — pressing hard on the *delaying*, the *loitering*, the *wavering*. Make *full proof of thy ministry*, O, my soul! Amen.

If some are *lost at last*, God clearly acquits himself of their blood. Tried hard that I might be *acquitted* too, in case that calamity should happen to any of my hearers. How men do *abuse* the *mercy* of God to his face! But how *patiently* does he bear with them, and await their *leisure* for repentance! — calls loudly upon them to *repent*, and *waits ;* — scores and scores and hundreds of times offers them *mercy*, and suffers them to *reject* it; — *repeats* the *offers* again, and again, till the sinner is *weary* of them. O God, how great is thy goodness! Repeats the *offers of mercy* again and again, till the sinner *loathes* them, *spurns* them, treats God and them with *contempt!* Alas! then cometh the end, and *vengeance* to the uttermost.

O, how terrible is that intimation in Hebrews 10 : 30, "*Vengeance* belongeth unto me, I will recompense, saith the Lord"! But it is a *flash* from that awful thundercloud, in the 26th, 27th, 28th, and 29th verses of the same chapter: "For, if we sin *wilfully*," &c. All sin that is *damnable*, is *wilful;* but all *wilful sin* is not *unpardonable*, because not *incurable*. But, as one remarks, "When

THE PATIENCE AND PROVIDENCE OF GOD. 267

it is *incurable*, it is the *special sin of hell*, the *badge* of devils, and of sinners damned." It cannot become *incurable* till "*the sin unto death*" is committed, I suppose. — 1 John 5 : 16, 17. Some sin against the Holy Spirit, doubtless, and under *superior illumination*. O, for a right heart to feel for sinners !

Dec. 11th. — Ay ! *Experience* and *necessity* teach more effectually than *theory*. Depravity, enmity, and unbelief, make a man *serious ;* and that *old serpent*, the Devil, *Apollyon*, leading them on, saying, " *Thus far, but no further ;* — and my soul replying, "Yes, and further ! so help me, O God, in Christ ! " Ay ! these things *sober* one, and *fancy and imagination* hide themselves from the *fight*.

* * * * * * *

To *hew a stone*, to *cleave a knotty block* that would not receive the *wedge*, and *to plough* upon a *rock*, were the great sorrow of an old preacher's ministry, of whom I once read, *dulling* his hopes, and *wearying* his spirit; and well they might. But they rendered him *serious as eternity*. Hard to be *lively* long without success, unless a man becomes *careless* of success; and then he has become *unfit* for the pulpit. O, for power from on high !

* * * * * * *

Mr. Wesley, I perceive from his journal, paid *Birmingham* numerous visits, and for several years with but *little success*. His visits, however, were of short duration, — a day, and off again. Perhaps that was the *reason*, — a *siege* or *battle*, instead of a few shot, or a skirmish, was what Birmingham needed *then* as *now*. But Mr. Wesley could not afford so much of his time in one place ; he flew, like an angel, through these kingdoms; a *necessity* was laid upon him, — the *care* of all the societies in Methodism. But, under date October 24, 1749, he writes: "After preaching again at one, I rode to *Birmingham*. This has been long *a dry and uncomfortable place;* so I expected little good here. But I was happily disappointed. Such a congregation I never saw there before; not a scoffer, nor a trifler, nor an inattentive person [so far as I could discern] among them; and seldom have I known so deep a sense of the divine power, and presence of the love of God. The same blessing we had at the meeting of the society; and again at the morning preaching. Will, then, God at length cause even this *barren wilderness* to blossom and bud as the rose?" Yes! O, immortal *Wesley!* it was even so in thy day, and we are hoping to see it more than ever so in these days, under the ministry of thy sons and successors in Jesus Christ! — even until *Birmingham* shall become as *the garden of the Lord!* Hallelujah! Amen.

Dec. 13th. — It is in vain to *foresee* for sinners what is coming upon them, if they refuse to open their eyes to *foresee for themselves*. A great point that to press home. *Conscience* will ring a terrible peal, by and by, in the ears of those who refuse to *foresee* and *act*, until the miseries of the death-bed are upon them! A few more have found mercy. *Tokens* encouraging.

Dec. 16th. — A severe attack of sickness, *short* but *severe*, like that which I had in York; — a *rough part* of the road to heaven, but it is *a part* of it, thank God; — the *uneven* as well as the *even*, the foul as well as the fair weather along it, the *troublesome* as well as the *easy*, the *perplexing* as well as the *plain*, all belong to the heavenly way, so great is its *variety!* What matter, seeing it happens so on the royal highway to the Jerusalem above?

Baxter says, "Remember that the school of Christ has a *rod.*" Ay! Jesus will not allow us to forget it! — to *feel* it, is a *remembrancer*, indeed! It teaches one to "*serve the Lord with fear*, and *to rejoice with trembling*," as enjoined in the book of Psalms. But the *rod* and the *honey* at the *end* of it go together with me. — 1 Sam. 14: 27. O, how often have I *deserved* the *rod*, but never the *honey!* — and yet the *rod* has never been *without* the *honey* since the day Christ and I were friends! "Whom the Lord *loveth* he *chasteneth*, and *scourgeth* every *son* whom he receiveth." — Heb. 12: 6. "Whom the Lord *loveth*," that is, the *honey!* Blessed be God! "Behold, he whom thou *lovest* is *sick.*" More honey!

And what *providential honey* have I, in having such a kind and experienced physician, — *Dr. Melson!* God bless him! he is so *attentive*, so *considerate*, so in *earnest* for my recovery! And such a kind *host* and *hostess!* O, my Lord! may my *heart* and *life* be good to the end of life's rough pilgrimage! Amen.

* * * * * * *

That is a sweet and cheering declaration in Rom. 8: 28, and relates evidently to the workings of *Divine Providence:* "*All things work together for good to them that love God;*" working *for* and *against*, apparently. like the *wheels* in my watch, I perceive; — for how contrary to each other do they seem to go! — one in *one direction*, and another in another direction, — such a *wilderness of confusion;* but all are working together for good. The good appears on the *dial-plate;* every *wheel*, however contrary in motion, *works* to the *same result!* It is so with *Providence!*

A man of God, now in glory, used to say that he often felt he would not be without the above *Scripture* for the world! — that, in time of *trial* and *sickness*, it seemed so full of *promise*, he thought, were there not another promise in the Scriptures, this gave an abundant supply of *consolation!* I think so, too, blessed be God!

CHAPTER XXXV.

IN THE FURNACE. — LETTERS
To ———.

* * * * * *

CONFINED to the *house*, but not to my *bed*. The attack was very sudden, similar to that which prostrated me twice in *York*, and once in *America;* and, as then, "in dead of night;" — the *fourth* attack of the same kind, and always at *night*, and with no previous warning; — as if Death, had he permission, would like to come suddenly upon me, and "as a *thief* in the night," — and so *sudden* as last night; — a *comment* upon those lines of *Charles Wesley*, which I copied in Quebec, from an old Magazine, brought over by an emigrant:

> "From sudden, unexpected death
>   Jesus thy servant save,
> Nor let me gasp my latest breath
>   Unmindful of the grave.
>
> "Unconscious of the yawning deep,
>   And death eternal nigh;
> O, do not suffer me to sleep
>   Till in my sins I die!
>
> "And summoned to the mountain-top,
>   Without a lingering sigh,
> Render my ransomed spirit up,
>   And to thy glory die.

> Wise to foresee my latter end,
>   With humble loving fear,
> I would continually attend
>   The welcome messenger."

* * * * * *

After about two hours of severe suffering, I staggered out of my room, and awoke *Mr. Wright.* Had great peace in the midst of *great pain.* When it seemed as if I could *endure no more and live,* was enabled to say to Mr. W., "*Death* has no *terrors,*— no *sting;* Jesus is precious,— tell my friends this, if I depart." However, I wished to live, should it please the Head of the church;— did not wish to die in a *strange land;*— affairs of a *temporal nature* not in a very tangible form,— my private *papers and journals* in a somewhat disordered state,— would like to live to *erase* this or that, and *rewrite* other parts, and not leave that to the judgment of others; but above all to call sinners to repentance, a while longer.

* * * * * *

To ———.

* * * * * *

Still *weak;* but my "beloved physician," *Dr. Melson* seems to understand my case perfectly, and has no fears. This *visitation* has done me good; could realize the truth of what one said: "It does not frighten a child of God to discover all the signs of *death* in his body, so long as he can see and feel all the signs of *grace* in his *soul!*" St. Paul, you remember, was in "a *strait* betwixt two *conditions,*— a desire to depart, and to be with Christ," or, to *remain* upon earth to *preach the Gospel a while longer.* "I am in a *strait;*" which Dr. Doddridge, I remember, renders, "*I am borne two different ways;*"— like a *ship* riding at anchor, yet under *stress of weather,* is likely to be forced from her anchorage, and driven out to sea. St. Paul's *affections* were *anchored* upon the *church,* yet the *desire* to depart, and to be with Christ, was sometimes too strong for his *anchor-hold.*

It is good to be familiar with death. "*I die daily,*" said St. Paul, in another place. No wonder, when, at last, he saw death approaching him in right good earnest, he calmly said, "*I am now ready to be offered, and the time of my departure is at hand;* — O, *Death!* where is thy *sting?*" Then followed the note of "victory!" But that was not the *first time* Paul had shouted *victory* over the *King of terrors!* He had become too *familiar* with Death, so oft had he approached him, to be afraid of that *conqueror* of conquerors. It is *Flavel,* I think, who illustrates the *benefit* of this familiarly, thus,— that a *lion* is much more dreadful to one who never saw him before, than he is to his *keeper* who sees him every day! — and a battle is more frightful to a *young recruit,* who never saw an engagement, than to an *old soldier,* who has long been used to them!

Well, it would seem as if the Lord would prepare my *cautioned* soul for the last *encounter,* which *may* come suddenly, and must surely come at one time or another. It is good to feel one's self intercepted now and then by *this passing shadow;* — for, O, when the *shadow* is nigh, the *substance* that caused it cannot be far off! — it is good —

> "To damp our earthly joys,
> To increase our gracious fears."

A *wise man* was that *Emperor* of *Constantinople,* who, at his *inauguration,* ordered a *mason* to bring *two stones* and lay them before him, with this question, "*Choose,* O, emperor, *which* of these two stones thou wilt have for thy *tombstone."* He renewed the ceremony on great *state occasions*, and upon feast days.

* * * * * *

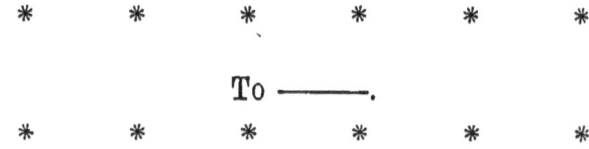

* * * * * *

No, it does not tire me to write, but rather *amuses* me, and is profitable withal. There is a great *feebleness* upon me, and *lassitude;* — thinking of what one said, "I am so weak that I cannot stand upon my legs, but I can cast myself into my Father's arms!" Blessed be God, I can do that!

But I feel much better, — trying to *buckle* on the *armor* again, with a glad and solemn heart; — cannot sympathize with him who, on returning from the gates of death, exclaimed, "I was as a *sheep* that had nearly entered the *fold*, but was driven back into the *storm* again, or as a *traveller* almost *home*, yet compelled to return again to *fetch something* he had *neglected;*" — or, he might have added, like a *ship* that had nearly entered her destined port, but ordered out to sea again by her owners!

O, but I am glad at the prospect of a return to the *battle-storm* of *soul-saving!* — glad to return to "fetch" more *holiness* with me to heaven, and many more poor, *neglected* souls besides! — glad to put out to *sea again*, as *long voyages* are apt to give *large returns* of profits, and *short voyages* the contrary!

He *wished* wisely who desired either to die *preaching* or *praying*. He spoke like a *Daniel*, who said, it became a *soldier* to die *fighting*, a *minister* to die *preaching*, and a *Christian* to die praying. Ay! I want to keep on *fighting, preaching, praying*, and then — go to heaven *by and by!*

Much have I passed through, so far on my *pilgrimage* and *warfare;* — many, many sore *mental conflicts,* — more than I can tell of upon earth; — but it was right, — all *worked for good,* although I was often to *blame;* — yet all so *overruled* as to make my *heart better* and holier, and my intellect *stronger, sturdier, hardier,* if you will allow me such words. Was once much comforted with those remarks of *Leighton,* that the *church* is God's *jewelry,* — his *working-house,* where his *jewels* are *polished;* and those he especially esteems, and means to make most *resplendent,* he has oftenest his tools upon them! This is enough for one letter. About to venture out for a short *walk,* — shall write again, — it refreshes me to write, and does not weary, — at least writing to you.

* * * * * *

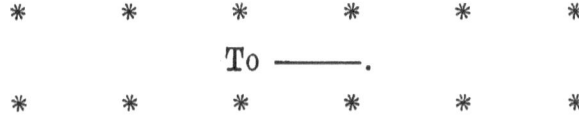
To ⸺.

* * * * * *

Have enjoyed a quiet meditative ramble, and all the better for it. What a wonderful faculty is *memory!* What food it affords to *thought* and *reflection,* — and for *regret* also! tempting one to wish, were it possible, to *try the ground over again,* — *revoking* time, that, by the light of *dearly bought experience,* one might shun the *rocks* that *jeopardized,* or find the *happiness* that *eluded.* Upon the whole, I felt unwilling, were it at my *option,* to *live my life over again.* The *second edition* of my short life might, perhaps, have more *errors* than the *first.* No! I do not wish to try the same ground over again; — too great a *risk;* — content with the present order of things; — that we must go *forward,* never *backward,* except by *reflection.*

Affliction seems to impart a singular *vividness* to the *memory.* Partly of the opinion of him who compared *memory* to a *mirror*, which *affliction* dashes to the earth and the fragments only multiply *reflection!*

* * * * * *

A poor night's rest, — *body* much out of order; but a gracious *season* in *private* and *family prayer*, — *heart full* of love to God, gratitude, and humility, — eyes full of tears. It is *mercy* all! Ventured to preach last night on Luke 15 : 10, — the joy of angels over repenting sinners; — hoping to get *fire* and zeal out of it for my own soul, — was not disappointed, nor angels neither; — many *saved!*

* * * * * *

To ———.

Birmingham, Dec. 20, 1845.

The work advances. *Public attention* is waking up and looking this way in right good earnest, and moving the *masses* this way; — inclined to *listen;* by and by to *feel.* Souls are finding mercy daily. Thinking of the Spanish proverb, which speaks of *time* and *patience* turning the *mulberry* leaf into *silk!* I like that couplet in *Burns*, —

> " Come firm *resolve*, take thou the van,
> Thou *stalk* of *carle-hemp* in man ! "

But I like St. Paul's motto better, "*I can do all things through Christ which strengtheneth me,*" — Phil. 4 : 13, — and his watchword, "*Put on the whole armor of God, that ye may be able to stand* against the wiles of the devil." — Eph. 6 : 11. There is no *carle-hemp*, or firm *resolve* in man, *aside from the grace of God*, can sustain and carry the soul and body of a preacher through such a scene of conflict to *victory!*

CHAPTER XXXVI.

RETURN TO THE BATTLE-STRIFE. — A SOUL-SAVING MIN-
ISTRY. — LETTERS.

To * * * * * *.

Birmingham, Dec. 22, 1845.

* * * * * *

URGING on the *battle-strife* once more, — for truth, — for Christ, — for souls; — in *weakness* fearing another attack of *illness*. But the doctor hopes it may be avoided, and does not forbid my *preaching*. God bless him for that! for, O, to be *passive* or *inactive*, at such a time as this, would require more grace than this *activity* for God demands!

Rom. 8 : 28, stands good, — "*All things work together for good to them that love God.*" The *fires* which *agitate* and greatly *try gold* and *silver*, work at the same time for their *purification, beauty, value, glory!*

But *truth* and the *sinner* are still *antagonists*. I see that! What an *expression* of resistance! Truth may be *dressed* up so *prettily* that the *sinner* will really *like* it; but no sooner does it appear in its real dress and uncompromising utterances, than he *frowns* upon it, and puts himself in an attitude to *repel* it. Well, I have not been "dressing up" truth since my arrival in *Birmingham*, God knows! — for I know precious little gain is it to the church in the long run, — "dressing up truth, as if it were to sell," as a Spaniard observed.

Dec. 23. — Truth cuts like a sword. It is well; it would wear out the body else, — the sword would cut through the *scabbard* at such a time as this; — best to keep *using* it! *Real truth* is a *real sword, dividing asunder the joints and marrow, the soul and spirit,* of wickedness; but not *painted truth!* A painted sword *cuts* not, nor a sword in the *scabbard*, nor a *muffled* sword, though equal to that of *Goliath* of Gath, that was "*wrapped in a cloth behind the ephod.*" — 1 Sam. 21 : 9. O, give me the *naked sword of truth*, with strength and courage to wield it, O, Lord God of truth! Amen.

To change the figure, truth is as a *serpent* to many. *Sinful men* cannot understand this; neither can some in the church, who profess to be better. It is enough, they think, that truth should be a *rod*, — even a *sword* is admissible, where the *sinews* of wickedness are hard and tough! — but that truth should be made to multiply itself so, and become as "fiery flying serpents" among the people, they cannot away with it; — fly from it; — and yet, strange to say, it has a fascination to draw them back to it! They forget that the *rod* of Moses was turned into a *serpent!* He fled from it; but when God commanded him to come back and take it by the *tail*, he did so, and it became a rod again, — his *friend*, indeed, by which he shook the throne of the *Pharaohs*. So, the Lord our God brings back again these *flying* sinners; — they venture to seize the *serpent* truth by the *tail*, keeping as far from its *bite* as possible, when, lo, it is but a *rod*, after all, in the hand of *schoolmaster* Law, to bring them to *Christ*, as Paul hints. Then it becomes their *friend* indeed, and by it, they shake all *spiritual Egypt around them;* and their *emancipation* from the slavery of the old Pharaoh of hell, becomes the order of the day of salvation! Hallelujah!

To *** ***.

Birmingham, Dec. 24, 1845.

Exactly so, my dear friend! — a *body* vigorous as the oak on yonder heights is needed! — like *Seneca's* man, with ribs of brass and bones of iron, and sinews of steel! O, but God can so empower and strengthen and inure the *body*, that brass and iron and steel might sooner wear out! — if man is *immortal till his work is done!* * * *

To *** ***.

Dec. 26.

* * * * * *

Ay! all that is true! — a *soul-saving* preacher requires a soul stern as the face of war; yet, in its *secret depths*, full to overflowing with the *gushing benevolence of Jesus*,— and of *the spirit of burning!* — Is. 4 : 4, — crying out unto God·

"Steel me to shame, reproach, disgrace;
Arm me with all thine armor now;
Set like a flint my steady face,
Harden to adamant my brow.

"Bold may I wax, exceeding bold,
My high commission to perform,
Nor shrink thy harshest truths t' unfold;
But more than meet the gathering storm.

"Adverse to earth's rebellious throng,
Still may I turn my fearless face;
Stand as an iron pillar strong,
And steadfast as a wall of brass.

"Give me thy might, thou God of power,
Then let or men or fiends assail,
Strong in thy strength I 'll stand, a tower
Impregnable to earth or hell."

He needs a *heart*, under some circumstances, like that of *Job's Leviathan*, that "*laugheth at the shaking of a spear!*" and, if you will allow me to *parody* a little upon that noble creature, the *Leviathan*, which even God himself so graphically describes in the *forty-first* chapter of *Job*,— such a *minister* needs to be "*firm as a stone.*" O Lord, my God, he does, and a *heart of fire*, giving a *flame* at the mouth, that *kindles coals!* — esteeming *iron* as *straw*, and *brass* as *rotten wood!* — fearless too of the arrows of sarcasm, ridicule, or criticism,— *counting sling-stones as stubble;* — *the sword of him that layeth at him cannot hold;* nor the *spear*, the *dart*, nor the *habergeon!* So firmly has God joined the *flakes* of his character and courage together, *they cannot be moved.* There are *breakings*, or *breakers*, *when he raiseth up himself*, so that even the *mighty are afraid, and purify themselves!* The onset leaves him unexhausted, for *his heart is firm as a stone*, and *in his neck there remaineth strength.* Out of his *mouth go burning lamps of light*, and words, like *sparks of fire, leap out;* — the *eyelids* of his understanding are *like the eyelids of the morning*, chasing away the darkness of hellish night,-- the harbinger of a glorious gospel day! His *path is a path of light, and it shines after him.* He stirs a population to its depths; — *he maketh the deep to boil like a pot*, and *a path to shine after him*, till one would think the deep to be hoary. *Opposition* is as nothing to him, for *the arrow cannot make him flee*, and *darts are counted as stubble* before the fire of his zeal, and *he laugheth at the shaking of a spear!* Why should it be otherwise, seeing that *he spreadeth sharp pieces of potsherd, and sharp-pointed things under him*, as ordi-

nary experiences, and regardeth them not; for he is called of God to *endure hardness*.

Ah, me! what a *bold* illustration is this I am *figuring with*! But the *Leviathan* is a *glorious creature of God, and upon earth there is none like him, who is made without fear;* — and a *glorious creature* is he, whom God has *called* and *prepared, fully qualified,* and *sent forth* to *shake the kingdom of darkness!* — to rescue from the powers of hell the *souls* for whom the Redeemer died; baptized with the Holy Ghost and with fire, and imbued with power from on high, which makes him *victorious* over all the power of the enemy. There is none among the *uncalled* like him upon the earth, whom God has made without *fear;* who fears *God* only, and *fears to sin,* and fears naught else besides in earth or hell. St. Paul considers such "*the messengers of the churches, and the glory of Christ.*"— 2 Cor. 8: 23. *Signal instruments* of good to the churches, and of advancing the glory of Jesus Christ in the world.

But, ah, sir, a messenger of this sort needs a peculiar *physical*, as well as mental constitution. For, although his are *moral*, not physical victories, yet the *body* must sustain the soul that wins them. A *mortal frame*, carrying about a *soul of fire*, needs a constant miracle to sustain it; as if insured in heaven! For it resembles the *bush in the wilderness,* — in a blaze, yet *unconsumed.* — Exod. 3: 2. "*A great sight*" it was to Moses that, and a great sight is such an one to angels and to men.

The head of the church raises up, and qualifies such extraordinary messengers. They appear, from time to time, in the churches' *need.* He endues them with extraordinary power and zeal, and thrusts them forth to *burn* and to *shine.* Such were Wesley, Whitfield, Fletcher, and many others in the eighteenth century; such was *Luther*, and a *host* in the *sixteenth* century. Nor is the *nineteenth century* unblest by them. They are designed to break up the ruinous *monotony* of the *churches*, and to awaken *men* to the concerns of eternity.

Usually, they are *short-lived*. Indifference, or opposition, breaks their heart; or hard constant labor wears them out soon, moaning with their Lord, as they disappear from among men, "*The zeal of thine house hath eaten me up.*' But the Lord raises up others of like spirit; for this is really the "*apostolical succession*," after all.

CHAPTER XXXVII.

PERSONAL EXPERIENCE AND PENCILLINGS ABOUT PREACH-
ING. — JOURNAL.

EVENING of Christmas day, Dec. 25th. — It is recorded of the *Macedonians*, that they always celebrated the birthday of Alexander the Great, having his *picture* suspended from their necks, set with *pearls* and *jewels*. And upon how many hearts, of late, has *the fair image of Jesus been impressed!* From their looks to-day, it was easy to gather that his *image* within was, indeed, set about with the richest *pearls* and jewels of their lately regenerated affections.

But how is it with *myself?* Long have I worn the loved *image* of Jesus in my poor heart; but, somehow, the *jewelry* of my affections around it have not been very bright or resplendent to-day. A singular *solitariness* and *stillness* have been over my spirit. The *body* has been out of tune, and the *soul* has sympathized with it. *Flavel* compared the two to a couple of *musical strings*, set exactly at one height; if the *one* is *touched*, the *other* trembles; they *laugh* or *cry*, are *sick* or *well*, together. I *feel* that. O, but there is a strange and mysterious *union* and sympathy in *this web of life!* How mutually do they affect each other! How *reciprocal* the influence!

I want to have matters more in harmony with St. Paul's

experience (2 Cor. 4 : 16), "Though our *outward man perish, yet the inward* man is renewed *day by day;*" the one going *prematurely* to the dust, *almost worn out*, while the other is "*renewed* day by day;" becoming more and more *like God*, and increasing daily in *vital power*, and *spiritual and intellectual strength*. A great help that; it acts upon one's *intellectual* and *physical* system, like that nice law of *compensation* in mechanics, and in the workings of the grand *machinery of the universe!* Preached *twice* to-day. Many *moved* and *saved*. Thanks be to God for the unspeakable gift of his *Son!*

Dec. 26th. — *Weak;* but *peace* and *comfort* in believing; the *honey* at the end of the rod,— which my heavenly Father allows me to eat without threatening me with death, as did Jonathan's father (1 Sam. 14 : 43, 44); realizing the *sweetness* of that remark uttered by one many years ago : "The sense of *pardon* takes away the sense of *pain*." Ay, blessed be God! So it is, as Isaiah says, "*The inhabitant shall not say I am sick; the people that dwell therein shall be forgiven their iniquity; then is the prey of a great spoil divided; the lame take the prey.*" — Isa. 33 : 23, 24. The prophet refers to a hostile nation, and victory over an *invading army*, forced to flee away before God's Israel, leaving *great spoils* behind, which even the *weak and the lame* may seize, forgetting their weak and crippled state, in the glorious opportunity of seizing the abandoned spoils of the enemy; they shall not say I am *sick* or *lame;* such transports of *joy* at such a *deliverance*, such a *victory*, over such *spoils*, and such prospects of future *peace* and *prosperity* as quite to absorb all sense of pain and disability; quite *forgetting* themselves, *surprising* themselves and others; the secret of it all being concealed in the fact of *their iniquity being forgiven;* God taking the part of those who *loved* and who *feared* him; thus, even then, causing *the weak things* of the *world to confound the mighty*, as St. Paul intimates, *that no flesh should glory in his presence.* It is so yet, blessed be God!

Dec. 27th.—The ancients compared *truth* to *salt;*—very significant; it makes the *old sores* and *new wounds* of professors and sinners *smart* again! All the better for that, if they keep temper. It hastens the healing. The spiritual *hurt* must not be healed *slightly*, as the *Head of the church* intimates by the prophet: "*They have healed also the hurt of the daughter of my people slightly, saying, Peace, peace,* when there is no peace." Ay, that deceptive practice is still continued. The wounds made by sin must be *probed, cleansed,* closed, before they can be healed with safety, without the risk of a spiritual *fester*, or of bleeding afresh.

But, what a work of God is breaking forth in every direction!

Dec. 29th. — A little more strength. The work spreads like a flame, — "*like fire among dry stubble.*" Hallelujah!

Dec. 30th. — Sinners are greatly *moved;* some say, "*frightened.*" What of that, if it be but a *sanctified fright*, set apart for *conversion!* when they shall be able to say, "God hath not given us *the spirit of fear*, but of *power*, and of *love*, and of a *sound mind*" (2 Tim. 1: 7); the result of a *sanctified fright;*—not like that which came down upon the *soldiers* who watched our Lord's sepulchre. They were wonderfully frightened when they saw a flaming angel roll away the great stone from the mouth of the sepulchre, while the earth shook and trembled, and they *fell*, almost scared out of their wits, and tumbled about like logs in a whirlpool; till, at length, they rolled themselves out of *sight and hearing*. Alas, the *fright* was not sanctified! A little *money* hired them to tell a *deliberate lie*, — that the disciples of Jesus came and stole away his body while they slept. — Matt. 28 : 13. "*Slept!*" A Roman guard *asleep!* — and *all* asleep, — asleep in the *open air*. So *soundly asleep*, as not to hear the *crashing motions* of such a stone in the removal, and the *full moon* shining in brilliancy, and the usual *passover* stir in and around Jerusalem! *Asleep*, and yet knew who took the body away! "*Slept!*" — as much as the *frightened* ones in my congregation slept last Sabbath night, during the reverberating thunders of the truth of the Omnipotent God!

Afternoon. — The work of God at York, and other places, was glorious. Have been trying to collect my *notes* of its *incidents and progress*, from journal, and note-books, and fragments of letters; but the whole are in such confusion, when collected, and item after item *dateless*, I find it difficult to *systematize* them. Ah, me! Ought to have taken more pains at the time. Cannot help it now. Many interesting things lost past recovery; and so also with this work of God in Birmingham; — instance the *effects* of the *Friday night* discourses on sanctification; — a large number of believers saved on those occasions.

Dec. 31st. — Well, 1845 is nearly gone; and 1846 seems as if stretching forth its hand to grasp mine; and it will grasp the hand of a *poor*, *weak*, *feeble* and somewhat *shattered* warrior of the cross; but much better than he was.

There is a great dea. said about *war, weapons* and *fighting*, in the Scriptures, -- *spiritual* war, weapons and fighting, I mean,— implying *enemies*, diabolical and human, of no easy *encounter* or conquest.

Every *unsaved sinner* is a *host* in himself; his *passions*, habits, carnal interests, ideas and idols, as so many *battalions* of a grand army, set in battle array against the *spiritual batteries*, &c. &c., of the pulpit.

A *sermon* is, or should be, an *army of ideas ;* — every *idea* a *soldier* of Christ, with some spiritual weapon or other in hand. *Divisions* are — what ? O, *three parts* usually; as the *right* and *left wing*, and *centre* of an army, on the rough edge of battle! Although I often prefer the *solid square* (a single *proposition*), in which my *rank* and *file* are *equal;* which, in *military tactics*, seems to stand upon the defensive, rather than the *offensive;* but, "at the word of command, my *solid square opens out in avenues of armed* thoughts, unmasking *concealed batteries*, which sometimes do tremendous execution !"

There is *great disorder* sometimes, and who ever saw a great battle entirely free from that ? My *sub-divisions*, regiments and battalions, and rank and file, go in for it in a holy *disordered order*. *Ideas and illustrations*, — what are they in military parlance ? O, *armed soldiers* of *Emanuel*, in *uniform* and *panoply divine !* — a *bannered host*, rushing forth, and doing battle for the Lord God of hosts ; the Holy Ghost *electrifying* them with his energy and power, and *sweeping* them along, or "*leading them to the charge*," as a military man observed, "*where the slain of the Lord were many;*" as on last Sabbath night. Hallelujah!

I like all the *chapels ; Newtown-Row, Belmont-Row, Cherry-street*, and *Wesley ;* — have held meetings in them all. Very easy to preach in them; they display much sound judgment in that respect; plain, substantial buildings; fine organs and good *choirs* and *congregational* singing; excellent bands of devoted and talented leaders and local preachers. The stationed ministers on both circuits are kind. *Rev. Joseph Wood* is truly at home in the revival. Praise the Lord!

CHAPTER XXXVIII.

NEW YEAR. — THE PROPHESYING TRUMP. — JOURNAL.

Hail, 1846! — *Farewell*, 1845! Thou, like the souls of our departed friends, art gone over to the *majority*. I hail thee, even thee, now numbered among the years of bygone ages, and the *years before the flood*. I shall *rejoin* thee again in that *duration* which is not measured by summer and winter, spring and autumn, or by the revolutions of the planets. Farewell, 1845, for a little while, till I meet thee, or thy *records*, where I hope to meet my friends, in the abodes of *the spirits* of just men made perfect. *Farewell!*

Held a *Watch Night* in *Cherry-street Chapel* last night. Text, "*This year thou shalt die.*" — Jer. 28 : 16. The New Year ushered itself in most *gloriously* to *some*, but most *miserably* in the apprehensions of others, — the *awakened*, the terrified, the despairing. Poor souls! reminding one of Petrarch's line,

"When *trembling Hope* was *frozen to Despair!*"

But I know the *Lord!* I know his *ways!* He always *kills* before he makes alive, — inflicts *death* before he infuses *life*, — and administers the *bitter* always before the *sweet*. The *Devil* reverses this, in whom he is working *damnation*. But this is *God's* order with those in whom he would work salvation. Poor *souls!* they do not seem to understand this, and *sob* and wail as if he really intended to damn them. But I have no *fear* of them, if they only persevere. "*The Lord will not always chide; neither will he keep his anger forever!*" No, blessed be his name!

As to my own providential path, "clouds, alas! and darkness rest upon it;" thick as over old Egypt, in the days of darkness. Well, let the *future* of my path here below remain so. What matters it, seeing there is *light* and *sunshine* in *Goshen*, and I *live* in Goshen! — my watchword, *Exodus!* — must be confident, and march on. *Darkness* and *difficulty* ever recede before the bold, the courageous, and faithful.

The *past* I know, and the *present;* but the *future* is an unknown; — my *feeling* this New Year's day! What of that? The Lord is worthy to be *trusted* by *me*, as well as by those "ghastly squadrons of despair," who passed away from our sight in Cherry-street, this morning!

There is a *light* for the soul, that shines not through the eyes of the body; — have often realized this, and do now. From this, I gather courage to press forward, through surrounding *providential darkness*, to the *day* of which this inward light is the *harbinger*.

Had a hard time in preaching, night before Watch Night, as I usually have, before some *great occasion*, when people are looking *forward*, instead of *up;* and so they go *down*, and the poor preacher with them. But, this usually *nerves* me for the *conflict*, when the *great occasion* arrives! However, we had a powerful time in the prayer-meeting. *Hard a time* as I had had in preaching, a *gentleman sinner*, from London, had it *much harder* under the *truth* which I found it so hard to deliver! He came forward to be prayed for, *trembling* like the *Philippian jailer;* "as if *conscience*, to the very centre of his being, had smitten him with a pain *irresistible!*" O, what a *tumult* was in that soul!

There is every prospect now of a *mighty work* of God, which, "like mighty winds and torrents fierce," will *turn*, and *overturn*, and *overcome* all opposing powers. A few *dams* have got to give way, and a few *barriers* swept out of the way, and then — *salvation!* O, for a fresh *baptism*, and *strength* of all sorts! A *crisis* is the time that *tests* the genius and fitness of a *general;* and *battle* tests the *soldier*, and such a crisis as this, the *preacher;* — and many such have I had.

"Arise, my soul, arise!"

*   *   *   *   *

Jan. 2d. — This is no time to *falter*, or to give *back*. The *iron* is hot, sparkling, and melting, and calls for the moulding-hammers. But *stronger blasts* and *hotter fires* are demanded for *other metals*, you may depend upon it. The *dead* are *awaking*, and require assistance and direction; but some have scarcely the motion of an *eyelash*, or a single pulsation of spiritual life. A louder *blast* of the *prophesying trump* is absolutely needed, even should it crack and go to pieces in the effort. God has other *trumpets* ready when this one is worn out. Till then, it is safest to obey the command, "*Cry aloud, spare not; lift up thy voice like a trumpet, and show my people their transgressions, and the house of Jacob their sins.*" — Is. 58: 1. "*Blow ye the trumpet in Zion, and sound an alarm in my holy mountain: let all the inhabitants of the land tremble: for the day of the Lord cometh, for it is nigh at hand.*" — Joel 2: 1. Ay! then, and not till then, may we expect the *seeing* of Zechariah the prophet verified:

"And the LORD shall be seen *over them*, and his *arrows* shall go forth as the *lightning;* and the *Lord God shall blow the trumpet*, and shall go with whirlwinds of the south." — Zech. 9 : 14. Read, also, the next verse; for my soul sucks *fire* out of these passages, and gathers strength for the *battle!* "The *Lord of Hosts* shall *defend* them; and they shall *devour* and *subdue* with *sling-stones;* and they shall *drink* and make a *noise* as through *wine*, and they shall be *filled like bowls*, and as the corners of the altar. And the Lord their God shall save them in that day as the flock of his people: for they shall be as the *stones* of a *crown*, lifted up as an *ensign* upon his land. For, how great is his *goodness*, and how great is his beauty!" — Zech. 9 : 14, 15, 16, 17.

*   *   *   *   *   *
*   *   *   *   *   *

Zech. 9 : 14—17, is a remarkable passage indeed. I never noticed it particularly before yesterday. When *copying* it, I knew not where to stop, every word and phrase seemed so full of meaning, and so thrilling. It is the Holy Spirit, *doubtless*, which, at particular times, infuses such *power* and *significancy* into the word of God, and as if spoken to *ourselves*. *Consider it carefully:* "*The Lord shall be seen over them*," — in some *conspicuous* and *unmistakable tokens* of his presence; — *presiding*, directing, controlling, overruling, and protecting us in our *enterprises* for him. Hallelujah!

Consider again: "His *arrows* shall go forth as the *lightning*." Mark that, "His *arrows*." Our God is not going to be an *idle spectator* of this conflict! No! 'his *arrows* shall go forth," *swiftly, silently*, and *directly* to the mark! Sinners shall be *hit and pierced* by an *unseen archer*, — shall not know who hit them, and shall

lay it all to the *humble archer* in the pulpit. Hallelujah!
"His *arrows* shall go forth as the *lightning;*" — *mark*
that, — with a *force* that is *effectual* as it is *irresistible!*

Consider further: "And the *Lord God* shall *blow* the *trumpet.*" *Mark* that also, — the *battle signal* shall be given by *himself!* He himself shall animate our troops, and sound the charge at the *crisis*, and lead us to the victory!

Consider again: What more shall our God do for us in the battle? "And shall go with *whirlwinds* of the south" Mark that, "*whirlwinds.*" Who can set limits to the might and power of a *whirlwind?* — that not only throws *chaff* and *dust* and *dead leaves* into tribulation, but tears in pieces every *bulkier object* that stands in its way; and, as if *one* whirlwind were not enough, *whirlwinds*, and plenty of them, is the promise!

Consider further: "And they shall devour and subdue with *sling-stones.*" Though fighting with *unequal weapons*, to what the Devil opposes us by, yet *victory* is of the Lord! — as David felt, when the sling-stone whizzed through the air against *Goliah*, as he stood like a pyramid of brass, armed with *sword*, and *spear*, and *shield;* — the *little stone*, like "a little sermon," slung with power, levelled to the dust that haughty and defiant Philistine!

Consider the sequel: "They shall *drink* and *rejoice*, and make a *noise* as through *wine;* celebrating the victory in *songs of praise*, and *shouts of triumph*, as on the day when the Lord God gave *Jehoshaphat* and the people of Jerusalem the famous victory over the combined armies of *Moab* and *Ammon*, without tinging the sword of a single *Israelitish soldier* with the blood of the foe; for *the battle was the Lord's*, and he fought for them, and caused them to return to Jerusalem with *joy*, and with sound of *psalteries*

25*

and *harps* and trumpets, unto the house of the Lord; because he had made them *to rejoice over their enemies;* or like the scenes of the *Pentecost,* when the wicked were *confounded,* — some *mocking* at what they could not understand, or rationally contradict, — others *accounting* for the glorious manifestations among the triumphant multitude, upon *principles* which *befooled* the objectors: " *These men are full of new wine.*" — Acts 2. " *Full* of new wine " ! " New wine " ! — who ever heard of people getting *drunk* on *new wine?* — *the newly-expressed juice of the grape!* Besides, such an article could not be had, " for love or money," at so early a season of the year as the day of Pentecost ! — to say nothing of the quantity for such a *throng of people;* — or, if they meant some other kind of wine, *nine o'clock* in the morning (the *Jewish third hour of the day*), it was too early an hour for such a multitude to get drunk, and all with one consent ! Peter took good advantage of that fact. At any rate, the silly *insinuation* was enough to cover such objectors with *derision,* and they sneaked away out of sight; while the more thoughtful and candid were *amazed,* and inquired, " *What meaneth this?*" O, but how much of all this shall we have in Birmingham, if the Lord our God will fight for us, as I believe he will, according to *Zechariah's prophecy!*

Consider its *beautiful allusions* in conclusion. " They shall be as the *stones* of the *crown;* " — we shall be precious in his sight, and in the sight of others, as the *crown of England,* with its *precious stones,* is to Queen Victoria and the government; — " as the *stones of a crown,* lifted up as an *ensign* upon his land; " — we shall be *effectual* and *influential* in the sight of the *multitudes,* as the *crown of England, brilliant with precious stones,* would be, if carried forth as an *ensign* before the army of Great Britain, going forth to defend the country against invaders, and to maintain its honor.

Then shall all know and acknowledge " How great is his *goodness*, and how great his *beauty;* " — how *infinite* in his goodness; how glorious in his beauty; — in his *goodness* to those who trust in him; and in the *beautiful* order of his divine providence towards his people, and in his *salvation!*

O, that our God may come speedily to our help, " with the *whirlwinds* of the south ! " — the most vehement storms which swept over *Judea* came from the *south;* from the *great desert* to the south of it; — a *revival whirlwind,* such as may tear up by the roots whole *forests* of the *Devil's planting!*

CHAPTER XXXIX.

AN EXPERIMENT REJECTED. — LETTERS.

To *** ***.

Birmingham, Jan., 1846.

YOUR "*observations*" are valuable; but, depend upon it, such a *method* would never accomplish much in Birmingham, or I greatly mistake the character of its people. It has been pretty well tried in Birmingham, and I have no heart to prolong the *experiment*, so well and so fruitlessly tested by wiser heads than mine.

The preaching that will please *carnal men* is about sure to please the *Devil* also; what one called "*gaudy allusions*, and *pretty gingles*, and *knacks of wit*, and *scraps* of *Greek* and *Latin*, and *shreds* of *fathers* and philosophy,— in *well-set* and *accurate speech;*" — ay! something to *tickle the fancy* without *touching the conscience!* No! by the grace of God, no! — a *thousand times no!* Better I was *concealed* once more in the *western wilderness*, than attempt such an *exhibition*. No! no! no! "Give me *souls*, or I die!" is the cry of my heart. But this is not the way to *win* them, nor any mode of preaching akin to it. No ——

* * * * * *

To the same.

*   *   *   *   *   *

Genteel efforts, and *polite endeavors*, will never *originate* a revival here, nor *sustain* it if begun; will never

"*Bow down stubborn knees*, and *hearts* with *strings of steel.*"

Nor can a *whisper* do what demands a *thunder*. A few *squibs* can never accomplish what demands a *grand battery of cannon!* A *breath*, a *zephyr* from a garden of roses, cannot move or overthrow that which requires a *breeze*, a *tempest*, a *tornado*, or the might of *ignited gunpowder!* The *strongholds* of the Devil are not to be taken and *pulled down* by "*gentle*," but by pretty *violent measures*, such as "*carpet knights*" and *tea-table champions* are never likely to engage in; but men of *nerve, courage, zeal*, and capable of *enduring hardness as good soldiers of Jesus Christ* (2 Tim. 2: 3); who are more anxious for *fighting* than for *drinking!*

Gideon, you remember, had orders to send all home who drank after a certain fashion; — down upon *all-fours*, by the river's brink, for a good comfortable drink, as if fearing a long expedition, and long abstinence; — so they resolved to *indulge*, and carry away a good *stomach-full!* — they thought more of their *stomachs* than of victory over the enemies of their God! *Nine thousand seven hundred* of them did so; and the Lord said, "*Send them home; they are unfit for this service!*" But there were *three hundred men*, who, instead of flinging themselves down upon *hands* and *knees* for a drink, were content to quench their thirst by taking up a little in the palm or hollow of their hand, without laying aside their armor, or being off their guard for a moment; and the Lord said, "By the *three hundred men that* LAPPED *will I save you.*" Those were the trusty soldiers; *hardy, fatigue-enduring, thirst-despising* men, who longed to *engage the enemy;* despising even *necessary refreshment* through zeal for their *God* and *country's cause.* — Judges, seventh chapter. But such, evidently, are the *officers* and *soldiers* of the cross, with which my God has surrounded me on every side! And now, by His help, they shall not have their *zeal quenched,* but in a great vi tory for the Lord of hosts! Amen.

* * * * * *

To * * * * * *.

* * * * * *

The soldiers of Christ are called to *endure hardness,* else they would not be the "*good soldiers,*" of whom Paul speaks. Every proper *revival effort* is a sort of holy, decided, obstinate *violence* against *sin, self,* and *Satan;* — against the *world,* the *flesh,* and the *devil;* — and, hardest of all, frequently, against cold-hearted, and fault-finding *church-members, sympathizers* with those who are *without.* But all these must be *moved, shaken, prostrated,* by a power from heaven, and by no very "*gentle measures,*" depend upon it.

The *judgments* of God must be rolled upon the ears of men; not "*theories* built of *gossamer,*" but stern, rugged, *devil-arousing,* and *sinner-piercing* truth; ay! and that with all the *energies* of the preacher, and with the power of God unto salvation.

Ah, sir! I know *human nature,* and *infernal nature,* and their *combined power,* too well, to miscalculate in this matter! — have been brought into *collision* with them too often to *underrate* their *power of resistance.* * * * *

To * * *.

*　　*　　*　　*　　*　　*

Weigh well what I am about to say,—but take it in connection with what has been already said,— a gentle touch will never accomplish what requires the *shoulder of an earthquake!* No! no! no!—but rather something after the *manner* of good old *Robert Bolton*, who hints that we must preach till the sinner *feels* he is in the actual grapple of the *King of terrors*, and is about to stand or fall at the tribunal of God ; as if he were about to drop into the fiery lake with a *senseless heart* and a *seared conscience*, or with the cry, "*Save, Lord, or I perish!*"—that we must preach till every sinner feels himself *now* in that predicament of peril and terror which he will certainly feel *hereafter*, when he would give *ten thousand worlds*, were they all turned into *gold, pleasures*, and *imperial crowns*, to have his salvation secured!—we must preach till the very heavens appear as if shrivelling together like a scroll,— as if the whole frame of nature were in *flames* about his ears ; — as if the great and mighty *hills* were starting out of their places like frighted men; — till he is ready to join in the *reprobate cry* for the rocks and mountains to fall upon him ; — till he feels that no dromedary of *Egypt*, nor wings of the morning, shall be able to carry him out of the reach of the avenging hand ; — till he feels that there is no *top of Carmel*, no *depth of the sea*, no *bottom of hell*, that can hide him from the wrath of a *sin-avenging God ;* — till he feels that no rock, nor mountain, nor the great body of the whole earth, can cover him from the *unresistible power* that laid the foundations of them ; — till he feels that no arm of flesh, or armies of angels, are able to protect him from those infinite *rivers of brimstone* which shall be kept in *everlasting flames* by the anger of God; — till he feels as if he is next to being chained, by the Omnipotent hand of God, among spirits damned, in a place of flames and perpetual darkness, where is torment without end, and past imagination; — that we must preach till he is ready to cry out, with the feelings of the damned, "O, that I were *annihilated*, or had but one more chance upon earth to obtain salvation!" — till he feels, upon returning recollection, that there is actually but one step between him and hell, — but the thin veil of the flesh [as *Baxter* observes] between him and that *amazing sight*, — that eternal gulf, into which sinners are stepping daily; — till he feels that his *breath* is about to be stopped by an *arrest* from heaven, and *justice* on the point of *surprising* his *unready* soul, and no assurance that he shall not be in hell in an hour; — till he feels some of those *piercing, griping, tearing thoughts*, which the consciously dying and the certainly damned do feel; — till there is an *outcry* for mercy from him and many others, which prove that the trumpet of the Lord has not been sounded in vain, nor in vain has his sword been wielded! Depend upon it, sir, this is the kind of preaching that is *needed*, if not "*asked for*," in Birmingham! And, if last Sabbath night bore any resemblance to it, to God be all the glory!   *   *   *

CHAPTER XL.

THE RENEWAL OF THE COVENANT, AND PROGRESS OF THE REVIVAL.

JANUARY 5th, 1846. — Yesterday, being the first Sabbath in the year, I preached in *Bradford-street* Chapel, from 2 Peter 2 : 9. A gracious time. The afternoon was spent in "the renewal of the covenant," one of the prominent New-Year's services among the Wesleyans in this country. The covenant was read, by one of the stationed preachers, most *impressively*. Was struck with the *introduction*, — exceedingly appropriate.

After the covenant, assisted in the administration of the *Lord's Supper*.

Preached again at night to a *crowd*. Was *sharp* and *convincing*, if *effects* are signs thereof. There were *fifty* saved, of whom *thirty* were justified, and *twenty* sanctified. It is well to preach every sermon as if it were one's *last*; or, as if one's *own life* depended upon it; — certainly it is life or death to the *hearer*, and that should *move* one, if anything would. My soul was *moved* indeed, and so were the *people*. Many saved.

Had much *joy* in my soul this morning in secret with God, and much after my return last night; one of those sweet and glorious *surprises*; what one calls "an excess of divine goodness." I sometimes call it *"revival joy,"* because it so frequently, with me, precedes, or *accompanies* at intervals, a great work of God.

Jan. 7th. Wednesday morning. — Preached at *Bradford-street* again last night. Chapel crowded, aisles and all. *Eighteen* found mercy, and *seven* or *eight* purity. After I returned, when alone with my Lord and Master, opened on Jer. 29 : 11, 14, and felt as if he was speaking to me.

What an amazing work hath the Lord wrought the last *ten* or *twelve* days! It is the Lord's doings, indeed, and marvellous in our eyes,—almost equal, in fact, to what we witnessed in *Doncaster* and *Macclesfield*. *Hallelujah!*

Afternoon. — Onward for victory. The Lord of hosts is with us. Sinners are slain on every side. The Gospel is the power of God unto salvation. But the power must be attended with an *unfaltering footstep*, a *bold heart*, and a *steady, trusty arm*, and a *fearless tongue*. The *French* poet spoke well, when he said,

> "O, he who in thy pathway treads,
> Must toil and pain endure!
> His head must plan the boldest deeds,
> His arm must make them sure."

Mr. Caughey speaks, in the above extracts from his journal, of the progress of the revival in Birmingham. The following, which we copy from a London newspaper, affords a better view of this extraordinary work, than can be gathered from the *glimpses* of it in the journal:

"BIRMINGHAM. — The Rev. Mr. Caughey has now been here for three weeks, and has preached in Newtown-Row and Belmont-Row Chapels, in the east circuit, and Wesley Chapel, in the west circuit. He was last week at Cherry-street, in the west circuit. The services in each of the chapels have been attended by overflowing audiences; and the work of God appears to be extending rapidly. Much good has been done, and much more is expected, for the Spirit of God is being poured out upon the people, and the impression made by Mr. Caughey's sermons is powerful and deep;—other denominations have caught the fire, and amongst the penitents have been recognized Baptists and Independents. The ministers, the leaders, and the local preachers, appear to be all animated with the spirit which has guided this servant of God across the Atlantic, and induced him to preach and labor in foreign lands.

"We believe the revival in Birmingham has taken deep root, and such an excitement has it created in the town on religious matters as was never before witnessed. Members of the church, who were dull and lethargic, have been aroused; sinners, who were deep in impiety, have been awakened and converted; and backsliders, whose case was thought almost hopeless, have again felt the efficacy of the redeeming blood of Christ. The scene which was presented in Cherry-street Chapel on Sunday night exceeds description. The chapel (which is the largest Methodist chapel in the town, and capable of accommodating more than two thousand persons) was densely crowded. The aisles, the pews, the space within the altar-rails, the vestries, and even the pulpit stairs, were crowded with anxious and attentive hearers.

"After the sermon, although many persons went away, the chapel was still crowded; and even the aisles were full. The prayer-meeting immediately commenced; and so great was the number of penitents, that the accommodation was totally insufficient, and the large school-room was filled. So deep is the interest felt in the progress of the revival, that some persons actually came twenty, thirty, forty, and even more than a hundred miles to hear Mr. Caughey preach. We are not in possession of the actual number of conversions, but they cannot be less than six hundred. Accurate lists are, however, kept, and we hope to be able to lay before our readers the actual result of Mr. Caughey's labors in Birmingham.

"BIRMINGHAM. — (Another account.) The revival of religion in this town now begins to assume a very encouraging and important aspect. The great amount of good which has been effected through the labors of that distinguished servant of God, the Rev. J. Caughey, from America, whose labors were so signally owned of God in several other large towns in this kingdom, has not been the less so here. In this town, Methodism may be considered far behind most of the other populous towns in the kingdom, compared with the density of its population, and it has oft been considered as an unfavorable soil for Methodism extensively to prosper. What from political agitation, mechanical ingenuity, which so greatly absorb the time and attention of the inhabitants, together with the prevalence of Sabbath desecration and intemperance, combined with infidelity and Catholicism, &c., render the simple story of Christ crucified a subject which they regard as beneath their attention.

"Although those hills may raise their heads, and appear to assume some prominence, yet it is written that the mountain of the Lord's house shall be established upon the tops of the mountain; she shall be exalted above the hills, and become the object of universal attraction, admiration, and delight; that all nations shall flow into it. And here, around our standard, we have not only Wesleyans, but members of different churches, and others who are of the world which lieth in wickedness, all pressing into our sanctuaries to listen to the powerful appeals, and to be made partakers of the quickening and soul-saving influence usually attendant upon the labors of this distinguished servant of the Most High. Not only is it that degraded sinners and backsliders, with dead, formal, pharisaical professors, are brought into deep penitence for sin by hundreds; but members and leading officials are raised to newness of life, and living in the comfort of the Holy Ghost, witnessing the truth of the apostle's doctrine, that the blood of Christ cleanseth from all sin. It was said, some two or three years ago, that Cherry-street Chapel was the mother chapel, and that she had grown old, and had ceased to bring forth children. But we now see it is not the advance of age, nor the pressure of infirmities under which she has labored from her heavy responsibilities, shall prevent her from bringing forth; but when overshadowed by the Holy Ghost, and the spirit of holy zeal is practically demonstrated by the church, then the barren shall bring forth, the solitary plain shall be made glad and blossom as the rose. Several hundreds have given in their names as having obtained pardoning mercy or sanctifying grace.

"On Monday evening, a missionary meeting was held at Belmont-Row Chapel, Dr. Waddy in the chair. The crowded audience was addressed by the Revs. J. Lawton and Tindal, in energetic, interesting speeches, followed by the Rev. J. Caughey, in strains both figurative and deeply affecting to the audience; after which, the Rev. J. Everett, from York, delivered one of the most interesting speeches ever listened to in the town of Birmingham. On the whole, it was considered one of the best missionary meetings that was ever held, and the collection about one fourth over last year. Mr. Caughey's labors have been continued at Cherry-street during the remainder of the week and an increased interest has continued to be exerted. The slain of the Lord may be said to be heaps upon heaps; the press of penitent seekers of salvation, and those seeking sanctifying grace, have been in such numbers, that the altar-rails were insufficient. The vestry and the large school-room have been frequently required, in addition, to accommodate them. Notwithstanding the powerful efforts displayed in the conversion of sinners of varied characters, from the degraded infidel to the formal professor, yet some would fain call it a mass of enthusiasm. Our worst wish to such is, that they may be brought under its influence, and be made the partakers of its effects, and be brought to possess that enthusiastic zeal which may lead them to present their bodies and souls as a living sacrifice to the Lord. If it be enthusiasm, it is that for which martyrs bled, which apostles and primitive Christians labored to promote, by converting sinners from the error of their ways. It partakes of the enthusiasm of the day of Pentecost, when, under Peter's preaching, three thousand were pricked in their hearts, and cried out, 'Men and brethren, what shall we do?'

"We are glad to add that the interest continues advancing; and it is pleasing to observe that many of the most talented and influential members are first and foremost in aiding in this great work. We hope this to only be the beginning of a most important era in the history of Methodistic revivalism in this populous town, and that similar energies will be continued, until its leavening influence shall be such as to affect the whole town, until the whole be leavened."

CHAPTER XLI.

NOTES OF CORRESPONDENCE AND PRIVATE REFLECTIONS.

A LETTER from one of my "field officers" in the late battles of *Sheffield and Chesterfield*,— fields of glory, where *laurels* were won that shall never wither! — good *John Levick!* But he writes himself down "*a disabled soldier*," but hoping soon to take the field again, as his *own* "*home* hospital," as he calls it, has in it an excellent nurse, in the person of a beloved wife. His soul is happy, and burns once more to be in the hottest of the battle for Christ and truth,—just as a disabled soldier of Jesus Christ should feel!

He reports good news from *Chesterfield;* — the labors of the *regular ministers* and their helpers greatly blessed,— souls saved *daily,— classes doubled* in numbers; — one minister has given to the winds his "*pulpit notes*," and speaks right out from the heart what comes next! — the *financials*, as might be expected. *Doncaster*, he says, is doing well, but the want of the church seems to be "a sanctified leadership." He writes, also, an exposition of 2 Cor. 1: 20, given by a *little girl* in the *Ebenezer* Chapel Sunday-school, Sheffield: "For all the promises of God in him are YEA, and in him AMEN, unto the glory of God by us." He asked the class of girls what they thought the apostle meant. It seemed to perplex all of them but one, a little girl of eleven or twelve years of age, who said, "I will tell you what I think it means. Now, if I were to ask God, 'Did not Jesus Christ suffer and die, to purchase all these blessings for *me?*' would he not say, '*Yea*'? and then if I were to say, '*Lord*, bestow them upon *me*, for Christ's sake,' would he not say '*Amen*' to my prayer?"

* * * * * *

But, alas! sad news from D—— of one whom I considered a spiritual child of mine, and of whom I had great hope;— but she has been suddenly called into eternity, under *painful circumstances.* *Mrs. H.* is no more! She and her sister, both intelligent ladies, sought and found an interest in Christ during my visit to D., and joined the Wesleyan Methodist church, and were both faithful for some time. At length, as a letter informs me, *Mrs. H.* became quite neglectful of class;— hoped she had found a way to heaven less *strict* and *precise*, and at length withdrew from the church; but not until her leader had again and again called upon her, with *invitations* and entreaties. But her mind was made up to walk in a way less narrow than that she had frequented, and his labors were in vain.

A few weeks since, on a Saturday evening, she retired to her room, not to prepare for the Sabbath, as she was wont, but to prepare for a *ball!* A *ball-dress* was to be got in readiness for the following Monday night.

Sabbath morning dawned, but the seat of *Mrs. H.* was vacant at the breakfast-table. A servant was dispatched to her room to make inquiries, when, alas! to her horror, she found *Mrs. H.* lying on the floor, a *corpse!* Her spirit had passed to the dread tribunal of God! The previous *Sabbath*, it appears, she listened to a very awakening discourse from 2 Cor. 6: 1,— "*We then, as workers together with him, beseech you also that ye receive not the grace of God in vain.*" Ah! this is a mournful case!

After reading the letter, I remembered having received a letter from one of these sisters, after I left D., but could not remember which; but, on turning to my note-book, I find it was from the *sister* of the deceased, and that the substance of the letter was, — *temptations* from former fashionable friends to return to the *pleasures of the world;* — that her reasons for refusing, when made known to them, they did not seem to understand or appreciate; — that they had used every argument that human ingenuity could devise, to turn her from that which they considered a *delusion*, — a term which these *fashionable* people applied to *conversion*. She concluded her letter by expressing her determination to resist all such temptations, and to be faithful until the end, adding: "We are wise, when we make a *choice*, after full conviction of its being best, to cast away *the means of return*. Thank God! my *choice is made,* — *my land is chosen,* — *I have crossed the stream, and I will break down the bridge behind me!*" Poor *Mrs. H.!* she could not withstand the temptations of a *flattering world*, — little knowing that *Death* was on the full march to meet her; — or, was it *the sin unto death?* — 1 John 5: 16, 17.

January 8th. — *Smooth words*, like round, smooth pebbles, do not *penetrate*, but roll off without making an impression. *Fine sentences*, and *handsomeness* of expression, do the same. They *please* men, but they *awaken* not, nor *wound* the conscience. *Words* and *sentences, angled* and *jagged* like *broken flints*, and *expressions* flying like *barbed arrows*, are the things for that. But, be it known unto thee, O my soul, against these, the world protests vehemently! Thou *knewest* it, and came forth with something *tastefully polished*, to the liking of flesh and blood. O beware!

However, the leaders have become *flames* of *fire* among *stubble*. But that is no reason why I should become a mere *phosphorescent*.

Engaged upon an Index for my "*Note Books;*" — in which I have noted many "items of interest," which it will be profitable to have at command, for the pulpit or for the press; — otherwise it *jades* the mind in hunting after them. My *tours* on the *Continent* have afforded me some rich material.

Have been looking back with gratitude upon the past year of my life; — a year of many *mercies*, and of considerable success to my ministry; — not less than between *four* and *five thousand* souls *justified*, and about *two thousand sanctified*, in the protracted services in which I have been engaged during the last *twelve months*. All glory to God! He doeth the works, and in every place he surrounds me with a *host of praying men* and *women*, to whom, under God, I owe much of my success. O, what a glorious *reward* awaits them above, if faithful to the end!

Jan. 9th. — *Wisdom* and *Prudence!* How necessary they should accompany burning *zeal!* Too much *prudence*, or overmuch *caution*, makes a cold and timid preacher, and *unfits* for such rough service as this; yet, a deficiency of these may lead a misguided *zeal* to spoil all. Lord, help me!

However, the work of God shows no pause. That text had great force, Psalm 16: 11, — "Thou wilt show me *the path of life:* in thy presence is *fulness of joy;* at thy right hand there are *pleasures for evermore.*" A sweet theme! — the *pleasures* of heaven! — the chief of which, a sight of *Jesus!* How that moves an audience! — especially when one can get such a view of Him, and language to express it such as the Holy Spirit alone can give the preacher, when that promise of *Jesus* has a fulfilment, "He shall *glorify me;* for he shall *receive of mine*, and will *show it unto you.*" But there is much we must die to know, even of Jesus and his glory. I believe with him who said, " Of all the objects of celestial blessedness, *Jesus* will stand first, the most conspicuous object of heavenly contemplation." The Psalmist was of the same opinion, when he exclaimed, " Whom have I in *heaven* but *thee?* and there is none upon *earth* that I *desire besides thee.*" He considered a sight of him, in heaven, the *loveliest, sweetest, grandest,* that heaven could afford; — so think I, and long to be there, to *see him as he is, and to be like him!* — 1 John 3 : 2.

> " Soon in heaven we 'll adore him,
> O, how he loves !
> Cast our glitt'ring crowns before him,
> O, how he loves !
> When the victory is completed,
> And around his throne we 're seated,
> Then we 'll sing, and still repeat it,
> O, how he loves ! "

A great move ; trophies of salvation many. Hallelujah !

Jan. 10th. Saturday morning. — *Sanctification* last night, — my usual theme on Friday nights. What a remarkable blessing from the Lord attends that doctrine ! What *want* or *dearth* is felt in that church or society where it is not preached, *fully,* clearly, *thoroughly,* heartily, and as a *present salvation*, attainable *now*, by faith ! *Mr. Wesley* was well persuaded of this when he wrote to one of his preachers thus : " When this is not preached, there is seldom any remarkable blessing from God, and consequently little addition to the society, or little life in the members of it. Speak, and spare not; let not regard to any man induce you to betray the truth of God. Till you press believers to expect *full salvation* NOW, you must not look for any *revival.*" Ay! and when that *grand doctrine* of the Gospel is thus faithfully preached, the effects are soon evident and glorious. "The *Gospel,*" as one observes, "will then be consulted as a *fresh charter* from heaven. *Promises,* which before were repeated with freezing accents, will now burn upon the lips, and will be *plead* with an *earnestness* that will open heaven." It was so, truly, last night. The work of *entire sanctification* (1 Thess. 5: 23, 24) has advanced with great rapidity and power the last few weeks; not less than *three hundred* persons have professed its attainment! A *noble pledge,* this, that these protracted services are not likely to leave the church *weary, wasted,* and *exhausted,* but rich in faith, and love, and holiness.

Jan. 12th. Monday morning. — I preached *twice,* yesterday, in the Islington Chapel, — a neat place of worship, in the suburbs of Birmingham. *Sixty* persons professed to find mercy, and *thirty* purity of heart. The scenes were indeed awfully grand and overwhelming, — such multitudes of wounded and distressed people crying for mercy! —

> " Deep wounded by the Spirit's sword,
> And then by Gilead's balm restored!"

Jan. 13th. — Delivered an address at the missionary meeting at *Islington,* last night, with considerable liberty and comfort, for *me,* — such a creature of circumstance am I on these platforms! English preachers are entirely at home there. They are the best *platform* speakers I ever listened to. I feel myself but a mere child there in their midst; and yet speak I must, if but as a child!

Mr. and Mrs. Greaves, from Sheffield, left for home to-day. They have been here a week or more, accompanied by *Mr. and Mrs. Denton*. They came over on purpose to enjoy the meetings. Mrs. G. has been the means of the conversion of one woman since she came. She happened to meet with her, and entered into *conversation*, telling her for what purpose they had come all the way from *Sheffield*. Nothing more was heard of the woman till a night or two since, when she arose in a meeting and declared what great things God had done for her soul, and how she happened to attend the meetings;—that a *lady* from *Sheffield* talked with her about religion, and told her how far they had come to hear "the stranger;"—that, pondering on the fact that such fine-looking people had come so far to hear him, it excited her curiosity, and she resolved to go herself; the word reached her heart, and she had no rest until she found the Saviour precious to her soul!

I am now entertained at the house of *Mr. Souter*, surrounded with comforts,—quite on the other side of the town, and nearer the chapels where we hold the services. The *Rev. George Turner* is the superintendent.

CHAPTER XLII.

DISPASSIONATE PREACHING.

To * * * * * *.

*   *   *   *   *   *

YOUR ideas of "dispassionate preaching" are all very well, provided there were no sinners here in danger of *hell-fire;* and no sleepy, inconsistent *professors* to be awakened out of their delusive dreams;—if all were holy, just and good; otherwise, such preaching may be unto them, what Ezekiel's was to a certain class in his day, —"*unto them as a very lovely song of one that hath a pleasant voice,* and can play well on an instrument." God himself used that figure in speaking with the prophet, adding, "*For they hear thy words, but they do them not.*"— Ezek. 33 : 32. It was no wonder the Lord commanded him to *smite with his hand, and stamp with his foot,* while speaking to them of the evil of their doings, and their *coming miseries.*— Ezek. 6 : 11.

There is a great plenty of such preaching as you admire; — allow one solitary preacher to differ somewhat, if upon no other principle than the old proverb, "*Variety* is the *spice* of life!"

Goldsmith, you remember, compared a certain class of minds to *liquors* that never *ferment,* and are consequently always *muddy.* But you will not allow the style you admire to be muddy;— well, perhaps it is not. It may be *clear* enough, and *cold* as clear! O, sir, give me the *fermented style!*—what St. Paul calls "*fervent in spirit,*" —that moves others also, and puts all the town in a *ferment!*

However, whatever *others* may do is nothing to me. My duty is plain,— to preach the whole truth of God with all my soul, mind and strength.

"*Perish discretion* when it interferes with duty."

What we do should be *done to purpose;* effect something; not only move ourselves, but move others — out of their sins to Christ; — move the church, and better it, and not be at an *everlasting stand-still.*

Erasmus tells us of a man, named *Rabirius*, who wanted his servant, Syrus, to get up, and called to him to *move*. "I do move," replied Syrus. "I see you *move*," rejoined the master, "but you *move nothing!*" Now, there may be much religious activity, and yet not a sinner moved out of his sins, and the church very little advanced in holiness. When we *move*, we should move to some purpose, and accomplish something!

* * * * * *

To the same.

Dean Swift used to say, preaching has two principal branches: 1st, to tell people *what is their duty;* and, 2d, to *convince* them that it is so. I think the dean should have had a thirdly:—to *move* them *to do* what they are *told* is their duty, and what they are *convinced* is their duty!

Now, with my *statements* regarding the duty of believers · and sinners you have no complaint; nor of my *arguments*, which effect *conviction;* but rather in my *manner* of moving them to act in accordance with their convictions.

Ah, my friend! if we were really *agreed* in head and heart about the great *end* of preaching, the *manner* of it, I fancy, would be of trifling moment, so that *truth is preached*, and *sinners are converted by it!*

If your neighbor's house were on fire, in dead of night, and the family fast asleep, and a neighbor, after a tremendous knocking and uproar, should succeed in arousing and saving them, you would be little disposed to *chide* him for the *manner* in which he did it. Your own good sense can make the *application*.

Whatever answers the *end* for which it was ordained is usually accounted good; the *air* we breathe, the *food* we eat, the *water* we drink, the *flower* we smell, the *bird* that sings, the *sun* that shines, and the *fire* that warms, — ay, and the *thunder*, and *lightning*, and *stormy winds*, which roll the clouds into heaps upon heaps, rending them into atoms, and which bring down the teeming shower over the thirsty land! You know the *design* of the Gospel; and that it is a *real good* only so far as it answers the *end* for which it was ordained. Is *that end* being answered now among the sinners of your great town? Surely, you cannot reasonably doubt! O, then, quarrel not with the *manner!* Let the *fruits* speak for themselves. I ask you to examine the *fruits*, whether they are *Gospel fruits*, or something else. Be assured of one thing, the "*dispassionate preaching*," of which you are so fond, would never have turned this tide of souls another way to that in which it was moving a month ago!

The *sword*, that gives the soldier *victory* on the field, is accounted trusty and true, inasmuch as it has answered the design for which it was made, and for which he *wielded* it, however *clumsily*, or *untastefully*, or *violently*, wielded. But what is *war* but a science of *violence?* The Gospel is a *sword* as well as a *sceptre* of mercy. St. Paul says it is *quick* and *powerful*, and *sharper* than any *two-edged sword, dividing asunder the joints and the marrow*, and is a *discerner*, or lays open the *very thoughts of the heart*, as the knife of the surgeon 'lays open the *seat of the disease*, or the *cause of death*. The Gospel is a science of *war*, against the world, the flesh, and the devil. Its *weapons*, though not *carnal*, as the apostle hints, are yet *mighty through God to the pulling down of strong holds, and casting down imaginations, and every other high thing that exalteth itself against the knowledge of Christ, and leading into captivity every thought to the obedience of Christ!* Such was *St. Paul's* idea of the Gospel; such it was in his day, and such it really begins to be in Birmingham.

In the hand of a Christ-sent preacher, the Gospel is a *sword* as well as a *sceptre ;* but of what use is a sword, however much adorned, if not *wielded energetically*, and if it *fail in execution?* "A sword that hath an hilt of gold, set with diamonds, is no good sword," says an old divine, "if it have no *edge* to cut, or want a good back to follow home the stroke." This was his illustration of *effective preaching!*

*   *   *   *   *   *

To the same.

But have you never considered Jer. 23 : 29 ? — "*Is not my word like as a* FIRE, *saith the Lord; and like a* HAMMER *that breaketh the rock in pieces?*" What! and laid on *dispassionately?* Nay, verily! when *fire* and *hammers* go to the work of *rock-breaking*, the thing is not done in *quietude* and *stillness*. But you will reply, "The *fire and hammers* of the Gospel have been going on quietly in Birmingham for years." Very well, and so they have; but have you ever seen so many *hundreds* of *rocky-hearted* sinners broken in pieces, as within the last eight or ten days, in Birmingham?

Ah, my friend, where the *Gospel fire* is kindled but sparingly, and the *hammers of truth* are laid on carelessly or coldly, they *effect* but *little, very little*. But I have no time for more. You must stand aside, out of the way of the sword and our artillery, if you cannot join in the fight. This is no time to falter. If it be the last battle for Christ and souls, allowed me in England, Amen!—but I shall push this forward with the might and energy God supplies;— *onward*, and sweep the *living storm of war* against the trembling ramparts of human depravity and diabolical power!— shall

' Keep back no *syllable of fire*,
Plunge deep the *rowels of our speech!*''

CHAPTER XLIII.

MORE PENCILLINGS OF THE REVIVAL IN BIRMINGHAM.

JANUARY 14th. — My style of preaching begins to be understood, and appreciated more and more. *Faith*, and the *sensibilities of faith*, dispose to this very *swiftly*. It requires a man to have *life* and *reason* to understand a *dissertation* upon life and reason. And the *sinner* must have some *spiritual life* and *sensibility* to appreciate what is called "*revival preaching*," which is *life* and *quickness* of perception and sensation. The more quickly are life and sensibility awakened and diffused among the masses, the more swiftly does the work of God progress. Many saved last night.

Jan. 15th. — How these daily effects of *truth* upon the consciences of sinners, do prove its *divinity*; — ay, and the soul's immortality, — its *depravity*, and its concealed sense of *accountability* after death, — *predisposing* it to sensibility and alarm!

Who can stand before the majesty and power of his *truth*, when accompanied by the *presence* of the SPIRIT of *truth?* But O, who can stand before it unflinchingly in eternity? None but *the pure* in heart; only such can enter that holy *elysium* above, the eternal abode of *truth!* I was struck with that sentiment of Dr. Chalmers, that heaven is a sanctuary guarded by all the holiness and by all the jealousies of the Godhead, and so repugnant to the approach of pollution, that if it offer to draw nigh, the fire of a consuming indignation would either check or destroy it. There is something of this perception, I think, always accompanies *truth*.

Jan. 16th. — A *moving point* that! — must return upon it with a new *impetus*, as perception is clearer, — it will bear it, — that *Theology* is the study of *Earth* and *Heaven* and *Hell!* He who refuses to study it properly here, shall be driven to it in *hell*, by the *arguments* of its flames and torments. A *terrible thought*, and true as terrible. He that learns not the *wisdom* it teaches *here*, must be taught it *there*, *necessarily*, but not *savingly* ; for imperfect consideration is *impossible* in hell; and equally impossible it should result in salvation. Ah! but it is a sad and terrible consideration, that *torments* will teach that which *mercy* could not! O, may this consideration *move my heart* to feel for sinners around me ! Amen.

An interesting letter from York says, " I am one of those new converts, confirmed * by you when in York, the Friday evening before you left us. I had been in the way before, but had *strayed*, in consequence of some unfortunate and perplexing events, over which I could exercise no control. I am now going on my way rejoicing. The following interposition of Providence for me and mine will interest you. I was out of a *situation* when you were here, and so for a considerable time; and all my applications were abortive, — self and family depending on casualty, and were enveloped in difficulty.

" One day, in *secret prayer* I determined to lay all my

---

* He refers to the somewhat peculiar service which I usually hold for the benefit of the young converts, which tends much to *confirm* and *establish* them in the grace wherein they stand.

affairs before the Lord. Did so, and plead my case, and that of my family, that my way might be opened for their *support;* that a door might be opened for me, which no man could shut. I put the whole matter into his hands, closing with prayer for spiritual blessings; resolved now to just wait and watch, for I felt I could do nothing more in the matter.

"At the end of *three weeks* a gentleman called upon me, from a quarter I least expected, and offered me a *clerkship,* where I am now in comfort. My *salary,* it is true, is only moderate, but I am *content.* '*Godliness, with contentment, is great gain.*' Some, sir, would call this *chance,* — that it just *happened* so. Yes, it did *happen!* but to me, who knew the circumstances, it appeared a species of *miracle* in answer to *importunate, believing prayer.*

"It has been said that prayer without effort is *enthusiasm,* and unavailing. It may be so, as a general rule, but my case formed an exception; — was left, like as when we pray for *dry weather,* we can only pray and wait, for we can do nothing more to bring about a change in the elements."

This good brother was like Noah and his family in the ark of the deluge; helplessly drifting on, they knew not whither, "till a dying surge, as by an angel's hand," found them bottom up on the *top* of one of the *Ararat mountains.* There are many wonderful illustrations of "*the prayer* of faith," among God's people, if one could but collect them together, but which now lie concealed in the memories of his faithful, but *hidden ones.* There will be a glorious telling of these things in *heaven,* by and by.

Jan. 17th. Saturday morning. — *Purity,* last night. That is, indeed, a *convincing* and *encouraging* text, — Acts 15 : 9, — "*And put no difference between us and them, purifying their hearts by faith,*" as it shows that purity of heart is *attainable*, and also *how* it is attained, — "by faith." The effect is fine when Mark 11: 24, is united with it: "Therefore, I say unto you, what things soever ye *desire* when ye pray, *believe* that ye receive them, *and ye shall have them.*" And, then, to show the difference between desiring purity *indistinctly*, and praying and believing for it *indistinctly;* and doing the same thing, but *distinctly;* that they might desire it, and pray for it with all the sincerity of a *Moses*, but if they did not *believe* for it *distinctly*, and *now*, to be received as a *present blessing* by *faith*, it would be but desiring and praying and believing in *vain;* so far, at least, as a distinct and conscious *reception* of the blessing is concerned.

This method brings *faith* before their eyes directly, and in the commanding position assigned to it in the *New Testament*. It is just saying of it, as the Lord God did of *Joshua* to Moses: "But *Joshua*, the son of *Nun*, which standeth before thee, he shall go in thither; *encourage him, for he shall cause Israel to inherit it.*" — Deut. 1: 38. *Works*, like Moses, had brought these *Birmingham* Christians to the *Jordan* of salvation; but *faith*, like *Joshua*, was to cause them to *inherit;* was to lead them over into the *Canaan* of purity and perfect love. Blessed be God! as *Joshua* led Israel over Jordan, dry-shod, into the promised land, so did *faith* much people, last night! There was a great move among the *tribes;* and a great consternation among the Canaanites, and the overthrow of many a towering *Jericho!* My soul might well cry out with Petrarch :

"Victorious *faith*, to thee belongs the prize,
On *earth* thy *power* is *felt*, and in the *circling skies.*"

Jan. 19th. Monday. — A great victory *yesterday*. Sinners are leaving the ranks of sin, *scores* following *scores !* —Wonderful ! O, how deep and pungent their *convictions* for sin ! How clear their sense of pardon ! How deep and tender their gratitude to God and man for so great a *deliverance !* and what unutterable humility and love ! O, who could doubt the genuineness of such a work as this ! *Hallelujah !*

The *Sheffield* brethren, noble souls ! are perpetuating that work of God there, nobly. Brother *Unwin* writes me, " I have sent out to be distributed to-morrow afternoon, within half a dozen streets of *Carver-street* Chapel, *five hundred* of the following bill :

"I shall go to-night to the Methodist Chapel,

" Because it is the LORD'S DAY, not mine ; and I must spend it so as to please HIM, not myself.

" Because I have a SOUL to be saved. I am a SINNER, under sentence of death ; and, unless I repent, I must perish forever.

" Because TIME is short : DEATH is sure : I may die to-morrow : and if I be not pardoned and prepared for Heaven, what will become of my poor soul ? '*The wicked shall be turned into Hell, and all the nations that forget God.*'— Psalm ix. 17. If I could have all the pleasures of this world, and enjoy them a thousand years, yea, for ten thousand ; yet, if I were to lose my soul — I should be a fool ; for Time is nothing compared to Eternity. O, ETERNITY, ETERNITY, ETERNITY ! Who can tell the length and breadth of Eternity !

" Because the Minister will tell me how to make my peace with God, to get my soul converted, and to find the way to Heaven. And then there will be a PRAYER-MEETING ! That is just what I need. O, I WISH I

COULD PRAY! Some of my wicked neighbors have gone to Chapel, and been converted: and now they are so changed! they are good and happy all day long. I wish I were like them; for I am miserable, and I AM SO AFRAID TO DIE. They are on the road to Heaven; I am on the way to Hell. But I MUST, I WILL REPENT; and I shall BEGIN TO-NIGHT; for 'NOW is the accepted time, NOW is the day of salvation.'

"Come! let us all go to the Methodist Chapel.*

"* *That is, if you are not going to another place of worship.*"

Jan. 21st. Wednesday. — Blessings come in *hurricanes* these days! These are Pentecostal days in Birmingham. Great liberty in preaching the word,

" And every feeling uttered, fully felt."

O, how evidently does the hand of our God *endorse* and attest the truth of his revealed will in the glorious Gospel of his Son! *Showers of blessings!* Hallelujah!

CHAPTER XLIV.

A MEMENTO.

* * * * * * *

YES, I had a hard time of it; *beating the air*, or as one throwing *feathers*; and I know the *cause* very well; and that is a *mercy*, otherwise I might have come to some rash or false *conclusion*.

It should be a *lesson* to me. This *lightness* of heart *before* preaching is not quite the thing; not *safe*, however *innocent*, — an innocent light-heartedness, as religious people would call it; but neither *innocent* nor *wise* in one who was about to stand between the *living* and the *dead*, — between *sinners* and *incensed justice*, and a *burning hell*, and a grieved Holy Spirit, and an interceding High Priest, and a justly offended God! "*He that winneth souls is wise*," says *Solomon*. Ay, but it is not wise to go about that work with a *loose* and *careless spirit!* This I know, and therefore I am *accountable*.

How liable I am to the *temptation* to *unbuckle* my *spiritual armor*, if I sit down for a *tea-table chit-chat*, even among good people; to *sheathe the sword of truth within*, and lay it aside, instead of burnishing it, and sharpening it, and looking at it, and at the *cause* for which it must be *wielded*, till my soul is fired "*to do exploits*," as the angel said to *Daniel*. And how such *tea-table sociability* smoothes down the *wrinkles of war*, and melts off the *horns,* and the *angles,* and the *spear-points* of *awakening truth* from the mind; so *sunny,* so *congenial* the atmosphere around approving friends! And then to hurry off to the pulpit without the proper time of being alone with God, or to *buckle on the armor anew,* and to *examine* the mind, as to the state of *truth* in it, around it, and upon it; and to see to my *sword,* — whether it has not *lost edge* in the sheath, or gathered *rust* in the soft, congenial atmosphere of the *tea-table.*

O, I did not get near enough to God! My views of *truth,* and of the *peril* of sinners, of *God,* of *Christ,* of the *Spirit,* and of my own *responsibility,* were far from being *intensified* as they ought. *Heaven, Hell, Calvary,* were not brought near enough to *arouse* and *alarm* me. Did not enter the *cloud* of the divine presence far enough to receive the necessary *unction* from above. Had not time. O, thou *sounding brass! thou tinkling cymbal!* let this be a lesson! — *must keep out of company,* and be much alone with God, *upon the holy mountain, walking up and down in the midst of the stones of fire;* then cometh the soul from thence, among the people, as *the anointed cherub.* — Ezek. 28 : 14.

If my spirit could not be allowed "*a holiday,*" it plead for a *light shoulder* at an *unseasonable hour;* and for that, it has gained an *additional weight* of the *old burden!*

"Keep thy soul loose about thee."

Nay, nay, my good old *Herbert!* that was the cause of my sorrow. My soul was *too loose* about me! Hard to preach so. The *bow* must be well bent, that speeds the *decisive arrow.* A *slack soul* has neither *energy* nor *unction,* — as one beating the air, truth leaving the lips like an arrow from a slack string. Ay, that was the *trouble!* and not for the first time neither! Alas, no! nor for the *hundredth* time.

The *arrow* that speeds to the *mark* and penetrates, must fly from a *well-bent* bow and a *tight string*. When one's soul is *bowed intensely*, the words fly like barbed arrows, straight to the *mark*. As a preacher in Germany remarked, "Your arrow should be shot from a *tight* bowstring of a perfect *inward confidence* and *certainty ;* then it becomes '*the arrow of the Lord's deliverance.*'" Ay, that is it! to feel that we are "*honest* in the sacred cause," not striving for *self*, but for *Christ*, and for *souls ;* that the *cause* is *His*. This gives great boldness, firmness and intensity. The message is *His* message. The *disclosures* we are making are *His will* and *desires* towards those who hear. To *believe*, to feel that this is His *own word* I am uttering, the very *thoughts of His heart* I am echoing ; to speak with this conviction, confers upon the soul a *tremendous confidence and energy.*

The *possibility* of the loss of a single soul, besides : lost by *misunderstanding*, or *misapplying* the message, or *presuming* simply upon it, or *rejecting* it ; or that this may be his *last call ;* the Spirit is giving him the last offer of mercy ; that within a very few days, he may be in "that lone land of deep despair, where none is found to hear or save ;" and the cold, heartless preacher, possibly, share the blame of his *damnation!* Ah! to *feel* these thoughts till the *body groans*, and the *soul* bows itself in an agony, and cries for help, and then goes forth from the *secret place* like a *Samson*, to feel for the *pillars* of scepticism, and pride, and sin, and unbelief; heaven, and hell, and earth looking on in an amaze, and hearkening for the *crash* of the temple of sin, and the cries of the slain of the Lord, as the soul of the preacher bows itself, crying, "Victory or death!" Ah me! such a *preparation* is seldom attained during a *tea-table chit-chat*, and religious pleasantry! Ah no! but *alone with God, crying,*—

> "My powerful groans thou canst not bear,
> Nor stand the violence of my prayer,
> My prayer omnipotent."

There, and there only, with rare exceptions, the arm of the soul is nerved with the energy of the God of Jacob. There, and there only, the whole man bows under the *stress* of his principles and emotions, "like a tight bowstring;" and then, look for the arrows of truth flying thick and fast, and sticking fast in the hearts of the king's enemies;—and the falling down of the people, and the consequent *cries*, prove that "*Thine arrows are sharp in the hearts of the King's enemies,*" O Lord God of hosts!—Ps. 45: 5.

O, who can *describe* the scenes which follow!—the effects of the word thus preached with the Holy Ghost sent down from heaven! St. Paul attempts it in Heb. 4: 12. Then it becomes "*the word of God,*" *indeed;* and not a *sword* only, but a *royal sceptre*, in the hand of such a preacher;—and more *potent* than all the *kingly sceptres* upon the face of the earth; for it *accomplishes* what all their power combined could never effect. "The *spirits* are subject unto us, through thy name." The place occupied by such a preacher is a *battle-field*, indeed! and his *pulpit a throne of power*,—and victory all around. "In one part of the field," as a German divine remarks, "spiritual restraints are imposed;—in another, *darts* and *hooks* are cast into the *heart;*—in a third instance, a *leviathan* is bound in chains of adamant;—in a fourth, the strength of the *wicked* is broken the *audacious* confused and ashamed, the *adversa-*

ries disarmed, *blasphemies* silenced, and the *licentious* forced back, at least, within the bounds of external order;— and, in a fifth instance, *Zion's banners* are encompassed by the *new subjects* of omnipotent grace;— and by such a preacher, effects like the above will everywhere and always accompany his word." I believe it, O my *German* brother! So have we seen it in *Birmingham*, and so shall we see it again, the same Divine Power assisting us. O, my Lord, preserve me henceforth from ever going into the pulpit in a careless spirit, and my *armor* loose about me! Amen. But, I suppose,

" Our *virtues* would be *proud*, if our *faults whipped them not!* "

However, it did me good! It is profitable to be well *humbled.* It leads to great " *searchings of heart,*" and drives the despairing and weakened soul to the feet of God,— *lays it low*, and *keeps* it low, and there! Amen.

I entered the pulpit the following night, with my *soul tight about me;* and had a precious time. O, what freedom and enlargement of soul! What ardor! O, but God did make my soul,

" As the rapt seraph that *adores* and *burns.*"

But, as *usual*—and O, how often it occurs!—upon retiring to my room, sunk into deep *humiliation* before the Lord, in view of my many *infirmities*, and *imperfections* as a speaker. The people are mown down like grass before the scythe of God's word. Not less than *thirteen hundred* sinners have been converted to God during the last *seven weeks;* and about *six hundred believers* have obtained *purity of heart.* All the glory be to God alone! He doeth the works, though in *infinite condescension*, he deigns to employ very weak and unworthy *instruments* in accomplishing his purposes of mercy.

The work is advancing with *unabated power* daily. There are some *adversaries* which spring up now and then, but are soon borne down by this inundating outpouring of the Holy Spirit. Hallelujah!

CHAPTER XLV.

GLIMPSES OF THE REVIVAL AND PRINCIPLES OF ACTION.

JANUARY 24th. Saturday. — *Sanctification* last night. A *heavenly calm* in the audience, so different from the *hurricanes* of emotions through the week. Had sweet *harmony* in my own soul,— the heart so in *unison* with the head, and a *breathing* like an air of Paradise within and around, increasing in power, till the listening multitude were stirred into an intense *breathing* after holiness. Many went away from under the word, like *Naaman* out of Jordan, cured of their spiritual leprosy.

Jan. 26th. Monday. — This driving the *knowledge of the head* down into the *heart*, creates strange scenes among the people. *Truth*, that has lain *dead* for years in the brain and imagination, when driven down upon the conscience, creates a wonderful uproar! It never, really, till then, becomes *effectual* to the salvation of the possessor. But "victory is of the Lord," and surely he did give us the victory, in the salvation of *scores* of precious souls!

Jan. 28th. — Pressed hard upon the *worldly-would-be-religious*, who, as one expressed it, "have nothing to offer God, but some *heartless service*, which the *world* can *spare*, and which are but the *leavings* of the flesh," — after the manner of *Cain* and his offering! — Gen. 4 : 3.

Jan. 29th. — Heavy, effective *ordnance*, in active operation, on our *spiritual batteries!* And what a dismounting of *sataniv-ordnance*,— carnal reasoning,— high imaginations,— prejudice,— ignorance,— error and folly; and as if, in the overturn, poor sinners would be torn into pieces!

The Lord grants me great peace of mind. Homely, but true, are those two lines of the old poet:

> "When all is done and said, in the end this shall ye find,
> He most of all doth bathe in bliss that hath a *quiet mind*."

And yet my soul retains its *antagonistic* energy, and the work advances in power. Last week, at Wesley Chapel, *one hundred and ninety* were saved. The week previous, at Islington Chapel, *two hundred and forty* were saved. So speaks the *Register*. What the Lamb's book of life in heaven speaks, we must *die to know*; and to know it with safety, or with comfort, or with joy, we must die in the Lord.

The people are *greatly moved*, and *easily moved*, now, and very *tender*; so easy to draw *tears*, and set them a *weeping* on every side! How wonderful the *change* which the Gospel can make in a people! The *eyes* which were dry as the sky, in the days of *Elijah*, during the three years drought, now weep tears of joy, like the same sky, after Elijah said to Ahab, "There is a sound of abundance of rain!" Bless thou the Lord, O my soul!

Have spent several *Monday* evenings past in assisting the brethren in town, at their missionary meetings; who considerately fixed upon that evening, as least interfering with the work. Had gracious assistance; and the *collections* were much in advance of last year. A writer considers the *sixteenth* century as the age of natural and scientific discovery; the *eighteenth*, the age of infidelity and revolution; and the *nineteenth* century, as illustrious for missionary effort for the evangelization of the world. In such an effort Birmingham seems determined not to be behind.

Jan. 30th. — Beware of *tinsel* and *finery*, O, my soul! — *dressing up the truth as if it were to sell!* as the *Spaniard* hinted; making it to appear a mighty fine thing, and you, J. C., a mighty fine preacher, and the people to think themselves "a mighty intelligent" people, to understand and appreciate it all! Alas! alas! *Admiration* is a poor substitute for *salvation!*

Jan. 31st. — *Holiness* last night. These *Friday* night discourses bring me back to the simplicity of the Gospel. They leave, also, a *sweet tincture* of *purity* upon my spirit; — make me feel with one, "I had rather be *holy* than be *eloquent;*" a sentiment that finds a sweet response within me this morning.

Matt. 21 : 22, is a noble and influential promise: *"And all things whatsoever ye shall ask in prayer, believing, ye shall receive."* It affords a fine field for the exhibition of the power of faith. It shows, also, why sincere desires after *purity* are not *gratified;* — *believing* is omitted. When we *believe* that we do *receive*, other things being equal, we roll the whole burden of our wants upon the veracity of Christ, of whom it is said, "Cast thy *burden* upon the Lord, and he shall sustain thee." Here is a strong point; but might have been rendered more *effectual* by being less *complicated.* O, for more *simplicity* in spirit and style!

Feb. 2d. Monday. — *Satan's captives* are extensively in trouble. It is evident he is fearing a *wholesale rescue*. To have them *damned without rescue*, was his *hope*. Our Lord Jesus Christ takes pleasure in rendering Satan *hopeless* in more ways than one! Glorious scenes yesterday!

Have just returned from a walk; — not *joyful*, but a *sweetness* in spirit; — a good thought that, that my *happy days* have far exceeded my *unhappy* ones, thus far in my Christian pilgrimage; — and my *peaceful times* have been much *longer* in continuance than my *times of war*; — and my seasons of *prosperity* more *numerous* than those of *adversity*; — that my *great troubles*, like days in *winter*, have been *short*, and, like *stormy days, few*; — and my *happy days*, like *summer* days, *long*, and, like *fair* and *pleasant days, many*, and by far the greatest in *number*, through all the years of my *spiritual life*, hitherto! Praise the Lord! And would it not have been otherwise, had not my gracious Lord sanctified my soul in 1831?

* * * * * *

A gracious time at the sacrament. What a *cloud* of *communicants*, scores, if not hundreds, of whom had never commemorated the Lord's death before!

It has done my own soul good; — I feel *stronger*, — as if new life, vigor, and zeal, had been infused into my soul. I usually feel so after partaking of the sacrament, and for *weeks*.

In ancient times, before *battle*, they used to show the *blood* of grapes and mulberries to the *war elephants*, to make them more *fierce* in battle. Well, a *sight* of these sacred emblems of the *broken body* and *shed blood* of my Lord stimulates my soul wonderfully to fight his battles, and gain victories!

Feb. 3d. — How quickly, after hearing a sermon or two, do persons of certain ranks and habits, disappear! So true is that remark of one, that there are those who will *play with the light*, who will not endure to be *melted by the fire!* But others come in their places, and so the truth is dropped into the more ears, and we know not which shall prosper, this or that.

To *** ***.

*   *   *   *   *   *

Birmingham, Feb. 6, 1846.

"Toiling on." To be sure! For what purpose did I enter the vineyard of my Lord, but to *work?* Certainly not to have a life of ease, nor to play, or to *amuse* myself or others! For what did I join the army of *Immanuel?* To *fight,* or enjoy an inglorious ease? To idle away my time? Nay, my dear friend, but to *fight* his battles, and to *endure hardness as a good* soldier of Jesus Christ! Or, if you will allow me the use of another figure, for what did I enter the *lists* upon the great *race-ground* of *preachers?* To run for the prize, or to *sit still* and *lounge?* Nay, but to run for the *prize,* — a double prize, — *heaven* and *souls.* Well, then, while I have breath in me, let me never lose the spirit of this! While I have *health,* may I never cease running for such a prize, — SOULS! While life and health do last, O, may I *work,* fight, run! — *true* to my *principles* laid down in the *onset;* to which the heart of my *fearful friend* cannot help saying, "Amen!"

To *** ***.

Birmingham, Feb. 17.

Laboring on with all my might, to make *sin bitter,* that the *Gospel* may be *sweet* to the sinner. Never can the Gospel be made truly *sweet* until the sinner is made to know and *feel* that it is *an evil thing and a bitter* to sin against God. — Jer. 2 : 19. Nor is *Christ* ever *sweet* till sin is turned into *wormwood.* Nor does Christ give *rest* to any, but to those who feel sin to be a *burden*. It is to those who *labor* and are *heavy laden*, Jesus gives the invitation to come to him and find *rest*, as we see in Matt. 11 : 28.

He invites the *heavy laden* to come unto him; those to whom the sense of unpardoned sin is a burden too heavy to be borne. It is my business, then, to *load* them down quickly as possible.

Well, I have been trying hard so to do; and to make the past and present *sins* of every sinner bitter, — ay, as wormwood, that the name of *Jesus* may be *sweet* and *desirable*, and sin heavy, — ay, as Byron said of it, as a *mountain* of *lead* upon the heart! — that they may be more anxious to get rid of their *burden!* After doing my best to bring all this about, I then preach unto them *Jesus;* and, O, how sweet he is to *their* souls, and also to *mine!* For, in making *sin* bitter and heavy to them, I cannot help thinking of *my own*, — sins of my youth and childhood, — sins before my conversion and after, — and much *unfaithfulness* in the past; and, though my *conscience* is assured of pardon, yet it would relapse into uneasiness and *the spirit of bondage again to fear*, if not met by a returning *faith* in that blood that has washed them all away. And so, when Jesus has thus become *their Saviour* and *mine*, O, what an ocean of sweetness do we all find in that wondrous *name!* And, then, how sweetly do we all sing:

> " Blest with the scorn of finite good,
> My soul is lightened of her load,
> And seeks the things above.
>
> " The things eternal I pursue,
> A happiness beyond the view
> Of those who basely pant
> For things by nature felt and seen ;
> Their honors, wealth, and pleasures mean,
> I neither have nor want ! "

Had a very awful time on the day of judgment, the other night, in *Wesley Chapel.* — Rev. 20 : 11, 13. When describing " the books " that shall be opened on that great day, I noticed the *Book of Privileges;* — *where* the condemned sinner lived and died; — the *light* under which he sinned; — *the means of salvation* within his reach; — the *sermons* he heard, or *might have heard*, had he pleased. Here an idea of *Horne*, which I had read many years ago, occurred to me,— that, on this great and terrible day of God, the sinner will be held as accountable for *what he might have known*, as for what he did know; — that, among all the subjects which might be said to belong to *speculative theology*, there is none more *terrible* than this.

Language of unusual *power*, with *vividness of thought*, were given me at this moment, such as I may never, possibly, have again; — was enabled to climb to heights which commanded much of the *judgment scene;* and the vast congregation climbed with me, — not one appeared to be left behind; — and, when at a certain point, and a *precipice* formed, the *alarming* thought that condemned men, in the judgment, shall have to account to God *for what they might have known*, as *well as for what they did know*, — O, it seemed as if we were all going over the *precipice* together! — till the feelings of the multitude gave way, in one *terribly convulsed* cry! O, I cannot describe it! — it was like the rushing sound of many waters, — crashing and breaking through dams and embankments, and all opposing barriers; till there were *groans*, and *shouts*, and *cries*, like the voices of the judgment! It was as if that day of terrors had really opened upon us, "and all beneath the cope of heaven in flames," — the risen dead assembled, the judgment set, and the books opened!

Never had I such a time upon the *last judgment;* never

saw such an *effect* produced by it. The prayer-meeting at the close was glorious in results. O, how evident it appeared to me that "*the times and seasons*" for such *extraordinary manifestations* "*the Father hath put in his own power!*" — Acts 1 : 7. But, doubtless, did I but walk as *closely* and as *steadily* with God as he requires, such visitations from on high would neither be few nor far between.

CHAPTER XLVI.

SANCTIFYING AND AWAKENING TRUTHS.

SATURDAY morning, Feb. 7th. — Christian *holiness* my theme last night. — Mark 11 : 24, is a rich *mine.* What *precious metal* may be dug from it in doctrine and experience ! It may be likened to a *magazine* also; for what *material* of war has it furnished me ? — that which has blown up and destroyed many of the strong works of the Devil ! O, when I can *persuade* the *people* to make it their own, what mighty *effects* do follow ! How it does sweep those hearts "where *passion* has woven its thousand thousand webs — its *webs* of thousand thousand threads, in grain and hue all different ! " What *tales* of *sorrow* and *deliverances* come to my ears ! *Spider-webs* give way not more easily before the sweep of the housewife's broom, than do these webs of passion and Satan, under the sweeping operations of that promise. A great move, last night, through the power of the Holy Ghost, in the promise. Hallelujah !

Feb. 14th. — Over *one hundred and fifty* souls saved since last date.

Holiness last night. For an *application*, Mark 11 : 24 is mighty. "What things soever ye *desire* when ye *pray*, *believe that ye receive, and ye shall have."* It is, indeed, *one of the exceeding great and precious promises, by which we are made partakers of the divine nature. —* 2

Peter 1: 4. It demands of the soul *immediate honor* to the *veracity* of Jesus. It shames unbelief, and amazingly humbles the *tardy professor;* he who boasted so much of his "Protestant faith," which "had ever honored the veracity of God in the Holy Scriptures," but now finds it very hard to put *implicit confidence* in the *veracity of Jesus!* Poor soul! it is well if anything will open his eyes to that cursed *unbelief* which reigns in his heart. Cursed it is of God, and a *curse* it is to the soul of him who indulges it.

Feb. 16th. Monday. — *Truth* is like *lightning* from heaven; the preaching of it is a *thunder*, which is "as the hiding of his power." There may be a *false fire*, an *Aurora Borealis*, quite amusing to the *curious;* but what does it accomplish? It cannot do the work of the *red lightning*, and the *thunder* crashing among the clouds. There may be a noise like thunder, or like the discharge of *cannon* without *ball*, which do *no execution*. But, when such a mass of *sinners* as last night were *struck down*, it is a *proof* that something fell along with the *lightning* and the *thunder*, which reached the soul, as the thunderbolt did that *shattered tree* in the hour of *storm!*

The glory of God does rest over Birmingham! Multitudes hear the voice of God within them, calling them to repentance; and *scores* and *hundreds* very lately have hearkened, obeyed, and turned to the Lord. Great is the rejoicing among God's people; and great their *power* with God, and with men!

Feb. 17th. — How some women *dress!* No wonder *colds, coughs*, and *consumptions*, are so rife! But is not the *pulpit* as much to blame as the *physician?* Should it not speak out against *tight-lacing, low-dressing*, and *slim-shoeing?* Is it not, as good Richard Baxter observed, setting the *body* against the *soul*, and the *clothing* against both?

Feb. 18th.—How evidently does it appear in some *countenances*, that it is not *spirituality* and *power* they came to hear and feel, but some other wonderful thing they had formed in their imaginations!

It will not do either for *preacher* or *people* to *play* with the *light* of the Gospel, *amuse* themselves with its *coruscations*, or those of the preacher's *genius*. To prevent this, there must not only be *light*, but *point* and *fire;*—that to *search*, and this to *penetrate*, and that to *burn ;*—making the hearers to "look out for themselves!"—a strange *predicament* for those who come out merely to gratify their *curiosity*, and while away an hour! No wonder such do not *return* again for some time; and not till they find the wounds made in their consciences are never likely to heal!

Feb. 21st. Saturday.—A great move, and successful, on holiness, last night. How evident that *full salvation* comes by *believing* they *do receive!*—even in the absence of all feeling, to thus *believe*, depending only on the *veracity* of Christ. "A hard spot" for some to get over, just there! For, when the *consecration* is entire, and the prayer extremely *earnest*, they refuse to *believe* until they *feel* so and so; and so the meeting closes, leaving them *unsaved*. "*Believe* that ye receive," says Christ. "Nay, but I must *feel* that I receive," say these; and so they and Christ *part* to meet again when they are disposed to think better of his plan of salvation. Upon no point does *unbelief* maintain its position more *obstinately* than upon this *requirement* of Christ. But, when it is fulfilled, in no position does *unbelief* ever receive a more signal and complete *defeat!*

The Holy Spirit always greatly assists me in pressing

home this point of doctrine. It often requires all the energy he bestows, to gain the victory. But when I do press it thus, regardless of the opinions of men or *devils*, the effects are remarkable. And, after all, what is it but preaching *a full and present salvation by faith*, in full accordance with God's own declaration, "Behold, *now* is the accepted time; behold, *now is the day of salvation*"? — 2 Cor. 6 : 2.

Afternoon. —

"A lark sent down its revelry."

In my ramble to-day was surprised and delighted with the singing of a *lark*, "soaring deliriously high, glittering and twinkling near yon rosy cloud;" upward and heavenward, turning all the air around it into music; and so much music — [pardon me, little *lark!*] — so much music in so small a *speck*. But the *philosophers* say, that is a part of *nature's art*, to crowd a vast perfection into "a puny point;" and here is an illustration of it. Honor to the little early songster!

"A bright gem, instinct with music, *vocal spark*,
With cloud and sky about thee ringing."

Did a happier bird than the *lark* leave the ark, when Noah left it, I wonder? O, how it did sing! What a revelry of gladsome notes, as if it would throw itself into delicious ecstasies! How he won my *admiration!* But little cared he for that; while rich

"In all the bliss a bird can feel,
Whose wing in heaven to earth is bound,
Whose home and heart are on the ground."

Ay, indeed! and, no disrespect to thee, little lark, but too many of our *professors* are too much like thee in *this*: who seem as if soaring heaven-ward, and all their affections there, but, alas! their "*home* and *heart* are on the ground;" and, like thee, they soon return to their centre of gravitation.

Amused with the suggestion of one, that *poets* feign how that birds steal their notes from the lyres of angels, and that the lark might be going up for a new lesson, bearing up from earth one of its own songs for their approval:

> " Up and away, with the dew on its breast,
> And a hymn in its heart,—
> To warble it out in his Maker's ear."

And, as an evidence, to observe how, the *higher it soars*, the *sweeter it sings*. Ay, indeed! and most probably from this fact, that he feels himself safer from the *annoyances* and *perils* of earth, and therefore all the happier. And the *happier the heart*, the *sweeter the song!*

And is it not thus with the child of God? The higher he ascends in divine and holy contemplation and adoration, the freer he feels himself from satanic perils and worldly entanglements; consequently the more happy, and the more *heavenly sweetness* there is in his song of praise, while he sings,

> " My soul, with joy she claps her wings,
> And loud her lovely sonnet sings,
> Vain world, adieu."

At any rate, this *song* of the lark is a pretty sure indication of the speedy approach of spring,—as *Mudie*, on British birds, observes,—that, as a *herald* of spring, there is a certainty about the lark which can hardly be predicted of any other songster of the early season; for though there may be an occasional song of this bird from a small height, upon one of those fine days wherewith a lingering winter is not unfrequently spotted, yet, when the lark mounts to the top of flight, and swells his song to the full power of his voice, one may rest assured that the spring has indeed arrived, and that any relapse into winter, which occurs after this, will not be either severe or of long duration.

Feb. 23d. Monday. — Yesterday was a great day, — a glorious Sabbath, — and glorious *news* to the *eternal Sabbath-keepers* above! Sinners converted on every hand; — had *clear* and *convincing truth*, — did not linger in heart and tongue, — *leaping* like *fire* in a conflagration! Hallelujah!

But, alas! a sudden death of a *backslider*. He heard me the other evening; was enabled to draw, what turned out to be his *picture*, to the life, though I knew nothing of the man by name, or otherwise. But he thought I did, and Satan took the advantage of it, and suggested that some unkind neighbor had told me all. This *hardened* and *irritated* him, and wounded his pride. Poor fellow! it appears to have been his *last call* to return to the God he had forsaken. But he was not in a *humor* for that, and left offended, *and died suddenly;* so I have been informed. That *Scotch minister* spoke truly, that Christ gives *last knocks;* and that, when the sinner's heart becomes hard and careless, then he should fear lest Christ *may have given his last knock!*

Feb. 25th. — "*Life* begetteth life, as fire kindleth fire," says *Baxter*. O, for more of this life of God in my soul! It is a *vexation* to the ungodly; they *feel* it, and *fear* it; it wakes the *conscience*, and starts it into *active life;* but, to some sinners, it is the life of a *rattlesnake* let loose. Multitudes are converted thereby; but many begin to kick and rail against it. More life, my Lord! more life Give me more of this life that begets life. I know the *consequences*. A preacher full of this divine life is a torment to the wicked; and they will surely try to "worry him down;" as those *dogs* did that *living creature*, while they passed by the *dead one*, untouched. It is not the *dead preacher*, but the *living one*, that is always barked at by the Devil's dogs.

Feb. 26th. — An interesting letter from the Rev. Mr. W——, of Shrewsbury, minister of another denomination. He tells me, some time since, he called upon a young lady, a member of his church, and requested her to become a *tract distributor;* but she declined, saying, "I cannot, sir; my engagements are so numerous, I have time for no more." Perceiving it would be of no use to urge the matter, he retired. About a week after, she called upon him to inquire whether he had obtained a *distributor* for that district. He replied, "No." She then offered her services. "You have disposed of some of your other engagements, then?" rejoined the pastor. "No, sir; but since I saw you last, God has graciously *cleansed my heart from sin*, and has blest me with the grace of holiness; and I find I can do more for Him now, than I then thought practicable." The pastor adds: "I saw, then, that the previous hindrance had been the state of her heart, and that, by the removal of sin from that, she was at liberty to attempt much more for God, and for the good of others." An excellent testimony for *holiness*, and a very good argument for it.

Feb. 28th. Saturday. — Endeavored, last night, to lead believers into the *deep things of God*, and very willing were they to go. Was struck with that sentiment of one, that, as the *deepest springs* yield the *sweetest water*, so the *heart* that is the most *deeply sensible* of God's love, yields the *sweetest praises!* A sweet thought, but never fully realized until we become deeply acquainted with "*the deep things of God.*" It is good to keep these things in the clear view of all such as would be entirely devoted to God; taking care, always, to show that *all these springs* are in *Jesus. The life of faith on the Son of God* must never be *severed* from such;— as well expect the stream to run, if cut off from the fountain. That is a sweet text for all this— Gal. 2: 20.

The following extract from the correspondence of a London religious paper, describes the progress of the great revival, of which Mr. Caughey speaks in this chapter. Some may think that what is said of Mr. Caughey is too flattering. Let that pass. The reader will have a striking view here of this wonderful work of God:

"Birmingham. — The Rev. James Caughey continues his labors in this town with increasing interest and success. Last week, although in one of the smaller chapels, namely, Islington, the number of names given in, as obtaining pardoning mercy or sanctifying grace, exceeded any former week in this town. Many conversions of an extraordinary character have been effected; restitutions have been engaged to be made; unholy alliances are being succeeded by marriage; and some are afraid to come under the sound of his voice. But, while his appeals are so terrific and alarming to the obstinate and persevering sinner, his persuasive encouragements are equally delightful to the repenting and returning sinner; the weak get strengthened and encouraged, believers sanctified, and the work of God is going on gloriously. We hope the revival here begun will be continued.

Ministers and local preachers are partaking of the reviving influence. What should hinder the continued progress of the work of God, if the same untiring energy and self-denying zeal and faithfulness be manifested in the discharge of duty? Is God partial to his workmen? Does he not say to all his commissioned servants, 'Go ye into all the world,' &c.; and, 'Lo, I am with you,' &c.? We want to get nearer to God, and to possess more of heavenly influence in our own souls, to be eminently successful. An honest Yorkshireman was asked why it was that Mr. C.'s labors were rendered so remarkably beneficial. 'O,' was the reply, 'he lives next door to heaven, and they acquaint him with secrets that they don't let everybody know.'"

CHAPTER XLVII.

GOOD NEWS. — HOW TO BELIEVE FOR A CLEAN HEART.

MARCH 10th. — *Gloomy.* "*Why art thou cast down, O my soul*"— and yet have *flashes of joy*, and all gloom again? Why is this? But the work of God advances in power. The numbers saved in *both blessings*, pardon and purity, up till this time, is about *twenty-three hundred*, *eighteen hundred* of whom are persons who have obtained *pardoning mercy*. Blessed be God! and the glory be unto Him alone, forever more, amen!

March 11th. — How a *worn-down body* affects the mind! It illustrates that idea of one, that a *mower* who has a good *scythe*, can do more in one day, than he that has a bad one can do in two; and that every *traveller* knows the difference between a *cheerful* and a *tired horse*. But the Lord reigneth.

March 12th. — Take care, my soul! — *finery* again! — *tinsel!* — away with it! That was not Wesley's style, but good, plain, sturdy *English*. That is what is wanted in *Birmingham*. Did it escape you how the *children* at —— admired the *books* with the *beautiful covers*, and *pretty pictures*, while they cared nothing for the *reading* in them? But there are hearers plenty who treat *sermons* thus. O, for *point* and power! that which penetrates the *conscience*, though it *kill admiration!* Amen.

March 13th.— Too much *paint* in one place, and too *pon-*

derous and *formidable* in another. Ah me! it is not *painted fire* that *burns*, nor a *painted sword* that *cuts*, nor a *dead lion*, however formidable and ponderous, that *bites*. O, a sermon may be all these!

March 14th. — *Holiness* last night. The *poets* feigned that the top of *Olympus* was always quiet and serene. They *mistook* the *mount*,— that is all! Its name is *Holiness!* It is not found in *Greece*, in particular, but among the *spiritual hills of Zion!* — Ps. 87 : 1. " *The mountain of holiness.*"— Jer. 31 : 23. Blessed be God! we have not to take a pilgrimage to *Greece* or to *Palestine* to find it. The path of every truly justified soul runs directly along its base; and there are voices continually inviting him to ascend. Let him only resolve, in the strength of God, to be *holy*, and commence the ascent immediately; and O, how soon he will be the *anointed cherub, that shall walk up and down with God upon the holy mountain, in the midst of the stones of fire, perfect in all his ways!* — Ezek. 28 : 14, 15. There the air is always pure and serene. Hallelujah! A noble company of souls made the ascent last evening!

> " And there may they always abide,
> And never a moment depart;
> Concealed in the cleft of thy side,
> Eternally held in thy heart!"

March 16th. — Beware, my soul! The accomplishment which the ancients required of a *physician* is not the best for a *preacher*,— " a good *conjecturing* ability." When there is so much of what one is *certain*, it is idle, I think, to canter off after the conjectural. Therefore, I lay upon this *fancy* of mine an *interdict*. Amen.

Curious minds, like *amateurs* in the fine arts, or like

antiquarians, "groping in the dark unsearchable of finished years," often try to draw me off to things more *curious* than *useful;* to *theories* and *speculations,* rather than to the *real* and the *practical.*

If *life* were but *circular,* one might have time for such things; but as it is *progressive,* and *direct* as an *arrow* through the air, I dare not waste it in such a *circuitous* and *problematical* method of doing good. Let my preaching be as *direct* as my progress to eternity. God help me! Amen. I believe with him who said, *men* are not catched in *spider-webs,* though *flies* are!

March 17th. — Received the following interesting letter from a minister of Christ:

"*Oldbury, March* 11, 1846.

"MY DEAR BROTHER: Allow me to call you so. I had many thoughts about writing to you, and have often wished either to have an interview, or, in this way, to lay before you some of the difficulties that have perplexed my mind, respecting Penitent Meetings, — calling (such persons) to the Communion Rail, and *Faith.* As to instantaneous sanctification, though I have had many reasonings about that doctrine, yet, about twelve or fourteen months ago, I cordially embraced it, and began to seek the blessing; but my views of *faith* prevented me from obtaining it. However, thank God, I have now got out of the fog, and into a clear atmosphere, and I see the glorious sun, and rejoice in his beams.

"On Friday evening last, I was in Birmingham, and heard you preach in Wesley Chapel, and at the close of your sermon, while on my knees with the congregation, I was enabled to *believe,* and realize *the blessing.* Glory be to God!

"I afterwards went into the vestry, according to your public request, to register my name.*

"My object in writing is to state to you my *difficulties* respecting *faith*, and how I got over them.

"Residing at *Oldbury*, I had not an opportunity of hearing you every week, and did not hear your sermon on the *Substitutes for Believing*, but fancy they would have suited my case.

"For years I have had great reasoning about *believing*, and though I have directed *penitents* to say, '*With his stripes we are healed*,' yet I never could bring my mind to approve and cordially receive the doctrine, '*Believe that ye receive, and ye shall have.*' To *believe* when they do not *feel*, I conceived to be *unreasonable*. I have argued with ministers and others, for hours together, without receiving any light;—it still appeared *obscured*, and, to a reflective mind, *impossible*. I maintained that the *object* of *faith* was *Christ*, his divinity, incarnation, sufferings, death, resurrection, intercession, &c., &c.; and that to *believe that we receive*, was putting the *blessing* in the place of *Christ*, and opening a door for enthusiasm and antinomianism;—that the Scriptures everywhere hold out *Jesus* alone as the *object* of faith, and assure us that when we believe *on him*,—not when we believe we *receive*,—we shall be saved;—that they nowhere exhort the penitent to believe that he is pardoned, but everywhere to believe on the Lord Jesus Christ.—Acts 16: 30. Rom. 10: 6—9. John 3: 14, 16, 18, 36. John 6: 47. 1 John 5: 10. In these, and many other passages, I maintained *Christ* was held out as the object of

---

* All who had then and there *believed* for *pardon* or *purity*, and had *received it*, were requested to pass into the *vestry*, and have their *names* recorded, that we might ascertain the nature and extent of the work, and afford them the necessary advice.

faith alone, and not pardon, or salvation; and thus, I conceived, I had the authority of God's word for rejecting the doctrine, '*Believe that ye receive.*'

"For many years did I maintain this view. But I did not see, at the time, that *pardon* and *salvation* were the chief *objects of desire* to the penitent, and that he must believe in Christ to receive these blessings,— so that after all, he must believe that he *does receive*,— receive for Christ's sake, through him, and on account of his atonement; — thus, both *Christ* and *salvation* become the object of faith to such an one,— the *atonement* as the redemption price, *liberty* as the blessing procured, &c., &c.,— that Christ must be believed on, because he is the *way*, the *truth*,— *life*,— the one mediator,— only sacrifice for sins,— only foundation,— the only name given: but that *our salvation* was the ultimate design of all, and that we must receive this through him, for his sake, — that merely to believe that Christ came into the world and died, could only affect us as matters of *history*, and an *affecting narrative*, but, as to *salvation*, would leave us where we were. But to believe that he died for *me*, paid *my* debt, was delivered for *my* offences, and rose again for *my* justification, and that by his stripes *I am healed*, is a very different thing, and makes the death of Christ *avail* for *me;* — then faith in Christ is *believing for salvation.*

"When this view began to open before me, I reëxamined the above texts, and soon discovered that the chief object with the jailer was *salvation*. His soul agitated with a sense of guilt, trembling and alarmed, he came to the apostles, saying, '*Sirs, what must I do to be saved?*' Salvation was the thing that filled his mind, and for this he was directed to *believe*,— '*Believe* on the Lord Jesus Christ, and thou shalt be *saved:*' — that is, '*when thou believ-*

est,' — so that he had really to believe that he did *receive.*

"I saw also, that in Rom. 10 : 4, 6, 9, the apostle was discoursing on the plan of salvation,— the way in which a man is justified and made righteous; and in this view is taught just the same thing,— ' Christ is the end of the law for righteousness to every one that *believeth;*' — that is, *faith* in Christ accomplishes the same object as *perfect obedience to the law would have done;* — it secures *life;* and that *believing with the heart,* and *confessing with the mouth,* was in order to *salvation:* so when those two texts were made plain, I saw that all others taught the same thing, and that it must be so, because ' *What shall I do to be saved?*' is the most important inquiry to a guilty, condemned sinner. I now wondered that I had not seen this before.

"But my difficulties were not all over yet. That which was the last to give way was the following. I will state it as clearly as possible. ' All *rational belief,* I argued, must be the result of *conviction,* and all conviction must be the result of *evidence,* and all evidence must arise from *existence.*' This appeared to me a matter of *intuitive* certainty, and therefore I further argued, ' No *evidence* can possibly outstrip *existence,* and no *rational belief* can go beyond the bounds of *evidence;* and therefore for a man to *believe* that he *receives,* before he *feels* that he does, is absurd and unreasonable, and, if not impossible, none but an enthusiast can do it.' This appeared to me so clear and plain, that I conceived it perfectly *unanswerable.*

" On the 6th of February, I went to *Birmingham,* to hear you, and your text was, Mark 11 : 24,—' Therefore I say unto you, *what things soever* ye *desire* when ye *pray, believe that ye receive them, and ye shall have them.*'

You preached in Cherry-street Chapel. In the course of your sermon you related an account of a conversation between a *Baptist* minister and a *Methodist* minister, upon this text, during which they examined the *original* to see if the translation was correct; and, finding the original word in the *indicative mood and present tense*, they saw that it was so. I remembered, at the time, that there was another reading marked by *Griesbach*, but did not recollect what was the strength of its authority; but I determined, on the following morning, if spared, to examine it for myself.

"At the close, you exhorted the people to test the promise, and called them to kneel. I thought, at all events, *I'll try*. I did so, and felt the power of God; but the knowledge that there was *another reading*, and always having explained the text by '*Ask, and ye shall receive*,' and the thought of the above argument, prevented me from fully taking God at his word. Again and again it came to my mind, 'This is attempting to do what is *unreasonable*.' Afterwards, a friend said to me, 'How simple!' Not wishing to discourage him, I replied, 'Yes;' but I thought, at the time, 'It may be so to *you*, but if you saw as I do, you would not think so.'

"On the following morning I examined the *Greek* text, and found the different reading to be in the *second aorist*, 'ἐλάβετε, and that it was *marked* by *Griesbach*, denoting that it was worthy of further examination, but *inferior* to the text. Now, thought I, whatever *my logic* may say, I must respect and believe the word of God, and I must come to '*Believe that ye receive*.'

"Now I prayed, and scores of times have I repeated the words πιστεύει 'Οτι λαμβάνετε και εσται ὑμίν; but all the time my heart hesitated, and my logic kept me in unbelief.

"Now l began to examine other texts, and I found that the parallel text not only said, '*Ask, and ye shall receive*,' but, '*every one that asketh receiveth;*' that we are invited to come *boldly to the throne of grace* to *obtain*, and to *find;* and that many other texts *implied*, if they did not *express, the present time*. Still the thought, 'No rational belief can go beyond the bounds of *evidence*, and no evidence can outstrip *existence*,' prevented me from *believing;* and thus I was perplexed and agitated *between a text of God's holy word*, and a *deduction of reason*.

"At one time, the thought, 'I do not honor and credit the word of God,' distressed me; and, when I was attempting to *believe*, the suggestion 'Now you are unreasonable; to believe without evidence is enthusiasm,' threw me down again; while the question, 'Is this submitting to God? Is this obeying him?' would increase my agitation.

"At length, in the midst of this perplexity, I began to think about the *prophecies*, and perceived that they foretold things that had no actual existence; and that, when I believed in them, I was allowing *my belief* to go beyond the bounds of *existence*, and so rest on the word of another. I had always thought of them before, and always satisfied my mind with saying, 'But they have an *actual existence* in the *purpose* of God, and they shall be, they are appointed, &c., &c.' But I believed them, and so was believing only upon the word of *another*, and *that word was my only evidence*. But I only perceived this faintly, as in a fog now, but it was of some relief to my mind. The *mist*, however, was never fully removed till I *believed*.

"I began to think there might be a similarity between the word of *prophecy*, and the word of *promise;*—that they both rested upon the *veracity* of *Jehovah;* and that that veracity was *evidence* on which I might rest without enthusiasm; and, if I believed the word of *prophecy* before it was accomplished, why not the word of *promise?* Besides, thought I, is not wishing to *feel* before I believe, like a person wishing to *taste* before he begins to eat? And may there not be as close a connection between the *former* as the *latter?* In this way, I tried to make myself submit to God. I prayed, and reasoned about the goodness, love, and faithfulness of God, the fulness and sufficiency of the atonement, &c., &c., while I sighed,

> 'Jesus, see my panting breast!
> See, I pant in thee to rest!
> Gladly would I now be clean,
> Cleanse me now from every sin,' —

till Friday night last, when you called the congregation to kneel with you. I remembered that you had stated that if we would 'touch the promise' [alluding to the figure you had taken from electricity], 'such a thrill of power and glory would run through your souls as you have never felt.' This encouraged me, and I ventured to touch, — steadily to believe, — *I do receive*, — I do, — I do now, — yes, I do! — and the thrill of *power* and *glory* was felt like a fire in my heart, spreading over my whole frame, — filling me, not with rapture, but calm joy, and peace, and gratitude.

"Instantly the thought came, 'Do not mistake this burning, &c., &c., for the blessing.' But as quickly this thought followed, 'In what way could the Holy Spirit witness with my spirit, but this? All my impressions from *outward* things are received through the body; and all my *inward* impressions must, in some way, affect the body. At all events I will not reason, — *I believe I do receive!* Glory be to God!' Yes, I did receive glory, and I have felt pleasure in confessing it publicly while preaching, and I feel it now, glory be to God! I fear lest the length of this letter should be tedious. In this respect, pardon me for trespassing on your time. I could not well be shorter.

"Very sincerely and affectionately yours,
"RALPH WALLER,
"Of the Methodist New Connection."

CHAPTER XLVIII.

JOURNAL CONTINUED.

MARCH 18th. — Sinners are breaking down on every hand; and some most *unlikely cases!*

Accountability to God, *now*, and *after death*, is one great *anchor-hold* of the *Spirit* in man. I find great advantage in taking *fast hold there*, in bringing the sinner to God. *Drop anchor* there, if possible, and you have the sinner. *Harpoon* him there, if need be, and his whole weight will soon be felt upon the line. He may flounce and flounder, and dive into the mud of infidelity and error, and make a great noise, and go off among his companions in a tangent, turning all his element into *foam ;* but, if the *harpoon* has stuck fast in the right place, and holds fast, he will soon reäppear, and be drawn alongside, as the *whalers* speak!

March 19th. — *Mental accountability to God ;* — did not lose sight of that. Looking into my watch, observed that every *wheel* works in allegiance to the given point on the dial-plate; all parts of the sinner have a strict relation to the *inward dial-plate*, accountability to God. And, even when the watch is all wrong in its motions, yet there are signs on the dial-plate which indicate what should be. The sinner knows, from the sense of *accountability* within, what he should be, both within and without. When all is *right* or *wrong*, with regard to that *inward dial*, all will be right or wrong on the dial of the visible conversaticn. The Bible is its grand *authority*. If my *watch* had sensibility, and could read its own *face*, comparing it with the *sun*, assurance of truth, or conviction of wrong, would be the immediate result. Christ Jesus is the *Sun of Righteousness*. St. John declares him to be "*the true* LIGHT *which lighteth every man that cometh into the world*,"—every man, whether he reads the Bible or not; for he shines, doubtless, upon this mental *dial-plate* [if I may so call it], ACCOUNTABILITY TO GOD.

March 23d. — The church of God has become a *moving flame of fire*, into whatsoever chapel she enters! How little can be done when she is not! But who may set limits to her influence when she is thus! *Three or four score of sinners saved on Sabbath, and half as many sanctified!*

April 3d. — The *Love Feast* was excellent. The new converts talked like *new creatures*, indeed!

"In joy triumphant, sorrow flown."

Had some noble testimonies to the blessing of *perfect love*. The spies of old (Numb. 13 : 23) brought out of Canaan *grapes, pomegranates*, and *figs*, such as Israel had never laid eyes on before; and they reported that it was, indeed, a land flowing with milk and honey; but they also reported evil of the land, of the strength of their walled cities, and *giant-like* population, among whom they felt themselves but as *grasshoppers*, and set the people a *murmuring*.

But these sanctified souls exhibited the fruit, and said, with *Caleb*, "*Let us go up at once and possess it; for we are well able to overcome it.*" The resolved multitude one and all exclaiming:

> "Rejoicing now in earnest hope,
> I stand, and from the mountain top
> See all the land below;
> Rivers of milk and honey rise,
> And all the fruits of Paradise
> In endless plenty grow."

While not a few sorrowing ones mournfully ejaculated:

> "O, that I might at once go up!
> No more on this side Jordan stop,
> But now the land possess;
> This moment end my legal years;
> Sorrows and sins, and doubts, and fears,
> A howling wilderness."

Those who enjoyed the blessing greatly encouraged and strengthened each other. The fellowship of purified minds is a *holy alliance!* for it is by this that HOLINESS *strengthens* and reinforces itself.

April 7th. — A note from Brother *Yates*, containing a vote of thanks from the quarterly meeting of the *Birmingham East* circuit, and recognizing this revival as "a remarkable outpouring of the Holy Spirit." Also, another from Brother *McTurk*, of a similar import, from "the quarterly meeting of the Birmingham West circuit," in the form of a *resolution*, moved by Dr. *Melson*, and seconded by Mr. *Wilkinson*, stewards, Rev. *George Turner* in the chair, and "carried unanimously," gratefully acknowledging the work to be of God, and rejoicing in the great prosperity of the circuit, spiritually and financially; and full of the kindest expressions towards me, his servant.

It is truly cheering to have the confidence and approbation of good men. But what is this just to hand? A *pamphlet*, and my name upon it in type large enough, surely, to make me appear *somebody!* * * * *

Have just looked it over; — quite a spirited opponent; — as if the writer, Mr. E., belonged to the corps editorial of *Blackwood's Magazine*, — so stately and eloquent! — thus, for example, he begins:

"REVEREND SIR: I think it must be admitted to be almost axiomatic that a courtier is not an impartial medium of conveying true and unbiased intelligence to his sovereign; the circumstances by which he is surrounded, the desire to please his master by communicating flattering intelligence, and '*ex parte*' reports, tends, I fear, too much to give a fictitious coloring to the waters transmitted through such a channel. Leaving, however, the court, and viewing the world in general, we shall see the same appearances still manifested, the same principle everywhere developing itself. Forgive me then, sir, when I tell you, that I fear the atmosphere by which you are surrounded bears too great an affinity to the dense air of the court; and that the medium by which you receive your information is of too partial and one-sided a character.

* * * * * *

"Sir, if I look around upon the beauteous manifestations of nature, if I view the glorious scenery by which I am on every side surrounded, the thought visibly presents itself that the Deity is a being of beneficence and goodness, and if I open your sacred oracle, the visibility of the fact is still further manifested; but, sir, you endeavor to clothe him with vengeance, to call up the Jupiter of the Grecians, and bid him scatter his thunderbolts around him, to tear the heavens asunder in the ire of his rage, hurrying forward impetuously to take vengeance on the world, and visit it with his severest chastisement and displeasure; in fact, to make him appear the God of the passions, not that being which nature so continually develops.

"I will not detain you by noticing the wild phraseology which you occasionally indulge in; I will not stay to point out the strangeness of the diction in which you enunciate your peculiar ideas; it is not my intention to throw down the gauntlet about mere form of words, however strange the verbiage, or wild and incoherent their phraseology; though, I would observe, 'en passant,' that, did I wish, I have a wide field to select from.

"We will conceive that the wild oratory is for a moment hushed! that the bright flashes of genius, purified at the altar, and offered up to the service of their Maker, have for a time ceased to emanate! that the pulpit is vacated for the communion rail, and that the word of exhortation is lost in the breathings of prayer. And here what manifestations are called into existence, what a medley of sound peals upon the ear! The storm (pardon my simile) which occasionally issued forth betokenments of its approach in the early part of the eve, now still more powerfully continues to develop itself, sound commingles with sound, until at last it arrives at its maximum of power."

The whole production displays considerable talent, but this polite breath of opposition will only serve to fan the *glorious flame*, that is consuming sin of every sort, wherever it sweeps! It seizes upon everything that stands in its way; — *ten, fifteen,* or *twenty,* saved every night, and *scores* on the Sabbath days, — of all ages and classes, chiefly from fifteen to thirty-five, and up to *seventy!* Great is our *God,* and great and marvellous his *goodness* to the children of men. Blessed be his name! And blessed be his *Son Jesus Christ*, who is Lord of all, and sees *of the travail of* his soul and is satisfied! And blessed be the *Holy Ghost*, that worketh the counsel of his will so wonderfully! Amen.

CHAPTER XLIX.

CHEERFULNESS AND COURAGE REQUIRED.

APRIL 2d. — My *health* is much better, thanks be unto Him who preserves it, as he did the *bush* in the flame. As to my spiritual state, he favors me with many a *smile*, and blesses me with sweet *tranquillity of mind*, — which an old divine calls *the cream of life* and *a bunch of grapes by the way!*

There is no use in yielding to *sadness*; for it leaves the soul very much like an instrument out of tune; and *Satan*, unlike all other *musicians*, has a great fancy for playing upon an untuned instrument!

Gladness! I like to cultivate the spirit of gladness! It puts the soul so in tune again, and keeps it in tune, so that Satan is shy of touching it! — the chords of the soul become too warm, or too full of heavenly electricity, for his infernal fingers, and he goes off somewhere else! — at least, thus I have ever found it. Satan is always very shy of meddling with me when my heart is full of gladness and joy in the Holy Ghost.

My plan is to shun the spirit of *sadness* as I would Satan; but, alas! I am not always successful. Like the Devil himself it meets me on the highway of *usefulness*, looks me so fully in my face, till my poor soul changes color!

I often think of a remark of a divine in *Switzerland*, —

that *sadness* discolors everything; it leaves all objects *charmless;* it involves future prospects in darkness; it deprives the soul of all its aspirations, enchains all its powers, and produces a mental paralysis!

An *old believer* remarked, that *cheerfulness* in religion, makes all its services come off with delight; and that we are never carried forward so swiftly in the ways of duty as when borne on the wings of *delight;* adding, that *Melancholy* clips such wings; or, to alter the figure, takes off our chariot wheels in duty, and makes them, like those of the Egyptians, drag heavily.

Gladness is the *musician* of religion. It surrounds the soul with an atmosphere of harmony; makes her

> " Forget her labor as she toils along,
> Weep tears of joy, and burst into a song!"

April 3d. — " *Courage!* " Yes! indeed, *courage* is indispensable in such a work as this; and must be maintained at any cost! What a *French officer* remarked in a letter to a friend, when with *Napoleon* in the campaign in Egypt, is not inapplicable. " Here we need *courage*, not only of the head, but of the heart and the soul." But *Jesus* never fails me. His grace is always equal to my day. As my day is, so is my *strength*, as the *promise* runs.— Deut. 33 : 25.

The world is of the opinion, says a great writer, that the end of *fencing* is to *hit;* that the end of *medicine* is to *cure*, and that the end of *war* is to *conquer;* and that those *means* are the most *correct which best accomplish the ends*. A better reply could not be given, with regard to the subject on hand; besides, the number of the *hit* that spread the ground must have decided that in your judgment; and the number of the *cured* and the *conquered!*

31*

And Mr. —— was really *hit* himself. There is no doubt of that, although he made out to get away; and days passed away before he ventured again within range of our shot. Nor would he have come again, but that the *wound* in the conscience would not heal. An "*apology*" would have been a poor *plaster*. It was not to be hoped for, unless the *preacher* could be convinced he was in the *wrong;* or that the "*random* shot" was anything else than what one called "*ā conglomeration*" of *truth*. If he will keep coming, he will get a better *plaster* for his conscience than an *apology* from me, even an application of that *blood that cleanseth from all sin.* — 1 John 1 : 7.

It requires *courage* to incur such hard epithets; but my Lord had worse. *Erasmus* said to the opponents of *Luther*, "Nothing is easier than to call *Luther* a *blockhead*, but nothing is more difficult than to *prove* him one!" Nothing is easier than to coin such *epithets*, nothing harder than to prove their just *applicability!* Nothing is easier than to call such and such *teaching* false, nothing harder than to prove that it is really so.

A *madman* in America said to me, "Sir, when ministers keep the Law, what a tremendous cudgel they have for sinners!" That is true, I replied, but how do you manage sinners yourself, when they are hard on you? "O, sir, I take hold of the *Divine Law;* they are not used to such big thoughts, sir!" Ah, there was both Law and Gospel in that which produced such results.

The end of *medicine* is to *cure;* and the end of *war* is to *conquer*, said the critic;—ay! and the end of the Law and the Gospel is to *conquer* and to *save*, — to *wound* and to *cure*. Surely, the scenes witnessed the last few nights prove how well both Law and Gospel are adapted to such a work; when accompanied by the power of the *Holy Ghost* sent down from heaven!

CHAPTER L.

PEACE OR WAR.

To * * * *.

Your ideas on "*peace*" are clever, both in conception and expression; and, were you arguing against the evils of *national wars*, would be most applicable and persuasive.

Animals coming into the world armed with *natural* weapons, while man is born *weaponless*, proving that God designs him to be a peaceable creature, is a good, though not an original idea; as Lord Bacon, I think, notices it. But how would you answer an objector, that though God has not chosen to send him into the world panoplied for war, like the inferior animals and insects of which you speak, yet he has endowed him with *reason*, and provided him with vast stores of *material*, out of which he may make weapons, *offensive* and *defensive*? The subject is not unworthy of reconsideration, if you have time. Such *materials* of war were very useful to the *Israelites*, when fighting what one may unshrinkingly call *the battles of he Lord*. But let that pass; for I am no apologist for war!

But what does all your "reasoning" prove? That the "*new creature* in Christ Jesus" (1 Cor. 5: 17), when "*born again*," is unarmed, — "not warlike, and ready to fight for the truth"? But how know you that? Suppose

I grant it; what then? Does it follow that the Holy Ghost does not call upon him immediately to "*put on the whole armor of God*"? — the *girdle* of truth; the *breastplate* of righteousness; the *feet shod* with the preparation of the Gospel of peace; the *shield* of faith; the *helmet* of salvation, and the *sword* of the Spirit; and to *watch* with all perseverance, as you may see by consulting Ephesians, sixth chapter. Man, what are we to make of all this? If this be not a *warlike* creature, I want to know what is! But of what use is all this panoply? Surely, not for mere *show*, like that upon officers and men in a mere *review?* Nay, verily, but wherewith to *defend* and to *fight*, — "*the good fight of faith*," — which many of these young *believers* are doing now, in right good earnest; which may they do always, until they win the last victory over the *world*, the *flesh*, and the *Devil*, and gain the *crown* of glory that fadeth not away!

The "*mischief*" that is being done is, indeed, a consideration; but if *needed*, and in the *right direction*, never mind; — to the spoiling of *principalities* and powers, and devastating the dominions of the Devil, and breaking up the *confederation* of sinners! If the *works of darkness* are being overthrown; if *lukewarmness, pride, unbelief, spiritual death*, and other notorious works of the Devil, are being destroyed; there is no cause for *mourning*, surely; — but much for acclamations of joy, and thanksgiving to God!

An old writer says, "War is mischief on a large scale." Such, I admit, is a great revival of religion; — it is *war* against the Devil and all his works, — *mischief on a large scale*, in that direction.

A friend of mine said to a young lady from a distant city, "Well, you have had Mr. Caughey preaching in your city." "O, yes; and he did a great deal of harm," was her reply. There was *harm* done, a great deal of harm, and all hell confessed it; — *one thousand* sinners converted! But that was not all the harm. Some *do-nothing* churches had their *congregations* thinned, — the *rub* was there; she only spoke as she had been taught. And there were many *united families* severed in their affections; *united* hitherto in serving the Devil. That unity was quite broken up, for Jesus Christ took a *remnant* out of them to serve him; and that created trouble, after the manner foretold by himself: "*I came not to send peace, but the sword. For I am come to set a man at variance against his father, and the daughter against her mother, and the daughter-in-law against her mother-in-law; and a man's foes shall be they of his own household.*" — Matt. 10 : 34, 36. "A great deal of *harm*" in all that! and the poor preacher comes in for a large share of the *blame*. However, better such troubles should occur here upon earth, than the *whole family* should be left to fall into *hell*, there to fight as fiends for ever and ever. The rich man in hell deprecated a reünion with his family in that place of torments: — "Send him [Lazarus] to my *father's house;* for I have *five brethren*, that he may testify unto them, *lest they also come into this place of torment.*" — Luke 16 : 27, 28.

To the same.

1. I like your signature, "*A man of peace;*" — and so am I, if one can have it with a good conscience; else, farewell to it, — *war* in preference!

Why did the *Greeks* name *peace* to be the *nurse* of *Pluto?* Because *Pluto* was their god of *wealth;* and they were well aware that *peace* increases the wealth of nations, while war *impoverishes*. Your allusion was pretty but you see I have stated it more *classically*, and with less prodigality of words.

2. *Peace!* I love the word;—peace with those who call upon the name of the Lord out of a pure heart. *St. Paul* enjoins that. *Peace* with the *membership* of the *general church* of Christ; and, of course, with every member of that particular *branch* of it among whom I labor. Peace! I *welcome* it, when they are what they ought to be; when they are at *peace with God, and at war with sin.* If not, the sooner peace retires from our midst the better. In this case, let *truth* declare for war. The sooner the better. Peace sometimes must be purchased by war. War, in order to a healthy and lasting peace.

3. *Peace* with *sin* and sinners! Then I reject peace. Otherwise, God himself would soon declare war against me. And right that he should. It would be wrong in me to risk it; wrong to them and to myself.

4. *Peace* in the church of God, other things being equal, is a grand source of spiritual health and prosperity. But peace with those who would be at peace with the world and its wickedness, and who would convert the church into "*the synagogue of Satan,*" would *impoverish* the church, even to spiritual bankruptcy and ruin. *War*, in such a state of things, is better than *peace*. War, in order to a lasting peace, is the way to enrich a church, in the estimation of God and angels.

5. To this end the Lord sent *Jeremiah*, the prophet, to *fight against his professed people* (Jer. 15: 19, 21); where God assures him, he should *stand before* him, if he would take forth the *precious* from the *vile*, and be as the *mouth of God* unto them; acting on this principle, *that they should return to him, and not he to them;* that is,

fur the sake of a *hollow peace*, he was not to *connive* at their *connivance* with the wicked world around them. God promises, on his part, to make him *a fenced brazen wall*, against whom they should *fight*, and not *prevail;* for that he should be in and behind the wall, so that the prophet could not be overthrown; with a sure promise of *deliverance* out of the hand of the *wicked*, and out of the *terrible!* No wonder Jeremiah was so *bold*, so *unflinching*, so *uncompromising* a witness for the Lord his God! Nevertheless, he had his troubles, and sore ones, out of which his God did deliver him always. Blessed be his name!

6. God is no less concerned for the purity of his church now. More of this by and by.

7. Mark what I am going to say. There never can be a *long peace* upon the earth in any nation, or among the nations, while a *majority* are in arms against God. Again and again did that thought oppress my heart when travelling in *Continental Europe.* I saw enough to convince me of that. But never, till we enter heaven above us, shall we know how often, in every generation of the nations, a voice of thunder gives power to the *angel* that sits on the *red horse*, "*to take peace from the earth.*"—Rev. 6 : 4. And mark further what I am going to say. Nor can any church, where many are guilty of *treason* against its Head, by conniving at the rebellion of the world against him (to say nothing more), have a long peace. No! the Almighty will send some *angel* to take peace from the church. Then commences "the tug of war." *Potsherds* striving with potsherds! Yea, and the *woe* of *man striving with his Maker!*—Is. 45 : 9. I said,—"to say nothing more;" but *more* might be said,—where there is "*a this and*

that," in great abundance, in direct *collision* with the will of Him whom we consider Head of the church militant.

8. The *church* must be in the *field*, to *war* against sin and wickedness; else God will enter the church, and war against it. Then woe be unto the church! Nor can the church of God ever be enriched with all the riches of God, till she is *pure within*, — "all *glorious within*," as the *king's daughter*, — and *pure* from *the blood of souls*, — *warring* as she ought against *the works of darkness!*

It will, indeed, never be well with the *world*, until it beats its *swords* into *ploughshares*, and its *spears* into *pruning-hooks*, and learns the art of war no more. On the contrary, it is never so well with the church, as when her *swords* and *spears* are in active hostilities against all the powers of sin and Satan! *Aggression* is the life of the church, and the grand means of her *true aggrandizement*. God help me, sir! I am endeavoring to carry out these *principles* with all my heart, and with all my soul; and *shall*, I trust, till my *Great Captain* sounds my *retreat* from the *battle-field* of life!

To the same.

Controversies during a revival I avoid, if possible. I have no heart for anything of the kind. The *spiritual temple* should be built, at such a time, without the noise of such hammers as these. It is best to let these *hammers* work elsewhere, by those who have a heart to use them. We have *better hammers* and *better work* for them to do, — to knock down and break to pieces all manner of sin and wickedness, in the church and out of it, the Lord our God being our helper!

A prelate of the Church of England advised *Mr. Wesley*

to let *debatable* subjects alone, and endeavor with all his might to overturn wickedness, and convert sinners to God; — *that* he considered an *undebatable good!* Ay, that is it! That is *my motto* also, sir. I press hard upon these *undebatable* things. The hammers of truth work wonderful changes; but no man, nor men, shall be able to change my hammers, or turn them to any other work. Must keep them all *agoing*, and with a sort of *trip-hammer* rapidity and *indomitableness*, if you will allow the word, to bend the *iron sinew* of rebellion, and break the rocky hearts in pieces before the Lord.

Peace, as you say, "in the eye, on the tongue, in the gesture," is "attractive and winning," no doubt; but if *self* happen to be the centre of attraction, instead of Christ, then *woe* to the preacher! Alas! *self* may become a *loadstone*, to draw people to *itself*, instead of drawing them out of their sins to *Christ ;* and what is that but drawing them from one devil to another? — for, *self*, that would be *idolized* at the expense of *Christ*, is little better than a devil, — "*a tame devil*," as one named it. O, but if I found *self* engaged in such an abominably selfish purpose, I would *knock it down*, and *nail it to the cross*, and let it die the death! I tell you, sir, if convincing and converting *truth* be shuffled aside, that the listening, unsaved multitude may be pleased and drawn to the selfish preacher, *self* reigns in the pulpit instead of Christ, and is proving itself a downright *traitor* to the *King of kings*. It resembles wily, politic *Absalom* at the gate, who, with fair words and gentle speeches, "*stole the hearts of the men of Israel*," and then dethroned his father, and drove him from his palace and his capital. — 2 Sam. 15. Such a *traitor-like self* deserves the fate of *Absalom* in the oak, and will certainly have a worse destiny, if it persist.

Byron, speaking of a fascinating preacher, hints that " he gained more *hearts* than *souls;*"—a striking distinction! Alas! it is to be feared, there is much of this sort of thing going on among the Christian churches. It is a mighty cause of *spiritual death* wherever it occurs. This *Dagon* must be made to fall before the ark of God!—again and again it must fall, till not even "*the stump*" of the abominable thing remains!—1 Sam. 5: 4.

Ah! sir, you little know, perhaps, how many *self-mortifications, overturnings*, and mental agonies, some preachers have to endure, ere this *Dagon* is reduced to *the stumps*, or till it is utterly destroyed. But when the thing is done, and this *sinful self* is slain, and numbered with the dead, and all the glory of his father's house redounds to Christ alone; then, and not till then, shall the glory of the Lord God of Israel be revealed in his temples here below.—1 Kings 8: 11. Is. 40: 5. O, who would spare this *Dagon*, with such a glory, and such consequences as are set before the eye of faith!

Our earth presents many a *sad sight;* but the saddest, I sometimes think, is where *self* has the ascendency in the house of God,—in the *pulpit*. It is not only bringing ruin upon itself, but blight and death upon the church of God. The *Head of the church* will surely contend with it; for he hath said, "*My glory I will not give to another.*" That is his fixed purpose,—his *unchangeable decree;*—a purpose, a decree, that awakens the echoes of heaven with, "*Thou art worthy, O Lord, to receive glory, and honor, and power*" (Rev. 4: 11), and vibrates in *judgments* upon the earth. May our God preserve me, and all his ministers, from this inward *Achan* of an *unsanctified self!* Amen.

To the same.

Very true. There was no *peace* for the unsaved that night! — no, nor rest in *my bones!* — no! for rebellion against the Holy Spirit was rife; — and how could there be *peace?* To them, and to the troubled preacher, another *Jehu* might have said, " *What hast thou to do with peace?* "— 2 Kings 9 : 19. Ay! "*tongue, eyes, hands, arms, body,*— all warlike,— so unlike an ambassador of the Prince of peace." And might I not say to thee, as the stripling David to his brother *Eliab* in the camp of *Saul*, " *What have I now done? Is there not a cause?* " — 1 Sam. 17 : 28, 29. *Cause!* yes, sufficient to stir the heart of the archangel Gabriel!

Ay! all was "*violent and warlike*" enough; — many an alarmed and wounded sinner felt the truth of that. Neither self nor subject were "burdened with the *loadstone* of attraction, but *repulsion* with a vengeance." Very true again! but how did you account for the fact, that so many scores of distressed sinners, of all ages, clustered around me, with tears and cries, and would not go away? Did that look like *repulsion?*

Ah! my "Friend," *truth* is a more powerful *loadstone* than *flattery*. But it cut through all concealment, like a very sword ; and *loaded* many a terror-stricken conscience with a weight of misery and guilt too heavy to be borne. In this sense, there was a *loading* indeed,— a *fearful loading*,— something like what the damned in hell feel, only there were *hopes of mercy*. O, what a piling up of sentences of condemnation! O, what a region of alarm was that of many a soul! O, what fearful-outcries! And yet, what expressions of hope and confidence in divine mercy through Jesus Christ! —

"Though my sins as mountains rise,
  And swell and reach to heaven,
Mercy is above the skies,
  I may be still forgiven:
Infinite my sins increase,
  But greater is thy mercy's store;
Love me freely, seal my peace,
  And bid me sin no more."

Be it so, then, that all was "*repulsion*," yet you are a witness how that the slashes of the sword of divine truth, which reached unto the soul, did the work required by the Gospel most effectually. You did not wait till the close of the prayer-meeting, most likely; but if you had, you would have acknowledged that they had not mourned and prayed and wept in vain, nor the preacher and his helpers labored in vain. Hallelujah!

CHAPTER LI.

EXTRACTS FROM JOURNAL.

APRIL 9th. — My *Birthday*. *Thankful* for the past, trusting my gracious Lord with and for all my future. Many *reminiscences*. The book of Providence, like Hebrew letters, must be read backwards, upon earth and in heaven; — a very profitable study. Have enjoyed a sweet walk, singing over and over again. with tears, that sweet stanza of Mr. Wesley:

> " What thou hast done I know not now,
> Suffice I shall hereafter know ;
> Help me my sinful head to bow ;
> That still I live, to thee I owe :
> O, teach thy deeply humbled son,
> Father, to say thy will be done ! "

The work of God does not flag. But, weak as I feel, and humbled to the dust as my soul is before God in private, always, yet in public, he does cause "the sword of truth to gleam like his own lightning !" O, he does ! Blessed be his name !

*　　*　　*　　*　　*

How soft and sweet is the breath of spring, in this country, with

> " Light leaves, young as joy ! "

Held a *private watch-night*. The Lord near. After midnight opened upon the Scriptures for a birthday expression from my Lord (Acts 7), where it is said, Moses "was a *stranger in the land of Midian!*" and Isaiah 44 : 26, "*That confirmeth the word of his servant, and performeth the counsel of his messengers; that saith to Jerusalem, Thou shalt be inhabited; and to the cities of Judah, Ye shall be built, and I will raise up the decayed places thereof.*"

April 10th. — *Preaching,* like *life,* should be *direct,* not *circular,* — but *direct* and *progressive.* Beware of this *circumlocution* and wordiness; cure it at once. However, that was a strong point, and worthy of a larger place in a future discourse; — that those who will not *weep* over a *sinning* friend, let them prepare to weep over a *dying* friend; — those who cannot *mourn* over an *unconverted* relative, may soon be called to mourn over a *buried* relative; — that the Christian world is full of such cases; — that *sinning on,* without repentance or conversion, is sure to shorten the days of the *sinner;* — that, for a professed follower of Christ to stand and *look on,* without *prayers* and *tears* for their salvation, is pretty sure to be followed up by such a painful retribution.

April 11th. — Yesterday being *Good Friday,* and a general holiday, I preached twice at Newtown-Row Chapel, on "*Let him now come down from the cross, and we will believe him.*" — Matt. 27 : 42. Had some liberty in the forenoon, and assisted at the Sacrament, after; but, at night, upon the same text, was much *fettered* and *stilted.* Another text would have been better for the crowd assembled. However, many were saved.

April 12th. — A great day yesterday at the *Islington* Chapel. Had what Baxter calls "a piercing quickness," with brisk life and power. Results glorious.

April 14th. — How little one can do without *zeal, fire,*

energy! O, how this shows — speaks to me like a trumpet, the necessity of working hard and steadily in the *soul-saving* way, while *physical* and mental vigor last! for, without these, it is to *rise up*, and be forced to sit down again, or something equal to that; for, O, how true is that observation of one, that, unless a minister preach, as if he determined, if the *sinner perish*, he *must perish* also, he can *move nothing, do nothing!* Lord Jesus, help me to work while health and vigor are vouchsafed!

April 17th. — Holiness night. That sentiment tells upon some consciences. It is not the *want* of faith, but a *lack of determination* to be cleansed from all sin, that prevents many from receiving the blessing.

Have spent this week in the chapel at *Islington*, in the suburbs of Birmingham, with signal success. But there is a deep *pensiveness* over my spirit; — a *raven-winged influence* overshadowing me, shutting out all the sunshine of the heart; and I really cannot tell why; —*fatigue*, perhaps. O, what a thing is a *dull heart*, and a decay of *vital energy* But the Lord is at hand to bless and support.

CHAPTER LII.

MORE NOTES OF THE REVIVAL.

SPEAKING of the progress of the revival in *Birmingham*, Mr. C. remarks:

The whole town seems moved. The *confederations* of sin are in considerable confusion; at their *wits' end*, some of them!—to preserve themselves from *dissolution*. Error flies before the revival, as chaff before the wind. *Drawing-room* circles are in an amaze. *Bar-rooms* and *beer-shops*, here and there, are vocal with lonely grumblers. The *wicked* are fretting and fuming, and the *pamphleteering presses* are groaning for them, poor souls!—ay, loud as their poor *consciences* are groaning for themselves.

However, we have vast masses of the people on our side. The Wesleyans, generally, are *true;* though some *shrink*, and *query* what all this is coming to; and whether the church of God shall be able to wash her face and robes clean, after all this bespattering from the wicked. They can bear to read how that the face of Jesus was covered with the spittle of the ungodly, and his person arrayed in a *mock robe*, &c., &c; but, to have the church of their choice despised and mocked, is too much for their pride or humility.

However, it is the *green wood* that shrinks. The *seasoned material* in the spiritual temple never *shrinks* in the *hot atmosphere* of *persecution* There is much of this *material* in the Wesleyan church in this town; — neither *ridicule* nor aught else effects such noble souls. They would be surprised to behold the *members* of an active, *aggressive* church crowned with *rose-buds*, while the Head was crowned with *thorns*.

How many professed *navigators* to the *heavenly port* have I known, who could not sail in *rough* and hazardous weather! — would rather make for the shore, at the risk of running *the work of God ashore*, and *Zion's ship* among the *breakers!* — "Any port in a storm," says the old proverb; — and there wait for calm weather, and clear skies,— and the *smiles of the world* for their sunshine! Then farewell to the revival!

It is hard for some to show their heads, unless they are sure the world shall cry, "*Well* done!" and this and that circle of "taste and intelligence" echo it. Then such are "on hand" for all that was good! But when the heavens lower, and the storm howls, and the *sea is troubled*, and the *waves* toss themselves about,— then "*discretion* is the better part of *valor!*" and they disappear!

Birmingham Methodists, generally, know how to "*rough it out*," sailor fashion, in all weathers; — out on duty, whether the heavens smile, or whether they frown; — men and women, who, I verily believe, would stand up for God, against a host, were the scenes of *Dura* to be reënacted!

True, they are in the *world*, and mingle in its business, and buy, and sell, and serve it, and make *money*, and acquire its *substance;* and the wicked say, "See, your citizens of heaven are as active and money-making as us, the citizens of the world, and who have our hope in this life!" To be sure they are! and I want to know who has a better right than they? Besides, they have families to provide for, and the treasury and cause of our Lord Jesus Christ to sustain;

Why should they not be *lively* and *active*, cheered as they are by the prospect of a better inheritance above? Their *hands* are busy here below, while their *affections* are in the *altitudes of heaven;* — busily engaged in the humble drudgery of life, while their *hearts* are lodged in the *tree of life*, and their thoughts among the angels, and "the spirits of just men made perfect." If outward appearances do make against them, it only illustrates what St. John says,— "*The world knoweth us not;* — and it doth not yet *appear what we shall be.*" No, blessed be God! "but we *know that when he shall appear, we shall be like him; for we shall see him as he is.*" That is enough! Till then, we can bear the *comparison* of a good man, of an *eagle* sitting upon a *low branch*, but her *nest* is *built on high;* or the *moon*, which, though seen in the *water*, yet has her *seat* in the *firmament!*

But the *wicked* do not understand these things; such thoughts are *too high* for them. But the time is coming when they *shall* understand them; ay, though they may have to look as high as *Dives* did from the depths of hell. What Jesus says to every disciple of his, he says to every wilful servant of the Devil, "What thou knowest not *now*, thou shalt know *hereafter*." Alas! alas! it will then be too late for such. O, may every *loyalist* of *heaven* buckle on the armor, firmer than ever, and rush upon these *brands* of hell, and pluck them out of the burning!

In the mean time, shout, earth and heaven, that prayer is being daily answered!

> "Like mighty winds or torrents fierce,
> Let it opposers all o'errun,
> And every law of sin reverse,
> That faith and love may make all one."

This is no time to *falter*. It is *truth* and tne *effects* of truth they are quarrelling with, and with *me for setting* it on against their *consciences ;* and yet, what could it or the preacher have done, but for the Holy Spirit who applied it? I must stand by the *truth*, then, and stand or fall with it; let it have an *open field and fair play*. If this is *my cross*, it must be taken up, and borne along with courage and faithfulness. *Luther* says, " Every true saint is *heir* to the *cross ;* " and I have come into the *possession* of mine with some joy and power.

The world never did understand that declaration of Jesus, " *Blessed are they which are persecuted for righteousness' sake: for theirs is the kingdom of heaven.*" Mark that, — "*theirs is,*" not theirs *shall be*, the kingdom of heaven. " Nay," says the world, " but *miserable* are they who are persecuted for righteousness' sake." Thus our Lord's decision is a little paradox, or a *contradiction* to the world, but perfectly in harmony with Christian experience.

A voice from heaven saluted John with " *Blessed are the dead which die in the Lord, from henceforth.*" Jesus says, "*Blessed are they which are persecuted,*" &c. Thus the same word which expresses the happiness of *departed* saints in heaven, expresses also the happiness of the *persecuted* saints upon earth.

But what are all the *beatitudes*, or *felicities*, in the fifth of Matthew, but as so many "*point blank bastions*" against the opinions of the world? *Christ* and the *world* never did agreee; but they are never found more widely apart than in that celebrated sermon of our Lord on the *Mount !*

April 18th. — Cheer up, my soul ! — *words* do not hit so hard as *stones !* In March 30, 1751, Mr. Wesley writes in his journal, "The last time I preached in *Birmingham* the *stones* flew on every side." But, under the same date, he exclaims, "O, how the scene is changed! If any disturbance were made now, the *disturber* would be in more danger than the preacher. I found God in the midst of the congregation, and afterwards preached on '*If ye be led by the Spirit, ye are not under the law.*' The hearts of the people were melted within them; so that neither they nor I could refrain from tears. But they were chiefly tears of joy, from a lively sense of the liberty wherewith Christ hath made us *free.*" Cheer up, then, O my soul! *Wesley's Jesus* is thy Jesus; his *God*, thy God;—the same *Gospel* he preached, thou preachest; and the same *Holy Spirit* carries it with power to the hearts of the people.

April 19th.—The *art* of *war* is best learned in actual war. It is upon the field of battle where *rules*, *tactics* and *artillery*, are tested; the *effectiveness* of this *battery* or that; and the *wisdom* or *folly* of this and that *position*. A *change of position*, upon the part of the enemy, often renders them all *useless*.

It is thus in *preaching*, which is truly a great pitched battle for the rescue of precious souls; especially when continued for months together. *Sermons* of mine, which appeared very well in private, and likely, as *spiritual batteries*, to rake the ranks of the enemy tremendously, the *positions* being the best imaginable; but, alas! when brought into action, were quite useless, and I have *lost the day* by *sticking* to them. Whereas, I have won many a day by abandoning them at once; and, seizing upon some "rough, crooked *cudgel of truth*, or other," as a crazy man hinted, and *storm* the *altered entrenchments* of wickedness.

What was the use of firing away from that *battery*, when

the shot curved high over the heads of sinners, or fell far short of their entrenchments? It ought to have been *abandoned* before wasting so much time and strength. I have erred so often here, it is strange I have not yet acquired common sense. When the *proper batteries* were heaved up for my acceptance, I had neither time nor strength to play them upon the enemy; had wasted both in working those which were *ineffectual!*

April 20th. — Amused with that sentiment of one, that sinners are often like dogs in the work of persecution; that when *dogs bark* at a passer-by, it signifies one of two things: either they do not *know* him, or they *dislike* him; but that, in either case, it is no sign he is a bad person; for such dogs will turn and fawn upon persons of the worst habits, and not bark at them at all. "*Without are dogs,*" says John. Lord help us to *beware* of them! The *work* is advancing with *unabated power.*

April 21st. — How much one learns in a revival, of *human nature*, of the *providence* of God in preparing the way for this and that conversion! How evidently Providence has been at work to bring about the salvation of many of these; with some for *years;* — has had to almost *break their heart* by *trying providences*, before their proud *will* could be broken down to repent and believe! So goes it with the world; and an "Almighty Providence" is, indeed, an "*exceeding thought,*" and its *chastisements* exceed all we know of them, till *developed* by a great revival.

April 22d. — I seldom *weep* in the pulpit, though my eyes frequently *fill*, and *swim* a little; but *tears* do not often trickle down. I like to feel them; it is a great comfort to feel that my *springs* are not dry, nor the *fountain* of *tears* dried up. — Hosea 13: 15. But, O, how *deliciously sweet* are tears, when in *secret audience* with

God! Some one remarked that sugar is sweetest when it *melts*, and that when the religion of a Christian dissolves into tears of gratitude and thanksgiving it is the *sweetest* of all.

How freely these penitent sinners weep, when *truth* touches them, as the rod of Moses did the *granite*! I liked that thought of one, though it seemed to have a little of the dash of romance : "Tears flowing from the eyes of the penitent, are like water dropping from *roses*, — they are very sweet, and very precious to God." *Tears* and *prayers* once drew down blessings in clusters upon the head and heart and crown of a *royal one*, whose life trembled upon the verge of eternity : " *Thus saith the Lord, the God of David thy father, I have heard thy prayer, I have seen thy tears : behold, I will heal thee,*" &c., &c.— 2 Kings 20 : 5, 6. Hezekiah speedily recovered, and enjoyed his *fifteen additional years!*

How many of these Birmingham sinners may have had their *doom* changed, their lives prolonged, by their plentiful prayers and tears yesterday ! When the Lord turned, and looked upon *Peter*, "he went out and *wept bitterly.*" Those tears were no enemies to Peter's *futurity*, nor to his place in the *sympathies* and *affections* of his Lord.

Chrysostom blessed God for the *laver of tears to wash in* ; so may these, especially as the fountain of their Redeemer's blood was open to receive them also; without which an *ocean of tears* would be of no avail to wash away a single sin from the conscience, or stain from the soul.

April 28th. — Last Sabbath *forenoon* in Bradford-street Chapel. Preached in behalf of the *Sabbath-school.* Collection, fifteen pounds. Text, " *Therefore, if any man be in Christ, he is a new creature : old things are passed away ; behold, all things are become new.*" — 2 Cor. 5 :

17. Never better *definition* of a *true Christian* ever given. Yet had something of a hard time for myself, and for *hearers* as well, perhaps ; — " spun the *subject* out, and *patience* out," as an old brother in America observed of a straitened preacher, like myself.

> " From his prudent lips shall flow
> Words as light as flakes of snow,
> Fall as soft as snow on the sea, —
> Are lost, —— instantly."

However, at night sin and folly had no *twilight;* but the full blaze of Gospel truth ! But I do not like this way of preaching in the morning in one chapel, and at night in another ; it *weakens* and *dissipates* me ; — cannot carry out my plans properly, and so fail in getting hold of the people. However, I have been singularly mournful and dejected for some days, although have had glimpses of joy between. But my soul has been *weak, tired* and *faint,* "yet pursuing" the great work, *the conquest of souls !* The work of God is onward, and sweeps everything before it. But this preaching *six times* a week for so many months, and to such amazing crowds of people, to say nothing of my *select meetings* for seekers of salvation, my *correspondence,* which is very extensive and burdensome, and much other writing besides, — O, it is *wearisome* and wearing ! Fight thou my battles, O Lord God of hosts ! Amen.

> " Only thy terrors, Lord, restrain."

April 29th. — Felt I was going on an *errand* for God ; — an *errand* implies a message ; — had a *message* from him to poor hell-exposed sinners ; felt I was going on an errand for Him, and knew *with what,* and *for what.* What *boldness* and *confidence* this conviction gives ! But it often brings trouble as a consequence. People do not understand it. There is no way to make the errand agreeable, and the consequences easy to be borne, but to aim at pleasing God fully therein. Then every word is *heart-deep*, in preacher and hearer; or as a strong-minded *Scotchman* observed, "then comes the *nailing of the subject to the wall.*" The slain of the Lord were many. The *nail* of truth, if it did not *pin them to the wall*, it did to the *floor*, as did the nail, in the hand of *Jael's wife*, the *head* of *Sisera*.

What a noble, large-souled old servant of God, is the *superintendent* of the east circuit, *the Rev. Alexander Bell!* God bless him!—the very expression of his countenance stimulates me to "*deeds of noble daring*" for the Lord our God. He knows the mission of *Methodism* well. How much a man may do for God, by what one calls "unconscious *influence*"! When he thinks he is doing little or no good, he may be accomplishing, silently, the greatest good! However, *Alexander Bell* is not silent; his voice sounds like a thunder in the thickest of the fight! O Lord, multiply by thousands such men in the battle-field of *Emanuel!* Amen.

CHAPTER LIII.

MISTAKING THE PATH.

APRIL 30th. — Received the following interesting letter. It tells a sad tale; — shows how easy it is to get out of the providential path, and how hard to get back into it again, and how perilous besides. It illustrates that observation of *Baxter*, that SELF in some cannot get its *heart broken*, until the *heart has been broken by sorrow*, and by the *keen rebukes* of Providence, with many and fresh *confessions*, and *plenty of tears!*

"*Birmingham, April 29th,* 1846.
" HONORED SIR : I believe it is under a sacred influence I address you. I have held myself in check till my grateful emotions can no longer be controlled. I have never had courage to answer in the affirmative, when you have asked me, ' Do you know your sins are forgiven ? '

" Religion has been a familiar thing to me since my childhood. At the age of *fifteen* I engaged myself determinedly to pursue it. I walked before God in *sincerity*, though in *obscurity*, during *six years*, when the Lord sent me the life of *Mr. Wesley*, to study in a sick-chamber.

" The *Spirit*, through this, showed me how far I had gone; — how far from original righteousness I now was. Deep, soul-rending convictions for sin seized me, which ended, in a few weeks, in a conscious sense of pardon ; my chains fell off, with that book in my hand; my heart was free, and I was free indeed.

"Previous to this, I had been a member of the Established Church, and felt opposed to the *Methodists*. Now my *prejudices* were laid aside. I read their works, attended their ministry occasionally; finally said, '*This people shall be my people.*' But, not being free from the control of others, I postponed it, contrary to my convictions; but still remained in a waiting position for *three years*, with much trial and fiery temptation, yet felt the life of God was kept alive in my soul. I doubt not I was eating the *honey of perfect love*, through all this time, though I knew it not. That promise, which I used to call peculiarly my own, '*I will instruct thee, and teach thee in the way thou shouldst go, I will guide thee with mine eye,*' was a sort of index to my state of mind.

"In the year 1841, I gained the desire of my heart, — the Lord placed me among the *Methodist* people. My congratulations had barely subsided, when *Satan laid a snare for me;* he was transformed into an angel of light. The *snare* was bewitching in its attractions. I mistook this for *providential indication*, and stepped out of the order of God, in a certain domestic arrangement. The thing might appear trifling in itself, but for the principle involved. — Prov. 3 : 6. And its long train of consequences has made me recognize it as a very important matter.

"Thus God's designs were thwarted, and my expectations, as well as those of my fellow-Christians, were, in a great measure, never realized; the wine was mixed with water. For a time my judgment was perverted, and learned to call *evil good, and good evil.*

"My mind was brought into a most awful state, and I besought the Lord to show me my real state; which he did.

I then pleaded for *external deliverance*. He granted this also. Then I felt the need of *internal deliverance*. My cry was, 'O, my *leanness!* my *leanness!* Restore unto the ears that which the canker-worm and the palmer-worm have eaten!' The Lord heard me, and delivered me, so far as I would permit. But I was not *hearty*, nor sufficiently sensible of my state. I *sought* for deliverance, but did not *strive* for it.

"During this time, I had many *strokes* from God; but he seemed to say in them all, '*Slow to anger.*' I did not come to the point he wished me; and, at length, heavier strokes were inflicted, and the stern look of his displeasure seemed to accompany them.

"My spirits began to sink; *mental anguish* took possession, — robbed me of all my moral ability to a great extent. My *spiritual bent of mind* remained, but all hope of happiness upon earth had departed. My mind had received the stamp of deep melancholy. I said, '*I will go mourning all my days.*' I was forming plans for leaving *Birmingham*, when you arrived, to see what a change of position would do, but did not; could not understand why the Lord hedged up my way; nor that he was about to bring me into a wealthy place. — Ps. 66 : 12. To his name be all the glory, so it proved to be.

"On Friday, January 23d, in Wesley Chapel, I was the character you described; and you asked, '*Is it enough?*' There my trouble ended; sweet peace again took possession of my heart; the tide turned in my favor.

"Since then I have been enabled to make good use of my advantages; have heard you on almost every occasion; strained every nerve, as it were, and pushed my points, and urged my conquests. It has been difficult work, but I have more than conquered through him that loved me. Praise the Lord for another introduction into the Canaan of perfect love!

"Many of those who were near and dear to me in the *Establishment* have been greatly blessed; savingly and gloriously benefited, and will, to-night, make public acknowledgment of it. You will be followed by the tears and prayers of many, whom you have had no public recognition of. I charge my soul ever to let your name and the remembrance of you act as a polar star to me. God bless you! * * The Lord reward you, and give me a humble recognition of your glorified spirit in the world of spirits!

"Yours, dear sir, in deep respect,
"A HUMBLE MEMBER
"*Of the Wesleyan Society.*"

Ah! the world is full of such mourners! but, as one has observed, the cloak of *indifference*, or the mantle of *concealment*, or the pall of *despair*, may hide these things from the world's unfeeling gaze; but the broken heart is not less surely there.

It illustrates that sentiment of another, that our *haps* and *mishaps* arise chiefly from the way in which we order our own *hearts;* that these toss the private state, and render life unsweet, leaving us 'midst the wreck of *Is* and *Was*, things incomplete, and purposes betrayed; troubles following, not *singly*, but in *battalions*, and we, at length, such students in *Disappointment's school*, that all our after life is swayed with *plenitude* of ill; thus

"The heart gives color to our destiny."

And I might add, *Noah's* dove, hovering and flying to and fro over that wild waste of shoreless waters, but *find-*

ing no rest for the sole of her foot, till she returned to the *Ark*, strikingly illustrates the experience of one who has enjoyed the blessing of *perfect love*, and lost it. Well, thank God for another trophy of salvation; and to him be all the glory!

CHAPTER LIV.

LINES IN PLEASANT PLACES.

(Ps. 16 : 6.)

MAY 1st. — The *revival* is onward still in power. O, the glory, the grandeur of this work!

I returned to *Sparkbrook House* some weeks since, from my other home on the other side of the town. I am surrounded with comforts. Surely *the lines are fallen unto me in the pleasant places!* We have fine weather. Lovely mornings. Blossoms wet with morning dews; and fanned with zephyrs breathing of Paradise. Pleasant walks through the grounds, — one especially, near the mansion, under fine *overshadowing trees*, my favorite walking-place, which they shade from the sun, leaving me the benefit of the western breeze; and, close by, the fine garden, with a pretty sheet of water, in which are a couple of *snow-white swans*, sailing majestically around, and, with all

> "———— the mantling spirit of reserve,
> Fashion their necks into a goodly curve;
> *Arches* thrown back between luxuriant wings
> Of whitest garniture."

One day I greatly disturbed her *swanship*, enjoying her *siesta* in the sunshine. Coming suddenly upon the green bank, before her floating sentinel had time to give her warning, I was close by her side, — opening her eyes, her alarm was terrible, frightening her out of all the proprieties of majesty, — rushing into the flood in the wildest disorder, and, if one might judge from the *noise* they kept up, it was long before they concluded to forgive or forget. Always after that, when I visited the banks, they put on a sort of haughty *reserve*, and, with more than usual of the rushing, "gushing impulse," cleaving the water in circles, nearer and nearer to the bank where I stood, but never forgetting for a moment their *dignity!*

As to myself, I have been floating about from chapel to chapel, the last two or three weeks; *Belmont-Row* Chapel, *Cherry-street*, *Wesley*, *Newton-Row*, and *Islington* chapels, with constant success. *Hundreds* converted, and great numbers sanctified throughout, body, soul, and spirit. Hallelujah to God and the Lamb!

Visited *Warwick Castle* some days since, in company with Rev. *D. Walton* and Mr. Alderman *James Meek*, of York. This ancient monument of feudal grandeur stands upon the banks of the river *Avon*, a pleasant drive from Birmingham. I desired much to see it, as it is the most interesting of the kind in England; seen from a distance, rising in a cluster of ancient towers, the effect is picturesque and imposing. We spent an agreeable hour or two in walking through its halls and rooms. One of the towers is said to be of *Anglo-Saxon* origin. *Cæsar's* tower is very old, and so is *Guy's* tower, which rises to the height of one hundred and forty feet, — "The Sir Guy, of *Warwick*, who figures largely in the wild history of Romances in days of chivalry."

The heart receives a lesson amidst such scenes it hardly ever meets with elsewhere.

We were shown the celebrated ancient Vase which was dug out of the ruins of the villa of the Emperor Adrian, at Tivola, in Italy, and sent to England in 1774; a beautiful specimen of Grecian art in the time of Alexander the Great It is really a study; — composed of white marble, nearly spherical in form; is capable of containing one hundred and sixty-three gallons; is wreathed with two vines, which, at their stems, form the handles of the vase, and then ingeniously spread and interlaced, with their tendrils, foliage, and clusters, — all sculptured out of the solid marble, with antique heads, — that of *Bacchus*, of course, the god of wine and of drunkards, with his Thyrsus and panther's skin, things which the old Grecians delighted to sculpture. But, farewell, Warwick Castle!

"In war renowned, in peace sublime!"

May 2d. — These Friday night discourses on holiness, seem to give that glorious doctrine an *impulse* through all the week.

But how many *unconverted members* of Wesleyan and other churches are being constantly awakened out of their *deception* and *saved!* — those "*wooden legs*," as *Baxter* called them in his day, — for so he named *unconverted* members of the Christian church; — *wooden legs!* Such a one, he would say, "is but as a *wooden leg* to the *body!*" "A *dead member* of a *living body*," was *Bellarmine's* notion of them! Though attached to the body, yet not of the body; or he would say, as the *hair*, or the *nails*, which, though *in the* body, yet not *properly members of the body*. *Chaff* among the *wheat*, was *Austin's* idea of them, — an *appurtenance* to the wheat, *but not the wheat*. *Chaff* on the *threshing-floor of the church*, was *John the Baptist's* idea, destined to *be burned with unquenchable fire;* — *tares* was Christ's figure for them, and *fire* the final instrument of their destruction. Those are strong words of the apostle. — Gal. 6 : 4, 5, 15.

That *distinction* between feasting upon "real solid comforts," and feeding upon "*airy delusory conceits*," was capable of profitable expansion, had I had time; as, also, between the comfort of the *spirit* and that of the *fancy*. But, O, how terrible that idea of one, that if we have but the *image of true religion*, we shall have but the *image of heaven* at last; — some dreams and self-created hopes of happiness, which may accompany us to the door of eternity, but there they will leave us to *everlasting horror!* Terrible thought!

May 3d. --- He that would continue to save souls, I find, must not depart from first principles; — he must dwell much on *first principles*, — the *essentials* of Christianity. This, some, whose *heads* have *out-travelled* their *hearts*, do not like; they want *variety* and *novelty*, and something to gratify *curiosity* in doctrine. To meet their case, one would need *another Gospel* than Paul preached. Shall I pander to such a taste? *Nay*, by the grace of God, never! O, never may I live to prove to sinful men that I think the *Gospel* has become *stale* and *uninteresting*, and, therefore, must lay the *sciences* under contribution, to make the Gospel *bearable* or *palatable;* and, as it were, work another Gospel, than *Christ crucified*, out of them, or a *diluted* Gospel, or *mongrel!* The present age is a tempter to this, and, it is to be feared, too frequently succeeds.

That *deprecation* of the apostle is a powerful *antidote* to me : "*But God forbid that I should glory, save in the cross of our Lord Jesus Christ, by whom the world is crucified to me, and I unto the world.*" — Gal. 6 : 14. St. Paul never interposed a "God forbid!" but upon some point of the highest importance, — and he used the phrase on several occasions. The scenes are amazing here! Glory be to God!

May 4th. — The *sun*, and *moon*, and *stars*, are sometimes *nearer* to the *earth* than at other times. ETERNITY, with its *Heaven*, and *Hell*, and *Spirits*, looms up, and sweeps nearer to men during a *revival*, I sometimes think, than during any other portion of the history of a population; so near, I often feel, as if one could almost hear the *shouts* of the *glorified* saints in heaven, and the *wailings* of the damned in hell.

It is then the *power* of God is felt; and the *truth* of God rushes out upon sinners, like the *lion* upon the children of Ephraim! and cries for mercy ascend from the smitten and the torn; and shouts of deliverance from the healed and the saved. Such is the state of things in Birmingham at the present time. Hallelujah!

May 5th. — What a necessity for a *storming time* that was! *Ordinary effort* would have been of no avail, but *Satan's triumph*. But how important to be ready for such a *divine intimation!* One should not have his *heart* or *wit*, or *courage*, to seek at such a moment; no, nor his *weapons*, nor his *faith!*

What a noble spirit is the Rev. *Joseph Wood*, of the *West* circuit, — full of faith and of the Holy Ghost! How sweet this union with his spirit!

CHAPTER LV.

INCIDENTS OF THE REVIVAL.

To * * * * * *.

Birmingham, May 7, 1846.

You desire to have some "particulars regarding the great work in *Birmingham.*" I hardly know *where* to begin, unless I were to copy a great part of my private journal. The scenes have been very wonderful, — many cases marked and striking, and remarkable in their effects upon others. Some notoriously wicked sinners converted!

You may remember I told you of a *temperance lecture* I delivered in the Town Hall.* A letter from a citizen lies before me, of which the following is an extract:

"I had been an advocate for *temperate drinking*, but had often been carried into the vortex of *intemperance;* — wanted to hear your *lecture;* — did, and was convinced that I was *wrong*, became *decided*, and took the pledge. I am now a practical *tee-totaler*. That meeting brought *deep convictions* into my mind. I was then breaking the *Sabbath* by keeping my *shop* open, and selling on that day; — alas! against the convictions of my own conscience! Mine was

---

* The reader will recollect that Mr. Caughey referred to the state of the temperance cause in Birmingham. Before leaving that town he attended several temperance meetings, and lectured on the subject. These meetings were attended with the most happy results. —*Editor*.

Sabbath-breaking of no common order, — it was against the *clearest light.* O, but I do feel it is through infinite mercy I was not sent to hell long since!

"But *Jesus* was my *interceding friend.* My face is now *Zion-ward.* Let others do as they may, by his help I will save my soul.

"To my excellent leader, *Dr. Melson,* I owe a debt of gratitude. He called upon me, and took me kindly by the hand. May God reward him!

"My *shop is closed* on the Sabbath, now, and ever shall be. My leader tells me the eyes of the world are upon me. I know it, and feel it. My fellow-tradesmen laugh at me, and *sneer.* They tell me I shall soon reöpen it. Sir, pray that I may be kept from *sin,* and from *falling,* and that the Lord would *increase* my *faith,* fill me with the *Spirit,* and perfect me in love, and confirm my hope. I pray much that your ministry may be blessed to thousands more, and that you may be filled with all the fulness of God, and conducted at length, through a sea of light, to the throne of the *Eternal One.* Affectionately,

"W. A. J." *

And here is a letter from a converted *Roman Catholic,* who ventured out some weeks ago to *see* and *hear* for herself, and then she says her "troubles began;"— that, after resisting the strivings of the Spirit for some weeks, she sought and found *the pearl* of great price; — says that *Jesus* is now her precious Saviour, and fills her heart with peace and gladness. FAITH,— justification *by faith,*— O what a word of *power* there is in that! —*justified by faith, without* the *merit of works!* When a Roman Catholic

---

* His full name is attached to the letter

understands and receives that doctrine, the effects are *immediate* and *glorious*. Luther once remarked, that it is by this *one piece of artillery* the *Papacy* is to be finally *overthrown* and destroyed; — that it is plain, if our sins may be taken away by our *own works, merits* and *satisfactions*, there was no necessity the *Son of God* should be given for them. But, seeing he was *given for our sins*, it follows that *we* cannot put them away by our *own works;* — so *great*, so *invincible*, so *infinite*, are our sins, it is impossible for the whole world to satisfy for one of them. But, as it is written, he "*gave himself for our sins,*— *according to the will of God and our Father*"(Gal. 1: 4), it shows the *power of sin*, and the impossibility of our being saved in any other way, in the *estimation* and *judgment* of our God. Thus, if the *Popish error* would overthrow the *necessity of the atonement*, the doctrine of *justification by faith* overthrows the *error!* *Luther* declared the opinion, before his death, that had the *Protestants* continued to preach as at the first,— "*justified neither by the righteousness of the law,* nor by our *own righteousness, but by faith in Jesus Christ only,*"— that this *one article* would have overthrown the whole *Papacy*, with all her *brotherhoods, pardons, religious orders, relics, invocation of saints, purgatory, masses, watchings, vows,* and *infinite other like abominations!* Blessed be God! it will. This saved *Romanist* is all gratitude, thanksgiving and praise; — signs her name in full, and has done with *Popery* forever; — says "*Jesus* has given me a complete victory over *fiery trials;*"— trusts that having put her hand to the Gospel plough, she will never look back towards spiritual Babylon and Sodom; — hopes that "the *prayers* of a *once distressed*, but now happy servant of Christ," will be answered for my continued success in bringing lost sinners to Christ.

Blessed be God! Why may I not *multiply my power with God by such petitioners?*

The *Roman Catholics* of Broad-street have lost their *Organist.* He and his wife have both found Christ; and so he plays there no more. It is not to be wondered at that the *priests* are so desperately opposed to their people attending our meetings. It is *perilous* to allow them to hear the *whole Gospel!*

* * * * * *

———

Mr. Caughey received a large number of letters, asking advice in matters of conscience. To some of these he replied. The following replies will be read with interest:

To an Apprentice.

Birmingham, May 7th, 1846.

My dear young Friend: Yours is to hand. You have *a body to support,* but you have *a soul to save.* You have a *master upon earth,* but there is a God in heaven. He has commanded you to remember the *Sabbath day to keep it holy;* and you are under *bonds* to the value of your soul to obey. *Suffering* you must endure, most likely, in case of your *master's displeasure;* but this, however severe, cannot be compared to the *effects* of the *displeasure of God,* which is *eternal.* Better suffer *death* than *sin against God.* Your *master* will be punished for causing you to sin; but you will have to suffer for your own *transgression.*

Having said thus much, I must leave you to decide as you may think best.

Yours affectionately in Christ,

J. C.

To a Clerk in the B—— Post Office.
Birmingham, May 7th, 1846.

My dear Sir: You have a *family* to support, and a difficult world to bring them through. But you have a *soul*. You cannot be happy in violating the holy *Sabbath*. You are under as great an obligation to *keep it holy*, as to be an *honest man*. The *health* of body and soul depends upon *peace of mind*, which you cannot well have in your present employment.

Having said thus much, I must leave you to take that course you may think best.

Affectionately yours in Jesus Christ,
J. C.

O, how much *wisdom* and *prudence* is needed in dealing with troubled consciences! It would be well, I suppose, to keep a full record of my *letters, conversations,* &c., &c., but it is extremely difficult to take the time to do so; and so *occasions* pass away, and the circumstances are forgotten.

* * * * * * *

CHAPTER LVI.

PERSECUTION.

MAY 8th.—A letter from my *Liverpool* host, *Mr. Banning*, of the Liverpool Post Office. He says, "The newspapers are determined,—perhaps not *intentionally*, but nevertheless are doing that which produces it,—to increase your popularity, and thereby your usefulness;—the statements of '*The Morning Chronicle*' * have circulated in all the newspapers of the *United Kingdom*, nearly, I should think!"

Amen! let them *write*, and *print*, and *circulate*, and make me out the greatest *fool* or *knave* that lives;—what of that, if I am neither a fool nor a knave? What care I, if the work of God but go on, and my *conscience* feels sure of his *approbation?*

PERSECUTION!—of the *pen*, of the *tongue*,—what signifies all *we* are called to endure in *this age*, however humiliating, compared with what the saints of *other days* have endured from the *hands* of the ungodly?—as the tickling of *flies*, when compared with the stings of *wasps!* —nay, as the stings of *wasps*, when compared with the *strokes of scorpions!* *They* bore *the cross*, indeed, upon bare, bleeding and lacerated shoulders; but we, of modern

---

* This paper became notorious in its opposition to the revival, but with what success, the reader may form some idea from what follows.—*Editor*

times, only bear the *chips* of the cross; or, if the *chip* happen to be a big and heavy one, and hit pretty hard, or sit heavy, we are not without *cushions* of many comforts to make them *tolerable!*

Nevertheless, some in modern times have the persecution of the *hand*, even unto *blood*. A *letter* lies before me, of which the following is the substance:

A *faithful wife*, the cause of the conversion of a wicked, persecuting husband.

She sought and found mercy. Her husband was displeased; but, finding her a *changed woman*, he *opposed*, and resorted to a variety of petty annoyances, hoping to discourage her. But she stood fast in her glorious liberty, and *would go* to the *Methodist* meetings, and serve God, notwithstanding his positive prohibition.

At length, he became *enraged*, and threatened to *horsewhip* her if she went any more to those meetings. This brought *tears* to her eyes, but did not drive *courage* from her heart. She replied, "*Husband*, have I done my duty to you as your *wife?* Is there anything left undone in the house, which ought to be done, in order to make you more comfortable?"—"No," he replied, "I have had no cause of complaint in such matters; but a *Methodist* you never shall be." To this she answered, "I have done my *duty* to my *family*, now I owe a duty to my God; and, if He strengthens me, I shall do that also." — "Well, if you do, *horsewhip* you I shall, when you return; that's all." — "Very well, husband, I shall do the will of God, and let him see to it." She went to meeting, and had a very happy time; the Lord blessed her abundantly, and prepared her for the *trial* of faith that awaited her.

When she entered the house, she met her *enraged* husband, *horsewhip* in hand, saying, "I'll do as I said;

strip!"—and, seizing her, he literally tore her clothes off her person, and applied the *horsewhip to her bare back*, until it became a *discolored, bleeding* mass. She bore it all without a *murmur*, which maddened him the more; and, when he gave her the last lash, pushed her from him.

She retired into her room, fell upon her knees, and began to pray for him. After a while he came into the room, and, seeing her on her knees, her back bare and bleeding, — the woman he had promised to love, succor, and protect, until death, — and heard her praying for him, and saying, "Glory be to God that I am counted worthy to *suffer thus* in the cause of my Lord Jesus Christ!—glory be to God!" At that instant, *convictions* of guilt seized his conscience, — the *Spirit* of God laid hold of the persecutor. He fell upon his knees by her side, imploring her *forgiveness*, and her *prayers* that God would have mercy upon him, and not send him to hell, as he deserved. "Forgive me," said he, "I have been worse than a *Turk*." Her prayer did ascend to heaven, and in a short time he found mercy, and joined the *Wesleyan Methodists* also!

What a *trial!* What a *victory!* The Devil, for a long time to come, will remember that *defeat* from a weak woman, and be ashamed of it before apostate spirits in hell!

* * * * * *

Last Sabbath day, I preached in *Bradely*, a few miles from Birmingham, to a multitude of *colliers*, and others. It was in behalf of the "*trust fund*" of their chapel;— had to preach in the *grave-yard* in the evening, the crowd was so great. We had a great time, forenoon, afternoon, and night; some *thirty-four* souls were saved. Collections over £80, or *four hundred dollars!* Bless thou the Lord, O, my soul!

* * * * * *

The time is at hand when I must leave *Birmingham*,—noble, *glorious Birmingham!* O, how I love the place, and its people! Hard to drag myself away from them Have been *consolidating* the work; strengthening and fortifying the new converts, and preaching *farewell sermons* in various chapels; journaling a little, and trying to keep up with my *correspondence*, which is no easy matter sometimes; but all with a single eye to His glory.

* * * * * *

Have had the pleasure of taking *tea* with the *ministers* and *leaders* of both the Birmingham circuits; told them all *I hoped* and all *I feared* regarding the *young converts;* and with the deepest humility, begged they would do all in their power to *preserve* them to the church, and to maintain the *honor* of this great revival.

We had *gracious seasons;* and they kindly assured me that nothing should be wanting, upon their part, in carrying out *all my suggestions.* I felt *greatly humbled* at the loving, hearty *deference* which they paid to one so *unworthy.* May the Father, Son and Holy Ghost bless them more and more! Amen.

This has been a glorious work of God, indeed; *thousands* have been saved. To God be *all* the *glory*, is the sure language of my heart. From the *registers*, kept by authorized and competent *secretaries*, on both "the east and west circuits," as they are called, it is ascertained that, since last December, about *two thousand eight hundred souls* have been justified by faith in Christ; and about *one thousand four hundred persons* sanctified, in the full sense of Acts 15 : 9,—"*Purifying their hearts by faith.*" Total saved, in both blessings, *four thousand two hundred* persons.

The names of all these persons were carefully registered as the work advanced, together with their respective places of residence. This was done to prevent exaggerated reports and that proper care might be taken of the subjects of the work. Many of the above were from the *country* around, as well as the town ; some were from ten to fifty miles distant. Other *churches* and *congregrations* in town were well represented, and doubtless have, or will, receive *accessions*. A large number, too, were members of the *Wesleyan church*, both of the justified and sanctified. Allowing these deductions, the numbers from the *world*, and now united with the Wesleyans, must be *very large*.

I have been most hospitably entertained at *Sparkbrook House*, by *Mr. and Mrs. Wright*, and at the house of *Mr. Souter;* the largest part of the time at the former place. Never shall I forget the kindness shown me by those two blessed families. May my Lord reward them much in time and in eternity!

> "Sweet is music's melting fall, but sweeter yet
> The still small voice of gratitude."

CHAPTER LVII.

CONCLUSION.

THE following *resolutions*, copied from the *quarterly meeting* journals of the Birmingham east and west circuits, will show the reader in what estimation the revival was held by the *authorities* of *Wesleyan Methodism* in *Birmingham*.

The *first* resolution was passed in March, some time before the revival had obtained its full and glorious *triumph*.

"*Birmingham, East Circuit, March*, 1846. — That, while this meeting expresses its thankfulness to Almighty God for the encouraging prosperity vouchsafed to this circuit during the last few years, it would more especially record its devout gratitude for the remarkable outpouring of the Holy Spirit, as manifested in the present extraordinary revival, — and it would also express its most grateful sense of the *most important services* of the Rev. James Caughey, as an instrument in the hands of God, in bringing about this most delightful extension of his work. — *Passed unanimously, signed by the Rev. Alexander Bell, Superintendent.*

"*Birmingham, West Circuit, June*, 1846. — That this meeting feels itself called upon to place upon record their devout and grateful acknowledgments to Almighty God for the unprecedented prosperity with which he has visited this society in its several departments during the last quarter. Its numerical prosperity is evidenced in the accession of two hundred and eighty-five members, out of three hundred reported on trial last quarter-day; and the future is cheering, inasmuch as two hundred and fifty-seven are now reported on trial in this circuit alone. The spiritual state of the society demands the gratitude of this meeting in the exhibition of a *greater* degree of *union* among the members, in the increased zeal and devotion of its officers, and in the desire generally manifested to promote, encourage and carry on the gracious revival, commenced under the ministry of the Rev. James Caughey, and continued to the present time in connection with our own ministry. Another delightful feature of this revival is exhibited in the *improved attention* of the old members, and in the *steadiness* of the new converts to their classes. — *Moved by Mr. Ratcliff, seconded by Mr. Edmund Heeley, and carried unanimously; the Rev. George Turner, Superintendent, in the chair; present, the Rev. Messrs. Burton, Hurt and Joseph Wood.*"

The following account of the closing exercises of Mr. Caughey's labors in Birmingham is from one of the religious papers of London:

" The public labors of Mr. Caughey terminated on Wednesday evening, at Cherry-street Chapel. Great numbers were unable to get in. Several souls were saved at the prayer-meeting. The following evening the local preachers, leaders and stewards, of the east circuit, met together; after tea, the meeting was addressed by Mr. Caughey. A similar meeting was held in Cherry-street school on **Friday** evening. The Rev. Alexander Bell, superintendent of the east circuit, presided over the meeting in Belmont-Row vestry; and the Rev. G. Turner occupied the chair on Friday evening. On both occasions, several leaders spoke of the benefit they had personally received during the revival; of the state of their classes; and, according to their statements, some of them have received to their classes more than twenty persons who had been, up to the visit of Mr. Caughey, in an unconverted state, but who, not having given their hearts to the Lord, had united themselves to his people. Notwithstanding the attraction of Mr. Caughey's labors to the new converts especially, yet all the leaders rejoiced in being able to state that their members never met more regularly, although rumors had been circulated, in London and elsewhere, that the class meetings were almost broken up. It is, therefore, a cheering fact that the regular meetings of classes have been all through the revival well attended. Mr. Caughey left our town for Nottingham on Saturday last, where he commenced his labors on Sunday; he will find a people prepared of the Lord. By his amiability of disposition, by his eminent piety, by his burning zeal, by his extraordinary usefulness, he has endeared himself to the Methodists of Birmingham. Long may he live to prosecute his holy work! If the local preachers and leaders of Nottingham hold up his hands, as they have been supported in Birmingham, prayer must prevail, and floods of mercy will descend upon the thirsty ground. And the character of Nottingham Methodism says it shall be so. Amen."

Mr. Caughey's closing remarks are worthy to close the volume·

"May 10th. — *Farewell, Birmingham! Fare-thee-well*, in every sense of the word, especially in the religious sense; and farewell, *my children* within thee! Their *times* of *trial* are at hand; the chaff to be driven from among the wheat; — that will be taken up as a reproach against the *revival*, although ever so much *wheat* may remain! And alas! the *wheat* may be driven away too, or *spoil* through *inattention* or *mismanagement!*

"But, O, let me hope for the best! — that I shall not have to mourn as Mr. Wesley had to, as we learn from his journal, under date April 4th, 1755, where he says, 'We rode to *Birmingham*, a barren, uncomfortable place. Most of the seed that has been sown for so many years, the "wild boars" have "rooted up;" the fierce, unclean, brutish, blasphemous *Antinomians* have utterly destroyed it. And the *mystic foxes* have taken true pains to spoil what remained with their new gospel. Yet, it seems God has a blessing for this place still; so many still attend the preaching; and he is eminently present with the small number that is left in society.' A sorrowful record that must have been to *Mr. Wesley.*

"It is well, therefore, to *glory* in nothing, — neither in *success* nor *influence;* for, O, how soon both may vanish away! It is safe only to '*glory in the Lord*,' and to meet the temptation to glory in anything else, with the apostle's '*God forbid that I should glory!*' Ah, that is the *safest, sweetest, happiest* state of mind!

"And farewell, ye *ministers* of our God, with whom I have taken sweet counsel! — and ye *leaders* and *fellow-laborers!* A *glorious band* of faithful men and women, who helped us much in the Lord; to whom, in fact, under God, much of the credit and honor of this great work of God is certainly due; for, what could we have done without them? *Farewell*, ALL! — ye blessed families, where I have been for months so generously entertained; all, too, who have showed the *stranger* kindness in *word* and deed. Blessings on you all! — *every blessing* from heaven above, and earth beneath, be upon you all. *Farewell!*

"And, to poor *sinners* whom I leave in their sins, can I say, *Farewell?* Alas, alas! how can I? — with what heart or prospect, if they go on resisting the Spirit of God, as they have been doing? O, Lord God, have mercy upon them, and bring them to *repentance!* Amen."

NOTE. — *Mr. Caughey* left *Birmingham* on the 10th of May, 1846, after a sojourn of about five months, during which time *thousands* were saved. He opened his commission the following Sabbath in *Nottingham*, where he spent a few *weeks*, preaching constantly, and *hundreds* of sinners were converted to God. From thence he hastened to the city of *Lincoln*, and thence to *Boston*, in *Lincolnshire*, spending *weeks* in each place, the Lord crowning the labors of his servant with abundant success; an account of which may appear in a future volume, should the present volume find favor with the PUBLIC.

35*

APPENDIX.

The two following letters from Mr. Caughey contain his views on Church Architecture They exhibit the results of his observations on the influence which certain styles of architecture exert over the voice of the preacher. They are worthy of consideration.

"<i>Hamilton, C. W.</i>,
"<i>Wednesday Morning, May</i> 8, 1853.

" To ―― ――.

" My Dear Sir: Yours is to hand. I rejoice in your prospects. You needed a better church in ――. You say, ' As we are about to erect an elegant and costly temple to our God, we desire the internal plans and fixtures to be as conducive to easy and effective speaking as possible. You know, sir, tastes differ as to order and general style of church architecture. We have our tastes and notions here, which, I suppose, we would not alter for anybody. But it is our wish, for all that, to avoid everything, in the internal construction and arrangement of the edifice, that would be prejudicial to an easy and successful delivery of the Gospel message. You, sir, have had considerable experience in these things, on both sides the Atlantic. You have noticed, doubtless, that some churches have been harder to speak in than others, and possibly you have detected the cause or causes. Would you do us the favor to state them, or, at least, what you would have us avoid?'

" To this I reply: Those churches which I have found most exhausting to voice, strength, &c., have had one or more of the following defects:

" 1. Position of the Church.— Painfully close to low houses and noisy children, mechanic shops; too near the street, especially if rough and much travelled, so that every passing carriage duly announced itself, and even the passing segar-smoker; so flush upon the sidewalk as to allow no fence, exposing the prayer-meetings in basement to outside gazers, if windows open,— if shut, ruining the meeting for want of ventilation.

" From such defects as these your good sense, I trust, will preserve you,— ay, even though the site should be offered as a gift.

"2. CHURCH PROPORTIONS. — Want of internal symmetry; either out of proportion in length or width. The wall of galleries too wide, placing the audience at a painful distance from the preacher,— tempting him, perhaps, to pitch his voice too high to begin with, and to speak louder than he need to. Ceiling too lofty, allowing the voice to ascend too high before receiving a returning impulse, such as a properly-constructed ceiling always affords. Concave ceiling always bad; but more on this by and by.

"3. THE PULPIT — *Its Position and Fixtures.* — Position: At the entrance, where winds and noises may annoy the preacher the readiest, whether administering in pulpit or altar. Too low, if ceiling lofty; too high, if ceiling improperly low. Fixtures: Lamps too near for safety or comfort, leaving the preacher no choice but submit. Recess behind: Too deep, always bad; or, if shallow, so abundantly supplied with whitewash as to leave the preacher no alternative but sit 'bolt upright,' like a boarding-school miss, or lean back for a moment, to rise like a powdered beau or liveried servant of other days. Drapery behind the pulpit: A nuisance evermore; it absorbs sound without returning it, as black absorbs the sun-rays without separating them; detains and deadens the voice. Foot-board: Too high or low for the desk or habit of the preacher, without means of lowering or raising his standing to taste; and so uneven and shaky, withal, as to 'creak time' with his motions. Times not a few I have had to fold my cloak and stand upon it, to avoid one or other of these disadvantages. Kneeling board or stool: Too low, so as to bury him to the shoulders when at prayer. Times without number have I been forced to press cloak or Bible under knees, as a remedy, or have prayed standing.

"These are small matters to some, sir, but they are often very annoying and weakening to a preacher.

"4. WINDOWS. — In particular, two or three facing the pulpit, dazzling the preacher's eyes on a bright or sunny day, without remedy. Windows, in general, uncorded, or but one here and there so honored; and so large as to require two men to lower or raise them for ventilation; or so tight that but one or two out of half a dozen could be opened at all upon an emergency; or so loose as, when winds were on parade, to remind the boys of drum-beat on training-day; and so open as to give them lessons in the whistling science.

"5. DOORS. — Perhaps I should have spoken of these first — but so wakeful as to announce arrivals and departures by creak or slam, with great faithfulness.

"6. PEWS. — Backs capped with a projecting ridge, or shoulder protuberance, and so upright and so narrow-seated, withal, as to force wearied hearers to sit sideways to the preacher at length, and with that wearied and displeased expression by no means inspiring to the preacher. And, besides, so inconvenient for kneeling as to induce a general habit of sitting or standing at prayer-time.

"7. LIGHTS. — Dim, or badly arranged; twinkling here and there like a stray star in a gloomy sky.

"8. TEMPERATURE. — In extremes of heat and cold, owing to want of judgment in the sexton, or absence of that invaluable appendage to our American churches, a good thermometer.

"9. VENTILATION — *Neglected or Mismanaged*. — Neglected: Air left unchanged after the congregation has retired, to be reinhaled by the next audience, — perhaps on a Sabbath morning, after having been imprisoned through the week, exhausted and poisoned on the previous Sabbath, and now to be breathed over again; voice making its heavy way through a loaded and leaden atmosphere, into the ears of yawning or sleepy hearers. Ah me! what sorrowful times have been my portion from this cause! Not one sexton in twenty has any rule against this evil. Mismanaged ventilation: Windows kept closed till the atmosphere becomes insufferable; then opened without judgment, wide and to windward, spreading discomfort and uneasiness in the vicinities. I have not found one sexton in ten who makes it a rule, in such emergencies, to open the windows the sheltered side of the church, keeping those to windward shut, or but very slightly open. What next? Windows re-closed; 'better bear the ills we have,' than suffer others to fly to us, 'that we know not of.' Thus the pure air — a friend, indeed, if prudently managed — has made 'cowards of us all.'

"10. A few words about CHURCH CEILINGS. — A ceiling immoderately high may have some advantages. It may, in the eyes of some, perhaps, look imposing. In hot weather, or when a large audience is present, may be somewhat refreshing, enclosing, as it does, a larger body of air for the breathers beneath. But, depend upon it, the preacher pays the tax upon such slight advantages, in an increased outlay of both voice and strength, besides a sensible diminution of his ordinary power, enjoyed under a ceiling of medium height. He feels it, sinks by degrees, or loses heart, and closes under the impression of 'a hard time.' Let him realize the same difficulty again and again in the same pulpit, and the apprehension will go far to weaken his faith in his usual preparation.

"If the ceiling be concave, or arched, the difficulty will be increased ten-fold.

"There is a singular sympathy, if I may use the word, between the voice and the ceiling. At least, the voice is singularly aided or retarded by the character of the ceiling. If it has to ascend high in space before it meets a substance to arrest, steady and react upon it, by a returning impulse, the preacher will sensibly feel the loss. It will force him to unusual exertion, risking the unnatural both in tone and manner. And this will exhaust. Remember this, my dear sir; every foot you poise your ceiling above an ordinary and reasonable height, you are preparing a proportionate tax upon the strength of your successive pastors.

"Above all, sir, let me caution you and your colleagues of the 'Building Committee' to reject, once for all, any plan which contemplates a sloped, or concave, or arched ceiling. I may not be using the proper architectural phrases, but you comprehend me. Either of these is almost ruinous to easy and effective speaking. I have tried them to my sorrow, and would warn you against them. Whatever advantages they might afford to *oratorios*, they are the bane of oratory, — that, especially, that *moves the soul* or *melts the heart*. He is a rare preacher that succeeds in hewing down sinners under such a ceiling. If it does not create an echo, — and it is sure to do so if the congregation be small, — it will attract the voice away from the audience assuredly.

"It goes far to rob the voice of its unction and power, returning an empty sound to the ears of the people. Vacant looks will tell the laboring preacher there is something wrong or wanting. Solomon says, 'If the iron be blunt, and he do not whet the edge; then he must put to more strength.' Just so! And he who preaches under such a ceiling will soon find voice and sentences blunt enough. If he love souls, — if he desire to constrain sinners to feel that they have need of everything that Jesus has purchased for them on Calvary, — he will 'put to more strength.' But 'there's the rub!' This is just the extra tax he is paying to the ignorance or caprice of the architect, or his advisers.

"I was holding a series of meetings, some time since, in a church of this sort — contending with these difficulties till my heart ached. And, to add to them, a recess behind pulpit, — not deep, but wide and lofty, in the form of a Gothic window, of 'dead wall,' — large as the eastern window of some Roman Catholic cathedral, and abundance of dead wall on either side of it — never better ally to the slopes above. I advised drapery, though opposed to it in general, hoping thus to interfere with the alliance. One evening, noticing the architect present, I consulted him. He doubted whether drapery would help the matter much; said he was aware such ceilings did attract the voice away from the audience, and recommended a sounding-board over the pulpit, as the best remedy.

"A couple of years ago, when travelling in the States, I preached in a small church of this sort, — seemed as if one was standing between two abutments of a bridge, underneath a high arch. It required the greatest manœuvring to coax the voice down to its office in the ears of the audience. I happened upon two others in the States somewhat similar — both bad; one has since been demolished.

"Happily, churches cursed with such ceilings are not numerous; but they are increasing, both in the United States and Canada. The Gothic has become quite popular of late years, — a style which offers the architect strong temptations to pitch his ceiling not only unduly high, but somewhat in conformity with the window-tops.

"Methodism has lately come into the possession of several specimens. Windows well enough for the Gothic; but the architect, not contented to extend his ceiling at the height which their extraordinary altitude demanded, sloped it parallel with the rafters, clear up to the vicinity of a roof-top by no means humble in its aspirations! Others I have noticed, — windows semi-Gothic, lofty, of extraordinary width and height, — all well enough, if made to raise and lower easy; which was not the case, for they required the strength of two men, and frequently in vain. But the architect, instead of spreading a plain ceiling at a reasonable height above the windows, sprang an arch a considerable height, carried it all around the edifice, as if contriving how best to tempt the voice to vagrancy, and suspended thereon a strip of common ceiling, affording 'a pretty play-ground' for the voice to excursionize before doing the work in the ears and consciences of the hearers.

"A preacher careless of effects — indifferent as to immediate results, not laboring for a revival, not anxious, not expecting sinners to be instantly awakened and converted under his ministry — may exhibit his talents in such places, with some satisfaction to himself, and to others, perhaps, of like mind. But he who has been groaning, weeping and agonizing, in secret places, for the conversion of sinners, will be made to feel there is an enemy overhead, bad as the devil and human depravity. Nor will he preach long there without becoming shorn of his strength.

"For my part, I avoid such churches for revival efforts, if notified beforehand. I have had souls given me within their walls, but with a will at fearful strife with things, and at a great expense of physical and intellectual strength.

"And now, sir, I have given you the result of several years' observation on both sides of the Atlantic. Please read this reply to the members of your 'Building Committee.'

"There is not one item in the above catalogue of defects which has not cost me sorrow or defeat, in one place or other, the last score of years. To such things, sir, rather than diabolical agency or human resistance, have I traced 'many a hard time,' which has sent me to my room to groan the night away!

"I have written this letter in great haste, without time to prune or polish sentences, as I have preached twice to-day, — and, for that matter, ten times a week the last seven months. But you may gather some 'cautions' from the above facts, — facts they are, and mournful defects, from which I pray God to deliver all ministers who are toiling day and night for the conversion of sinners. The work of God is advancing here in glorious majesty.

"With affectionate regards to yourself and family, I am, dear sir,
"Yours, in the bonds of the Gospel,
"JAMES CAUGHEY.

"P. S. The further you project your pulpit into the congregation, if the chapel be large, and you can afford it, the better. It is that advantage which renders the large Wesleyan chapels in England so easy to preach in. On that account, I have no objections to the orchestra behind the pulpit, if its front be a couple of feet higher than the preacher's head when standing; if lower than his head, it is injurious, as it divides and weakens the voice. Such an orchestra, besides, has this advantage: If the choir be disposed to whisper or 'read' music, they will not annoy the preacher by seeing them nor he offend them by reproving. J. C."

Mr. Caughey, in a letter to us dated London, C. W., Feb. 3d, 1855, adds:

"The *Wesleyan* Methodists in Quebec, L. C., have erected a large noble and elegant Gothic church, at an expense of fifty-five thousand dollars, ay, and at a urther COST, not to be estimated by dollars and cents, or p'unds, shillings and pence, — the *strength*, *voice* and *effectiveness*, of their preacher, in attempting to fill 'waste and unoccupied space' spread around with surprising prodigality.

"First of all, the CEILING, — to say nothing of the liberality of *pew-room*, and *aisles* roomy enough for an English cathedral, and the 'waste places' on the galleries, three or four cavern-like breaks for 'grand stairways,' which the voice is allowed to sound to the depths, and 'far in the distance,' where scores might stand, is an *empty space* in rear of the gallery sittings, as if designed to give importance to a prodigious Gothic window, — like an *area* before some palace façade; another tax upon the preacher's capabilities. But the ceiling! what shall I say of the ceiling? Imagine a succession of semi-hoops of a mammoth hogshead, plastered between tight as a drum, and bent to the altitudes, — a vast *magnet* to the voice, drawing it up and away from the audience, as the magnetic influence commands the direction of the needle in the mariner's compass — to say nothing of the devouring disposition of the vast space through which it has to travel and ascend before it receives a *return action*, and then to be waylaid and led into captivity by ruffian echoes, hardly noticeable, indeed, to the hearers, except in some loud key, but cruelly felt by the baffled preacher, especially if the church happen not to be well filled, — an evil too frequent in large churches. But, if he set out to *move* the people, and raise his voice like a trumpet, 'he will find his match;' the voice will not *go down* with point and energy among the people, but reverberates and runs to and fro, — a sound of words and sentences tripping upon sentences, void of the secret *unction* that moves and melts and wets the cheeks of an audience; at length he is forced to modulate and manage his voice as best he can, and be content to make them *hear*, and let *feeling* alone for this time. And so he hobbles on, restrained and embarrassed, to the close. So it was with me last winter, till my health gave way, and was confined to my room. When able to venture out again, a few friends had taken the matter in hand, and covered the *well* of the galleries with two large sails of a ship, lent for the occasion by *Mr. Henderson*. I stood in the altar and to fine audiences preached the word of life, until we had hundreds of souls converted and sanctified, an account of which you may one day meet in my printed journal."

Mr. C. adds: "I am now in London, C. W., preaching in a new and beautiful Gothic Wesleyan church, lately erected at a cost of *thirty thousand dollars*. But, alas! with an *extravagance* of space almost equal to that in Quebec. The ceiling, indeed, is somewhat different, reminding one of — pardon me, ye architects! — *a great flat bot'omed scow, inverted*, and poised to an extraordinary height, 'the hola thereof' painted in imitation of oak, — an accomplished *light-absorbent*, by the way, — which, aided by galleries of like color, renders the house sombre and gloomy, although enlightened by *one hundred 'gas-burners'!* O, gentlemen of 'the Building Committee,' how much more lightsome and pleasant had been your temple, had you draped it in modern, modest *white*, — and a saving on your gas-bill, withal! — a thing you might have readily anticipated by a little RE-FLECTION upon a similar talent *more* or *less* distributed among *colors*.

" The same difficulty is felt here as in Quebec, as regards the unsteadiness and vagrancy of the voice; unless the church is perfectly filled, it seems like '*beating the air.*' A minister remarked to me, the other evening, ' When I pray in that pulpit, it seems as if that vast vacancy above eats up my words.' Yes, and quite exhausts and disheartens before one is half through with prayer or sermon, especially if one desires to have '*power* with God and *with men*,' and to *prevail*. — Gen. 32 : 28. The pulpit does not project into the audience, after the manner of ' the home Wesleyan pulpits,' and which afford the English preachers such a manifest power over their vast audiences, but is set back to the wall. The *orchestra* is, indeed, *behind* the pulpit, but in a recess built to the church, to which there is a vast Gothic opening in the wall behind the preacher's head. This recess is lofty, and vaulted like the main building, which, with the organ, seats fifty or sixty persons, — another draft on the preacher's strength, in a wasteful and voice-dividing direction; and uselessly expended, for most of the choir leave it after singing, complaining that they cannot hear there. Directly opposite the pulpit, at the other end of the church, is a large Gothic window, and a wide, lofty, empty space to keep it company, — another demand upon the voice.

" Now, all this inconsiderate tax upon a preacher's strength I consider ' simple folly,' — nay, *sinful*. O ye people of Canada ! have mercy on your preachers! Betray not thus the cause of God! Weaken not, dishearten not, destroy not, the health and effectiveness of your ministers. Tempt them not thus, or the time may come when ' *the twenty-five minutes' sermon* ' may be as rife in Methodist churches as in English and Continental cathedrals; ' the long-drawn aisles ' and stately columns, and ' avenues of pillared shade,' vaulted like another sky, discipline the preacher to

> The clear harangue, and, cold as it is clear,
> Falls soporific on the listless ear ;
> Like quicksilver, the rhetoric they display
> Shines as it runs, but grasped at slips away.

" After preaching a few times in this church, and baffled and disheartened, I began to repent my visit; felt strongly inclined to retreat to some other town, where my labors might be more successful in winning sinners to Christ, without *shattering my health* as last winter. It was suggested that a *sounding-board* over the pulpit might relieve from the difficulty some, — and has *considerably*. The error is regretted by the *trustees*, not only from the fact of having wasted a *thousand dollars* upon this misconstructed ceiling, — and which only a perverted taste could pronounce ornamental, — but because it would require *seven* or *eight hundred* dollars to replace it with a proper ceiling. Perhaps, brother Wise, these remarks, going forth with the book, may be useful elsewhere, in this church-building age. As the Methodist people grow rich, it is to be feared such-like *vagaries* in church architecture will be neither few nor far between, — when the *eye* will be more consulted than the *ear*, when *pulpit effectiveness* must give way to *architectural appearances*, — a fact which has contributed largely to the *heartless preaching* which prevails in English and Continental cathedrals. One has only to listen to a sermon in one of them to be convinced of the truth of the remark.

"But to return to my subject. To add to the disagreeableness of the place, no ventilation could be had from a single window; the 'design' of the architect forbade such a vulgarism! Gothic throughout, every window was as solid as *lead* and *glass* could make it. A little *fresh air* might be coaxed in by the doors and through some auger-like perforations in a few small pendants in the ceiling; *fresh* air from the attic! — *foul air*, ascending there, cooling, and accumulating, to be returned and re-breathed again, unpurged of its noxious qualities, — and so in process continued.

"The large lecture-room below was in a similar 'fix.' After holding meetings a week or two, the air became *intolerable*, and I *protested*. So the architect had his '*design*' marred by determined men, who cut a passage for the pure air through his 'majestic Gothic windows,' and *fifteen hundred* people may now breathe comfortably, and hear the word with profit.

"They have also kindly 'closed in' the space in front of the large window, leaving an outline thereof upon the cloth screen. This alteration, with a *sounding-board* of extraordinary dimensions, has lessened the difficulty considerably. Nevertheless, it is still an *exhausting place* to the speaker, and will so continue while the *lofty curse* hangs overhead, and the cavern-like orchestra, as it is, behind.

"However, the Lord has poured out his Holy Spirit upon us the last few weeks, and *hundreds* of souls have been converted, and *scores* of believers sanctified. But, O, how exhausting and wearying is the effort! Affectionately in Jesus, thy Lord and mine,
"JAMES CAUGHEY.

"*London, C. W., Feb.* 3, 1855."

RECOMMENDATIONS.

REVIVAL MISCELLANIES. — Altogether, this is a remarkable volume. All of its author's peculiarities of style and composition, varied in subject; rich in expression, striking in illustration, vigorous in thought, forcible in manner, stirring in zeal, and glowing with a high and holy spirituality, it will make its mark on the heart of the reader, augment his anxiety to know more of God as he works out the good pleasure of his goodness in the depths of the soul, and elevate him by its own earnestness to a richer and profounder knowledge of the grace that is in Christ Jesus.

The title-page of the volume does not "hold a promise to the ear, to break it to the hope." It is a true and faithful index of the book as to its subject, as reliable as the hands of a well-regulated time-piece; and as well furnished with the appliances of moral quickening and godly edifying as any volume of its size to be found. We are quite sure that the volume deserves, and will receive, an extensive circulation. — *Richmond Christian Advocate.*

REVIVAL MISCELLANIES. — This book is quite miscellaneous in its character but full of the strong and original traits of the author, who is one of the most remarkable men of our times. All who have read the preceding volume will be interested in this as much, if not more. It will do good. — *Herald and Journal.*

REVIVAL MISCELLANIES is the title of a remarkably successful book, the publishers having sold over *eighteen hundred* copies in fifteen days after its publication! It is a book for the times; full of burning thoughts, and admirably calculated to guide earnest and inquiring minds into the attainment of "the faith of assurance," and into such paths of extraordinary usefulness as were trodden by a Page, a Martyn, a Wesley, or a Payson. — *New Bedford Standard.*

THE sermons of Mr. Caughey were preached during the great revivals he witnessed in England. They were taken down by stenographers and committed to the press, and had a very extensive sale. They contain many passages of great beauty, force, and power; rich in illustration, direct, and earnest. His thoughts on revivals, holiness, &c., in the second part, are deeply interesting, and cannot be read without moving the heart. We believe the book is calculated to do immense good. — *Writer in the Western Christian Advocate.*

A BOON TO THE CHURCH. — Of the many new books which, for a long time past, have been brought before the notice of the public, there is not one we have read with so much interest or profit as the "Revival Miscellanies." Part I. contains eleven of those "Revival Sermons," which, under God, have been instrumental in the awakening and conversion of hundreds, if not *thousands*, of souls. Part II. is exceedingly miscellaneous, and contains some of the best thoughts we ever met with on matters and subjects of vital importance to the interests of religion and the salvation of the world. *Thoughts and style are Mr. Caughey's own.* No plagiarism here. Everything here bears the manifest impress of Mr. C.'s bold, original, unique and fruitful mind. We have read it, much to our spiritual profit. The happiest hours of last Sabbath were spent in its soul-thrilling and spirit-stirring pages. We verily believe it has aroused us to deeds of more daring valor against sin and hell.

Now, we want every minister of the M. E. Church to get a good supply of this work. Let him scatter it amongst his people, accompanied with the advice that they read it with much prayer, that the holy unction which it breathes may descend unto their own soul. This being done, our church will become the theatre of such agonizing and prevailing prayer, — combined, earnest and successful effort, --- saving and converting power, as hath not been witnessed since the day of the Pentecostal rain. If ever we did meet with a book we wished to see

RECOMMENDATIONS.

put in the hands of all our people, it is the one now before us. It ought to have a more extended circulation than even "Methodism in Earnest," for really it appears to be more *earnest* even than that. Now for a general rally. All hands to work. Let us scatter this book like the leaves of autumn. — *From a correspondent of the Herald and Journal.*

THESE are extraordinary compositions, well adapted to awaken the slumbering, and alarm the careless. They are pointed, imaginative, impressive, and powerfully exciting. — *Wesleyan Association Magazine, London.*

CAUGHEY'S EARNEST CHRISTIANITY ILLUSTRATED. Being Selections from the Journal of Mr. Caughey, and containing several of his Sermons, etc., etc. With an Introductory Sketch of the Life of Mr. Caughey, by Rev. DANIEL WISE. This is a new work of Mr. Caughey's, never before published, and is about the size of his "Revival Miscellanies," got up in the best style. The Fourteenth Thousand. Retails for $1. The following are a few of the many favorable notices of the work:

"Like all other works from the pen of Brother Caughey, it will do good wherever it goes, and to all who, with a sincere and pious heart, will peruse its pages." — *Dr. Elliott, of Western Christian Adv.*

"It will hardly be possible to read these thrilling pages of unparalleled revival efforts and success, without feeling the soul fired to deeds of bolder daring against sin and hell. All such as are seeking after higher Christian attainment, should make this book, next to their Bible, their closet companion." — *Correspondence of Zion's Herald.*

"This volume will fall not a whit behind its predecessors in awakening the interest of its readers, and enlivening their spirituality. It has many strong points, exciting incidents, and is full of an intense and transforming spirituality." — *Dr. Lee, of Richmond Christian Advocate.*

"Like the 'Revival Miscellanies,' it will make the heart of the reader better — the head wiser — and thereby purify and intensify the Christian character. Like the mystic wheels in the Prophet's vision, the 'spirit of life' is in it. We are not surprised (and it augurs well for the Church) that an edition of *four thousand copies* was nearly exhausted in a week after it made its appearance, uncommon as are such occurrences even in the annals of the most successful authorship." — *J. V. Watson, of the North-western Christian Advocate.*

The demand for the above works is unprecedented in the history of Methodist publications. Multitudes have been aroused from their spiritual slumbers by reading them. They are books for Ministers, Class-Leaders, Young Converts, Christ's tempted ones, and for all who desire to be *useful* and *holy*. A large number of ministers in all parts of the country are engaged in selling them. For sale at all the Methodist Book Depositories, from Canada to California. For the retail price, they will be sent, by mail, to any part of the country, free of postage.

SHOWERS OF BLESSING
FROM CLOUDS OF MERCY.
SELECTED FROM THE JOURNAL AND OTHER WRITINGS OF THE
REV. JAMES CAUGHEY.

CONTAINING stirring Scenes and Incidents during great revivals in Birmingham, and other places in England, under his ministry — Several of MR. CAUGHEY's awakening Addresses and Sermons — Thoughts on Holiness — Notes of Personal Experience — and Observations upon Persons and Places Visited. Retail, $1.

This is an entirely new work of Mr. Caughey's, and will be found full as interesting as his other works, which have had such an extraordinary sale. His "REVIVAL MISCELLANIES" has reached its forty-third thousand.

☞ Large profits made in selling these works, as a very large discount is allowed. *Presiding Elders* and other ministers are engaged in their sale all over the country. For sale at all the METHODIST BOOK DEPOSITORIES. Books can be easily sent from Boston to any part of the country.

Address Rev. R. W. Allen, No. 5 Cornhill, Boston, Mass.

Choice Books.

POPULAR OBJECTIONS TO METHODISM CONSIDERED AND ANSWERED: or the Convert's Counsellor respecting his Church Relations; with Reasons why Methodist Converts should join a Methodist Church. An Antidote to certain Recent Publications, assailing the Methodist Episcopal Church. By Rev. DANIEL WISE, A. M. Seventh Thousand. Retail, Sixty-two cents. A book for every family. For sale at all the Methodist Book Depositories. Read the following:

"We hope to see it in the hands not only of every young convert, but of every Christian who would enjoy a feast and grow in grace." — *North-western Christian Advocate.*

"I hope it may have an extensive circulation." — *Bishop Simpson.*

"Here is a book for the times. Let it be circulated in every direction." — *Nashville Christian Adv.*

PRECIOUS LESSONS FROM THE LIPS OF JESUS. — Containing Cautions, Counsels and Consolations, for such of the Disciples of Christ as are seeking to be like their Lord. By REV. DANIEL WISE, A. M., author of the Path of Life. Just from the press, and selling rapidly. The Sixth Thousand in press. It is got up in two styles, one of which will retail at twenty-five cents, and the other at thirty-one cents. Read the following recommendations:

"A small book, but filled with very great truths. We commend it cordially to all." - *Northern Christian Advocate.*

"We commend this volume as a fit companion for those who love Jesus, and are seeking to know more of him." — *Western Christian Advocate.*

"A tiny book, but rich in good things." — *Christian Advocate.*

"Its topics, all on important themes of Christian life and duty, are presented in lessons, rich in illustrations variously expressed, and happily combining instruction with edification. We have read some of its lessons with great interest, and we think, also, with profit; and can recommend it as well adapted for general circulation." — *Richmond Christian Advocate.*

"It is a pithy little book, abounding in the well-known excellences of its author's able pen. Few writers have a happier tact at illustration. Some of his 'figures' are devices for the worker in gold. The religious tone of the volume is of the highest order. It is a good presentation book." — *National Magazine.*

"It is admirably adapted to promote the instruction and spirituality of the reader." — *Christian Guardian.*

LOVEST THOU ME, Etc. — By REV. DANIEL WISE, A. M. A new edition of this exceedingly popular little work is now in press, and will be ready in a few days. We know of no work which ministers can circulate to better advantage among their people than this. The Thirteenth Thousand. It is recommended as follows:

"This manual of devotion is a companion for the pious, whose gentle teachings are pure, and full of comfort and encouragement. Its study will mend the morals and adorn the heart." — *Richmond Christian Advocate.*

"This is an intrinsically delightful and mechanically beautiful volume, from the prolific and versatile pen of Rev. Daniel Wise. It is just one of the gift books for the holidays which no one, who desires to quicken the flow of friendship, should omit to purchase, and send to some friend, as a token of affectionate interest in his spiritual welfare. It possesses every quality of adaptation to such a sweet and silent mission of love and spiritual refreshing." — *North-western Christian Advocate.*

"It may be read with pleasure and profit by every Christian." — *Christian Guardian*

Got up in two styles; retailing at twenty-five and thirty-one cents.

LIVING STREAMS FROM THE FOUNTAIN OF LIFE. — Containing a Scripture Text, a choice Aphorism, and a Verse of Poetry, for every day in the year. By REV. DANIEL WISE. Just from the press. Got up in two styles; retailing at twenty-five and thirty-one cents each.

SACRED ECHOES FROM THE HARP OF DAVID. — A choice volume for spiritual Christians. By REV. DANIEL WISE, A. M. Just from the press. Retailing at twenty-five and thirty-one cents.

☞ For agencies address REV R. W. ALLEN, NO. 5 CORNHILL, BOSTON.

www.ingramcontent.com/pod-product-compliance
Lightning Source LLC
Chambersburg PA
CBHW030541300426
44111CB00009B/820